Daily Demonstrators

YOUNG CENTER BOOKS IN ANABAPTIST & PIETIST STUDIES

Donald B. Kraybill, *Series Editor*

Daily Demonstrators

The Civil Rights Movement in
Mennonite Homes and Sanctuaries

Tobin Miller Shearer

THE JOHNS HOPKINS UNIVERSITY PRESS
Baltimore

© 2010 The Johns Hopkins University Press
All rights reserved. Published 2010
Printed in the United States of America on acid-free paper
2 4 6 8 9 7 5 3 1

The Johns Hopkins University Press
2715 North Charles Street
Baltimore, Maryland 21218-4363
www.press.jhu.edu

Library of Congress Cataloging-in-Publication Data

Shearer, Tobin Miller, 1965–
Daily demonstrators : the Civil Rights Movement in Mennonite homes and
sanctuaries / Tobin Miller Shearer.
p.   cm.
Includes bibliographical references and index.
ISBN-13: 978-0-8018-9700-9 (hardcover : alk. paper)
ISBN-10: 0-8018-9700-9 (hardcover : alk. paper)
1. Mennonite Church—History—20th century. 2. Civil rights—Religious
aspects—Mennonite Church—History—20th century. 3. Race relations—Religious
aspects—Mennonite Church—History—20th century. 4. General Conference
Mennonite Church—History—20th century. 5. Civil rights—Religious aspects—
General Conference Mennonite Church—History—20th century. 6. Race relations—
Religious aspects—General Conference Mennonite Church—History—20th century.
7. Civil rights movements—United States—History—20th century. I. Title.
BX8129.M5S54 2010
289.7'7308996073—dc22   2009052702

A catalog record for this book is available from the British Library.

Special discounts are available for bulk purchases of this book. For more information,
please contact Special Sales at 410-516-6936 or specialsales@press.jhu.edu.

The Johns Hopkins University Press uses environmentally friendly book materials,
including recycled text paper that is composed of at least 30 percent post-consumer waste,
whenever possible. All of our book papers are acid-free, and our jackets and
covers are printed on paper with recycled content.

Contents

Preface

We want you to come and learn to love white people.
—Nettie Taylor, African-American head usher,
Bethesda Mennonite, St. Louis, 1957,
when asked if "colored people" were welcome
in a church with a white pastor

Shifting from the Streets and Sidewalks

In a conversation with a white Mennonite leader in 1959, Martin Luther King Jr. asked, "Where have you Mennonites been?"[1] King's theological studies made him aware of Mennonites' long-term commitment to peacemaking, their racially egalitarian pronouncements, and their sacrificial efforts to bring about justice in the United States and throughout the world. King posed his question because he was looking for resources, both theological and human, to further the work of demonstrating for civil rights. Mennonites seemed like a logical group to join him in protest on the streets and sidewalks. Unbeknown to King, a small but identifiable group of Mennonites had been demonstrating for some time. They did so, however, in a manner King did not then recognize. They demonstrated at home and inside the church.

The five adults who gathered at Bethesda Mennonite Church in St. Louis on a Sunday morning in November 1957 were taking part in a civil rights demonstration (see figure P.1). Rather than marching with protest

Fig. P.1 Nettie Taylor, Susie Smith, June Schwartzentruber, Louis Gray, and Rowena Lark,
Bethesda Mennonite Church, St. Louis, November 1957
St. Louis Argus, November 29, 1957, 2C. Photo courtesy of *St. Louis Argus*, St. Louis, MO

signs, the five Mennonites held open bibles and Sunday school quarterlies.
They did not need to carry placards to attract public attention: a reporter
from the *St. Louis Argus*, one of the country's oldest black newspapers, was
writing a profile of their interracial fellowship. Like most observers of the
civil rights movement, the reporter did not identify these Bethesda members as civil rights demonstrators. Even as he featured their fellowship, he
failed to see the meeting as a deliberate action taken to disrupt the status
quo. As the focused attention of June Schwartzentruber, Louis Gray, and
Rowena Lark made evident, the carefully staged photo sent the message
that an African-American woman like Nettie Taylor could command authority in an intimate, interracial gathering. The members of this Sunday
school class thus took part in a civil rights demonstration, an organized
event meant to disrupt the lives of a wider audience to bring about an integrated society. Their demonstration inside the church confronted those
on the outside with an image of integration achieved.

The photo of this integrated Sunday school class thus represents *Daily
Demonstrators'* thesis. Civil rights demonstrations that took place in the
streets have received significant attention. In the intimate settings of
homes and churches, a different kind of civil rights demonstration took
place, one that challenged racial segregation in a less dramatic way. By ex-

amining the actions, beliefs, programs, and pronouncements of Mennonite groups like the Bethesda congregation from 1935 through 1971, this book shows how relationships, communal boundaries, cultural practices, and core religious convictions contributed to societal change. It does so by attending to the actions of Mennonites in their living rooms and meeting-houses. In those intimate, sacred locations, the slow, often contradictory process of religiously motivated, interpersonal exchange made possible a historic transition in post—World War II American society.

In *Daily Demonstrators* I explore new sites that expand our understanding of demonstration to include off-street action. By shifting attention to less public but no less significant environs, I show how racial change unfolded as co-believers took communion, sat down to dinner, and discussed marriages. Rather than sites of escape from the civil rights movement, living rooms and sanctuaries become arenas of racial agitation. Those who ventured across racial lines in intimate settings displayed courage equal to that of demonstrators who faced fire hoses and attack dogs. Children who traveled hours to stay in rural homes with strangely dressed white people braved unknown dangers as real to them as southern sheriffs were to voter registration workers in Mississippi. The pastor who faced down livid congregants after inviting an African-American preacher to his pulpit showed as much daring as students who faced down restaurant owners after sitting at a lunch counter. Demonstrators in sanctuaries and on sidewalks thus look surprisingly similar. All took risks, challenged assumptions, and longed for an egalitarian future. This church history of the civil rights era brings together home and congregation to show how religious practice in intimate environments interacted with higher-profile movements.

Because demonstrations on the streets and sidewalks attracted so much more attention, this intimate, religious form of demonstration remains largely absent from studies of the civil rights era. Historians, social movement theorists, and contemporary activists study the thousands who demonstrated for racial justice to gain fresh insight into mechanisms of change. Scholars and organizers alike examine the charismatic leaders, campaign strategies, political maneuvers, and organizational resources that encouraged so many to march.[2] The firefighters who hosed demonstrators off sidewalks in Birmingham, the police dogs that attacked activists on the streets of the same city, and the state troopers who bludgeoned marchers on the road to Selma offer high drama that further fixes historians' attention on cement surfaces.

The story of the civil rights movement also unfolded, however, in carpeted sanctuaries and living rooms. By wearing the distinctive costume of her religious community to worship services, Rowena Lark, the African-American Mennonite woman pictured on the right in figure P.1, countered the assumption that only white people could be Mennonite. June Schwartzentruber, in the middle of the same photo, modeled new ways of relating across racial lines when she sought the counsel of African Americans while sitting in their living rooms. Over meals at the dining table, Nettie Taylor, the object of Lark's and Schwartzentruber's attention, along with her children and other African-American youth, prompted white church members to rethink their racial stereotypes. Bethesda members and their allies challenged their white co-believers to pay racial reparations as they preached on Sunday morning. These intimate civil rights demonstrations challenged racial segregation by upsetting racial norms.

This study seeks to shift the gaze of civil rights movement historians from paved roads and concrete sidewalks to overstuffed couches and hardback pews. Although I recognize the importance of marchers, I argue that other less dramatic actors within home and church environments also contributed to the civil rights movement by amplifying, modifying, and sometimes opposing pronouncements made in the streets. I attempt to answer the question, How did the civil rights movement bring about change? by demonstrating that relationships, cultural practices, evangelical initiatives, and core religious convictions operated alongside street marches to bring an end to legalized segregation. Unless we understand the means by which actions in the home and sanctuary intersected with organized racial advocacy, our view of the long civil rights movement remains incomplete and skewed toward the street.[3] By observing Mennonites in their living rooms and meeting houses across a thirty-six-year span, the slow, often contradictory, and messy unfolding of religiously motivated, interpersonal change in intimate, sacred locations is brought to light.

Pairing Home and Church

I was prompted to study Mennonites' daily demonstrations by scholars who have broadened our understanding of political resistance and religious practice. In his book, *Race Rebels*, historian Robin D. G. Kelley deepens our understanding of how black working-class resistance in the workplace, on public transportation, and at sites of commercial entertainment supported organized political action. Kelley unifies formal political protest with everyday actions like stealing from an employer to protest low wages and spitting in the face of a bus driver to challenge segregated transit.[4] I follow Kelley by noting the political significance of daily acts of resistance but expand his reach by attending to religious actors in their homes and in church buildings. Kelley only briefly mentions religious groups and, like many other writers in African-American history, ignores those African Americans who went to church with white people. The attention I pay to the everyday action of religious adherents was likewise prompted by the work of religious historian Robert Orsi on "lived religion." Orsi argues that the best way to understand religion is to study religious practice "in all the spaces of experience," not just in the formal sites of sacred gathering.[5] Taken together, these writers invited me to explore new sites of demonstration to include off-street action and to show how religious practice in intimate environments interacted with high-profile marches.

To further that exploration, I have deliberately paired home and sanctuary. At first glance the two settings appear disconnected. Home-based encounters are marked by an intimacy and close personal contact seldom associated with formal Protestant religious practice. Furthermore, although Mennonites' religious forebears and their contemporary Amish cousins held worship services in their homes, the subjects of this study went to church at separate meetinghouses designed for this purpose. Little seems to link the home with the sanctuary. As I paid attention to the interactions of white and African-American Mennonites in the 1930s, '40s, '50s, and '60s, however, I soon noticed that many white Mennonites presumed a physical familiarity with African Americans not limited to the home environment. African-American Mennonite women, for example, referred to white co-congregants who touched their hair in both homes and churches.[6] Other African-American Mennonites recalled times, in those same settings, when their white co-believers stared at them with unabashed fascination or assumed friendship where none existed.[7] Although inappropriate by contemporary standards and at the very least insensitive according to period mores, such familiar acts linked the home and sanctuary. Therefore, rather than treat the home as a private space definitively separate from semipublic worship settings, I have paired the two to examine how these presumptions of familiarity affected the interactions between African-American and white Mennonites.[8] Among the Mennonites studied here, conversation and contact could be just as intimate and intense at a churchwide meeting or Sunday school class as in the living room.

This purposeful connection of home and sanctuary allows for careful study of Mennonites' close social networks. Because by 1970 the community included only 180,000 adult members in North America, the effects of churchwide decisions can be traced to individual congregations and households, a difficult task in large denominations like the Presbyterians, which counted more than 4 million members during the same period.[9] Historical records connect, for example, the decision by a midwestern Mennonite congregation to deny membership status to an African-American young adult with homes and churches in Lancaster, Pennsylvania, Goshen, Indiana, and Gulfport, Mississippi. Mennonite social networks reveal mechanisms of racial change amid a dense but traceable web of familial, personal, and congregational relationships.

The stories chronicled in *Daily Demonstrators* present homes and churches as active sites of, rather than staging grounds for, civil rights activity. Most civil rights scholars view racially progressive congregations as the support base of the civil rights movement. Historian David Chappell traces how "enthusiasm moved out of the church and into the streets." In the same way, Alisa Harrison capably documents how women in home environments supported street actions.[10] In both studies, the actions taken by civil rights supporters in churches and homes are counted only as staging grounds for the real action that took place elsewhere. I treat the intimate environments of home and sanctuary as sites of civil rights struggle worthy of their own study rather than as ancillary points of inquiry.

This home- and sanctuary-centered analysis opens up new vistas into the mechanisms of change inside intimate environments that have been glossed over by otherwise exemplary civil rights scholars.[11] Actions in living rooms and Sunday school classes had political effects. For example, short-term, home-based hosting ventures prompted church leaders to travel to the White House, and pastors of integrated congregations appeared before Congress. In addition to affecting the political arena, the actors featured here changed the church community. Interracial relationships nurtured over cups of coffee, for instance, prompted action against sacred segregation. Yet most of the intimate actions described here reveal much more subtle and complex change processes. One couple's interracial marriage prompted some of their co-believers to reconsider folk notions about race, while for others it reinforced stereotypes. Vincent and Rosemarie Harding's activism called their colleagues to courageous action even while complicating the church's theology of nonresistance. The Mennonite church that welcomed African-American members struggled to allow their young adults to socialize across racial lines. As these instances suggest, the stories told in *Daily Demonstrators* are fraught with contradiction, complicated by imperfection, and indicative of human limitation. Nonetheless, those same stories reveal the messy but no less substantive contributions to social change of personal relationships, theological commitments, and communal boundaries.

These richly complex narratives also challenge Mennonite histories of the twentieth century by bringing African-American Mennonites from the margins to the center of historical inquiry. Two of the most comprehensive twentieth-century historical works on Mennonites, Paul Toews's *Mennonites in American Society* (1996) and Perry Bush's *Two Kingdoms, Two Loyalties* (1998), refer to African Americans in the Mennonite church only in passing and underestimate the impact made by African-American leaders like Curtis Burrell, Vincent Harding, Gerald Hughes, Rowena Lark, and Roberta Webb. Rather than sitting silently on the sidelines, African-American Mennonites vociferously challenged their faith community to show integrity of word and deed. Only by incorporating stories like those told in this volume does twentieth-century Mennonite history become complete.[12]

Choosing among Mennonites

Among the many religious communities available for study, I have chosen to examine the two largest denominations of the Mennonite community—the (Old) Mennonite Church and the General Conference Mennonite Church. The (Old) Mennonite Church was the larger of the two denominations during the period of this study, with 88,947 members in the United States as of 1971. Although not an official designation, the term *(Old) Mennonite Church* was adopted by many members of both denominations to refer to the larger group. I follow this practice to avoid confusion between the two denominations.[13] By the time this study opens,

(Old) Mennonite congregations clustered most heavily along the eastern seaboard, particularly in Pennsylvania and Virginia, and in the Midwest, in Ohio, Indiana, and Iowa. From these locations, (Old) Mennonites eventually came in contact with African-American communities in northeastern cities and throughout the South. Culturally, white members of this community were predominantly of Germanic-Swiss heritage and tended toward more strict interpretations of church doctrines in the area of distinct dress and practices such as the holy kiss, a gender-segregated greeting given within the confessed community. Similarly, many constituent groups belonging to or connected with the (Old) Mennonite Church employed strong bishop-centered authority structures. Church hierarchy and the subsequent ability to enforce a centralized position on racial matters would prove critical to interracial ministry and church positions.

By contrast, the General Conference Mennonite Church counted only 36,458 members in the United States in 1971. Congregations from the General Conference were clustered most heavily in Kansas and Nebraska but were also found in Ohio, Pennsylvania, and Iowa. Owing to their concentration in rural communities in the Midwest, General Conference Mennonites came into contact with African Americans far less frequently than did (Old) Mennonites. The denomination sponsored some mission work among Native American communities but had little formal connection with African-American groups, save through the work of Camp Landon in Gulfport, Mississippi. The membership of the General Conference shared Germanic-Swiss roots with the (Old) Mennonite group but also included a large contingent of Mennonites with roots in Prussia and southern areas of Russia. The General Conference polity was more congregationally autonomous, was less defined by distinct dress codes, and, though committed to missions, worked more extensively in rural than in urban settings. A less robust church hierarchy also led to a greater variety of theological positions on racial matters among General Conference congregations.

I selected the homes and sanctuaries within these two denominations because the tensions inherent in Mennonite service left a clear record of their motivation for working across racial lines. By the middle of the twentieth century, these Anabaptist heirs of the sixteenth-century Radical Reformation, who eventually, in 1683, found their way to Germantown, Pennsylvania, confronted three primary tensions. First, having witnessed many Mennonite men choosing noncombatant or frontline status rather than conscientious objection during World War II, church leaders redoubled their efforts to promote the community's historic commitment to peace.[14] Concurrently, through the 1960s most church leaders prohibited members from joining nonviolent street marches because they saw all demonstrations as fundamentally coercive and therefore against the church's nonresistance doctrines.[15] At the very point when Mennonite leaders sought to increase congregants' peace commitments, they decreased support for the highest-profile exercise in American nonviolence of the twentieth century. For the first time, Mennonites felt a tension between their commitment to nonresistant principles and their opposition to nonviolent marches.

Second, although they opposed civil rights marches, Mennonite leaders protected their increasingly fragile reputation as racial egalitarians. From the colonial period forward, Mennonites opposed the practice of slavery and cherished the memory of having done so.[16] Mennonite leaders also referred to having been the first denomination to admit a black student to a private Christian college in the South.[17] Although they took such early measures to oppose racial oppression, Mennonites had little success in evangelizing African Americans. By the end of the nineteenth century, only one African-American family had joined a Mennonite church in Pennsylvania, and only a few others trickled in during the first few decades of the twentieth century. Through World War II, few other African Americans joined the church.[18] In addition to balking at the sectarian demands placed on converts, African Americans also shied away from formally aligning themselves with a group that often displayed overt racial prejudice.[19] By the middle of the twentieth century, although more than a thousand African Americans worshipped in Mennonite churches on Sunday mornings, many fewer had officially joined. As of 1953, Mennonite congregations listed only 282 adult African-American members in a church that counted nearly a hundred thousand baptized congregants.[20] Despite such limited engagement with African Americans, white Mennonites continued to consider themselves racial egalitarians because of their early opposition to slavery.

Third, the church leaders who tried to prove their racial tolerance, even as they opposed civil rights marches, found their efforts further complicated by the Mennonite doctrine of nonconformity. Throughout their history in the United States, Mennonites had struggled to separate themselves from sinful social temptations by adopting distinctive clothing, avoiding worldly practices like dancing and attending movies, and refusing to join fraternities, secret societies, or labor unions. Although by the 1950s the most visible of these prohibitions had begun to weaken in many Mennonite communities, leaders continued to seek out ways to call their constituents to faithful, separatist conduct.[21] As a result, many Mennonites felt torn between a desire to serve the African-American community and concern that such contact would stain them with worldly contagion.[22]

The tensions born of protecting a reputation as racial egalitarians while promoting nonresistance and nonconformity reveal the motivations of civil rights—era religious actors. As noted, many Mennonites opposed marches because they believed that nonviolent demonstrations relied on coercion and, therefore, contradicted their doctrine of nonresistance. Others, like African-American convert and Mennonite minister Vincent Harding, felt that marching in the streets was the only way to restore integrity to the nonresistance doctrine. The ongoing debates within the Mennonite community over how best to support racial justice while remaining true to core tenets left an uncommonly clear record of motivations, beliefs, and rationales missing from other racially egalitarian groups. The Methodists, for example, focused more on internal integration than on civil rights activism owing, ironically, to a relatively successful record of African-American evangelism.[23] As a result, their motivations for civil rights activism are less clear. Likewise, the Society of Friends had long advocated for African Americans and, like Mennonites, sought to serve the world while remaining separate from it. Unlike Mennonites, however, Quakers readily participated in civil rights demonstrations and therefore had less need to debate and clarify their motivations. Amid debate, discussion, and intense soul-searching, Mennonites demonstrated a startling and transparent honesty about what they did and why they did it.

Finally, because of accidents of history and deliberate mission strategy, white and African-American Mennonites found themselves at revealing moments and strategic sites in the history of the long civil rights era. Mennonites in Virginia in the 1940s instituted and then struggled against a policy of sacramental segregation well before the 1954 *Brown v. Board of Education* ruling. In a deliberate challenge to the civil rights activists who sought racial justice in New York City in the 1950s, Mennonites promoted their own means of achieving an integrated society by organizing "Fresh Air" vacations for African-American children in white rural homes. Vincent Harding became a close ally of Martin Luther King Jr. and other civil rights leaders in Atlanta in the early 1960s. As King brought his civil rights campaign to Chicago in 1966, Mennonites sought to integrate previously segregated congregations. When James Forman threatened in 1969 to take over white churches and synagogues if church leaders refused to pay racial reparations, Mennonites in rural Pennsylvanian congregations used the occasion to solidify their commitment to nonresistance, a move that displaced racial issues in the church for the next two decades. In all of these high-profile locales and historical moments, Mennonites acted to bring about change in ways that have long gone unstudied but reveal much about the slow, persistent, interpersonal complexities undergirding the civil rights movement.

The particular tensions in Mennonite motivations did not, however, make Mennonite action unique. Like many other mainline Protestant evangelists in the late nineteenth and early twentieth centuries, Mennonite missionaries to African Americans practiced paternalism toward new converts.[24] Like most Mennonite churches, individual Protestant congregations—as well as many Roman Catholic parishes—had a difficult time achieving and maintaining racial integration through the period of this study.[25] White Mennonite congregants, like their contemporaries in Presbyterian, Methodist, and Episcopal churches, hesitated to support the nascent civil rights activism of the 1930s and '40s and only reluctantly lent support to the organizing efforts of Montgomery and Little Rock of the late 1950s.[26] When Protestant and Catholic groups began to support the civil rights movement in earnest in the early 1960s, church leaders became involved to a greater degree than white grassroots members, a pattern evident in Mennonite churches as well.[27]

Comparative issues aside, Mennonites also proved disproportionately influential across the nation. In 1967 U.S. congressional representatives heard of the example set by "robust" Mennonites serving sandwiches and soda pop to children in inner-city Harlem.[28] Martin Luther King Jr. met with Bishop Paul Landis to learn about the Mennonite commitment to nonviolence.[29] National leaders from the Lutheran and Presbyterian denominations praised the (Old) Mennonite Church's 1955 race relations statement.[30] Reporters in Lancaster, Pennsylvania, Moundridge, Kansas, and Yankton, South Dakota, wrote favorable articles on Mennonites' various interracial service programs.[31] Members of this small, often reclusive denomination impressed leaders within and outside of the Christian community with their record of evangelism and service across racial lines. Long before tourists flocked in huge numbers to peer at conservatively dressed Mennonites and their Amish cousins, Mennonites drew attention for their interracial ministry.

Mennonites opened new windows into the civil rights movement because they acted like many other Protestant groups but explained their motives with uncommon clarity. As they responded to key civil rights events in the context of a close-knit community, they revealed intimate mechanisms of change in home and sanctuary often obscured in other religious groups. Although shifts toward a racially inclusive church and society seldom came easily or without conflict, both setbacks and successes entered the historical record. It is the tumultuous, messy, and at times rancorous chronicle of their debate, rather than a pristine record of racial equality, that recommends Mennonites for study.

A New Civil Rights Movement Story

From these demonstrations of Mennonite racial exchange a new story appears, one that highlights a movement less dependent on charismatic male leaders focused on legislative change. Following an overview of Mennonite racial history, the second chapter of this book shows the emergence of African-American and white women as vibrant organizers who often flummoxed white male church leaders by pursuing their own means of achieving racial integration. Similarly, as chronicled in the third chapter, African-American children challenged white adults to confront the church's racial naïveté and prodded their elders on to the White House by bringing the movement into rural environs. When men take center stage in chapter 4, charisma becomes less important than the skill of straddling racial and religious borders. In the arena of interracial marriage examined in chapter 5, the efforts of members of integrated congregations to bring about changes independent of Washington officials reveal the limits of legislation. Those same congregations, taken up anew in chapter 6, brought about changes in segregated streets by first integrating pews.

As argued in chapter 7, on the Black Manifesto, the unintended consequences of grassroots civil rights actions in rural Mennonite churches appear as important as the legislative triumphs claimed by national leaders.
In contrast with the dramatic, heart-thumping marches, the quiet but no
less forceful actions of women, children, border straddlers, evangelists, integrated congregations, and rural pastors demonstrate that street-initiated
change came to fruition amid the complexities of home- and sanctuary-
centered response. This book, then, speaks to a major absence in American
religious studies, namely, the remarkable role that religious outsiders like
the Mennonites have had in making possible key transitions in the depth
and spread of social movements.

Finally, this history of white and African-American Mennonites
shows that church leaders who sought to maintain religious boundaries
during the civil rights era often visited harm while desiring to do good.
To a degree, those who define sacred space inclusive of some invariably
exclude others.[32] Even those church leaders, African-American and white
alike, who invoked the beloved community as a symbol of inclusion often
drew clear lines between themselves and committed communists, practicing homosexuals, and professed atheists. The well-documented suspicion
directed toward organizer and activist Bayard Rustin, a gay man with a
history of involvement with "red" groups, is only one example of how religious boundaries could alienate and marginalize.[33] The beloved community, like most religious groups, necessitated exclusion.

In addition to such overt boundaries, Mennonites also maintained subtler lines of demarcation that thwarted the very goals they claimed to support. The professed desire to separate from society to form a redeemed
community that would prove attractive to African-American believers
often kept those converts from joining. Similarly, nonconformist doctrine
militated against full confession of racist practice. A community whose
identity hinged on integrity of word and deed hesitated to acknowledge
that, in the arena of interracial contact, they were not as separate as they
claimed. Even in the midst of historically significant support for civil
rights efforts, the fault lines and fissures of Mennonite race relations reveal the manner in which boundaries set by religious communities exacted
a human cost despite church leaders' egalitarian aims.

Although not intended as a guide to transcending racial boundaries,
Daily Demonstrators does offer a practical message. The stories herein vali-

date those who care about racial justice but refrain from marching. It is a theme that I did not originally intend to develop. As an occasional activist, I was initially interested in recounting street drama. Sunday morning worship services, midweek supper table conversations, and prayer coverings held little attraction. Yet the more I studied Mennonites, the more I recognized that they sat in pews and ate at tables to bring an end to segregation. As I prepared their narrative, I became concerned that the story of the civil rights movement in Mennonite homes and sanctuaries might undermine street protest. In the end, I have set that concern aside. The narratives of Montgomery, Birmingham, Selma, and Memphis show that nonviolent protest has toppled oppressive regimes. Alongside those protestors, the Mennonites featured in this book took part in the civil rights movement while staying at home and going to church. Their story merits attention because it reveals a younger, less street-centered, and more conflicted civil rights movement. At the same time, this story provides examples for those who by choice, temperament, or conviction do not take to the streets but may instead learn to act as daily demonstrators.

To tell the story of the new kind of civil rights activism featured in this text, I have drawn on diverse sources that highlight Mennonites' civil rights experience. To begin, I visited more than a dozen archives, libraries, and personal collections in Indiana, Kansas, Mississippi, Pennsylvania, and Virginia to examine letters, minutes, diaries, and journals of white and African-American Mennonites. Through these sources, I placed people in time, sketched the official story of Mennonite race relations, and—in some wonderfully surprising instances—discovered previously unexamined records of exchanges between white missionaries and African-American proselytes. Those records also pointed me toward interview subjects. More than forty people answered my queries about their motivations, the circumstances of their engagement with the civil rights movement, and memories of conversations with friends, family, and church members. These personal reflections added detail, internal perspective, and illustrative anecdotes that I then checked against the written record. To supplement these written and oral sources, I also examined hundreds of photographs of white and African-American Mennonites. In addition to chronicling the official representation of program supporters and church officials, I learned much from accidental photographic evidence—the expressions, postures, positions, and arrangements of those photographed.[34] This pictorial evidence, in turn, focused my attention on

PREFACE

xxi

the material culture of Mennonite costume.[35] The significance of the color, positioning, size, fabric, and shape of the distinctive Mennonite prayer covering, for example, tell a story absent from accounts based on written and oral evidence. Together, these four sources—written archival documents, oral histories, photographs, and material culture—open up a narrative of religious actors who participated in the civil rights movement even though their contributions, for the most part, have gone unnoticed.[36]

Few desired to demonstrate on a daily basis more than Louis Gray, Rowena Lark, Nettie Taylor, June Schwartzentruber, and Suzie Smith at Bethesda Mennonite in 1957. They came together in the heart of a housing development literally falling apart, owing to the very legacy of racial inequity that the civil rights movement sought to overcome. Although not all Bethesda members opposed marches, they sought racial change within the confines of their fellowship as well as on the sidewalks of Pruitt-Igoe. In the intimacy of an unadorned Sunday school room, they defied the social boundaries that made interracial encounters like theirs so worthy of attention. Although, as this history shows, Lark and her contemporaries knew firsthand the cost of crossing boundaries within the church, they nonetheless made such interracial spaces possible through their actions and beliefs. The chapters that follow tell how groups like those gathered at Bethesda led daily demonstrations in the intimate spaces of living rooms and sanctuaries and, in so doing, changed the streets and sidewalks of the world around them.

ONE EARNS MANY DEBTS in writing any book. Mine have piled deep in preparing this manuscript. My primary interlocutors have long been Josef Barton and Cristina Traina of Northwestern University, and I am grateful for their gracious insight. Martha Biondi, Curtis Evans, Felipe Hinojosa, Fred Kniss, Don Kraybill, Jarod Roll, Michael Sherry, Sarah Taylor, and the anonymous external reviewer at the Johns Hopkins University Press have given perspicacious feedback. The knowledge of archivists and librarians Harold Huber, Jim Lehman, Erin Miller, Joe Springer, Dennis Stoesz, John D. Thiesen, Carolyn C. Wenger, and Nate Yoder has made many a historical insight possible. Financial support from the Louisville Institute, Northwestern University, and the University of Montana has also been invaluable. Finally, I owe a debt to my family. Cheryl, Dylan, and Zachary—you are amazing.

Daily Demonstrators

A Separated History

It was thought best to have a separate [mission] work for the colored.
—Merle W. Eshleman, white pastor, Philadelphia, 1936

T he Reverend Rondo Horton understood white Mennonites. Since
he began working for a Mennonite Brethren evangelist in the Blue
Ridge Mountains of North Carolina in 1917, Horton moved in a
religious community he would come to call his own. This ordained African-American minister and moderator of the North Carolina Mennonite
Brethren Conference did not limit himself to one group of Mennonites.
He thought of himself as "just a Mennonite."[1] Demonstrating his commitment to the broader Anabaptist community, Horton traveled to Chicago in 1959 and Atlanta in 1964 to participate in inter-Mennonite race
relations conclaves. The official assembly photo shows Horton, dressed
in a three-piece suit and a dapper necktie, sitting in the front row with
Vincent Harding and Delton Franz, sponsors of the 1959 conference. His
prominent position reflected his leadership role. Having observed white
Mennonites evangelize African Americans, he knew that many of his
coreligionists prided themselves on their racially egalitarian stance.[2] He
also knew that white evangelism of black people left the underlying problem untouched. So Horton challenged the gathered assembly to switch
directions. "In working for better race relations," he noted, "we begin at
the wrong place. We should not begin working with the Negro. Mennonites should start working with the white people in the South." Referring
to the core Anabaptist values of discipleship and nonresistance, Horton

concluded, "Teach them the way of love. Teach them that segregation is wrong."[3]

Horton's comments focused on southerners but also applied to Mennonites across the country. Interlacing their egalitarian record, a history of separation kept white Mennonites at a remove from their African-American co-believers. Horton knew this history firsthand. In the late nineteenth century a group of Mennonites known as the Krimmer Mennonite Brethren emigrated from Russia to the Midwest and on to the West Coast. Although they had been in the United States for far shorter a time than the African Americans they would soon work among, the Mennonites who first affirmed their religious faith in Horton's home community nonetheless labeled their 1886 evangelistic endeavor to North Carolina a foreign mission.[4] The local African-American community welcomed the Mennonite Brethren missionaries, who, despite intense opposition from the local white community, founded an orphanage for African-American children in the Blue Ridge Mountains. By 1925 the white evangelists switched from tending orphans to founding churches and developing local African-American leadership. Eleven churches emerged and eventually formed the North Carolina District of the Mennonite Brethren Church.[5] Although separated by distance—most members of the Mennonite Brethren community remained west of the Mississippi—and by designation—the community was a foreign mission within the United States—the separation itself appears to have made the contact possible. Mennonite Brethren failed to start missions to African Americans in their home communities during this era. What was possible to do at a distance remained too controversial at home.

Separation also defined the interaction between African-American and white Mennonites in the early 1970s, long after Horton's appeal had been forgotten. The Minority Ministries Council, a group of African-American and Latino Mennonites, met without white oversight and challenged racial subordination in the church. Although relatively short lived, lasting in official form from 1969 through 1974, the council nonetheless pushed African-American and white Mennonites into close contact through separation. Because council members had been able to separate, they stayed in the church. Members of the Minority Ministries Council talked frankly with their white co-believers in part because they could withdraw to their own organization after venturing into the white-dominated world.

Here again, separation, although of a different kind than that employed by the Krimmer Mennonite Brethren, allowed for a measure of interracial exchange. In this case, African-American and Latino Mennonite caucuses fostered scarce contact with white people amid the racial splintering of the late 1960s and early 1970s. If not for the Minority Ministries Council, many Mennonites of color would have left the church.

Mennonites, like most of their Christian cousins in the United States, thus embodied racial contradictions through much of the twentieth century. As Horton knew, white and African-American Mennonites first connected, ironically, through separation. Decades later, the practice continued. Only a religious group that was also a racialized community could engender such paradox. This chapter highlights the religiously motivated and racially conflicted history of separation and contact between African-American and white Mennonites between 1918 and 1971. Although this book focuses on the period from 1935 through 1971, the following overview of post–World War I Mennonite history provides important background to the study as a whole.[6] As Horton's ministry as "just a Mennonite" spanned more than half a century, so too does this historical overview. Through this summary, the paradox of separated contact serves to explain the complexity of motives and methods that made daily demonstrations possible.

Unlike the other tightly focused chapters of *Daily Demonstrators*, this chapter covers a broad swath of time to trace a theme of racialized separation. Although the history told here focuses on African-American and white Mennonites, it is not the only racial history of this quietist community. White Mennonites also came into contact with Latinos/as, Native Americans, and Asians. The work of historian Felipe Hinojosa on the Latino Mennonite community in South Texas and of sociologist Jeff Gingerich on Asian and other ethnic communities in Philadelphia tell important stories that fill out the history chronicled in this text.[7] The ironies, contradictions, and continuities of exchanges between African-American and white Mennonites nonetheless offer critical insight. After a brief introduction to the Anabaptist roots of the Mennonite community, this chapter describes six periods in Mennonite race relations between African Americans and whites. The daily demonstrators described herein came from a religious community that found ways to connect across many racial lines despite and because of a desire to separate from the world.

Anabaptist Roots

The Mennonites Horton would grow to know so well arose out of the Radical Reformation in sixteenth-century Europe. Early Anabaptists argued that Martin Luther had not pushed his reforms far enough and challenged other reformers, like Ulrich Zwingli, to separate the church from state oversight. By 1525 a small group of believers in Zurich, Switzerland, had, in defiance of the local city council, met and rebaptized one another to demonstrate their belief. This emergent community of Anabaptists—literally, rebaptizers—put the authority of the scriptures before the authority of the state. Despite persecution, imprisonment, and execution by European state authorities, the movement continued to grow throughout the sixteenth and seventeenth centuries. This free-church tradition eventually gave rise to the Hutterites, who followed their own path of communal living beginning in 1528; the Amish, who broke away from Mennonite groups in 1693 over matters of church discipline; and the Brethren, who merged Anabaptist and Pietist strands from 1708 forward. In the midst of this early diversity of religious practice among Anabaptists, the impulse to separate from one another and from the world remained strong.

The early Anabaptists articulated a set of core beliefs that shaped Mennonite doctrine. Menno Simons, an influential early church leader, left the Roman Catholic priesthood in 1536 to join the upstart movement that eventually bore his name. Simons and other early church leaders first articulated their belief in the primacy of the scriptures before all other authority. This belief, in turn, fostered a conviction against bearing arms that became known as the doctrine of nonresistance. In the area of church life, Mennonites promoted mutual accountability, known as discipleship, to encourage all community members to daily replicate the ethic of love modeled by Christ. Perhaps most important for this study, Swiss–South German Mennonites felt that they should separate themselves from society's sinful influences, a belief that eventually became codified as the doctrine of nonconformity. As governmental officials persecuted those Mennonites who refused to bear arms or recognize the state's authority, church leaders sought lands where they could practice their beliefs without interference from the world around them.

By 1683, one group of German Mennonites had settled in Germantown, Pennsylvania, where in 1708 they built the first Mennonite meetinghouse. Members of this community spread to the South and West during the eighteenth and nineteenth centuries as they sought new land and economic opportunities. Other groups of Mennonites, like the Krimmer Mennonite Brethren who would go on to proselytize Rondo Horton, came to the United States from Russia and settled in the Midwest and on the West Coast during the late nineteenth century. By the end of the twentieth century, nearly forty different groups of Mennonites populated North America, totaling nearly a quarter million members. As noted in the preface, I have focused on the two largest Mennonite denominations in the United States during the middle three decades of the twentieth century, the (Old) Mennonite Church and the General Conference Mennonite Church. In comparison to their religious cousins, both groups have had relatively greater involvement with African Americans. More strictly sectarian Mennonite groups, such as horse-and-buggy-driving Old Order Mennonites, had far fewer interactions across racial lines. As a result of a strong interest in service and evangelism to the poor and oppressed, (Old) and General Conference Mennonites moved outside communities defined by racial and theological homogeneity and encountered African Americans.

Attending to racial dynamics in the (Old) and General Conference communities, this project notes the particularities of each and yet contends that the racial experience of African Americans within both denominations was strikingly similar for the span of time under study here. (Old) Mennonites, especially in the large and wealthy Lancaster (Pennsylvania) Mennonite Conference, led the entire Mennonite community in ministry to African Americans by being the first Anabaptist group to baptize black converts into the church in 1897, when Robert and Mary Elizabeth Carter and their son Cloyd joined the Lauver Mennonite Church in Cocolamus, Pennsylvania.[8] Members of that same regional conference body also started an industrial training and outreach mission to an impoverished African-American community in the Welsh Mountain area of New Holland, Pennsylvania, the following year. No similar activity took place among the General Conference Mennonites at this time, but African-American Mennonites testified that their experiences with Mennonites from the two denominations did not feel substantively different. Despite significant differences in how the two groups evangelized African Americans and separated themselves from the world, patterns of paternalism

and prejudice proliferated in both communities. The brief historical out-
line that follows traces the history of both (Old) and General Conference
Mennonites as they related to African Americans.

The Segregation Era, 1918 – 1943

The years 1918 to 1943 involved deliberate segregation, overt participation in the racial order, and initial resistance to change. Even as they sought
to separate from the influences of a world they deemed sinful, (Old) and
General Conference Mennonites followed the example of secular society
by practicing racial segregation. From the end of World War I through
1943, African Americans like Rev. Rondo Horton would not have been
welcome at most white Mennonite churches in the United States. Those
who did venture into white congregations often found themselves
shunted to one of the "colored missions" opened in this period. At Broad
Street Mennonite Church in Harrisonburg, Virginia, and Pennsylvania
mission churches in Lancaster, Philadelphia, Reading, and Steelton, (Old)
Mennonite mission workers made deliberate decisions to segregate their
urban mission efforts, usually after failed attempts at racial integration.
For example, after holding integrated summer bible school classes "for a
number of years," church workers in Philadelphia reported in 1936 that
"it was thought best to have a separate work for the colored."[9] During this
time, General Conference Mennonites sponsored no organized missions
to African-American communities. Such efforts would not occur until after World War II. As a result, the General Conference congregations remained racially homogenous owing to the restrictive housing covenants,
sundown laws forbidding blacks to be out after sunset, discriminatory
realty practices, and other overt methods that protected white communities from black infiltration during the segregation era. Throughout both
Mennonite denominations, the initial welcome promised by early baptism of African-American believers in Pennsylvania dimmed as the realities of Jim Crow laws in the South and de facto segregation in the North
confronted the Mennonite community.

During this period Mennonites drew their evangelistic techniques from
external sources and also asserted that racial problems stemmed from the
same. In the former instance, missionaries involved in interracial ministry
were far more influenced by the methods and theology of evangelicalism

than by Anabaptist credos.[10] Having come relatively late to both domestic and foreign mission fields, Mennonites followed the example set by their more experienced white Protestant counterparts.[11] Early Mennonite missionaries thus followed the lead of other evangelists who had set up separate stations for blacks and whites. Similarly, Mennonites from both denominations described racism as an issue external to the church community, an irony noted by the African-American Mennonites diverted to segregated churches.[12] Mennonites, declared writers during the period, had only to avoid racial epithets and hatred to keep racism from entering their faith community.[13] Although fewer than 150 African Americans had joined the church by 1943, these members quickly became aware that life on the inside of the church often did not match their leaders' public claims of separation from the world's sinful influence.[14] In many instances, racially oppressive practices loomed even larger in the eyes of African-American converts because the church claimed to be separate from those practices.

Most white Mennonites in this period accepted the racial norms of their day in both the North and South. Despite articles in the church press cautioning against such action, overtly racist acts were relatively common. In the most dramatic case, the Virginia Conference acted to segregate receipt of sacraments by race in 1940. Three years later, Daniel Kauffman, the white Mennonite editor of the (Old) Mennonite Church national weekly, the Gospel Herald, drew upon eugenic thought when he warned his readers about the danger of "hordes of colored (and renegade white) races" overwhelming white Christians who used birth control.[15] Through 1943, leaders of urban missions, bible school programs, and retirement communities maintained segregated mission sites. Although a few integrated groups managed to survive, racial segregation prevailed from Philadelphia to Sarasota. Even as Mennonite missionaries followed evangelistic methods and mores adopted from outside the church, they followed external patterns of racial segregation as well.[16]

A few Mennonites objected to such ready acquiescence to racial subordination by protesting segregation policies and advocating for the rights of African-American converts. In the early 1940s, white mission workers Ernest and Fannie Swartzentruber vehemently opposed the Virginia Conference's segregation decision, a stance that eventually led to their dismissal. In 1943 another white mission worker, Sem Eby, advocated on behalf of an elderly African-American woman who had been denied access to a retirement community run by Mennonites in the village of Welsh Mountain, Pennsylvania.[17] New African-American converts such as Roberta Webb and Rowena and James Lark carved out a space for themselves within the church through protest and social networking. Long-held Mennonite traditions of hospitality, concern for right relationship, and service to the poor and oppressed could also lead to egalitarian conduct. Values internal to the community did at times call believers to counter racial subordination, but the process was as fragile as it was rare.

Those who resisted and those who cooperated with racial segregation during this era seldom received enthusiastic support from mission boards. Most of the church's missions had only begun to develop revenue streams before the Great Depression, and they struggled to survive through the 1930s. Responding to the economic instability of that decade, mission boards terminated assignments more often than they extended them.[18] Nonetheless, the Eastern Mennonite Board of Missions and Charities of the Lancaster Conference did manage to send four missionaries to eastern Africa in 1934.[19] Here, as in the case of the Krimmer Mennonite Brethren who witnessed to a young Rondo Horton in North Carolina, evangelizing dark-skinned peoples at a distance drew significant attention and, in many cases, proved more successful than venturing across racial lines close to home. The same mission boards that managed to raise funds to send personnel across the Atlantic found it more challenging to raise funds in support of missions among African Americans in the United States. At the same time, mission boards seldom interfered with individually initiated efforts to minister to urban populations, migrant communities in the South, or rural communities in the Northeast.

From 1918 through 1943 church members set relational and institutional patterns that would confront African-American and white Mennonites for the next quarter century. White Mennonites from the (Old) and General Conference denominations consistently viewed African Americans during this time as sullied representatives of the world from which they sought to separate. Although a small group of evangelists reached across the color line in the (Old) Mennonite community, they brought with them the same paternalistic attitudes and assumptions of cultural superiority that defined much of white evangelistic contact across racial boundaries through World War II. In stark contrast, the Communist

Party generated good will and no few allies within the African-American community because of its demonstrated commitment to ending racial discrimination and illusions of white superiority. Mennonites would take far longer than their communist adversaries to gain similar standing as they carried forward the legacy of segregation.

The Era of Evangelism, 1944–1949

During the next six years, Mennonites read reports about churches planted within African-American communities, listened to debates over the problem of how best to respond to racial diversity in the church, and peered at the spectacle made of new converts. Meanwhile, African Americans like Rondo Horton struggled to build a home for themselves within the Mennonite community. By the end of the 1940s, largely owing to stronger mission agencies and the energetic and visionary leadership of African-American Mennonites James and Rowena Lark, eight new African-American and racially integrated congregations appeared across the country.[20] Although two new congregations were begun in Pennsylvania during this period, the center for this new growth and evangelism shifted from the East to the Midwest as the Larks founded Bethel Mennonite in Chicago in 1944; the following year James Lark became the first ordained African-American minister in the Mennonite church. The Larks generated interest across the church community in their mission efforts and by 1949 had brought forty-six new African-American converts to full church membership.[21] In Ohio and Illinois, regional conference bodies expressed new interest in planting integrated churches, an effort that bore fruit in the founding of Lee Heights in Cleveland and Rockview in Youngstown in 1947. The Ninth Street Congregation in Saginaw, Michigan, founded two years later, also added to the shift westward.

Although the General Conference denomination did not show the same interest in church planting among African Americans at this time, individual white members ministered to impoverished African-American families in Gulfport, Mississippi, at the Camp Landon mission. After the Civilian Public Service unit in Gulfport closed at the end of World War II, Camp Landon administrators switched from constructing privies to conducting recreation programs, summer bible school sessions, and weekly sewing and woodworking classes for children. Although by the 1950s volunteers would work exclusively with African-American children, during this period the camp held separate programs and open houses for whites and blacks.[22] Local Mennonite congregations supported the camp's segregated mission and practiced a racial separation of their own. Members of Gulfhaven and Wayside did not at that time welcome African Americans into their fellowships.[23] General Conference leaders supported the Camp Landon ministry through the Mennonite Central Committee, the inter-Mennonite relief and development agency begun in 1920 to provide famine relief to Mennonites in Russia, and would later confront the legacy of segregation when they took full responsibility for the project in 1957.

Mennonites from across the country joined the Camp Landon volunteers in grappling with segregation. In Pennsylvania, the Lancaster Conference's Eastern Board continued to segregate mission work in Steelton in 1944 and decided to segregate the Newlinsville mission in 1946.[24] In the Virginia Conference, segregated receipt of sacraments remained in force, and in 1947 the conference-run Eastern Mennonite College refused to admit Ada Webb, a daughter of African-American convert and Broad Street member Roberta Webb. In 1944 theologian and professor Guy F. Hershberger, speaking on the topic of race relations at Goshen College, a Mennonite liberal arts school in northern Indiana, chided white Mennonites for expressing attitudes of racial superiority, hesitating to welcome African Americans into their fellowships, and espousing a belief in racial equality that they did not embody.[25] Whether enforced through mission policy or enacted through individual choice, racial segregation infused the church during the 1940s.

Nonetheless, some Mennonites opposed segregation in their religious communities. In 1945 students at Bethel College, a school sponsored by the General Conference in Newton, Kansas, raised money for an African Methodist Episcopal choir that included a student who had attended the college four years earlier.[26] White Mennonites from both General Conference and (Old) Mennonite communities called for an end to prejudicial behaviors in the church and urged racial unity, noting that "we are all part yellow, part brown."[27] At the same time, leaders from the (Old) Mennonite Church strictly interpreted the doctrine of nonresistance as they cautioned against involvement in "interracial movements and organizations who by political pressure or nonviolent coercion seek to raise the social status of the Negro and other racial minorities."[28] Such a separatist stance, however, allowed for other internal changes. In 1948 the Eastern Board of the Lancaster Conference recommended ending segregation in all of their retirement communities.[29] Although not enforced for years to come, the conference's recommendation paralleled the Virginia Conference's decision to admit African Americans in 1948, a decision that led to Ada Webb's enrollment at Eastern Mennonite the following year.[30] Debates over segregation in congregations and sacramental practices continued through this period, but tentative signs emerged that African-American converts like Louis Gray, Susie Smith, and Nettie Taylor, from Bethesda in St. Louis, would be welcome at a few more Mennonite institutions. In these initial actions against segregation, Mennonites mirrored similar steps taken by other white Protestant denominations.[31]

Concurrent with these small changes, church press editors presented African Americans as spectacles for their readers. Staff of regional conference magazines and national journals highlighted photos of mission work with African Americans in Illinois, Michigan, Mississippi, New York, Ohio, Pennsylvania, and Virginia, with captions that pointed to the novelty or exoticism of African Americans' relating to white Mennonites, a pattern common throughout many white-majority denominations.[32] Through this period, the (Old) Mennonite Church's annual yearbook identified African-American mission stations with the parenthetical label "(Colored)."[33] Similarly, a photo of a wedding at Broad Street Mennonite Church in Virginia appeared beneath the caption, "A Mennonite Colored Wedding"; a picture of church planters James and Rowena Lark dressed in distinctive Mennonite plain attire appeared above the terse title "Zealous Larks"; and a 1948 photo caption described "boys and girls with . . . big black wistful-looking eyes . . . so polite and orderly" yet not knowing "what it is to play a real live game."[34] As the Reverend Rondo Horton would point out several years later, the novelty of Mennonite missions to African Americans underlined a final message of the period: the solution to the sin of racial discrimination lay in saving the souls and improving the physical condition of the African-American community. Press attention emphasized the spectacle of that ministry rather than racial subordination within the Mennonite church.

Alongside the focus on racial spectacle, the doctrine of nonconformity came to play a central role in evangelism across racial lines. Although leaders from both (Old) Mennonite and General Conference denominations had long interpreted nonresistance in similar ways, the two groups codified nonconformity differently. Through this period and beyond, General Conference polity allowed congregations significant autonomy. As a result, congregations interpreted nonconformity standards in their own terms. The (Old) Mennonites, however, took a more uniform approach. In 1943, as Mennonites grew ever more acculturated, one of the denomination's national working groups, known as the General Problems Committee, proposed that nonresistance and nonconformity be established as tests of church membership. Members of the committee recommended that anyone who bought life insurance, belonged to a union, dressed immodestly, wore jewelry, attended the theater, or went to movies should forfeit his or her member status.[35]

Delegates eventually tabled the proposal in favor of a more conciliatory approach, but the action revealed (Old) Mennonite Church leaders' continued concern about the need to curtail worldly behaviors.[36] In response to these concerns, a few evangelists argued that such an emphasis on nonconformity complicated efforts to bring African Americans into the church. For example, writing from her work assignment at the Philadelphia Colored Mission, white "sister worker" Emma Rudy wondered in 1945 whether the doctrine of separation had "some bearing on small memberships" at the various African-American missions.[37] Although white Mennonites born into the church tested the limits of the nonconformist restrictions, African-American converts discovered quickly that church leaders gave them less leeway to challenge the dictate. A nonconformity conference held in Chicago in 1948 made no mention of the emerging double standard.[38] In subsequent years, the racial disparity would become even more pronounced.

During the era of evangelism, white Mennonites approached African Americans with a mixture of hospitality, fascination, and rigidity. Peggy Curry, an African-American member of Broad Street Mennonite Church, would later describe the attitude of her white co-believers as an "iron fist [in a] velvet glove."[39] Although the evangelistic impulse brought Mennonites out of their white enclaves to serve and proselytize, their commitment to maintaining a separated order—especially evident among (Old) Mennonites—combined with assumptions of racial superiority to result in restrictive and controlling behaviors toward African Americans. James

and Rowena Lark countered this trend by starting churches in which conservative dress standards mattered less, but even their efforts could not
counter in full the "superiority attitude" that theologian Hershberger as-
cribed to his co-believers.[40] The promise of evangelism unfolded amid the
hazards of separatist doctrine and segregationist attitudes. Only a few in
the church imagined and embodied a more egalitarian community defined
by the "way of love" that Horton would come to promote.

Racial Interventions, 1950 – 1955

The years 1950 to 1955 were a period of focused racial interventions, including organization, conferences, and correction. As the 1950s opened,
African-American converts demonstrated their allegiance to the church.
Like Rev. Rondo Horton, the new members claimed that they were "just
Mennonite[s]." In accord with their assertion of Anabaptist identity, African-American Mennonites joined their white coreligionists to start new
organizations, plan racial conferences, and correct racial grievances. White
activist and scholar Guy F. Hershberger played an especially prominent
role in fostering such initiatives. During this time, Mennonites also began to debate how best to respond to racial inequity. Denominational and
congregational leaders in both General Conference and (Old) Mennonite
communities no longer concurred that focused evangelism and provision
of material resources would suffice. This lack of consensus expressed itself
in debates over whether nonviolent campaigns like the 1955 Montgomery bus boycott contradicted the Mennonites doctrine of nonresistance.[41]
In short, discussions about race in the Mennonite church intensified.

Stronger institutions supported such race-focused conversation. As
1950 opened, the (Old) Mennonite Church counted only 150 adult African-American members, but white Mennonites' interactions with African Americans increased through eighteen African-American congregations and new home-based mission programs.[42] With even greater fervor,
Mennonites founded more than thirty-five new international missions
through the course of the decade.[43] Some Mennonites in rural settings, unable to leave their farms and businesses for overseas mission work, heeded
calls to join the burgeoning missions movement by inviting children from
the inner city into their homes. Most important, the Lancaster Conference
began to send African-American children and youth into congregants'

homes for short summer stays through a Fresh Air rural hosting program enacted by the Colored Workers Committee in 1950. Although white children at first outnumbered African-American and Latino participants, program sponsors prioritized ministry to African-American children, and the program soon reflected that emphasis. The Woodlawn Mennonite congregation in Chicago also founded a General Conference–based Fresh Air program during this period. In addition to home-based ministry, the Lancaster Conference's Eastern Board expanded their witness "to the colored" in 1950 and soon afterward started a racially integrated home for the elderly in Philadelphia.[44] Meanwhile, General Conference leaders began to administer the Gulfport, Mississippi, Camp Landon service program in 1953, thereby lending stability and legitimacy to the longest-running African-American mission effort in the denomination. Such organizational attention brought new resources to previously cash- and resource-strapped mission stations.

National conferences also lent new authority to race relations ministries. In particular, gatherings organized in 1951 and 1955 by the Committee on Economic and Social Relations, under the leadership of Guy F. Hershberger, attracted the church's attention. The 1951 event, held at Laurelville Retreat Center in western Pennsylvania, concluded with a call to "abolish" racial segregation and discrimination "wherever it may exist within our brotherhood."[45] At the time of the conference, a rumor spread that the church's mission board had refused to rent a property to an African American for fear that doing so would reduce the property's value.[46] Whether or not Hershberger had this particular instance in mind when he raised his call matters less than the force of his position. He knew of many instances of individual and institutional discrimination in the church body. Hershberger used the authority of his position and the occasion of the conference to excoriate them.

Although segregation at many mission stations continued despite such egalitarian calls, other of his co-believers joined Hershberger in demanding an end to segregation and oppression. Women like white mission worker Leah Risser raised objections to racial divisions at the Steelton, Pennsylvania, station and elsewhere long before local administrators finally put an end to mission segregation.[47] Other congregants from the (Old) Mennonite community involved in evangelistic outreach to the African-American community pointed out inconsistencies between church proclamations and members' actions.[48] Appeals based on scripture and on science appeared frequently.[49] One writer captured a common sentiment of the era when he asserted, "Science has . . . confirm[ed] Paul's view of the human race . . . [that] race is a biological unity."[50] General Conference writers noted similar inconsistencies and appealed to common humanity, but they had less practical experience to offer.[51] With the exception of workers from Camp Landon in Mississippi, General Conference members faced a far more theoretical than practical question when they called for racial reconciliation.

This national and local attention to Mennonite racism opened the door to more extensive discussion during the 1955 Hershberger-initiated conference on the campus of Goshen College. At least 120 participants gathered in northern Indiana to hear an integrated slate of speakers representing the Mennonite church and other Protestant communities.[52] Although no woman gave a plenary address, African-American Mennonite church planter Rowena Lark presented a short testimony, and Rosemarie Freeney, an African-American school teacher from Chicago who would later marry historian and activist Vincent Harding and figure prominently in civil rights work in the South, offered a devotional.[53] Although clearly responding to the 1954 *Brown v. Board of Education* Supreme Court decision, conference organizers nonetheless dealt forthrightly with a broad range of racial issues inside the church based on carefully crafted, biblically informed presentations.[54] Conference participants drafted a statement on racism that the (Old) Mennonite Church passed later that year. In addition to echoing the biblical and scientific arguments about racial unity that had been prominent in church publications for the previous four years, the statement called for corporate confession to the sin of racism and, perhaps most significant, asserted that there was no scriptural basis for opposing interracial marriage.[55] Local and regional leaders acted on the statement's appeal for confession and right conduct by rescinding the Virginia Conference's segregation policy later that year.

Despite this organizational upswing, church leaders enforced dress and grooming codes far more strictly among African-American converts than among their white counterparts. The concern for adhering to a strict code of nonconformist behaviors had not abated among many (Old) Mennonite Church leaders, and the pressure built with particular intensity in the Lancaster Conference. In that setting, bishops struggled to maintain their authority in the face of growing acculturation and a burgeoning renewal movement brought to the United States by missionaries on furlough from ministry in Africa. Returning mission workers like Phebe Yoder and John and Catherine Leatherman emphasized grace over works, a message the bishops felt undermined their efforts to enforce nonconformity.[56] Rather than follow the mediating influence of the African revivalists, white mission workers from the Lancaster Conference echoed the bishops. Pastors and mission workers used doctrinal statements and Sunday school lessons to instruct African-American women to wear the distinctive Mennonite prayer covering and cape dress, while church leaders also enforced male grooming restrictions. For example, during this period more than one Mennonite bishop required an African-American man to shave his moustache before baptism.[57] In one instance, a bishop took an African-American man into a separate room and cut off the man's moustache with a child's blunt safety scissors.[58]

Similarly, during a 1954 Colored Workers Committee meeting, participants were asked, "Do we ask our new mission members to dress much plainer than members of home congregations?"[59] The white mission workers in attendance decided in the affirmative. They stated that stricter requirements proffered a "blessing rather than a hindrance" to the African-American converts.[60] Owing to the growth of African-American missions—twenty-nine congregations listed African-American members, and Sunday morning attendance reached nearly fifteen hundred—more African Americans came into contact with church strictures.[61] By their own account, white Mennonites in the Lancaster and Virginia Conferences as well as other regions of the (Old) Mennonite Church thus sought to control African-American converts through dress and grooming restrictions.[62]

The period from 1950 through 1955 also saw an intense focus on interracial marriage. At this time, an overwhelming majority of white people in the United States opposed intermarriage, while African Americans proved more tolerant.[63] A cadre of white Mennonite writers, debating the issue in the church press, focused on social rather than theological objections to couples' marrying across racial lines and typically used the example of a black man marrying a white woman.[64] The author of a General Conference article articulated the question he heard most often: "Do you want your daughter to marry a Negro?"[65] Such examples reveal much. The writers first assumed that men, regardless of their racial identity, found white women more desirable than African-American women.[66] The writers also accepted the notion that white men did not desire African-American women, despite centuries of evidence to the contrary.[67] The women's sexual interests did not register on writers who assumed that both African-American and white women passively accepted male advances.[68] These assumptions carried a potent message. The writing and discussion of the period implied that a white Mennonite woman could not remain unsullied if she married an African-American man. Thus when committed church workers and life-long Mennonites Gerald and Annabelle Hughes celebrated their interracial marriage in 1954, leaders from the Ohio Conference expressed their displeasure by refusing to extend ministerial credentials to Gerald the following year.[69] Few who knew of the Ohio Conferences' censure against Hughes missed the irony that the national denomination passed a statement the same year removing all biblical censure against interracial unions.

The racial interventions from 1950 through 1955 often contradicted one another. Even as Freeney, Hershberger, Lark, and Risser condemned racially oppressive practices in the church, bishops and evangelists from the (Old) Mennonite denomination strictly enforced nonconformity dictates among African-American converts. While some leaders overturned segregation policies, others sustained objections to interracial marriage. Intensified discussions of race relations included both assertions of human unity and the feared threat of black encroachment. The volunteers who staffed the high-profile ministry to African Americans at Camp Landon often attended local Mennonite congregations that rebuffed African Americans. The many contradictions of this period sprang from a church theologically committed to evangelism and racial equality while culturally immersed in separatist behaviors and prejudiced attitudes. No wonder then that Rev. Rondo Horton enjoined his coreligionists to discontinue evangelizing African Americans in favor of teaching white southerners "the way of love." He knew that the Mennonite church could often prove unwelcoming, if not hostile, to the African-American community.

Pastoral Era, 1956 – 1962

More than any other era in the twentieth century, the seven-year stretch from 1956 through 1962 held great promise for the hope of racial integration and the possibility of fresh engagement with racial justice. Pastors like Delton Franz, Vincent Harding, Orlo Kaufman, and Vern Miller played dominant roles during a time when organizational interventions from the previous period bore much fruit. Such domestic activity matched ongoing growth and development of overseas missions by both General Conference and (Old) Mennonites.[70] Although leaders from the Lancaster Conference remained concerned that such robust evangelism threatened the separated community, missions and missionaries garnered the attention and finances of the church.

The promise loomed large in the church's periodicals and public pronouncements. During this time the Reverend Martin Luther King Jr. moved on to the world's stage fresh from the success of the Montgomery bus boycott, and African-American leaders from across the country leveraged cold-war rhetoric to gain unprecedented access to halls of power, even as they distanced themselves from radical calls to economic reform. White Mennonites ministered in African-American communities with a fervor equal to that shown by King and his contemporaries. Articles touted the large number of African-American children attending vacation bible school programs at mission churches like Diamond Street Mennonite in Philadelphia. In 1959, four years after their (Old) Mennonite counterparts had done so, the General Conference Mennonite Church passed a statement on racism that lacked specificity on issues like interracial marriage but nonetheless represented a significant step forward in a denomination with far fewer opportunities for contact with members of the African-American community. The Lancaster Conference bishops followed suit in 1960 by issuing a race statement of their own. Mennonites made public their opposition to segregation, their support for racial equality, and their belief that, in the words of the Lancaster statement, "no race is inferior or superior to any other."[71]

Church members matched their pronouncements with public action. Fresh Air programs continued to proliferate as the Lancaster Conference leaders increased their promotional efforts in 1958, and Camp Landon staff started their own program in 1960. Faculty at Goshen College in northern Indiana hosted King that same year. New and continuing African-American leadership also came to prominence as longtime evangelists James and Rowena Lark moved to St. Louis in 1957 to plant yet another African-American congregation, Bethesda Mennonite; Billy Curry, an African-American member of Broad Street Mennonite Church in Virginia, where integrated communion services had been allowed to resume only a half decade before, took ordination vows as a deacon in the Virginia Con-

ference in 1961; and evangelist and church planter James Harris spoke on
the doctrine of separation to other members of the Colored Workers Committee in Lancaster in 1962. Congregations ministering to African-American communities began in eleven different states: Alabama, California,
Florida, Georgia, Indiana, Kansas, New Jersey, New York, Ohio, Pennsylvania, and South Carolina.[72] Groups from the General Conference and the
(Old) Mennonite denominations traveled to talk with Mennonites in the
South and to learn of African-American struggles for justice.[73]

   This burst of interracial ministry stemmed from evangelistic and political convictions. Those white Mennonites who brought the gospel message to African-American communities held fevered belief in the Great
Commission to spread Christianity around the world. At the same time,
other Mennonites echoed cold-war anticommunist sentiment as a reason
to minister to African Americans and counter racial prejudice. Although
most Mennonite leaders did not go so far as more patriotic Protestant
evangelists who equated communism with the "kingdom of Satan," they
did express concern that racial segregation at home might undermine overseas missions.[74] One writer applauded leaders of the 1957 Montgomery
bus boycott for fostering "moral issues" and denying communists "good
propaganda."[75] Although most Mennonites avoided political entanglements, the pairing of evangelism and anticommunism attracted many.

   This programmatic and theological activity received further support from integrated ministry sites. In particular, Harding and Franz, at
Woodlawn Mennonite in Chicago, caught the attention of their General
Conference denomination and the entire North American Mennonite
community. The two men hosted the race relations conference in 1959
during which Rev. Rondo Horton called on Mennonites to minister to
white southerners. The conference also featured the most racially diverse
slate of speakers the church had yet presented. Similarly, racially integrated congregations such as Bethesda in St. Louis, Lee Heights in Cleveland, Newtown Chapel near Sarasota, and Good Shepherd in the Bronx
received much attention. With the blessing of their congregation, Vincent and Rosemarie Harding left Woodlawn in 1961 to move to Atlanta,
where they founded and led the integrated Menno House. This center
for support of the civil rights movement increased the Hardings' already
significant profile as Vincent traveled extensively throughout the country
and gave a speech at the 1962 Mennonite World Conference. On the local

level, a previously all-white congregation in Markham, Illinois, received their first African-American visitors. Integration had come of age.

Church leaders concerned about the integrity of a community known for its peace stance and, increasingly, its racial egalitarianism began to pay more attention to street-based civil rights activity. In 1960, the year Martin Luther King Jr. visited Goshen College, more than twenty-five articles on the civil rights movement and the tactic of nonresistance appeared in the church press. The authors brought mixed perspectives. Guy Hershberger enjoined his readers to "take an open stand against segregation" even as he critiqued civil rights groups like the NAACP and the Congress of Racial Equality for promoting strategic rather than ethical nonviolence.[76] Budding theologian Norman Kraus noted the lack of uniform attention to the "Christian motivation for nonviolent action" even as he expressed admiration for students who maintained self-control when hecklers poured "hot soup . . . into their laps."[77] In his 1962 address to the Mennonite World Conference, Harding invited Mennonites to come to Albany to "share the experience" of being arrested with him.[78] Although they never roused the bulk of their community, during this period of promise a few leaders in the church experimented with and exercised nonviolent direct action.

Yet a seam of sobering withdrawal and limitation ran through the period. Ongoing debate over the codified standards of conduct stemming from some interpretations of nonconformity intensified attention to the doctrine and its racial implications. For instance, several leaders noted that the nonconformity doctrine supported racial separation by encouraging Mennonites to remain aloof from social strife. In 1959 Harding stated, "We must confess that we have let a doctrine of separation become an escape from responsibility to our brother men."[79] In the same year, Eugene Stoltzfus, an undergraduate from Eastern Mennonite College in Harrisonburg, Virginia, highlighted the contradiction between bold proclamations about nonresistance and tepid support for a nonconformist "stand on the race problem."[80] Furthermore, Harding noted, white Mennonites had confirmed a tendency to withdraw in the face of racial strife the previous year, when leaders of the General Conference seminary moved the school from a troubled African-American neighborhood in south Chicago to the suburban, small-town environs of Elkhart, Indiana. Harding described this seam in his 1962 World Conference address: "We let our Mennonite culture become our God, and we refuse to accept outsiders in to our fellowship."[81] Harding and a few of his contemporaries called on the church to understand the dangers of separation from the racial struggles of the world around them.

Despite the attempt by Harding, Stoltzfus, and others—including Rondo Horton—to harness church doctrine for egalitarian ends, some Mennonites continued to market a racial ideology that undercut the promise of the period. Although protests against interracial marriage and articles debunking the idea of race diminished, congregants continued to link church doctrine with racial constructs. In 1960 a constituent wrote to Guy Hershberger in support of segregation, explaining that Christ's "pure love" kept the races separate because God had created "pure" racial groups as defined by "pigment of hair, skin etc." and "blood content."[82] Even young children encountered racially charged images. In 1962 a vacation bible school speaker at a Mennonite church in Reading, Pennsylvania, told a story about a boy named Tom who "gave his heart to Jesus and the blood washed it white and pure as snow."[83] Embodied color-coding linked to church doctrine thus came to emphasize rather than diminish the racial hierarchy of the day at the very time when new African-American voices had begun to challenge white supremacy in the church.

Through the remainder of the period surveyed in this study, the church would never again experience such high racial promise. The partnership of Delton Franz and Vincent Harding symbolized the hope for an egalitarian and inclusive future. Following Horton's lead, Mennonites from both the (Old) and General Conference communities employed nonconformity doctrine to counter racial subordination rather than sustain it. Although leaders had not arrived at a unified response to the nonviolent tactics of the burgeoning civil rights movement, individual members engaged in a wide variety of actions to counter the racist attitudes and behaviors yet present in the church. Southern tours, integrated worship services, African-American deacons, new church plants across the country, and a speech by Martin Luther King Jr. at a Mennonite college in a former sundown town marked the breadth of that activity. By 1962, few from the church may have marched with King in the streets, but many pushed against a separatist past by demonstrating in their homes and churches.

Crisis and Debate, 1963 – 1965

The brevity of the period from 1963 through 1965 belies the far-reaching impact of its intense activity. Urban racial rebellion, summer protests, the

Birmingham civil rights campaign, and the Mennonite response to these events captured the attention of the church. The frequency of race-focused articles in the church press reached an all-time high in 1963, as more than eighty-five reports, editorials, profiles, and opinion pieces explored the racial turmoil in the nation. Because of the Hardings' involvement in the Birmingham campaign, Vincent's prolific pen, and his ability to use Anabaptist theological terms, every church leader in both the General Conference and (Old) Mennonite denominations had to deal with his critique if they wanted to address race relations in the church. In the remaining two years of the period, Harding continued to frame much of the debate about the manner in which the church should respond to the crisis precipitated by the civil rights movement.

Alongside the internal demonstrations described at length in the following chapters, the church responded to national crisis by calling meetings, sponsoring tours, passing statements, and emphasizing service initiatives. Activists and church leaders hosted six race-focused gatherings in Georgia, Indiana, Kansas, Missouri, Ohio, and Virginia. Harding spoke at the first four, called for the fifth, and was quoted at the sixth. In each setting, participants debated how best to respond to the civil rights movement. In response, some poured their energies into challenging vestiges of segregation inside the church. Peter Ediger, Vincent and Rosemarie Harding, Guy Hershberger, and Vern Preheim—church staff and executives from both the General Conference and the (Old) Mennonite Church— toured the South and invariably discussed congregational segregation, even when their original intention had been to evaluate Camp Landon's service program. Others responded by passing statements, an action taken up by at least four different Mennonite groups in 1963 alone. Mennonites also publicized white volunteers assigned to African-American communities, often in service to African-American children. For example, editors of the Lancaster Conference's promotional newsletter, the *Volunteer*, abruptly began to feature many more photos of white volunteers interacting with African-American service recipients.[84] First and foremost, Mennonites responded to the civil rights crisis by intensifying existing service and mission activity among African Americans.

This burst of activity in response to street-based civil rights demonstrations paralleled the church's response to independence movements in Africa and elsewhere. North American missionaries had to change their

strategies and programs in countries like Congo and Somalia, where independence movements and internal warfare undermined their initiatives.
Those who had once commanded broad authority and local politicians' respect found their social status diminished and their mission work threatened.[85] Even as white Mennonites scrambled to demonstrate their racial
egalitarianism in response to domestic agitation, Mennonite missionaries
scrambled to demonstrate their openness to indigenous rule in response to
international agitation. From Birmingham to Mogadishu, quietist Mennonites tried to make their way forward in the midst of foment and unrest.

In this volatile environment, a degree of organized political activism
found traction in the church. In 1963 denominational peace executive Ed
Metzler called all local peace committees to take new legislative action in
response to the example set by Vincent and Rosemarie Harding. General
Conference editor Maynard Shelly and pastor Lynford Hershey traveled
to Mississippi in 1964 and took part in demonstrations there.[86] Even participants in a 1964 conference, organized to examine race relations in the
church, that included many of the figures encountered in this historical
overview—the Hardings, Hershberger, Bethesda Mennonite pastor Hubert Schwartzentruber, Camp Landon staffers Edna and Orlo Kaufman
and Harold and Rosella Regier, and North Carolina Mennonite Brethren
moderator Rondo Horton—could not keep from debating whether participation in street demonstrations was appropriate.[87] That same year, Mississippi jailers severely beat Eli Hochstedler, a young white Goshen College
student then studying at Tougaloo College, who had become involved in
several civil rights demonstrations.[88] Members of both Woodlawn and
Community Mennonite congregations in the Chicago area participated in
marches led by Martin Luther King Jr. Finally, in 1965, Mennonites from
throughout the East and Midwest attended meetings held in Youngstown,
Ohio, and St. Louis, Missouri, where participants offered cautious but deliberate support for civil rights involvement. Without a doubt, some members of the church took to the streets.

Yet other Mennonites opposed such overt involvement. Most Mennonite church members neither actively opposed nor engaged street-based
activism, although many more participated in demonstrations in their
homes and sanctuaries. Others took more oppositional stances. The Lancaster Conference's bishop board, for example, continued to oppose in-

volvement in civil rights demonstrations throughout the period. In 1965 white Mennonite Sanford Shetler opposed civil rights involvement outright and called for Mennonites to stay away from demonstrations of any kind, even while declaring his opposition to racial segregation.[89] Shetler joined a sizable contingent of church leaders who raised theological objections to demonstrations and street marches because such tactics, even when strictly nonviolent, still coerced change. Although Guy Hershberger expressed deep respect for civil rights leaders like King and nonviolence strategist James Lawson, he continued through this period to oppose coercion of any kind.[90] Like many of his contemporaries, he professed a belief that love alone should compel people to repent. Less sympathetic voices in the church turned support for a strict interpretation of nonresistance into active opposition to civil rights leaders. Also in 1965, a member of a racially integrated congregation in Harlem declared that "a church of largely white members located in a Negro community in contemporary America offers potentially greater gains for the claims of Christ than . . . ten civil-rights marches led by Rev. M. L. King, Jr."[91] The debate over the civil rights movement had not resolved.

The intensity of the crises and debates present within the church from 1963 to 1965 moved racial issues to the center of the Mennonite community. Although the promise of the previous period dissipated in the middle of discord and turmoil, white Mennonites discussed racial issues more frequently than at any time in the past. Just as they had often reflected the racial attitudes of those around them, Mennonites now reflected the new attention to race relations. Yet the reflection was particularly Anabaptist. Whereas members of other white Christian groups opposed demonstrations because they disrupted law and order, Mennonites disapproved of marches because they used coercive methods. Unlike Methodists, who lobbied legislators without pause, Mennonites objected to political entanglements. In contrast to Presbyterians, who appealed to patriotic values to condemn segregation, Mennonites opposed Jim Crow laws with biblical injunctions. The new focus on race relations did not displace core values that had both supported and blocked movement toward a more racially egalitarian community during the previous four decades. Like Rondo Horton, Mennonites continued to interweave their racial engagement with clear doctrine.

Reaction to Black Power, 1966–1971

From 1966 through this study's finish in 1971, the Minority Ministries Council emerged in the (Old) Mennonite Church as a prophetic voice for change both emboldened and debilitated by the rhetoric of black power. During this period, warmly affirmative comments about white Mennonites' engagement with African Americans gave way to harsher, more accusatory commentary. The shift toward assertiveness and confrontation within the church reflected the rise of black nationalism, the black power movement, and a rejection of tactical nonviolence on the part of groups like the Student Nonviolent Coordinating Committee and the Congress of Racial Equality. The affinity some white Mennonite leaders felt with nonviolent leaders in the racial justice struggle quickly dissipated in the face of direct and pointed challenge. Leaders of white mainline denominations experienced a similar sense of dislocation and, at times, betrayal.[92] Even assurances from long-time African-American members such as Rondo Horton could not quell the turmoil.

Three historical developments gave rise to the Minority Ministries Council. First, white Mennonite magazine editors turned their attention to the black power movement. In 1966 several writers introduced black power themes of racial autonomy and power analysis in largely pejorative terms.[93] Their commentary about black power, however, set the stage for African-American Mennonites like Lee Roy Berry, Curtis Burrell, Gerald Hughes, and John Powell to gain new power in the church as they and their white allies noted how few African Americans sat on church boards and committees. The 1968 assassination of Rev. Martin Luther King Jr. and subsequent urban turmoil increased interest in racial issues as numerous writers lamented the loss of a nonviolent leader and revisited themes unaddressed since the previous round of racial rebellions in 1963. Most important, however, in 1969 Powell confronted (Old) Mennonite Church delegates in Turner, Oregon, with a call based on James Forman's Black Manifesto, asking the church to invest significant financial resources in programs for racial justice. Powell and his colleagues in the Minority Ministries Council then used the promise of substantial funding to challenge the racist practices they encountered within the white Mennonite community. Although no similar body emerged among General Conference Mennonites at this time, executives and grassroots members alike paid close attention to council activity and even appointed representatives to the group's advisory committee.[94]

Direct and vociferous critiques of white Mennonites' racism led to African-American withdrawal from the church and increasing criticism of the council's efforts by white Mennonite leaders and their constituents. In 1967 Harding returned from partial exile to address the Mennonite World Conference on the topic of the church's nonviolent peace witness in an age of revolution. His speech both galvanized and divided the delegates as they listened to him criticize the "power of whiteness" within the Mennonite church.[95] The positive voices initially raised in response to Harding's critique began to dissipate in the wake of rising black nationalism and continued appeals for financial support of the Minority Ministries Council. Although the volume of articles on racial themes in the church press spiked to a five-year high in 1968, by 1971 they had fallen back down to levels not seen since the early 1950s. On the heels of this rapid retreat, white church executives ostracized Minority Ministries staff members, and a survey revealed that a majority of Mennonites in the United States did not yet support racial integration.[96] By the end of the period, the Minority Ministries Council had received less than a tenth of the $2.5 million originally sought. Without finances to support its prophetic critique, the organization soon collapsed.[97]

The legacy of the council nonetheless remained. Although churchwide discussions of racism diminished after 1971, African-American Mennonites and their white allies resisted ecclesiastic racism in terms defined by Minority Ministries members like Hershey and Powell. Two decades later, the church again turned its attention to racial issues and drew on the power analysis that council members had originally introduced. At that time, Hershey, Powell, and others rejoined the church and took on new leadership roles. Those who had been pushed aside and separated for challenging the church's history of separation entered again to renew their critique. The story of Mennonites' daily demonstrations continued to unfold.

Changes and Continuities

Significant racial changes occurred during the fifty-three years reviewed here. By 1971, fewer Mennonites displayed visible markers of separation from society than in 1918. Fewer women wore head coverings or refrained from cutting their hair. A smaller number of men wore the plain coat. More Mennonites watched television and listened to the radio, and some had begun to attend and appear in plays. As these examples suggest and historians of the Mennonite experience in North America have noted, an increasing acculturation took place over the course of the twentieth century but especially in the post–World War II era. Mennonites looked more like those around them than they had at any time in the previous seventy years.[98]

When examined through a racial lens, that acculturation looks less distinct. For most of the twentieth century, white Mennonites had, in the main, accepted society's opinions about, approaches toward, and distance from African Americans. Although a group of leaders consistently pushed against patterns of racial subordination, prejudice, and overt discrimination within the church, even they seldom drew on distinctive Anabaptist doctrine to make their case. Those who, like Rondo Horton, used principles of nonconformity and other core theological professions to oppose racist practice left the church early, as did Rosemarie and Vincent Harding, or grew frustrated over the slow pace of change, as in the case of Harold and Rosella Regier of Camp Landon. The same church that cherished its racially egalitarian image also practiced racial discrimination that, upon closer examination, looked very similar to that practiced by their neighbors outside the church community. In the area of race relations, Mennonites did not become more acculturated during the twentieth century; they already were.

Yet Mennonites came by their racially egalitarian reputation honestly. The (Old) Mennonite Church removed all scriptural objections to interracial marriage in 1955. Theologians like Guy Hershberger became more open to the possibility of at least limited involvement in street-based activism. Hundreds more African Americans appeared on membership roles, and dozens more churches ministered in African-American communities. In the main, church leaders more readily acknowledged that the Mennonite church had "too long overlooked its own racism" than had its grassroots congregants.[99] Although yet token in their representation, African-American Mennonites like Gerald Hughes from Lee Heights in Ohio overcame resistance to their leadership abilities and accepted appointments to key national committees. Amid the continuity of acculturation to racial discrimination, some in the church embraced new inclusion and confession.

The changes that kept people like Hughes in the church and the continuities that kept people like Vincent Harding away shared a theme of separation. To be certain, through the course of their history in the Americas white Mennonites had been far less socially separated than their distinct attire would suggest. Attitudes that supported white racial superiority had proliferated since evangelists segregated their mission sites in the first half of the twentieth century. Nonconformity dictates amplified assumptions of superiority by suggesting that racism existed only outside the redeemed community. Harding noted the depth of those attitudes, and when he found them intractable, he left. At the same time, separatist values born of an urge to remain distinct from a sinful world opened doors to Hughes. Leaders like Guy Hershberger called for nonconformity to racial prejudice and segregation. Other Mennonites, like Hughes's wife Annabelle, ventured beyond homogenous enclaves because a separated church had instilled within them the value of service. Hughes gained opportunities to serve the church because Mennonites also believed that nonconformity to the world could necessitate opposition to discrimination. In these instances and those to follow, the impulse to separate complicated Mennonites' engagement with the civil rights movement, at times supporting and at other times diminishing active participation.

The chapters that follow trace the demonstrations that Mennonites mounted during this conflicted history of separation. That white Mennonites held many of the same ideas about African Americans as their white neighbors through much of the twentieth century makes their demonstrations in home and sanctuary all the more worthy of examination. That those demonstrations resulted in identifiable change makes their methods historically significant. The drama of civil rights movement street campaigns can no longer receive all our attention. Within the church, where the words spoken, relationships built, and actions taken echoed for years, new drama awaits. The daily demonstrations of Mennonites who, like Rondo Horton, confronted racism inside the church opens a new perspective on how this country began to overturn its own apartheid system. Alongside those who pounded the pavement, another set of marchers strode through sanctuaries and loped through living rooms. Through the history of Mennonites, this book tells the story of that latter kind of marching. The lives of two women, one black, one white, launches that narrative in chapter 2 as prayer coverings, communion, and interracial cooperation come to the fore.

Prayer-Covered Protest

*I am not challenging the devotional covering . . . but the attempt to introduce our
particular version into a culture and on hair different from our own.*
—Paul Peachey, white Mennonite pastor, 1957

Prayer Covering as Movement Medium

On a nameless country road in 1939, Rowena Lark and Fannie
Swartzentruber stand relaxed and contented in each other's presence (see figure 2.1). Lark, on the left, and Swartzentruber had
been working together for two years at the Gay Street Mennonite Mission in Harrisonburg, Virginia, when a photographer took their picture.
Although Lark was nearly two decades older than Swartzentruber, the
two women had developed a close and lasting attachment, as suggested by
the photo. Both women smile, their covering-clad heads cocked at opposing but symmetrical angles. The women appear as comfortable with each
other as with the clothing they wear. Although the fabric differs, the cut
and styling of their cape dresses—traditional nonconformist Mennonite
garments tailored with modesty panels—match as closely as the prayer
veils they wear on the back of their heads. In a southern county bound by
Jim Crow practice, Lark and Swartzentruber appear at ease beneath their
white lace head coverings.

The prayer coverings these women wore were an integral part of their
struggle to end segregation within the Mennonite church, as were other
types of civil rights–era protest taken up by African-American and white

Fig. 2.1 Rowena Lark and Fannie Swartzentruber
with Homer Swartzentruber (held by Fannie) and
Nancy Swartzentruber, 1939
R. M. Mullet, "Broad Street Church in Review, part IV,"
Missionary Light 21, no. 4 (July–August 1961): 8–10. Photo
courtesy of Virginia Mennonite Conference, Harrisonburg, VA

Mennonites. Through the interlocking life stories of these two women,
the history and form of Mennonites' daily demonstrations emerge. An integrated group of Mennonites used common religious resources like cloth-

ing and ritual to protest racial exclusion. Their demonstrations took forms unfamiliar to most students of the civil rights movement, such as wearing a religious symbol, as well as forms more familiar, for example, participating in street marches—although in the latter case not on the expected scale, in the expected place, or at the expected time. Together, these two forms of protest—one subtle and understated, the other direct and unequivocal—extended the reach of traditional civil rights demonstrations into a community that external observers deemed racially disengaged. In that community, women transformed the prayer covering into a medium of civil rights protest.

The variously tragic and hopeful story of Swartzentruber and Lark's challenge to their church from 1935 through the end of the 1960s reframes women's resistance to the racial order in the United States. Although other social groups also pursued common goals across racial lines, Christian communities often claimed that interracial cooperation should be the norm rather than the exception.[1] Though rarely acknowledged in U.S. church history, the expectation nonetheless brought African-American and white Christians together. Scholars of religion have studied high-profile events such as eighteenth-century Moravians worshipping across racial lines in eastern Pennsylvania, early twentieth-century Pentecostals hosting interracial gatherings at Azusa Street in Los Angeles, and white and African-American Christians working together at Koinonia Farm in Georgia in the latter half of the twentieth century.[2] Those same scholars have unfortunately ignored interracial partnerships that, while less visible, altered religious communities and quite often lasted much longer than the high-profile encounters. Lark and Swartzentruber's story also demonstrates the particular resilience of women's relationships across racial lines. As other scholars have noted, women played a key role in sustaining and advancing the civil rights movement.[3] The narrative that unfolds here adds to this growing body of scholarship by demonstrating the complex ways in which two women in a long-term interracial relationship faced religious and political changes during the long civil rights era. Together, Lark and Swartzentruber built a friendship across racial lines that led to a different kind of freedom struggle, one marked by distinct yet intertwined daily responses to oppression.

This chapter opens new vistas into the history of the American Mennonite experience. The few studies that have attended to racial issues among Mennonites have paid more attention to men than to women.[4] By foregrounding male experience in the Mennonite history of race relations, scholars have missed the reasons that African-American women joined the church. When undergirded by church doctrine, lifelong interracial relationships brought African-American women into an often unwelcoming church. Similarly, the women featured in this chapter excoriated racial discrimination in the church, did so earlier than many of their male counterparts, and sustained interracial fellowship longer than many men.[5] Mennonite women resisted the most oppressive forms of racial subjugation in their day. With their words and bodies, women in the Mennonite church thus built a foundation on which race relations in the community would both thrive and falter.[6]

Wearing clothing that marked them as Mennonites was one way the two friends built that foundation. The prayer covering, in particular, drew attention within and without the church. With origins in the Palatinate folk custom of eighteenth-century Europe, the covering took on religious significance in the late nineteenth century, as church leaders established it as an ordinance on par with communion and baptism.[7] Church leaders promoted the covering based on a New Testament passage: "Any woman who prays or prophesies with her head unveiled disgraces her head" (1 Corinthians 11:5). Leaders used the same Corinthians text to assert that the covering represented male authority.[8] In response to this mandate, Lark and Swartzentruber wore prayer caps daily, in a practice that two decades previously had been limited to church services and personal devotions.[9] In the post–World War II era, women and men would increasingly debate the meaning and necessity of the prayer covering, but at the time this story opens, Lark and Swartzentruber demonstrated their church membership by donning the covering every day.

Their choice to wear distinctive religious garb required more of women than it did men. As in other religious groups, church officials policed women's dress.[10] Although some Mennonite men wore a collarless "plain coat," church leaders did not enforce this practice as closely as they did the prayer covering.[11] Furthermore, those men who wore the plain coat rarely did so on a daily basis. Lark's husband, James, shed his during business trips to town.[12] By the end of the 1930s, however, few Mennonite women on the eastern seaboard had the option of taking off the prayer veil. To show proper piety and avoid censure, women wore the prayer covering at all times.

Yet those who wore the prayer covering did not automatically acquiesce to male patriarchy. As scholar of religion Saba Mahmoud points out, women who don religious garb also pursue their own interests. Some Muslim women, for example, teach others how to embody piety while wearing the hijab, a formal religious veil, creating intimate space where they decide how they will move in society.[13] In that space, men, ignorant of the practice, have diminished authority. In the same way, Mennonite women who wore the prayer covering controlled the shape, size, styling, and positioning of the covering. The choices they made about the prayer veil challenged the authority of Mennonite bishops and ministers.

From the start, Lark's choice to wear the covering differed from Swartzentruber's. Within the African-American community, hats and head coverings carried deep cultural significance.[14] Especially during a Sunday worship service in an African-American church, a woman's hat sent both a religious and a fashion message.[15] Rather than making an uncomplicated switch from one kind of head covering to another, African-American converts like Lark used a highly symbolic mode of dress as part of a strategy to counter racial exclusion.[16] Because she broke with one tradition to join another, Lark's choice to wear the covering becomes all the more significant. As this chapter makes evident, Lark and other African-American women wore the covering to claim belonging in a church that frequently denied them full status.

At the time they posed in front of a Ford Slantback in 1939, Lark and Swartzentruber sought to create a more racially egalitarian church through a shared passion for African-American missions. Swartzentruber's eldest son recalled his parents' visiting Lark and her husband, James, during the Swartzentrubers' move from Delaware to Virginia in late 1936.[17] Early the next year, soon after arriving in Virginia, Swartzentruber and her husband, Ernest, invited Lark to join their ministry to African Americans in the northeast corner of Harrisonburg.[18] With the support of the Virginia Mennonite Conference mission board, the couple extended an official invitation to "the colored sister from Washington" to participate in their vacation bible school program, an evangelistic effort common in the period that focused on providing scriptural instruction to neighborhood children through classroom activities, crafts projects, and outings.[19] Lark led songs, told stories, and energized the gatherings.[20] She would later look back on the time spent at Gay Street as "glory-filled days when we labored together for the Master."[21]

The women dressed alike during their shared ministry in Harrisonburg, even though they came from different backgrounds. Having been raised in the Amish community until her parents joined the more liberal Mennonite church, Swartzentruber had long worn the prayer covering. From an equally young age, she had expressed sensitivity to the marginalized. Early exposure to prejudice directed at an adopted sister of Italian heritage may have motivated Swartzentruber to take up the unpaid Gay Street matron responsibilities.[22] Once in Harrisonburg, she entered a community where enough Mennonites resided that women who wore the white prayer veil attracted little attention. Lark had already been a part of the (Old) Mennonite Church for more than a decade when Swartzentruber and her husband contacted her. Lark first began attending Rocky Ridge Mennonite Mission near Quakertown, Pennsylvania, in 1927.[23] When the family relocated in 1935 to Cottage City, Maryland, near where Lark taught in the public school system, she and James joined the Brentwood Mennonite congregation.[24] By the time the Swartzentrubers recruited her, Lark had adopted the prayer covering and cape dress as her daily attire.[25] When she came to Harrisonburg, she entered a community in which a black woman wearing the covering was a rare sight.

The women's similar dress belied the image of a racially egalitarian church. Following early twentieth-century attempts at integrated missions, Mennonite urban church workers in the North segregated their churches.[26] For example, the Philadelphia Colored Mission in 1935 started a separate mission for African Americans only two blocks away from the first white congregation.[27] Although African-American children had attended summer outreach programs for several years, in 1936 the white mission workers wrote that "It was thought best to have a separate work for the colored."[28] As mission boards became more active following World War II, they maintained those patterns of separation, in some cases through the early 1960s. Similarly, although they had not yet legislated segregation, leaders of the Virginia Mennonite Conference followed their northern co-believers by separating white and black Mennonites, as Lark observed in her periodic travels to Harrisonburg in 1937.[29] As a 1939 photo from one of Gay Street's first vacation bible schools attests, church leaders kept African-American children separated from their white counterparts on the other side of the city (see figure 2.2).[30] Nonetheless, Lark and Swartzentruber worked side by side and dressed alike. Although church leaders segregated churches, they did not mandate different clothing.

Fig. 2.2 Gay Street Vacation Bible School, Harrisonburg, Virginia, 1939

Virginia Mennonite Conference Archives, Papers of the Virginia Mennonite Board of Missions and
Charities, box Harold Huber's Papers, Broad Street Mennonite Church Materials (History, etc.).
Photo courtesy of Virginia Mennonite Conference, Harrisonburg, VA

Initial Protest and Response, 1939–1943

From the start of her time at Gay Street, Lark tested the limits set by her
adopted church. Some of her co-believers appreciated the solos she sang
during evening meetings.[31] Others found her introduction of African-
American musical tradition troubling. Although Mennonites in the area
enjoyed four-part a cappella singing, they disapproved of the prideful attention solos invited. Lark also used one of the few public speaking opportunities open to women to test the boundaries of approved behavior.
Rather than limit herself to telling children's stories during vacation bible
school programs, Lark gave "stirring message[s]" while wearing the prayer
covering that gained the attention of mission and conference-wide leaders

alike.[32] In his 1939 report to the annual meeting of the Virginia Mennonite Board of Missions and Charities, the sponsoring body for the work
at Gay Street, Ernest Swartzentruber made specific mention of only one
name. He referred to Rowena Lark, the "colored sister from Cottage City,
Maryland," who had assisted in the vacation bible school program.[33] As
she claimed Mennonite status while wearing the covering and challenged
Mennonite practice by exercising leadership in song and sermon, Lark
quickly gained the attention of Virginia Mennonites.

Lark's efforts to claim equality with white Mennonites parallel African-American laborers' efforts to defeat racism during the 1940s. Black
union members participated in the Double V campaign to end fascism
abroad and racism at home.[34] They sought to use the social dislocation
brought about by World War II to realize dual victories on the domestic and international fronts. Like Lark, they offered skilled labor, found
themselves in high demand, and remained committed to their sponsoring
organization—in the case of the unionized African Americans, the house
of labor; in Lark's case, the Mennonite church. African-American laborers lent their sweat and toil to the country's war effort in hopes of ending
racial disparity in society. Lark offered her services to the church's mission enterprise in order to stop racial oppression in the church. Although
no evidence exists that Lark modeled her efforts after those mounted by
unionized African-American laborers, her efforts inside the church reso-
nate with those exerted by advocates of the Double V campaign.

Lark and the Double V participants had one more thing in common.
They all encountered significant backlash, despite demonstrated commitment to church and country. In Lark's case, leaders from the Virginia
Mennonite Conference responded to her high-profile ministry by officially segregating church sacraments. In late 1940 the executive committees of both the Virginia Conference and its mission board passed "definite
policies to govern" interracial relationships.[35] Claiming a desire to promote
"the best interests of both colored and white," the joint executive committees voted to segregate the rites of baptism, foot washing, the holy kiss,
and communion.[36] Notably, the official sacramental segregation centered
on the most physically intimate of the church sacraments. At no point did
the policy call for racially differentiated prayer coverings, for instance. Although Lark agreed to dress like white Mennonites, she no longer could
share a communion cup with them.

Lark and Swartzentruber responded to the segregation pronouncement in different ways. Along with her husband, Swartzentruber challenged her supervisors to identify a scriptural basis for the dictate. In response, the bishops declared that some decisions did not require scriptural backing, an uncharacteristic statement from leaders who called for biblical guidance in all other areas.[37] Swartzentruber and her husband viewed the bishops' explanation—that "as a matter of expediency we must make some distinction to meet existing conditions"—as a significant setback for their work.[38] The latter portion of the mandate particularly irked Swartzentruber, since it broke with the long-standing tradition of sharing a common communion cup.[39] By contrast, Lark chose a less public role. In the difficult period following the bishops' mandate, Lark offered to travel to Harrisonburg to assist the Swartzentruber family after an accident left Ernest in the hospital for a stretch of ten days. Lark assured Swartzentruber of "the complete sympathy and service of the Lark family" and enjoined her to "not worry my dear."[40] Rather than direct challenge, Lark supported her friend's efforts while continuing to wear the covering in a subtler kind of protest.

The combined witness of Swartzentruber's direct protest and Lark's clothing-based strategy drew new members to the mission, despite the church's segregation policy and doctrinal demands. Although by 1942 as many as ninety children had begun to attend the congregation's vacation bible school program, many fewer adults participated on a regular basis, and men were more likely than women to join.[41] As already noted, men had a less demanding sartorial barrier to overcome in that they experienced greater flexibility in the wearing of the plain coat.[42] By contrast, in addition to facing nonconformist dictates, such as those forbidding life insurance policies, women bore the extra requirement of needing to adopt the cape dress and covering upon their baptism.[43]

At the beginning of 1942, Swartzentruber reported that seven adults, only one of them a woman, had joined the congregation as of that year.[44] At this initial stage, the congregation broke the trend common in most African-American congregations in which women constituted the majority. Clothing requirements thus may have dampened women's receptiveness to the mission's early outreach efforts. Nonetheless, during her frequent trips to Harrisonburg, Lark demonstrated that African-American women could join the church and wear the veil. In response to her example, Roberta Webb, a talented teacher and community organizer, became a member in early 1943.[45] Following her baptism, Webb began to wear the prayer cap and cape dress (see figure 2.3). She explained that she did so because of the "very deep desire to treat our people [African Americans] as brothers" evidenced by mission workers like Swartzentruber, who on June 8, 1943, accepted another year's reappointment as matron at Gay Street.[46] Lark and Swartzentruber together overcame some of the racial barriers constructed by the church.

This chapter begins by setting out to explain how prayer coverings became a medium of civil rights protest. Lark's and Swartzentruber's narrative thus far highlights four developments crucial to that explanation. First, during World War II, at least some African-American and white women in the church developed strong relationships. Second, during the same period, the increasingly high-profile African-American missions that grew out of those relationships prompted formalized segregation. Third, though a measure of paternalism undergirded their relationships, Lark, Swartzentruber, and contemporaries like Webb wore the same clothes as they struggled against racist practices in the church. Finally, as they wore the same clothes, African-American and white women used different types of protest to counter Jim Crow practice. Swartzentruber directly confronted bishops about their segregation decision. Lark stepped into leadership roles that indirectly challenged gender and racial expectations. Both women pursued their protest strategies while wearing the prayer veil. Thus at this point in the narrative, the women wore the same religious garb and made similar claims on church membership even while pursuing different protest strategies.

Diverging Paths and Intensified Protests, 1944–1945

Lark continued to mark her Mennonite identity through dress when she moved west to minister in Chicago. In the summer of 1944, at the age of fifty-two, she and her husband, James, traveled to the Near Southside neighborhood of Dearborn Street in Chicago, an impoverished African-American community, to lead vacation bible school.[47] Lark's reputation as an enthusiastic and effective leader of children's programs again drew attention. While carrying out her new responsibilities Lark continued to wear the prayer veil and cape dress, though Mennonites in the Chicago

Fig. 2.3 Roberta Webb and daughters, Harrisonburg, Virginia,
circa 1943
Virginia Mennonite Conference Archives, Papers of the Virginia
Mennonite Board of Missions and Charities, Box Harold Huber's Papers,
Broad Street Mennonite Church Materials (History, etc.). Photo courtesy
of Virginia Mennonite Conference, Harrisonburg, VA

area did not enforce dress restrictions with the same rigidity as in Virginia
and Pennsylvania. For example, she and James dressed far more conservatively than their white co-workers even though both couples had relocated to the Chicago area from the more conservative East (see figure 2.4).

Whether Lark continued to dress plain because of her fidelity to church teaching or as part of a deliberate, long-term strategy to gain acceptance and full-member standing in the church matters less than the impact of her dress decision on those with whom she came in contact. As she transitioned from bible school helper at Gay Street in Harrisonburg to pastoral leader at the emerging Bethel Mennonite congregation in Chicago, Lark made visible her denominational affiliation.[48]

Back in Harrisonburg, Webb followed Lark's sartorial strategy even as she intensified protest against the church's Jim Crow practice. At the time of Lark's move, the Virginia Conference—sponsored Eastern Mennonite College in Harrisonburg maintained a whites-only policy. Administrators segregated their institution because they feared that admitting African-American students would create "trouble."[49] Webb, however, viewed the policy differently. Her brother John complained that "they accept you in the church . . . yet, they won't accept your children in their college."[50] Webb noted this hypocrisy in letters to church leaders even while contacting other Mennonite colleges to see whether they would accept her daughters.[51] Even as she protested through writing letters, she also made clear through the clothes she wore that she was a Mennonite. Her co-believers had to acknowledge her commitment in part because she dressed like them.

In the midst of her ever bolder protest, Webb lost her most vocal ally against the conference's segregationist policies. Having bid farewell to Lark, Roberta Webb said good-bye to Swartzentruber as well but under far more controversial circumstances. In the fall of 1944, Swartzentruber lost patience with the practice of segregated communion.[52] She had been overruled by supporters of sacramental segregation, watched Lark leave the Jim Crow South, and witnessed school administrators deny Webb's daughter's enrollment bid. At every turn the church's segregated practice blocked her efforts to evangelize African Americans. Swartzentruber could not fully welcome potential converts into a church that claimed to include all but, in its most sacred rituals, excluded some. Even those African Americans who, like Lark and Webb, marked their separation from society by the clothes they wore could not fully participate in physically intimate sacraments where believers kissed cheeks, shared a cup, washed one another's feet, and entered together into baptismal waters. Emboldened by Lark's departure and Webb's entry, Swartzentruber made a deci-

Fig. 2.4 Paul and Lois King, Rowena and James Lark, Chicago, 1953
J. D. Zehr, "The Brotherhood of the Saints," *Christian Living* 3, no. 5 (May 1956): 17–19.
Photo courtesy of Mennonite Publishing Network, Scottdale, PA

sion to take to the streets. Before communion ended on a Sunday morning, she gathered her youngest daughter Rhoda into her arms and stormed out of the service. Rather than wait for her husband, she walked four miles to their farm just north of Harrisonburg. When Ernest joined her, Swartzentruber declared that she would never again sit through such a service.[53]

Swartzentruber's long walk home in her covering and Sunday best symbolized a singular entry into a form of protest anathema to most white Mennonites but already common among African Americans. In 1941, for example, civil rights activists A. Philip Randolph and Bayard Rustin made plans for a massive march on Washington to protest the exclusion of African Americans from wartime defense industries. In response, President Franklin Delano Roosevelt signed Executive Order 8802, ending racially discriminatory federal hiring practices. In a move prompted in part by this kind of street-fueled activism, the Supreme Court struck down the all-white southern primary in *Smith v. Allwright* in 1944, the same year that Swartzentruber protested the segregated communion service.[54] Although Swartzentruber was not connected to the organizers who brought about such legal and political change, her spontaneous march from the church into the street reflected organizers' labor- and legal-focused tactics. Swartzentruber modeled a proactive means of challenging racism in the church using methods similar to those employed outside the faith community. For many years few Mennonites would follow her example. Yet by marching out of a communion service while wearing sacred garb, she set a precedent that others would later follow.

Leaders from the Virginia Conference responded to Swartzentruber's singular demonstration by shattering her congregational foundation. Although in May 1944 the Swartzentrubers had been reappointed for another year's term, on January 5, 1945, only months after Swartzentruber stormed out of the communion service, the executive committee of the Virginia Mennonite Board of Missions abruptly removed the Swartzentrubers from their posts as matron and superintendent.[55] In the space of a few minutes, the bishops forced Swartzentruber to leave a church community into which she had poured the best of her energy and passion. Family members expressed concern about the couple's well-being and witnessed their emotional devastation. A niece remembered hearing about the dismissal when she was about eight years old and thinking that "something awful" had occurred.[56] Although Ernest continued to work at a local hatchery and Fannie and the older children kept the farm running, they felt spiritually adrift.[57] The dismissal from Gay Street left them so distraught that the Swartzentrubers contemplated leaving the Mennonite church and for a short while considered joining an independent bible church in the area.[58]

The bishops' decision to dismiss Fannie Swartzentruber can thus be understood as a move to rid the community of an internal, prayer-veiled threat during wartime. Mennonites in Virginia knew that conscientious objectors from their community had been imprisoned and harassed during the Civil War and World War I.[59] Those tales of persecution remained fresh as church leaders administered a nearby Civilian Public Service camp for Mennonite conscientious objectors to World War II.[60] Although church doctrine required that they accept reprisal for their pacifist belief, it made no similar demands that leaders risk antagonistic response for their racial convictions. Leaders from the Virginia Conference had already decided to cooperate with the "general attitude of society in the South toward the intermingling of the two races."[61] Swartzentruber's protests invited racial antagonism toward members of the conference when wartime persecution remained a possibility. That she made her protests while wearing the covering only served to emphasize the threat she posed. Church leaders could not dismiss her as an outsider. Given that northern Mennonites had not yet organized to oppose ecclesiastical segregation in the South, the Virginia Conference leaders made an easy choice.[62] By severing Swartzentruber's official connections to Gay Street, the bishops dismissed the person most likely to upset the precarious balance between racial acquiescence and military demurral.

The bishops' authoritative move also reflected their interest in reining in mission workers at home and abroad. Leaders in the Virginia Conference and the nearby Lancaster (Pennsylvania) Conference felt threatened by returning missionaries who introduced cultural relativism as they questioned the appropriateness of mandating European dress styles in African, Asian, and South American contexts.[63] These bishop groups and others like them across the church struggled to protect distinctive Anabaptist practices and beliefs from encroaching acculturation. At a time when their attempts to codify and enforce nonconformity doctrine met both passive and overt resistance from longtime members, the bishops had little patience for those who advocated for change on behalf of new entries to the church.[64] By threatening to upset the racial status quo, Swartzentruber had also disrupted doctrinal stasis. Although she and Lark both cooperated with sartorial dictates, the pressures resulting from African converts who did not cooperate with those practices seems to have led to stricter enforcement of all doctrines at home.[65] In 1946 Swartzentruber further diminished the threat she posed by moving with her husband to Greenwood, Delaware.[66]

Spectacle, Success, and Outspoken Women, 1946–1952

While the bishops tightened racial restrictions and dismissed their most vocal critics, white Mennonite leaders in the Virginia Conference and elsewhere highlighted African Americans dressed in nonconformist garb.

As Lark and Webb had demonstrated, conservatively dressed African-American women claimed belonging by showing that they looked like any other Mennonite. Church leaders initially confounded the women's strategy, however, by putting dark-skinned converts on display. Countering any assumption that only older African-American converts like Lark and Webb wore the prayer veil, a 1947 denominational magazine featured a photo of a conservatively dressed wedding party beneath the heading, "A MENNONITE COLORED WEDDING" (see figure 2.5). In the photo, the bride's covering stands out with particular clarity atop her bowed head. Through his racially specific caption, the editor emphasized the rarity of an African-American wedding. Moreover, the photo amplified the spectacle of African-American Mennonites dressed in nonconformist attire. The photographer stood in front of the congregation during the ceremony to take the picture, a practice at odds with Mennonite rules of decorum. As the surrounding text made evident, the couple's race, rather than the photographer's ritual violation, made the event notable. Other Mennonite editors also featured prominent photos of plain-dressed Lark and her husband.[67] The attention given to photos of African Americans in sectarian garb suggested that they merited public display but not full inclusion.

Amid such visual spectacle, Swartzentruber and Lark fostered their relationship and their connections with Broad Street as they sought to end Jim Crow in the church. In 1948 Swartzentruber stayed at home with her children to make it possible for her husband to serve as the vacation bible school superintendent at Lark's congregation in Chicago.[68] In a reversal of their previous assignments, the Swartzentrubers had become Lark's helpers, a position that placed them under the authority of African Americans. At the time, few white Mennonites would willingly have accepted such arrangements.

Lark also nurtured connections with the Broad Street congregation by assisting Webb's daughter Ada. Despite Webb's protests, officials from Eastern Mennonite College had refused to admit the young woman in 1945. Undaunted, Webb arranged for her daughter to study at Hesston College, a two-year school in rural Kansas.[69] In November of 1947, Ada moved to Chicago, where the Larks welcomed her to their congregation. The following year, again with the support and encouragement of Lark, Ada took evening courses at Roosevelt College in Chicago.[70] While she studied in the Windy City, other parts of the church began to challenge

Fig. 2.5 Ruth Peachey, Estella Lang, Lewis Madden, Paul Yoder, Harrisonburg, Virginia, 1947
S. Shenk, "A Mennonite Colored Wedding," *Gospel Herald* 40, no. 36 (December 2, 1947): 782,
Virginia Mennonite Conference Archives, Papers of the Virginia Mennonite Board of Missions and
Charities, box "Harold Huber's Papers, Broad Street Mennonite Church Materials (History, etc.), folder
"Broad Street History." Photo courtesy of Virginia Mennonite Conference, Harrisonburg, VA

segregationist policies. In 1948, for example, white mission workers in the Lancaster Conference appealed to their mission board to allow African Americans into the Welsh Mountain retirement facility.[71] Changes in Pennsylvania foretold changes to come in Virginia. In early 1949 Ada returned home to Harrisonburg and became the first full-time African-American student enrolled at Eastern Mennonite College.[72] Through careful maneuvering within the Mennonite community, Swartzentruber, Lark, and Roberta Webb witnessed the end of one expression of segregation within the Virginia Conference at a time when other Protestant denominations in the South had not yet integrated their educational institutions.[73]

In the wake of Eastern Mennonite's desegregation decision, Lark challenged the racial and gender stereotypes then restricting women's roles. In

Chicago, a city grown increasingly African American in the aftermath of white flight, Lark donned her prayer covering each morning as she ran a woman's sewing circle, conducted bible studies, and kept "[the missions at] Dearborn St. and the work at Bethel going" when her husband took ill for a period of several weeks.[74] In 1949 the Bethel congregation, a group that then accounted for nearly a third of the adult African-American members of the (Old) Mennonite Church, had begun to outgrow its facility.[75] Before the mission board produced a fund-raising brochure, Lark mobilized the women of Bethel's sewing circle. Through rummage sales on March 12 and April 9, the women raised more than $150.[76] With evident pride Lark noted that this was the "first time in the history of the church" that a group of African-American Mennonites had contributed to a church-building project or major mission endeavor.[77] Even though some white Mennonites in Chicago resented the Larks' leadership and marketed in stereotypical descriptions of African-Americans' "emotional extremes, . . . poor housekeeping, . . . lassitude, and immorality," Lark continued to invite other African Americans to join the Mennonite church.[78]

Lark extended her ministry to African Americans outside Chicago and, in so doing, rivaled the authority of white bishops. For the summers of 1952 and 1953, as Jim Crow ruled the land, Lark traveled from Chicago to Philadelphia to assist in vacation bible school programs. One church leader recalled Lark's "vivacious" presence as she encouraged young African-American women to wear their hair "naturally" under the prayer covering.[79] In her atypical commitment to natural hair styling, Lark not only challenged the standards of respectability that had prompted many middle-class African-American women from the 1920s forward to straighten their hair but also claimed cultural space outside the bishops' purview.[80] The bishops could demand that female converts wear the covering and refrain from cutting their hair, but they had no knowledge of hair relaxers or how to discuss African-American hair care, a culturally specific practice steeped in history and tradition.[81] In the vacuum created by the bishops' ignorance of culturally specific hair care, Lark led where the bishops could not follow.

Lark's support for natural hair styling also bolsters the argument that she deliberately chose to wear the covering and cape dress as a strategy to claim church membership. As of the early 1950s, Lark expressed little interest in conforming to white norms. Her opposition to hair-straighten-ing practices makes this evident. As she chose hair treatment on her own terms, so she chose dress standards. She dressed in plain attire even when not required to do so in order to establish religious rather than racial credentials. That is, Lark embraced a Mennonite dress code, not a white one. Unlike the many white women in the church who sought ways to circumvent clothing directives during the early 1950s, Lark embraced the covering. Although the historical record does not indicate whether Lark ever articulated this strategy, her actions leave a convincing trail. It appears that Lark wore a cape dress and a covering, at least in part, to send the message that she was a Mennonite even though many in the church did not treat her as one.

Lark's sartorial strategy to claim belonging in the church inspired other members of the growing African-American Mennonite community to do the same. Although in 1950 only 150 African-American adults had joined the (Old) Mennonite Church, by 1953 that number had doubled, and Sunday morning attendance had risen to more than one thousand.[82] Several decades would pass before African-American Mennonites approached the 10 percent membership mark achieved by black members of many white majority Protestant denominations at the time, but Lark nonetheless helped bring about a significant increase.[83] Lark spoke in congregations, led vacation bible school programs, and organized bible clubs and sewing circles among the burgeoning African-American Mennonite community.[84] Photos from the period show both young and older African-American women in Pennsylvania, Virginia, and Illinois having adopted the dress patterns Lark had long chosen to model.[85] Yet Lark did not dictate her strategy. Neither she nor her husband required converts to dress plain, and some of the newcomers demurred.[86]

Double Standards, Testing Grounds, and Women as Objects, 1953–1955

During Lark's high-profile ministry, discussions about race in the Mennonite church intensified. During the early 1950s, many white Mennonites recognized that African-American converts had come to stay. Church leaders and mission workers responded by tightening restrictions on African-American women's dress and using African-American churches as missionary testing grounds while also passing church statements against racism and channeling new resources into African-American missions. Mennonite leaders also discussed how best to respond to the burgeoning civil rights movement. Denominational and congregational leaders encountered new divisions in the church over whether evangelism and material relief or lobbying and direct action offered the best witness to their faith. Such internal discord intensified as leaders and lay members alike debated whether support for nonviolent campaigns like the 1955 Montgomery bus boycott upheld Mennonites' doctrine of nonresistance.[87] In brief, race commanded the church's attention.

During this period Lark and her African-American contemporaries focused less on street-based strategies and more on church-based change. They first encountered racial double standards in the church's dress codes. White mission workers in the Lancaster Conference admitted in 1954 that they required African-American converts to "dress much plainer than members of home congregations," but they decided that the restrictions offered "a blessing rather than a hindrance."[88] Workers at the Andrews Bridge congregation in southern Lancaster County corroborated the double standard, as did a 1955 nonconformity survey distributed in Virginia.[89] African-American converts also struggled to garner formal leadership posts. In 1953 white workers serving in African-American mission stations contended that turning leadership over to new converts would "loose the bears to ruin the world."[90] Not much had changed three years later when a church leader objected to African-American leadership by declaring that "A good thing can be overdone."[91] Personal slights added to the institutional restrictions. At a conference on race relations in 1955, Lark reported that her white co-believers frequently asked to touch her hair. Although she could not understand their request, Lark explained that she "graciously let them feel it."[92] In the wake of the 1954 *Brown v. Board of Education* Supreme Court decision that struck down "separate but equal" legislation, her anecdote influenced delegates to pass a race relations statement in 1955 that called the church to repent of "prevailing customs of discrimination."[93] Supported by such a proclamation, Lark and her contemporaries confronted those who treated their bodies as material curiosities rather than the sacred tabernacles symbolized by the prayer coverings that many of them wore.

Lark's African-American coreligionists in Virginia and Pennsylvania also encountered white missionaries preparing for African field service.

Throughout the first half of the twentieth century, Mennonites followed the example of their Protestant contemporaries by channeling human and financial resources into overseas missions. The African mission field, in particular, captured white Mennonites' attention, imagination, and pocketbooks.[94] That fascination fueled mission efforts throughout the African continent during a period when dozens of mission workers were getting ready to cross the Atlantic in a missions boom.[95] To prepare workers for service in Ethiopia, Kenya, Somalia, Tanganyika, and other overseas mission posts, Mennonite agencies began to apprentice neophyte missionaries at African-American mission churches. Some African-American members noted the pattern and felt that their congregations had become "testing ground[s]," an observation confirmed by congregational records.[96] Ironically, while church leaders attempted to use black Mennonites to prepare white missionaries for African evangelism, African leaders requested that the Mennonite church send African-American missionaries to work alongside them.[97] Rather than African-American missionaries, however, the church sent more white Mennonites, a significant number of them white women who had prior experience with African-Americans in the church.

Mennonites concerned about ending segregation and racial discrimination in the church had plenty to do. In addition to countering stringent dress codes, they built churches open to integration. When not challenging restrictions on African-American leadership, they counseled overseas missionaries. If no one was groping their hair, African-American converts still had to prove they belonged. Such activity required time, energy, and thoughtful consideration. Well before street activism drew the attention of the nation, African-American Mennonites and their white allies demonstrated daily. On the inside of the church, they ran their own movement.

Two Types of Protest, 1956 and Beyond

In the middle of this activity, the African-American Mennonite community blossomed. Especially during the later half of the 1950s and the first several years of the 1960s, new congregations arose, and church agencies invested money in domestic missions. From 1952 to 1962, mission workers planted more than twenty-six African-American congregations, many of them supported by funds from the newly flush coffers of the national Mennonite Board of Missions and Charities, an evangelistic arm of the (Old) Mennonite Church.[98] While President Dwight D. Eisenhower stepped up federal support for public school desegregation efforts in Arkansas to counter criticism from his cold-war adversaries, Mennonite mission administrators increased domestic evangelism budgets as African partners and returning missionaries found fault with domestic evangelism efforts.[99] Some Mennonites also called for an end to segregation in the church to counter "communist propaganda."[100] Leaders of both the federal government and the Mennonite church wanted to restore integrity to their initiatives abroad by addressing racial inequities at home. By 1964, 53 of the 818 Mennonite congregations in the United States listed African-American members, a fourfold increase over the 13 African-American missions in place as of 1950.[101] More than any other era in the twentieth century, the seven-year stretch from 1956 through 1962 held great promise for the hope of racial integration in the church.

Lark and Swartzentruber kept on challenging the church and dressing plain even though the geographic and experiential distance separating the two women grew wider. From 1956 through 1962, Lark and her husband completed their ministry in Chicago and then moved through St. Louis and on to Fresno, California. Just before this period, Swartzentruber and her husband had relocated to Schuyler, Virginia, where they engaged in a low-profile rural ministry. In Schuyler, Swartzentruber groused about the dress standards placed on women but continued to wear the covering. In Fresno, Lark offered no complaint about the distinctive clothing and veil she donned each day.[102] The contrast between Swartzentruber's complaints and Lark's compliance belied an underlying unity of purpose. Both women sought to challenge racial exclusion in the church and the patriarchy that helped maintain it.

In particular, Lark's long-term strategy to claim church membership by wearing Mennonite attire bore fruit. In 1959 Lark marked her sixty-seventh birthday, in Fresno. She continued to wear a prayer covering, though few Mennonite women in that part of the country did the same. Following her example, many other African-American Mennonite women donned the prayer veil. Photographs from this period show African-American women in Cleveland, Harrisonburg, and Chicago wearing prayer coverings in both church and home (see figures 2.6, 2.7, 2.8).[103] Lark had con-

Fig. 2.6 Claudia Watkins and Lee Heights Sunday school class, Cleveland, 1961
V. Vogt, "Emergent Church in Cleveland," *Christian Living* 8, no 7 (October 14–17, 1961): 34–35.
Photo courtesy of Mennonite Publishing Network, Scottdale, PA

tact with women in each community.[104] At a Colored Workers Committee
meeting in 1962, where memory of Lark's trendsetting example continued to loom large, African-American mission worker Willie Mae Thomas
led a session promoting the prayer veiling.[105] Rather than chafe against
prayer covering dictates, as had become even more common among white
Mennonite women during the 1960s, African-American women donned
the church's most visible symbol of church membership in order to call
other Mennonites to treat them as bona fide members. Peggy Curry of
Broad Street and Mattie Cooper Nikiema of Diamond Street, two more
African-American converts, both affirmed that they wore the covering as
a sign of inclusion and belonging.[106] Like Lark, many African-American
women during this period viewed wearing plain dress as an opportunity
to establish membership rather than a hindrance to the same.

    Swartzentruber and Lark continued to nurture their friendship despite
different approaches toward issues of patriarchy and racial exclusion in the
church. In an early 1963 exchange of letters, the two women described the
details of their respective ministries.[107] A mutual affection shone through
as the seventy-year-old Lark wrote to Swartzentruber, who was then in
her early fifties, that she thanked "God upon every rememberance [*sic*]
of you."[108] Even though Swartzentruber carried the burden of her abrupt

Fig. 2.7 Peggy and Billy Curry and their children, Broad Street
Mennonite, Harrisonburg, Virginia, 1961
Virginia Mennonite Archives, Box Broad Street 1936–1979 Richard &
Virginia Weaver Billy and Peggy Curry & Family, 1961. Photo courtesy
of Virginia Mennonite Conference, Harrisonburg, VA

dismissal from Gay Street and remained disengaged from African-American ministry in Virginia, she stayed connected with Lark through such
regular correspondence. In Lark, a woman by then widely respected and
valued by church leaders, Swartzentruber found a sympathetic listener
ready to reminisce with her about their shared "beautiful days of old" and
"fine Christian fellowship."[109]

Fig. 2.8 Seymour family at devotions, Chicago, 1962

K. Aschliman, "Living Family Worship," *Gospel Herald* 55, no. 24 (June 12, 1962): 538. Photo courtesy of Mennonite Publishing Network, Scottdale, PA

Even as the two women connected across diverse experiences and geographical distances, white and African-American women around them pursued various paths in response to the prayer covering. Swartzentruber and Lark had long before helped clear those disparate trails. In Swartzentruber's case, she had repeatedly railed against the covering in the intimacy of her home by noting that "God put the mark on the man, not the women," an allusion to the Genesis passage where Abraham underwent circumcision as a sign of separation from the world.[110] Although Swartzentruber continued to wear the prayer covering as mandated by church officials, the unequal, gender-based dress restrictions struck her as inappropriate and unjust. Acting on similar sentiment in the early 1960s, some white women reduced the covering's size, styled their hair beneath the covering, and repositioned the covering on their heads. One Mennonite bishop strenuously objected to those "Christian women" who made use of the "services of professional hairdressers."[111] The length and specificity of his instruction on how to cut hair and wear the covering indicate that, by 1962, enough women had begun to challenge nonconformist dress dictates as to evoke official response.

White women's overt protest contrasted with African-American women's covert strategy. From 1963 through 1965, African-American women accepted the prayer veil, as had Lark before them, but embraced the covering with an aesthetic sensibility unimagined by Lark or white church leaders. Even as officials in 1964 expressed approval of "the chaste and simple European veil as the most suitable application of the New Testament command for women to be veiled," new converts reinterpreted the covering as a fashion accessory.[112] An African-American convert to the Diamond Street Mennonite congregation in Philadelphia asked for a covering with strings because she thought that the "ribbons," considered a conservative sign by established Mennonites, looked pretty.[113] In the same community, other African-American Mennonite women refused to wear the strings because they did not like how they looked.[114] An African-American member of a Kansan congregation wore a prayer covering to church one Sunday morning in the early 1960s along with dangling gold earrings.[115] Throughout the United States, African-American women transformed the church's primary symbol of separation from the world on their own terms.

Even as African-American women appropriated Mennonite religious costume to serve their purposes, white women objected to the covering in new ways. Some wore the covering but coiffed their hair.[116] Others stopped wearing the covering to work but not to church.[117] Some stopped wearing it altogether, although through the 1960s few took this riskier step.[118] In one instance, a member of a youth ministry team appeared on the front cover of a national Mennonite magazine with an airbrushed covering; at the time the photographer snapped the picture, the church worker had not been wearing a prayer veil. The editors, deeming the veil mandatory, airbrushed a prayer covering in place (see figure 2.9).[119] They were willing to misrepresent the truth of the original photograph to promote the wearing of a religious symbol that white women had begun to challenge.

A Mennonite in Atlanta followed Lark's example as late as 1970. Betty Gwinn, the spouse of the incoming pastor of Berea Mennonite, wore a

Faith at Work
JANUARY-FEBRUARY 1966 78 YEARS OF PUBLICATION / FIFTY CENTS

FAITH CAN BE FUN PAGE 13
Can Prayer Bring Peace? PAGE 45

Fig. 2.9 Vel Shearer (with John Shearer), with air-brushed
covering, 1966
Faith at Work, January–February 1966, 1. Photo courtesy of Mennonite
Publishing Network, Scottdale, PA

black covering when she posed before a newspaper photographer along
with her husband and the outgoing pastoral couple (see figure 2.10). The
reporter assumed Gwinn chose the black covering to make a racial statement.[120] Gwinn later attested, however, that the she had donned the black
covering simply because she liked the color.[121] Although she had a white
covering as well, she chose the black one because of personal preference

Fig. 2.10 Gary and Marian Jane Martin, Betty and Macon Gwinn, Atlanta, 1970
"Countian Pulled Down Atlanta's Racial Bars," *Intelligencer Journal*, March 19, 1970, 48. Reproduced
with permission from *Intelligencer Journal*, Lancaster, PA

rather than religious conviction. Fashion again displaced doctrine. Rather
than a statement about her status as an African American, Gwinn's dress
made a statement about her status as a Mennonite.[122] Gwinn did not aban-
don the covering, she merely adapted the way she wore it. Gwinn wore
the covering, she later said, because she had "given her heart" to the Mennonite church.[123] To wear the covering was to stake her claim as a Mennonite. Lark's legacy survived.

The white woman who posed alongside Gwinn also made a statement. Like Swartzentruber before her, Marian Jane Martin pushed racial boundaries while wearing the covering. She supported Gwinn and
Gwinn's husband despite resistance from leaders in the Lancaster Conference. Those same leaders later forced the Gwinns to leave Berea after

the couple introduced African-American music and worship to the integrated congregation.[124] In a moment of promise before the suspension, Martin posed with Gwinn wearing a covering that also challenged the status quo.[125] Against the bishops' wishes, Martin coiffed and styled her hair and, in the process, moved the covering forward. In comparison to the traditional setting of the prayer covering on the back of the head, the covering now sat perched much higher. Although she had not removed the covering, she challenged tradition by repositioning it. While not obvious to most outsiders, Martin had nonetheless registered an internal protest. Swartzentruber's legacy also survived.

On March 5, 1970, the same month the photo and article featuring Gwinn's black and Martin's repositioned prayer coverings appeared in print, Rowena Lark died at the age of seventy-eight, leaving behind her husband, six children, and multiple grandchildren. The bulletin distributed at her funeral featured a photo of her wearing a covering.[126] A life of service and commitment to the Mennonite church had been capped through to the end by the prayer covering, demonstrating her commitment to the church.

Swartzentruber grieved the passing of her longtime friend but lived another twenty-nine years, most of them while wearing a prayer covering. Following a tearful reconciliation with representatives of the conference that had dismissed her so abruptly in 1945, Swartzentruber mourned the death of her husband in 1986.[127] Swartzentruber continued to wear the covering until she retired to a new community in northern Indiana. Once settled, Swartzentruber walked away from her church just as half a century earlier she had walked away from a communion service. For the six years following her departure from the Mennonite church until her death in June of 1999, Swartzentruber attended a Baptist congregation where leaders did not require women to cover their heads.[128] Although she chose to adhere to the dictate to keep her hair long, she finally found space to act out her lifelong complaint about the covering.

Protests Initiated, Amplified, and Modified

Rowena Lark, Fannie Swartzentruber, and their contemporaries open a conversation about the nature of protests in homes and sanctuaries during the civil rights era. These women first show that actors inside the religious community initiated protests in places untouched by traditional civil rights strategies. Swartzentruber's protest against segregated communion services drew attention to a form of segregation left unchallenged by the demonstrations then being mounted against civic Jim Crow practices. Ada Webb's matriculation at Eastern Mennonite College, an act made possible by Webb, Lark, and mission workers like Swartzentruber, came six full years before the 1954 *Brown v. Board of Education* decision. The women featured in this chapter thus protested and planned strategies when and where civil rights movement leaders had not thought to look.

The women's actions also amplified initiatives taken by civil rights leaders. When Lark testified that other Mennonites touched her hair, she presented evidence of racism inside the church to a community that had heard only distant echoes of racial injustice from outside the church. White Mennonites could ignore civil rights challenges when promoted by external activists like Ella Baker, Fannie Lou Hamer, and A. Philip Randolph but found it much more difficult to do so when a member of a conservative Mennonite church confronted them. Lark thus amplified Baker, Hamer, and Randolph's critique of white exclusivity in a way that demanded the attention of white Mennonites.

Lark's challenge to white Mennonites also amplified the risk she took. Unlike some African-American activists who had long since broken ties with white organizations, Gwinn, Lark, Webb, and their contemporaries maintained relationships with their white co-religionists even while addressing racism in the church. Although many high-profile civil rights leaders challenged the white church while worshiping in the safety of black congregations, African Americans in majority-white denominations challenged their white co-believers and then kept on worshiping with them.[129] Lark, Webb, and Gwinn not only refused to conform to the obsequious stereotypes often associated with African-American women who worshiped in white organizations, they also confronted the church from the inside and braved the resulting backlash.[130]

The daily demonstrations of the women profiled in this chapter also reveal modified forms of civil rights protest. Rather than carry a placard for a demonstration that lasted a few hours, Lark wore a covering for days on end. In so doing she used religious symbolism to craft a lasting kind of demonstration. Although other African Americans brought civil rights rhetoric to bear on a variety of cultural practices including hairstyles, hats, and haberdashery, few moved beyond Afros, *kofias*, and dashikis to bring African-American identity to bear on the religious symbolism of a major-ity-white Protestant denomination.[131] The African-American women who transformed the prayer veil into a fashion accessory by calling conservative covering strings pretty and matching coverings with worldly earrings also modeled new forms of protest. Although less obvious to outsiders than street marches, they nonetheless brought about significant change. The incongruity of coverings set off by gold earrings and prayer veils called fashionable often led to a relaxing of rigid dress requirements.[132] Rather than counter the growing threat directly, ministers in some parts of the Mennonite church simply let the covering go.

When seen as culturally creative resisters, Lark and her African-Amer-ican coreligionists have much in common with Ron Karenga, founder of the black nationalist Organization US and creator of the Pan-African cel-ebration Kwanzaa. Like Karenga, these women countered white domi-nant racial norms by creating new forms of cultural protest. Karenga did in secular academic settings what Lark and her contemporaries did in the re-ligious milieu: they used clothing to assert identity. Although the women were not Afrocentric black nationalists, they nonetheless acted in ways that resonated with Karenga's cultural movement when they wore Men-nonite garb without denying their racial identity. They created religious practices as a way to be "black and Mennonite."[133]

Once converts like Rowena Lark and Roberta Webb joined the church, they defined themselves as Mennonites through the protest strategies identified in this chapter. Lark's example makes the point. Thanks to her quarter-century tenure as a public school teacher and her husband's suc-cess as a church planter and entrepreneur, Lark did not draw on the ma-terial aid that Mennonites offered service recipients and new converts. Lark instead financed missions and prompted African-American converts to contribute financial and human resources to the church. She also chal-lenged racial and gender assumptions by daily dressing in conservative attire. The covering and cape dress did more to establish her credentials as a Mennonite than did any other aspect of her church life. More than the words she spoke, the songs she led, or the money she raised, the clothes she wore and the religious symbol she donned each morning sent the message that she was a Mennonite. She continued to dress in a plain manner even when other church members stopped using clothing to mark Mennonite identity. Lark remained faithful to core church markers even as others discarded them.

At root, Lark's and Swartzentruber's gender, avocation, clothing, and interracial friendship undergirded their protest strategies. As women, they cooked and raised children together during vacation bible school sojourns. As mission workers, they brought African-American converts into the church. Both also wore plain attire in public, a practice that connected those so dressed. While washing dishes, evangelizing new believers, wearing the covering, and leading others to do the same, Swartzentruber and Lark forged a long-term relationship that supported their protest against racial and gender-based restrictions. Although the women protested in different ways, they supported each other through shared activities and regular correspondence. Throughout their lives, they reminded each other that it was, indeed, worthwhile to stay in the church. As a white person, Swartzentruber offered Lark the same kind of support that moderate white southerners offered civil rights activists during campaigns in Birmingham, Little Rock, and Montgomery.[134] Swartzentruber played a similarly supportive role in Lark's campaign to establish herself as a full-fledged Mennonite. Friendships, clothing, and shared ministry thus contributed to changing racially oppressive practices in the church.

Swartzentruber's and Lark's narratives also explain the reasons for Mennonite women's resistance to the racial order in the United States. The relationships themselves called the women to take risks. Mennonite bishops dismissed Swartzentruber from her appointment at Gay Street Mennonite Mission because she protested communion restrictions placed upon her friend, Rowena Lark. Lark stayed in the church despite numerous encounters with Mennonite racism because there she found friends like Swartzentruber. Yet relationships alone do not explain the multiple motivations for resistance evident in the women's lives.[135] Religious convictions also account for why the women spoke up, walked out, and stayed within the church. Swartzentruber cared deeply about demonstrating integrity in her testimony and action. Lark ordered her dress and speech based on church teachings. These religious values acted in various ways upon the women. At times they pulled both women out from society by separating them from a sinful world. That movement away from the world also brought them together as they shared dress styles and head coverings. Such a nonconformist impulse also pushed them apart, however, as they sought racially appropriate means to counter oppression in the church. They thus joined their daily demonstrations with various and at times contradictory efforts to follow the church's teachings.

Lark, Swartzentruber, and those they emboldened left a legacy. With the support of her white ally, Lark showed that an African American could live and die as a Mennonite. In so doing, Lark invited African Americans to stay in the church. Some of them responded. As of August 2006, Calvary Community Church in Newport News, Virginia, a predominantly African-American congregation located a few short hours from Harrisonburg, where Lark and Swartzentruber first worked together, listed more members than any other Mennonite congregation in the United States.[136] Although leaders from that congregation struggled to establish themselves as legitimate Mennonites, they made those claims based on strategies modeled by Lark.[137] Calvary members did not wear coverings, cape dresses, or plain coats, but they did claim membership by staying in the church, promoting church doctrine, evangelizing other African Americans, and drawing attention to white Mennonites' prejudice. Lark had done the same.

In the chapter that follows, the story of four young African Americans reveals additional protest strategies within the Mennonite church. Unlike Swartzentruber and Lark, the children who participated in Mennonite-run Fresh Air programs had little opportunity to enter into sustained relationships across racial lines. The intrepid young visitors who entered the homes of white strangers disrupted the lives of their hosts to such an extent, however, that they changed their hosts' racial attitudes and prompted some of them to support the civil rights movement. Although their story, like those of Lark and Swartzentruber, abounds with contradiction, irony, and the uncertain interplay of egalitarian intention and prejudiced conduct, new forms of civil rights protest nonetheless emerged.

CHAPTER 3

Fresh Air Disruption

When Gulfport comes into our homes, we have a problem.
—Dr. Henry A. Fast, white church leader, Newton, Kansas, 1963

Disruptive Demonstrators

Margie Middleton could not contain herself. The unexpected separation from her best friend, Pat, was too fresh. During the weeks leading up to her country vacation from New York City in the early 1950s, no one explained to Middleton why her previous year's hosts only invited Pat to return. Despite her disappointment, Middleton entered into the lives of a new Fresh Air family in rural southeastern Pennsylvania. Part way through her two-week visit, she attended yet another Mennonite church service where she expected to be "the only black person" in the sanctuary. As the hymn singing began, however, Middleton noticed new faces around her. Several congregations had combined for an extended worship program. As she turned to see who else sat in the sanctuary, she caught sight of Pat several rows behind her. The two girls leaped up without thought to the service proceeding around them, rushed to the center aisle, and started "jumping up and down and hugging and kissing each other and saying how good it was" to see each other.[1] Their two host families quickly moved to quell the commotion. As the rest of the congregation looked on, the hosts informed the girls that they should have waited to express their joy. Middleton and her friend returned to their pews, and the congregants returned to their singing. The hosts had contained yet another Fresh Air disruption.

Nearly twenty years later, another African-American Fresh Air child caused a different kind of disruption. As a participant in a rural hosting program based in Gulfport, Mississippi, Jerry Smith had traveled far to spend two weeks with his host family.[2] Twenty-four hours in a school bus with no air-conditioning left him sweaty, tired, and eager to join the four Voth children on their Newton, Kansas, farm. Smith delighted in playing with toy tractors, taking rides on real tractors, and joining in the bustle of farm life. His host mother commented to an acquaintance that he got along so well with their family that "his hair might turn blonde one of these days."[3] Toward the end of his stay, however, that close connection threatened to become more demanding than his hosts had anticipated. With one short phrase, Smith pushed against the eleven-day time barrier built into the program: Smith asked his hosts to adopt him. Whether offered lightly or with serious deliberation, the request caught his hosts' attention.

Children like Middleton and Smith and their white hosts tell a civil rights–era story of intimate demonstrations that unsettled rural lives. Between 1950 and 1971, Fresh Air children left the familiar surroundings of their homes to travel to unknown rural Mennonite families for one- to two-week stays. The actions they took during those stays met all the marks of a demonstration: intention, organization, dramatic production, and disruption.[4] The children easily met the first three marks by intentionally showing that they knew their manners, organizing themselves to deflect personal inquiries, and recognizing that an observant Mennonite audience watched their every move. In disrupting that audience, however, they excelled. In Kansas, Pennsylvania, South Dakota, and Virginia, they confronted adults who did not know how to comb the children's hair, used racially offensive epithets like "niggers in the woodpile," and assumed that their young charges had little intelligence.[5] As the children taught their hosts proper hair care, shamed the adults into forswearing offensive speech, and displayed their mental aptitude, the children brought a new kind of demonstration into the home—one marked most clearly by the disruption of daily life and prior expectations.[6] Although the adults held significant power over their young charges, the children nonetheless changed their hosts' racial stereotypes, challenged the adults' racial naivete, and, in a few cases, prompted their hosts to advocate for civil rights legislation.

At the same time, Fresh Air program promoters used the children's presence in the host home to protect the church's racially egalitarian status. During the 1950s and '60s, civil rights advocates within and without the church challenged white Mennonites to set aside concern for separatist conviction and embrace racial struggle. In the face of such a threat to nonconformist practice and belief, church administrators used visits from young, deloused, and meticulously vetted African-American children to claim that their methods of building relationships through short-term hosting programs trumped activist measures taken by civil rights organizers. Under the innocuous guise of home-based missions, Fresh Air leaders sent children into Mennonite homes and sanctuaries to protect themselves from mounting criticism in the streets.

The two programs featured in this chapter used the children in different ways but to the same protectionist end. The first program—hosting children like Middleton—relied on white Mennonites from the Lancaster Conference, the (Old) Mennonite Church regional body that encompassed the largest geographical grouping of Mennonites in the United States during the years of this study. Although administrators in this program had earlier treated the children as dangerous and corrupt influences in the home, the program promoters increasingly spoke of their charges as unblemished innocents capable of overcoming racial unrest.[7] In keeping with their denomination's hierarchical and authoritative structures, Fresh Air administrators from the Lancaster Conference began to limit visits, set age caps, and discipline the children's bodies and minds. As they did so, program promoters amplified the image of the children's innocence and in so doing created an even more effective guard against external criticism. The second program—sponsoring Smith and other children like him—came out of the General Conference–run Camp Landon ministry in Gulfport, Mississippi. Rather than respond to the children's actions through restrictive program policies, leaders of the Camp Landon Fresh Air programs protected their racially egalitarian status by rotating the children through a series of Mennonite communities, thereby avoiding the frictions that arose from long-term relationships. General Conference leaders maintained a positive public image by shifting the children from community to community and household to household across the Midwest. One-time visits allowed for maximum public attention and minimal internal disruption.

The record of these Fresh Air ventures unearths a seldom-told civil rights—era story of children changing adults and adults changing children. With a few exceptions, historians of this period have focused on adult actors at both national and local levels.[8] Children do appear in dramatic accounts of Birmingham sheriff Bull Connor turning water canons and attack dogs on young marchers in 1963, but even these narratives play down the children's agency by focusing on the strategists who sent them "into the streets."[9] The children are presented not as courageous and significant actors in their own right but as powerless puppets used by leaders to heighten civil rights tensions. By contrast, the narratives presented here treat children as central actors in the civil rights story by emphasizing the process of mutual exchange between African-American children and their often racially naïve Fresh Air hosts as they determined living arrangements and work expectations.

Four children's stories organize this chapter and bring to light the intimate home and sanctuary environments where adults and children disrupted each other's lives. Margie Middleton first entered Lancaster Mennonite households in the 1950s. Albert Potts traveled from Mississippi to a Kansas home in 1961. Four years later, an article about a fictional Fresh Air child named Sammy opened a window onto the experiences of children like him who traveled to Lancaster farms in 1965. Like Potts, Jerry Smith also traveled from Mississippi to stay with a Kansas family, but his trip in 1969 came at a time when the programs appeared ready to fizzle and die. At key turning points across the two decades of this study, these stories reveal the source of the children's Fresh Air enthusiasm, the means of their in-home demonstrations, and the details of the adults' response to the children's actions. By highlighting the children's disruption of the status quo and the adults' protection of the same, these four stories show how demonstrations in homes and churches at times supported and at other points collided with demonstrations taken in the streets.

Margie Middleton and the Mennonites

Margie Middleton came to disrupt a rural Pennsylvanian church service in the 1950s through a century-old Victorian belief. Social reformers of the mid-nineteenth century held the conviction that the natural world offered inherent benefits to urban dwellers.[10] Based on that belief, late nineteenth-century philanthropists, Protestant urban evangelists, and their rural ministerial partners began to send children from the city for short stays in the country. Dubbed Fresh Air programs in recognition of the salubrious benefits of the country environment, the short-term hosting programs proved popular from the start. One of the largest programs in the nation, the *New York Herald Tribune's* Fresh Air Fund, began sending children from New York City to the country in 1877. Rapid growth in that program mirrored similar efforts by Mennonite church workers in Chicago. Five years after his organization first sent children to the country in 1896, Mennonite mission worker George Lapp bemoaned the children's reunion with their parents because they had again come under "the contaminating influences of this city."[11] Like their Protestant mission partners, the Mennonites who hosted Middleton and her peers also believed in nature's cleansing power.

The nature-centric program in which Middleton participated focused from the start on African-American children. Lancaster Mennonites like John Mellinger brought white ethnic children from New York City to their home in the 1890s but did so through the Fresh Air Fund rather than their own church-based program.[12] The Great Migrations of African Americans from the South to urban centers in the North and West had not yet changed the complexion of the inner city. When racial demographics began to shift in the first half of the twentieth century, Mennonites changed their mission efforts as well. The evangelistic efforts led by Rowena and James Lark and stronger post—World War II mission agencies made race-specific church starts possible. African-American children soon began to attract church workers' attention. As the church press reported on Fresh Air ventures operated by the Larks' Bethel Mennonite congregation and by other Chicago churches, program administrators in Pennsylvania began to pay attention.[13]

By the time Lancaster Conference leaders started their own program, city demographics had, in their minds, transitioned from white to black. On October 11, 1949, members of the Lancaster Conference's Colored Workers Committee called for a Fresh Air program "for colored children of our city missions" by appealing "to the brotherhood to open their homes."[14] Although white children would participate in the program through the first ten years and at times outnumber the African-American participants, the focus from the start was on the black children.[15] More than any other program in the history of the (Old) Mennonite and General Conference denominations, this venture brought African-American and white people within the church into close and intimate contact. Following a publicity blitz that promoted Fresh Air programs as a way to win "the Negro of America to Christ," forty-two African-American children from Mennonite city missions prepared to visit white rural hosts in the summer of 1950.[16]

The start of Fresh Air programs by the Lancaster Conference brought African-American children closer to white Mennonite constituents. In 1929 the conference's mission board appropriated funds to provide "warm meals to the colored children" in the geographically isolated African-American community of Welsh Mountain, Pennsylvania.[17] Soon after committing their support for this relatively distant mission effort, white Mennonite missionaries founded South Christian Street Mennonite Church in the late 1930s in the heart of Lancaster, Pennsylvania. Five siblings from an African-American family had attended a series of evangelism meetings, requested baptism, and needed a church home. Rather than send the Jones children to the Rawlinsville Mennonite congregation in the town where the children lived, mission workers in 1933 transported the children thirteen miles north into Lancaster City to attend a racially segregated Sunday school class organized for their benefit.[18] Other children from the neighborhood around South Christian Street began to attend the Sunday school class and thereby forced the conference to invest more time and money into a segregated mission effort. Although they worshipped in the heart of a county densely populated by Mennonites, the children remained separated by race.

Similarly, in 1936 Lancaster Conference mission workers in Philadelphia segregated their mission efforts because of the large number of African-American children that had begun attending their church.[19] As they took part in Sunday schools and vacation bible school programs, African-American children continued to appear in church periodicals and receive attention during mission board meetings, but they remained at a distance from most white Mennonites, a pattern prevalent in the few other Mennonite missions focused on the African-American community.[20] When conference leaders began their own Fresh Air program in 1950, they brought African-American children from segregated missions and distant communities into Mennonites' bedrooms, living rooms, and sanctuaries. Because of these efforts, for the three decades following the inception of the Lancaster Conference Fresh Air program white Mennonites in rural congregations came into closer contact with African Americans through these exchange programs than through any other means.[21]

Middleton and her peers responded to the new program with unbridled enthusiasm. From 1950 onward, children eagerly vied for the opportunity to spend a coveted vacation in the rural homes of Mennonites from the Lancaster Conference. Children chosen for their attendance records, good behavior in church, and recommendation by local mission workers gathered en masse before setting off for the country (see figure 3.1). Although they often did not know their host families, they anticipated the visits for weeks. Writing as an adult, Middleton mused that "the best part of Fresh-Air was the families . . . We had a lot of good times with them."[22] She praised her hosts for the deep concern they showed her. "By the end of two weeks I was calling them Ma and Pa and I was crying because I didn't want to leave," she added.[23] For many children, the most important thing about a Fresh Air vacation was that they had fun.

The Mennonite hosts operated from a set of more racially focused interests. As noted in chapter 1, Mennonites had long nurtured a reputation as racial egalitarians, stemming from their participation in the 1688 formal written protest against slavery in the colonies.[24] Mennonite leaders also referred to having been the first denomination to admit a black student to a private Christian college in the South in 1948.[25] At the same time, their doctrines of nonconformity and nonresistance left Mennonites concerned that service to the African-American community would lead to coercive, worldly ways. Bringing African-American children into their homes for short visits afforded white Mennonites the opportunity to express their commitment to racial justice without compromising their beliefs. As a result, hosts paid close attention to the children's racial identities. In 1951 a Brother Gehman contacted program administrator Paul Kraybill about his interest in "[hosting] Colored to prevent racial barrier."[26] That same year, E. G. Horst wrote of her experience hosting an African-American child, "It has been a blessing to us as it makes us feel there is no difference in color or race."[27] While many of the hosts paid first attention to the children's urban genesis, they frequently commented on the children's color. The

Fig. 3.1 Fresh Air children from Seventh Avenue Mennonite Church awaiting departure,
Harlem, circa 1960s
EMM Record Room, file cabinets middle aisle, drawer marked Information Services Picture File, file
cabinets—Home Ministries, Children's Visitation Program. Photo courtesy of Eastern Mennonite
Missions, Salunga, PA (www.emm.org)

contrast between conservatively dressed white Mennonites and African-
American children from the city rarely went unremarked.

Middleton's story thus begins with the interwoven interests of three
groups: the hosts, the children, and the children's parents. When Middleton and her peers arrived at their destinations, they were greeted by hosts
eager to demonstrate their willingness to risk crossing racial lines. In keeping with the burgeoning zeal for missions then present in the Lancaster
Conference and through the (Old) Mennonite Church, the adults sought
to be "missionaries right in our own homes."[28] The prevailing mission
model present at the time thus guided the hosts' actions. They assumed
that they could correct, clean, and save the children and, in the process,

maintain their egalitarian reputation. The children, however, expressed far more interest in the adventure, escape from segregation, and free travel of a country vacation. Seldom did they evince excitement about staying with a white family. Unlike their hosts, they focused far more on the rural setting. As one participant exclaimed, "A farm is the most interesting life I have ever lived for just 10 days."[29] The guest children simply enjoyed their country vacations on their own terms.

Finally, the children's parents sent their offspring to Mennonite missions to provide them with bible instruction, to obtain short-term child care, and—in some cases—because the African-American parents had come to trust the earnest, oddly dressed white people who moved into their neighborhoods.[30] Although owing to the demands of relocation and work as well as remaining uncertainty about Mennonite worship norms many of the children's parents did not attend mission services, they nonetheless expressed concern about the attitudes of their children's temporary caretakers. Middleton's mother, for example, instructed her daughter, "Any questions they ask you about your homelife, don't answer them. If they persist, tell them what goes on in our house stays in our house."[31] She and the other parents knew that Fresh Air hosts assumed their young guests came from poor, sinful, and worldly households.

The very queries that Middleton's mother anticipated would come her way dampened Middleton's excitement about the Fresh Air visits. Many of the hosts she stayed with during the 1950s asked incessant questions about the kind of house she lived in, where she went to school, and whether her parents lived together. Middleton could not understand why anyone would need such detailed information. She noted, "There were parents who lived together quite naturally and there were parents who didn't live together; mothers who raised their children alone and fathers who raised their children alone."[32] Like most of her peers, Middleton refused to quench her hosts' thirst for more and more personal information.

Middleton had less patience with the judgments her hosts made about her life and her community. She remembered overhearing a conversation between her mother and one of the white members of the Seventh Avenue Mennonite Church in Harlem. Her mother expressed her appreciation for the trips Middleton and other children took each year to the countryside but explained that she and other parents "felt the Fresh-Air parents shouldn't implant in . . . [children's] minds that the city was wicked." The children returned home bothered by activities like dancing and mixed bathing that had never before concerned them. Middleton soon came to realize, however, the inconsistency of her hosts' judgment. She noted that her hosts "said it was possible to be a Christian and live in the city, but all of them remained in Pennsylvania on farms."[33] Although only six the first time she visited a Fresh Air farm in the early 1950s, Middleton had to figure out the best way to respond to her hosts' judgments about life in the city. She grew tired of having to decide, upon returning from each Fresh Air visit, whether she would wear earrings, listen to the radio, or go to a public swimming pool.

Middleton's peers in the Fresh Air program faced similar judgments. In the second year of the Lancaster program, a host noted, "These children should be encouraged to help [and] learn to work, lest we encourage laziness, which I have learned since the New Yorkers are noted for."[34] That same year, a host in Lancaster who had worked with African-American children since 1939 bitterly complained of a Fresh Air child who purportedly stole a handkerchief.[35] Whatever the truth behind the accusation, hosts such as these often made assumptions about their charges based on the language used by Fresh Air program administrators to promote the exchanges. Promotional materials referred to "these needy children," "these needy city children," and "these underprivileged children" in 1951 and for many years to follow.[36] Although Middleton and many others came from homes where they received more than adequate nutrition, clothing, and love, the young children had to interact with adults who assumed from the start that they would steal, avoid chores, and arrive in need of nourishment.[37]

Yet the harshest judgment against Middleton and her peers came from the program's administrators. Administrators did not conduct background checks or health tests on the hosts or their children, but they required Middleton and all the Fresh Air children to undergo humiliating examinations for lice and other communicable diseases, a practice in keeping with white stereotypes that cast African-American city dwellers as disease carriers.[38] Although lice checks may have made sense based on past experience, program administrators still did not conduct background checks on host homes, even after a host parent sexually abused his charges.[39] The administrators moved decisively to reduce the chance of disrupting host homes with a lice infestation but did far less to ensure that the children's lives would not be damaged by inappropriate behavior on the part of their hosts.

Within two years of the Lancaster program's start, this double standard became even more pronounced. In 1952 Paul N. Kraybill, a program administrator from the Lancaster Conference, wrote to the Fresh Air Fund to see whether their personnel tested participating children for sexually transmitted diseases. Apparently some Mennonite hosts had contacted Kraybill to express concern that the young Fresh Air children might bring venereal disease into their homes.[40] In his letter Kraybill did not discuss the manner in which a six- or eight-year-old child might have contracted or might spread such a disease, but he carefully queried program administrators about their practices. Again, the hosts' concerns came first.

Middleton soon came to realize the irony of these efforts to protect Fresh Air homes from outside influences. She recognized that many homes already had problems of their own. Looking back on her experience as a young Fresh Air child, Middleton emphasized two things. First, she once thought that all Mennonite families embodied perfection. Middleton wrote, "My impression of Mennonites, each time I came back, was that they had lots of money, big cars, and lots of children, they never spanked their children, the husband and wife never had any arguments, and they were a perfect family."[41] Yet Middleton came to understand at a young age that other problems stood alongside that apparent perfection. The impression left by her hosts "that only Mennonites went to heaven" rankled her even then.[42]

More specifically, she remembered that the first family she stayed with abruptly separated her from her best friend. During that first visit, Middleton and Pat stayed with the same hosts. The following year, as mentioned in the anecdote that opens this chapter, the host family asked Pat alone to return. Middleton could not understand what had happened. She and Pat had both enjoyed their visit; both came from African-American families; and both had made decisions to accept Christ as their savior. At the time, the hosts offered no explanation for excluding Middleton. Only years later did Middleton learn of the reason for their decision. Pat had started to wear the traditional white, Mennonite prayer covering. Middleton had not.[43] As a young girl, Middleton knew only that hosts she had come to trust had punished her unjustly.

Middleton's disappointment highlights an additional inconsistency in her hosts' behavior. The devotional prayer covering stood for church membership and male hierarchy; moreover, especially during the first half of the 1950s, as one of the community's most visible signs of separation from the world it bestowed special status on women. A national church statement passed in 1955, however, instructed church leaders to refrain from pressuring children to join the church until they became responsible for their moral decisions, at or about twelve years of age.[44] Although the hosts knew that some white Mennonite girls did start wearing the covering before they turned twelve, their decision to exclude a seven-year-old child because she chose not to wear a covering flew in the face of official church doctrine. Evidently, Middleton's hosts held her to a stricter standard than the broader church held white Mennonite girls.

Middleton's story therefore ends where it began, inside the sanctuary. When Middleton greeted her friend Pat in the midst of a worship service, the two young girls revealed tensions implicit within the early Fresh Air programs among Mennonites in Pennsylvania. The girls' disruptive reunion after an extended separation in an all-white environment can hardly be blamed on lack of social graces or proper manners. Rather, Pat's hosts' overzealous application of church doctrine created a situation in which the girls felt a strong need to reunite, regardless of how disruptive it might be to the adults around them. That moment of disruption and containment captured the conflicting interests of the children and adults. The children had come to enjoy a country respite but had to deal with adults who sought to minimize disruption in their home and church lives. The adults desired to evangelize their guests but had to deal with children who refused to share information about their homes and carried the perceived threat of contagion. The children accepted the tensions as part of their payment for a summer vacation. The adults sought to lessen the tensions by tightening restrictions. In the ensuing years, repeat visits like the one enjoyed by Middleton's friend Pat became less common. As the repeat visits declined, so did the possibility of forceful disruption. The story that follows traces these initial signs of change to a second Fresh Air program, where children like Middleton experienced both love and disappointment.

Albert Potts and Country Living

Albert Potts proudly held his camera as he perched on a bike next to a cement-block garage in Inman, Kansas. Potts had reason to be proud. He had braved a twenty-four-hour bus trip from his home in Gulfport, Mississippi, to spend two weeks with Elmer and Linda Voth and their sons, Stanley and Eugene, in July of 1961. Rather than sit timidly inside, Albert prepared to venture out into the small, rural town of Inman to chronicle what he saw there with the help of a camera given to him by his host parents (see figure 3.2). As a Fresh Air child from another Mennonite-run rural hosting program, Potts came to stay with hosts who had been told only of his need. As in the case of Margie Middleton, Potts refused to meet their expectations.

Potts traveled to Inman under the sponsorship of a high-profile Mennonite program that had been working with African-American children in Mississippi since the mid-1940s. Camp Landon, situated just outside the town of Gulfport, Mississippi, only a few miles from the Gulf of Mexico, began in 1945 as a program site where young Mennonite men served out alternative military service assignments. Although program volunteers first worked to improve sanitation in the area by constructing outdoor privies, within a year of Camp Landon's founding volunteers began to work with children.[45] After the alternative service program ended, other young adult Mennonite volunteers conducted weekly metal shop and sewing classes, Sunday afternoon bible classes, and, in the 1950s, release-time bible instruction and recreational periods in the public schools.[46] By 1957, long-time Camp Landon director Orlo Kaufman had begun to recruit volunteers by centering on the camp's outreach to children.[47] Through the 1950s, the larger Mennonite church, with the General Conference denomination offering the most consistent backing, supported Camp Landon by contributing money, sponsoring volunteers, and sending Christmas gifts to Gulfport children from as far away as Illinois, Kansas, and Pennsylvania.[48] As the Southern Christian Leadership Conference drew the attention of white people across the country for their high-profile organizing campaigns, so Camp Landon drew the attention of thousands of white Mennonites in the Northeast and Midwest for their service programs.[49] By the end of the 1950s, Camp Landon had built a reputation for work with children in the Gulfport community that ap-

Fig. 3.2 Albert Potts outside the home of Elmer and Linda Voth,
Inman, Kansas, 1961
L. Voth, photo of Albert Potts with camera and bike, July 24, 1961,
Mennonite Library and Archives, VII.R.GC Voluntary Service, Series
11 Gulfport VS Unit, box 5, folder 196, Photographs. Photo courtesy of
Mennonite Library and Archives, Bethel, KS

pealed to the ethnically homogenous and racially insulated General Conference constituency.

Albert Potts came to Inman courtesy of a Fresh Air program initiated by
Kaufman in 1960. Kaufman sought to bring African-American children
from Gulfport into contact with white Mennonite families in the North as
a means to encourage interracial relationships. Although the administrator
of a similar program run out of Woodlawn Mennonite Church in Chicago
warned Kaufman that many of the Fresh Air children's parents expressed

great reluctance to send their offspring to unknown white Mennonite families, Kaufman's record of work with children through Camp Landon assuaged the fears of parents in Gulfport.[50] Whereas parents of children involved in the Lancaster-based program appear to have researched relatively unknown Fresh Air organizers through informal inquiries, Gulfport parents seemed to have felt less need to do so, given their long experience with Kaufman and Camp Landon. For the program's debut in 1960, Kaufman and his staff gathered twenty-one children, including three with the Potts surname, to travel to Kaufman's home territory in Goessel and Moundridge, Kansas, nearly a thousand miles to the north.[51]

Potts had a grand time during his stay. He did not go to the same town as his relatives had the previous year but instead stayed with the Voth family in the nearby town of Inman. Soon after his arrival, Potts teamed up with the Voths' son Eugene to ride bikes around town, swim in the local pool, and attend church and Sunday school at a Mennonite congregation. During the Voth family's daily devotions, Potts joined in the discussion and shared insight he gained from attending Camp Landon's bible study classes. He also earned money by feeding chickens, sweeping the Voths' garage, pulling weeds, and mowing the Voths' lawn.[52] Potts joined in the celebration of Elmer and Linda's silver wedding anniversary, where he met the couple's relatives. Like Middleton before him, Potts greatly enjoyed his Fresh Air host family (see figure 3.3).

Potts had heard others' glowing reports about their Fresh Air trips, so the Voths' warm reception came as no surprise. Upon returning from Kansas the year before, the Gulfport children had heaped praise upon their hosts.[53] They exclaimed over the rural sights they encountered and the good food they ate. Indeed, many young people gained weight in the course of their stays. Others returned home proud to have learned how to milk a cow, steer a tractor, or drive a car.[54] The children's interest in these agrarian pursuits pleased their rural hosts and fit well with those influenced by the Booker T. Washington school of thought, which emphasized trade and agricultural training over intellectual scholarship. Many children mentioned that they wanted to go back again the following year, often for a longer period of time.[55] Although Potts had not learned to drive a car, as had some other children, he had learned how to shoot a camera. His pride in the accomplished task came through clearly as he posed for a picture holding the camera by the Voths' garage (figure 3.2).

Fig. 3.3 Stanley Voth, Albert Potts, Eugene Voth, Linda Voth, Elmer Voth,
Inman, Kansas, 1961

L. Voth, photo of Albert Potts with host family, July 24, 1961, Mennonite Library and Archives,
VII.R.GC Voluntary Service, Series 11 Gulfport VS Unit, box 5, folder 196, Photographs.
Photo courtesy of Mennonite Library and Archives, Bethel, KS

Such glowing reports did not mention, however, the manner in which the children disrupted their hosts' expectations. As had Middleton, Potts remained silent when his hosts queried him about his home life.[56] Potts's hosts also expressed surprise at his polite behavior, noting that he put them "to shame at times" with his proper conduct.[57] Other Fresh Air children from Gulfport encountered similar reactions when they took good care of themselves and worked as hard as the white children they visited. In 1960 one host expressed surprise at the cleanliness of the children spending time in their community: "We found that they were just as lovable and clean as our white friends."[58] Another was enthusiastic about the "clean shiny black faces scattered thru out the Eden Church on Sunday morning."[59] In addition to proving their ability to maintain basic hygiene, the children also surprised their hosts by demonstrating their intelligence.

One child's host showed him how to do various tasks around the farm, with the assumption he would have to repeat himself before the child completed them correctly. When the Fresh Air child finished the tasks without error the first time, the host replied in wonder, "He is a very smart boy."[60] Through their actions, the children challenged their hosts' assumptions that African-American children had inferior intellects and did not know how to care for themselves.

In some cases Potts's peers also had to contend with adults who blamed their guests for unsettling their own children and for failing to express adequate appreciation. One Fresh Air participant enjoyed telling ghost stories that left at least a few of the host children in his household "scared to sleep alone at night."[61] His stories provoked understandable correction. Other children, however, dealt with host parents who offered less reasonable criticism. Host parents criticized the children's play, their interest in dancing, and their "onery" personalities.[62] One girl's host felt that her guest "came from too wealthy a home to really appreciate" the family's possessions and material provisions.[63] The young girl responded by behaving as properly as she knew how and demonstrating once again that she understood the basics of good hygiene. In the end, the host conceded that her guest had been "well behaved," "very neat and clean," and "never caused any trouble while she was here."[64] Many of the children in the Gulfport program struggled with hosts who assumed from the start that the children would bring disorder to their household.

The challenge of living in households that both welcomed and judged them left the Gulfport children with mixed emotions as they prepared to return home in the summer of 1961. Some looked forward to being relieved of work demands placed on them by adults who apparently had a very different idea of what a "vacation" entailed.[65] A few of the Gulfport children cherished positive memories and tried to forget judgments made on them for dancing, having "wild imagination[s]," or spending their money "foolishly."[66] They grew sad at the end of an enjoyable time spent in recreational activities with new friends. Others, like Potts, looked quietly back at their host families as the prospect of a twenty-four-hour return trip in a hot school bus loomed.[67] A few Fresh Air participants chatted excitedly about the prospect of returning again to host homes that had welcomed them particularly well.

Reverend Arnold Nickel and the Freedom Riders

Such return trips did not, however, appeal to those local planners who expressed greater interest in besting civil rights demonstrators than in developing long-term relationships with the children. At the time Potts visited with the Voths, freedom riders captured the nation's attention. As these groups of African-American youth and their white allies took organized trips through the South in bids to test Jim Crow laws, they often encountered violent reprisals. Mennonites in Kansas and throughout the country paid attention. In an article that appeared in a local Kansas newspaper soon after Potts and the rest of the Gulfport Fresh Air children arrived, the Reverend Arnold Nickel, pastor of Eden Mennonite Church in Moundridge, Kansas, told a newspaper reporter that Mennonite Fresh Air hosts approached "the racial problem with moderation" in contrast to the direct challenge posed by the freedom riders. Nickel added, "We work toward creating better relationships and better understandings."

Although Nickel made clear that Kansas had its own racial problems, he also pointed out that Mennonite hosts gave the Gulfport children experiences they would never have in the South, such as living with a white family or worshiping in a white church.[68] Yet Nickel's desire to promote "better relationships" with the children did not extend past the period of eleven days. In a letter to Camp Landon administrator Orlo Kaufman that same year, Nickel cautioned against sending children to the same home year after year because "familiarity in this case might lead to certain problems."[69] In particular, Nickel appeared to fear interracial sex, a particularly unsettling prospect to Mennonites during this period as is noted in chapter 4. The better relationships Nickel promoted in public evidently lasted no longer than a week or two.

Nickel's fear of disruptive "problems" thus dampened any desire expressed by Potts to return to the Voth family in Inman, Kansas. Although Nickel left the naming of those fears to other less circumspect Fresh Air hosts, his words resonated with concerns expressed by adults involved in hosting and planning the trips.[70] In the following years, Camp Landon continued to shift children among Mennonite towns and, by the end of the 1960s, to states even farther north. Seldom did any Fresh Air child from Gulfport, regardless how clean or well-behaved, get a chance to return to the same home twice. Even though General Conference members emphasized relational solutions to the racial unrest then sweeping the country, their most prominent interracial program intentionally curtailed long-term relationships.[71]

Nickel's 1961 letter to Kaufman demonstrated an assumption fundamental to the Fresh Air program: a little went a long way. Administrators did not regularly recruit host families interested in bringing children into their homes for months at a time. They recruited hosts willing to bring small children into their homes for short stays. Ultimately, the Fresh Air program focused more on limiting interaction than creating relationships. If Potts wanted to travel again to Kansas, he would have to risk entering a new home that could prove to be as relatively welcoming as the one he visited or as overtly judgmental as those experienced by many of his friends. Short stays at multiple sites limited relationships that might otherwise have proved sustainable. By contrast, many of the freedom riders criticized by Nickel developed longer-term relationships across racial lines while organizing protest rides, participating in sit-ins, and conducting voter registration drives in southern Mississippi under the auspices of the Student Nonviolent Coordinating Committee.[72] Ironically, committee members may have been best suited to boast of better relationships. Fresh Air programs built on small children and short stays could rarely outdo an organization that attended to entire communities—children and adults alike—for months at a time.

Potts traveled back to Mississippi with a new camera, good memories, and the prospect of racial change sandwiching him between civil rights leaders and his Mennonite hosts. In 1961 much seemed possible as civil rights leaders planned strategies to force a new president to intervene in segregated southern towns like Albany, Georgia, or Potts's home in Gulfport. The Mennonites who hosted Fresh Air children in Kansas that year also placed great hope in their strategy. Although the relationships they touted as a better alternative to politically focused street marches may not have been as superior as they claimed, Fresh Air administrators would come to recognize that the children they brought into their homes even for such short stays still managed to wrest change from a quiescent community. Like their Fresh Air sponsors, Potts and the other Fresh Air children did not realize what they had done and would yet do through their daily demonstrations in Mennonite homes. As he took pictures and rode bikes, surprised his hosts with good hygiene and remained mum about his home environment, Potts created a temporary living environment where neither adult nor child entirely controlled the agenda. Although he did not bring about civil rights legislation by traveling to Inman in 1961, Albert Potts did disrupt adults' lives enough that they began to pay more attention to the segregated world from which he came.

Sammy and the Innocence of Children

Four years after Albert Potts climbed back on the Camp Landon bus and nearly ten years after Margie Middleton caused a commotion in a Sunday morning service, a story about a young Fresh Air child and his host family made race the central issue of the ongoing Pennsylvanian program. The 1965 article in the Lancaster Conference's flagship missions magazine described how one family decided to invite an African-American child to their home: Anne Smith, the host family daughter, exclaimed one evening, "Mother, let's have a Negro child this year."[73] Her proposal highlighted a change since Middleton first began visiting Lancaster Mennonite homes. By 1965, African-American children had come to dominate the Fresh Air program. White flight from the inner-city New York locales where Mennonite mission outposts vetted Fresh Air participants left few white candidates. So common had the presence of African-American children become that at least one editor in 1965 refrained from adding a caption to a photo of two Fresh Air visitors and their white Mennonite hosts (see figure 3.4). The editor assumed that readers knew why two African-American boys would walk across a swinging bridge with a white Mennonite woman and her daughter. In the 1965 fictionalized account, Anne and the rest of her family joined hundreds of other white Mennonites in welcoming an African-American child into their home.

The article appeared at a time when racial rebellions destabilized many urban communities and Mennonite leaders and lay people alike debated how best to respond to criticism from civil rights movement activists. By the mid-1960s in nearby Philadelphia, movement leaders had begun to turn toward self-help strategies that had little room for white-run hosting programs.[74] African-American adults in Baltimore, New York, Philadelphia, and other urban centers from which Fresh Air children traveled grew increasingly impatient with white service providers, regardless of how well intentioned.[75]

Fig. 3.4 Fresh Air children and members of unidentified
host family
D. Harly, *Volunteer* 8, no. 6 (June 1965): cover. Photo courtesy of
Lancaster Mennonite Historical Society, Lancaster, PA

Within the Mennonite community, the debate in 1965 often proved
intense. African-American Mennonites publicly queried, "Why do white
folks hate us?"[76] In response, some white Mennonites advocated walking on picket lines, while others proclaimed that the solution would "not

come through marches and picketing" but by evangelizing "underprivileged Negroes."[77] Within the Lancaster Conference and (Old) Mennonite denominations more broadly, the debate over activist involvement in
the civil rights movement merged with disagreements over nonconformity
dictates. Some argued that to join a march was to countermand biblical
injunctions to separate from the world.[78] For a people long known for
their racial egalitarianism, the emerging debate over the problem of how
to maintain that reputation and respond with integrity to racial unrest left
many grasping for ways to move forward.

Young Fresh Air children like Sammy offered a particularly attractive
way to uphold Mennonites' record of racial egalitarianism while avoiding complications introduced by older Fresh Air participants. Like their
co-religionists in Kansas, Mennonites in Pennsylvania stayed true to their
belief in nonviolence and their commitment to bridging racial divisions
by continuing to host Fresh Air children, staying away from marches, and
emphasizing the benefits of "practical experience in race relations" gained
through the rural hosting programs.[79] As the earlier expressed fears that
Fresh Air children might carry sexually transmitted diseases suggest, however, African-American children from the inner city still posed a threat of
sexual entanglement with host siblings and neighbors. Especially as the
children grew older and, in the Lancaster-based program, returned to the
same homes over time, that threat increased. Adolescent Fresh Air guests
thus introduced a new set of problems even as they helped protect white
Mennonites from activists' criticism. Program administrators soon found a
way to keep the Fresh Air benefit without introducing teenage complications by turning to ever-younger children.

The author who described Sammy captured the innocence sought by
Fresh Air program promoters. By the mid-1960s, administrators no longer
expressed concern that the city children would bring venereal disease into
host homes. Instead, they emphasized the children's innocence. During
the Fresh Air visit described in the 1965 article, Sammy listened to "the
wind talking to the ripened wheat," found a nest of rabbits, collected eggs,
drank fresh milk, explored a groundhog burrow in clean earth, and lay
on his back to gaze at puffy, white clouds.[80] The wholesomeness of these
agrarian activities and of the child who experienced them proved singu-
larly appealing to white Mennonites. They found it easy to welcome such
innocent children into their homes and did so with renewed vigor.[81]

As a purported seven-year-old, Sammy represented a shift toward sending younger participants into host homes while shunting teenagers and preteens to camps. Already in 1961, a host in Kansas recommended that the program administrator not place teenage boys in homes with girls near their age.[82] In another instance, a longtime host family in Pennsylvania stopped inviting a female Fresh Air guest to their home after the hosts' teenage daughter grew jealous of their Fresh Air guest's budding physical maturity.[83] By the mid-1960s, African-American preadolescents and early teens rarely received invitations to Fresh Air homes.[84] In lieu of home visits, mission administrators gave the young people applications to attend camp. The teens and preteens responded with an enthusiasm that, in turn, raised another alarm. As African-American youth began to travel to church-sponsored camps, church leaders expressed some fear at the perceived encroachment. A white Mennonite mission worker lamented in 1963, "Missions Camp at Hebron is getting darker and darker each year."[85] Yet most mission staff and Fresh Air administrators supported the shift of older children to the structured and somewhat more distant camping environment. The following year a missions newsletter featured a photo of one of those preteen African-American campers fishing by the side of a pond (see figure 3.5). Like the author of the article who described Sammy's agrarian innocence, the photographer of the straw-hatted angler emphasized the rustic though stereotypical innocence of the boy's fishing pursuit. At camp, older children could still gain the benefit of country life without threatening Mennonite homes.

The six- and seven-year-old children who did spend time in family homes prompted Fresh Air hosts to change the length of the program. To be certain that their readers got the message that the Fresh Air program placed only young children in family homes, the editors of the 1965 article about Sammy and his host family included a photo of four kindergarten-age children, two white girls and two dark-skinned boys.[86] As program personnel placed such children in family homes, the young visitors showed greater signs of exhaustion at the end of their two-week stays than had the older children during the previous decade. As the children grew tired more quickly, hosts complained, and, in response, program administrators reduced most stays to one week.[87] The shorter visits led hosts to wonder whether they should continue expending energy on exchanges only seven days long.

Fig. 3.5 Unidentified camper fishing at Camp Hebron, Halifax, Pennsylvania, 1964
"It's Quiet Now at Camp Hebron," *Volunteer* 7, no. 10 (October 1964): 11. Photo courtesy of
Lancaster Mennonite Historical Society, Lancaster, PA

The children who tired so quickly of Fresh Air living proved irresistible to their hosts, however, because the adults came to believe that their
young charges could lead the way through racial tumult. The author who
described Sammy and the Smiths made that belief apparent. In the summer of 1965, the Smith family decided to invite Sammy and one other
Fresh Air child to their home. Host daughter Anne wanted a girl to play
with, while the Smiths' son Bob wanted a boy. In compromise, "Mother"
Smith offered a solution. "Well, why not both?" she asked.[88] Nevertheless
"both" did not mean two African-American children. Against the statistical odds—white children made up less than 10 percent of the partici-

pants in the Lancaster-based program by this point—blonde-haired Jennie also appeared in the story.[89] She, too, became part of the Smith family for a short while and learned of the wonders of agrarian bliss alongside Sammy. The message of the story came through clearly. Very young Fresh Air children could draw the church forward to a better world as headlines warned of race riots and made white Mennonites wary. Mennonite hosts placed great stock in their young charges and the innocence they had come to represent.

Children like Sammy did offer change and hope to their hosts but often not in the form the hosts expected. Although the program administrators' decision to invite younger participants had removed the older children most capable of challenging their hosts' prejudices, the younger children still forced their hosts to come to terms with their racial naïveté. One host, for example, could not at first bring herself to comb and plait the hair of her Fresh Air guest. As she struggled to overcome her reticence to touch the hair of an African-American child, the host "grew" from the experience and came to a new realization about her racial conditioning.[90] Such encounters often left hosts feeling uncertain about their interracial commitments. Although the hosts had removed older Fresh Air children from their homes, they had not removed a source of ongoing challenge. In the midst of the agrarian bliss so cherished by the Fresh Air program administrators, white Mennonite hosts found that even the youngest of their charges upset their lives and caused them to reconsider assumptions about their racial progress.

Smith, Adoption, and the Possibility of Return

By the time Jerry Smith asked his hosts to adopt him, white Mennonites in the Midwest showed less enthusiasm for Fresh Air ventures. Eight years after Albert Potts snapped pictures from the streets of Inman, Kansas, Smith arrived in nearby Newton to a church and in the middle of a country unsettled by criticism from black power advocates. By the summer of 1969, the racial dynamics, even in a small rural Kansas town like Newton, had undergone significant change. As black power advocates raised their voices, white Mennonites came under new criticism. The General Conference's publications featured articles that referred to the threat of "revolution" against the "white racist institution" of the church and called for sending money into the city rather than taking children out of it.[91] Facing challenges similar to those encountered by white missionaries overseas at the end of the 1960s, those who had dared to call Fresh Air efforts superior to freedom rides in 1961 offered no similar boast of dominance over the black power movement in 1969.[92] In the face of direct challenge to their record of race relations, some white Mennonites began to question their involvement in the Fresh Air program.

Yet Smith faced larger concerns than growing criticism of the Fresh Air program. He had traveled twenty-four hours north from Gulfport for respite from a segregated and threatening environment. The previous year Albert Potts had outgrown Fresh Air vacations and joined a local program also designed to give him new opportunities. As in the case of the Fresh Air program, however, those opportunities often came fraught with trauma. In the summer of 1968, Potts and a group of five other African-American boys had accepted a ride home from a white boy who worked with them at a high school summer employment program. Not long into their trip, a county patrolman stopped the car. Evidently, the teen had been driving erratically. The patrolman listened to the young driver explain that his car lacked second gear but did not ticket him. Instead, the officer ordered the six African-American boys out of the car, used offensive racial epithets against them, and ordered them to start running back to North Gulfport. As the boys left, the officer fired two shots above their heads. Upon hearing the gunfire, Potts and the other five young men ran as fast as they could to their homes. The story spread through the entire Gulfport community and eventually led to a cursory apology from the patrolman's supervisor, but county officials allowed the policeman to keep his job.[93] As Smith prepared to travel to Kansas the following year, the opportunity to leave behind the kind of harassment experienced by Potts overshadowed the dangers pointed out by critics of Camp Landon's Fresh Air program.

No wonder then that Smith thrilled to a farm experience free of the threat of police harassment. He quickly learned the names of his four new host siblings and followed them around the farmyard even before eating breakfast on the morning of his arrival. He got to perch behind the wheel of the Voth family's diesel tractor, to ride bikes with the Voths' sons, and to meet their extended family.[94] Smith even received a visit from one of his former vacation bible school teachers who, like Marietta Voth herself, had traveled from the Newton, Kansas, area to serve in the Camp Landon ministry. Smith, confronted with the same kind of prying questions about his family life that Potts and Middleton had faced before him, tactfully evaded the questions. Such small nuisances seemed a fair trade-off for a few weeks away from Gulfport.

Smith's positive experience with the Voths appeared to offer an ideal rebuttal to the Fresh Air program's multiplying critics. Everything seemed to have gone well. Marietta Voth, Smith's host mother, later wrote to Kaufman that she thought they had "gotten about the best one on the bus" and that hosting Smith had given them "a rich and rewarding experience."[95] She did admit that, owing to harvest demands, her husband spent little time with the family during Smith's stay and that Smith and their middle son did not always get along. Voth also noted that she felt "on edge" during Smith's stay, as she did whenever her children had overnight guests. Nonetheless, she concluded her letter to Kaufman by emphasizing again how positive the experience had been. "Before the bus was out of sight," she added, "our children were all 4 begging and making plans to have Jerry back."[96] After hosts and Fresh Air administrators learned of Smith's matching enthusiasm, as made clear in his request to be adopted, they had all the more reason to ignore the program's critics. In lieu of adoption, a return visit seemed certain.

Yet Smith and the Voths did not know how unrealistic return visits had become. Already in 1966, Kaufman and his staff from Camp Landon found it difficult to recruit host families. As the years progressed and reports of bad experiences spread through the Mennonite community in Kansas, fewer and fewer hosts volunteered, while more and more Gulfport children applied.[97] Exaggerated tales of theft, misbehavior, clashes over appropriate dress, and other cross-cultural misunderstandings diminished the enthusiasm of potential hosts. Even after relatively positive visits like Smith's, hosts in the Gulfport program seldom invited Fresh Air children to return. Evidently the visits had proved more disruptive to some of the hosts than to the Voths. Rather than accept that a once popular program had run its course, Kaufman looked even farther north to Mennonite communities in South Dakota as potential hosting sites. The same year that Smith and a smaller group of Gulfport children entered host homes in Newton, a group of fourteen children traveled thirty-six hours to Freeman, South Dakota, where their hosts and the local press welcomed them.[98] Although Kaufman allowed a few teens to travel to Kansas and South Dakota, he had begun to send older children to camps and retreats. As fewer white host families volunteered and Camp Landon staff sent children farther north, Smith's return to the Voth family seemed less and less likely.

The possibility that Smith would return to a Fresh Air home further diminished owing to waning support for both the Camp Landon and Lancaster Conference programs. By 1971, Lancaster administrators limited their program to six- to eight-year-olds.[99] They made official what Sammy's 1965 story had already implied: Lancaster Mennonites would take only the very young and innocent into their homes. With the drop in age came a reduction in overall numbers. After an initial spike in host participation that mirrored the move to younger children, hosts dropped off quickly. By 1971, the Lancaster program had decreased in size by more than 35 percent, from a high of 302 participants in 1951 to 191 in 1971.[100] That same year, critics within the Lancaster Conference echoed a growing black nationalist critique by calling for the program's end. They stated that Fresh Air ventures reinforced "patterns of racism in our brotherhood" and proved "detrimental to the self concept of participating children."[101] Reduced numbers and internal criticism likewise plagued the Gulfport program. Echoing concerns similar to those of parents in the Northeast, Marietta Voth wrote to Kaufman that two-week stays kept hosts from requesting return visits because the visits lasted "too long."[102] Subject to criticism both external and internal, the Fresh Air programs seemed ready to fade away.

Yet the children kept the programs active well beyond their prime. Hundreds of children at both sites continued to clamor for an opportunity to visit a Fresh Air home. Despite growing criticism about the program's length, implicit paternalism, and extent of required commitment as well as increasing reluctance from white families to invite even the youngest of African-American children into their homes, administrators kept on distributing applications to the children and invitations to the host families. Camp Landon staff continued to send children to the North through the mid-1970s, and Lancaster administrators placed children from the city in rural homes through the mid-1990s.[103] Those children, in turn, encouraged their own offspring to visit Fresh Air homes. When Margie Middleton sat for an interview in 1977 to describe her Fresh Air experiences, a photographer snapped a picture of her with her daughter Karen who, like Middleton, also had traveled to a Pennsylvanian farm for a Fresh Air visit (see figure 3.6); and in 1972, a graduate of the Camp Landon program asked staff to include her young child in the group that would travel north that year.[104] If not for generations of Fresh Air children inundating promoters with requests, administrators would have long before shut down the programs as too expensive, exhausting, and fraught with contradiction to continue.

Smith cared little about the critique mounted by civil rights activists. He had found a place where he did not have to worry about police officers forcing him to run home beneath a hail of bullets and a community that welcomed him because of his racial identity rather than in spite of it. The Voth family farm beckoned him with fresh air, exercise, and mechanized marvels of midwestern farm life. One of his peers considered walking back to his host family. The following year Smith's fellow participant asked of his trip to South Dakota, "How long does it take to walk 1400 miles?"[105] Smith may have considered a similar thousand-mile trek to return to his rural haven in Kansas. He thought a permanent relocation to live among white Mennonites would be ideal.

Yet no one told him what might happen if he did stay longer. African-American teens who traveled north to build on positive Fresh Air ventures rarely experienced the same welcome. During weekend visits to friends' homes, students at Bethel College in Newton, Kansas, encountered racial slurs.[106] To be served in segregated Newton during the 1950s, one student had to pretend he was Japanese.[107] Members of a Mennonite church in that same town told several Bethel students from Gulfport in 1963 that they would not be allowed to become associate members there.[108] Although by 1969 some African-American students felt welcomed at Bethel, others continued to feel that they were "not always treated fairly."[109] Similar evidence of overt prejudice by white Mennonites emerged when African-American students began to attend Lancaster Mennonite High School from the mid-1950s forward.[110] While some completed coursework at Mennonite colleges in Kansas or at Lancaster Mennonite High School in Pennsylvania, other students left early or refused to return after a semester or two.[111] For those who returned to communities that had once welcomed them, memories of the Fresh Air experience grew stale quickly.

Unfamiliar with these older students' encounters with white Menno-

Fig. 3.6 Margie Middleton and her daughter Karen, Harlem, 1977
M. Middleton and R. Y. Wenger, "Fresh Air Reminiscences," *Missionary*
Messenger 54, no. 3 (July 1977): 12. Photo courtesy of Eastern Mennonite Board
of Missions and Charities, Salunga, PA (www.emm.org)

nite racial prejudice, Smith traveled back to Gulfport, where an uncertain
future awaited him. Some Fresh Air children went on to succeed in high
school and college.[112] Others dropped out of school and married at a young
age.[113] A few remained in contact with Camp Landon staff into adult-
hood.[114] Others no longer maintained connections with Gulfport Mennonite personnel after their trip, in part because their presence at local Mennonite churches caused great controversy and therefore limited ongoing
relationship.[115] Smith's future, as promising as some and as imperiled as
others, remained uncertain. Whether his Fresh Air trip would contribute
negatively or positively to the path before him was equally unclear.

Yet as the summer of 1969 came to a close and the Camp Landon bus pulled away from Newton, Smith faced at least one near certainty: he would not be adopted by the Voth family. Voth had already hinted in her letter that, despite the children's enthusiasm, Smith would not be return-ing. She expected that Smith's mother would not respond to her letter and closed out the relationship by looking for a way to return a shirt and a pair of Smith's jean shorts.[116] Voth gave no indication that she knew of the intense opposition to interracial adoptions within the African-American community that would gain widespread attention through a 1972 state-ment by the National Association of Black Social Workers.[117] She focused instead on how Voth's visit with them, though fulfilling, was nonetheless exceptional, a one-time event. The rest of Smith's future—his prospects for good schooling, the possibility of a steady job, and the duration of his Fresh Air memories—would unfold without the Voths to intervene or Smith to change their minds. With a thousand miles between them, they would live out different futures.

The Fruit of Disruption

Many of the hosts mentioned in this chapter remained disinterested in the racial lessons proffered by their young guests. In most cases, children like Middleton, Potts, Sammy, and Smith entered homes where white Men-nonite adults knew little about relating across racial lines. When it be-came apparent that their guests had much to teach them, the hosts often resisted further learning. Some hosts, including many of those involved in the Camp Landon program, simply did not ask the children to return. Other hosts sent older children to the less intimate camp settings where professional staff restrained interracial contact across gender lines. As they withheld invitations, shunted older children to camps, and denied their naïveté, the adults made clear that they did not always appreciate the les-sons taught by their young charges. Given the tremendous control the adults exercised over their guests, it is astounding that the children coun-tered their hosts' assumptions at all. That so many of them failed in their efforts to challenge the adults' racial assumptions does not surprise.

By resisting their young guests' instruction, Fresh Air hosts and ad-ministrators responded to civil rights initiatives like many of their white peers. African-American activists already noted that many white people in both the South and the North seemed to be more concerned about law and order than ending segregation.[118] When African Americans threatened to transcend racial boundaries by breaking laws and refusing to conform to segregation, even liberal and moderate whites objected to the disruptive behavior. In the same way, adult Fresh Air hosts often appeared to be more interested in maintaining ordered lives than pursuing racial justice. Rather than opening their homes to African-American children on a recurring basis, the hosts limited stays and catered to young children, whom they assumed would be least disruptive.

Despite their similarity to those white people who balked at the methods used by civil rights activists to end segregation, white Mennonite Fresh Air hosts nonetheless ventured down one of the few integrated avenues accessible to them. At the grassroots level, practicality mattered most. In most cases, adults opened their homes out of genuine interest in the young children. The hosts frequently expressed concern about the burgeoning racial crisis in the United States and welcomed an opportunity to minister to young children affected by that calamity. The task proved especially appealing because, by the mid-1960s, the young children appeared much less threatening than older African-American city dwellers. Furthermore, few hosts could interrupt their exhausting summer farm tasks to attend a civil rights march. Fewer still had the desire or ability to develop adult interracial relationships outside their immediate community. Tied to the demands of farm life, the hosts had found a practical way to become involved in a kind of civil rights initiative. Fresh Air program promoters did not need to proclaim that hosting African-American children would protect hosts against civil rights critics. In the end, Fresh Air hosts became involved because a two-week visit fit more readily into the practical demands of rural living than did a trip to participate in an organized street march.

Fresh Air ventures did, however, offer a deliberate measure of protection to the leaders who planned, promoted, and sustained the programs. Like most Mennonite church leaders in both the General Conference and the (Old) Mennonite communities during this period, the Fresh Air program administrators found themselves in a bind. They sought to protect and promote a nonresistance doctrine that called the Mennonite community to abstain from coercive demonstrations and at the same time to demonstrate their concern for racial harmony.[119] Caught between the desire to minister to "the least of these" and the concern that they might become compromised in doing so, the leaders had limited options.[120] Fresh Air programs provided a means to satisfy both desires. By hosting young African-American children, Mennonites could minister to those they perceived to be in need without being compromised in the process. Having found an excellent solution to their evangelical dilemma, church leaders promoted the program most heavily at a time when their lack of involvement in civil rights initiatives came under heaviest attack. A month before the 1965 article about Sammy came out, for example, another author excoriated white Mennonites for remaining "aloof from the larger civil rights movement."[121] Fresh Air programs allowed administrators to demonstrate race-related action, if not civil rights advocacy.

Yet the protection sought by the Fresh Air promoters disrupted the children's lives. As noted throughout this chapter, the hosts exercised significant power over their charges. They required their guests to work according to their schedule and style, dress by their standards, refrain from dancing, eschew earrings, and return home as required. Throughout the two decades of the Fresh Air ventures sampled here, administrators kept the visits short, the children deloused, and the host homes free of inspection. Such control exacerbated the hosts' overt prejudice as they used racial epithets, expressed surprise at the children's appearance, and sometimes refused to invite children to return. Although the children gained experience in travel and adventure, they did so at the cost of having their lives upset by hosts who often tried to make them conform to a worldview based on prejudice and racism.

The children nonetheless disrupted the lives of thousands of adults across the church community. As they entered unfamiliar spaces, Fresh Air children defied racial stereotypes that cast them as dirty, ill-mannered, slovenly waifs. When they arrived on a rural farm, the Fresh Air travelers surprised their hosts by demonstrating good hygiene, proper conduct, and careful grooming. The children from Gulfport and New York City also tutored some adults in crossing racial boundaries. The rural host mother who did not know how to care for African-American hair eventually gained proficiency through her young guest's instruction. Every time they confounded their hosts' preconceptions, the children forced the adults to move beyond their racial naïveté and enter an unfamiliar world. During the two decades of this study, Fresh Air programs brought more white Mennonites into intimate contact with African Americans than any other church initiative. By 1970, only fifty-six Mennonite congregations in the United States listed African-American members, but hundreds of congregations and thousands of individuals had hosted African-American Fresh Air children.[122] Despite hosts' efforts to control the children and keep the disruption to a minimum by inviting only the youngest participants, the Fresh Air guests refused to be ignored.

Even those young children, however, forced the adults to live with limits. Middleton, Potts, and many other Fresh Air children refused to supply the intimate home details their hosts craved.[123] Although they rarely showed disrespect toward the adults, the children resisted white Mennonites' efforts to control them. Like Rowena Lark and other African-American converts, the children exercised power in ways often unacknowledged by their contemporaries. Every time young Fresh Air participants refused to give intimate information in exchange for their vacations, they controlled a small but significant measure of the interracial exchange. Rather than acquiescing to pressure from their hosts, the children set limits that the adults eventually came begrudgingly to accept. The hosts found their lives disrupted once again.

The adults who found their lives and perspectives unexpectedly altered by the Fresh Air children who came to live among them responded with a surprising mixture of activism and withdrawal. Most often, their interactions with Fresh Air children did not lead white Mennonites to protest the racial inequities faced by the children in Gulfport, Lancaster, New York City, and Newton. They continued living out their lives with little thought of taking to the streets or writing letters to Congress. Some wrote checks to Camp Landon; others, to Lancaster Conference's Fresh Air program. Once in a while, Fresh Air hosts gave a small gift to their guest during the home stay or at Christmas time.[124] Most hosts responded with actions that remained separate from the world of politics.

The Fresh Air children did, however, motivate a few hosts to take deliberate political action. This chapter closes with one of the most striking of those instances. On December 4, 1963, a group of Mennonite men gathered in Newton, Kansas, the rural town that Jerry Smith had visited. The men had come together to discuss the churches' response to the race crisis in a tumultuous year for the civil rights movement, one that had seen Birmingham fire hoses turned on young people and adults, witnessed the deaths of four young girls at Sixteenth Street Baptist, and marked the assassination of President John F. Kennedy. Among those who gathered in the room were Orlo Kaufman, the Camp Landon Fresh Air program coordinator; Delton Franz, a Fresh Air coordinator from Chicago; and several pastors who had helped host Fresh Air children. The rest of the twenty members of the Board of Christian Service came from congregations that had either sent or hosted Fresh Air children.

Although no children joined the conclave, the presence of Fresh Air youth was nonetheless clear. At a meeting that would provide the theological and programmatic basis for many General Conference and some (Old) Mennonite Church members to write letters to government officials in support of civil rights legislation and even take to the streets in years to come, the board's executive secretary, Dr. Henry A. Fast, voiced his motivation for seeking to become more involved in civil rights activism.[125] He stated simply, "When Gulfport comes into our homes we have a problem."[126] In 1963 Gulfport, Mississippi, came into the homes of white Mennonites in Kansas in one way only, through the Fresh Air program. Fast recognized that he and his racially egalitarian fellow church members had failed in their attempts to cross racial lines in the intimate settings of their homes. He remembered the disruption more than the fanfare.

The failure troubled him and other Mennonites so greatly that he knew something had to change. Less than six months later, for the first time in the church's conflicted race relations history, a white Mennonite leader participated in a national civil rights event. Although at that time members of the General Conference remained more open than (Old) Mennonites to political involvement, Fast nonetheless entered a new arena of politics. Prompted by the experience of Fresh Air children to enter a struggle from which he and his colleagues had sought to remain separate, this same Henry Fast attended a civil rights meeting for national religious leaders in Washington, D.C., two months before the vote on the 1964 civil rights bill. During the gathering, Fast attended a smaller meeting with President Lyndon B. Johnson. Fast gave Johnson "a good mansized handshake" and told the president, " 'We are all for you' (meaning on the civil rights issue)."[127] The children had pushed Fast to the highest levels of government and, in the coming months, they prompted other Mennonites to match such public affirmation with letter writing and lobbying for the 1964 civil rights legislation.

Henry Fast, a white Mennonite church leader, was moved to enter the civil rights arena by his experience with children thought to be too young, too powerless, too innocent, and too invisible to matter. His case shifts our gaze to the intimate home environments where a more expansive understanding of the civil rights movement begins to emerge. To be certain, the movement primarily relied on and worked through mass protests and forceful, adult-centered organizing and oratory. Yet alongside those dramatic, high-profile events, African-American children nonetheless prompted at least a few white religious actors to take new action in support of a racially integrated and just society. Although the adults often used the children for their own purposes, they did not stop the children's interpersonal, deliberated, disruptive, and focused activity.

The next chapter focuses on an activist whose ministry gripped Mennonites in part because of Fresh Air children. Although African-American Mennonite Vincent Harding did not participate in Mennonite-run Fresh Air programs, he found an audience prepared to listen to him because of children like Middleton, Potts, Sammy, and Smith. White Mennonites initially engaged with Harding because the children had carved out a space where race mattered in new ways. As the children challenged their hosts to look at their prejudices, the young participants established a precedent: white Mennonites had begun to learn—even if on a limited and contingent basis—from African Americans. The four children highlighted in this chapter may have protected some Mennonites from critics in the civil rights movement, but they also prepared the community to attend to a voice that could stir them to venture beyond the protection that the children offered.

CHAPTER 4

Vincent Harding's Dual Demonstration

*This revolution will never be complete until the church does what it was called
upon to do in the first place.*
—Vincent Harding, African-American Mennonite pastor, Newton, Kansas, 1963

On the Border

On September 14, 1963, at a hastily organized civil rights meeting at Prairie Street Mennonite Church in Elkhart, Indiana, four African-American men spoke before Vincent Harding ever said a word. Each of them called for action. Ed Riddick, a member of Woodlawn Mennonite Church in Chicago, cajoled the assembled midwestern Mennonite leaders to "apply the gospel to the whole man . . . [including his] civil rights."[1] Gerald Hughes, a Lee Heights Community Church leader from Cleveland, Ohio, spoke of the "agonies of the racial problem" that required "action programs." Following Hughes, seminarian and future Woodlawn pastor Curtis Burrell proposed interracial exchanges to bring about "greater faithfulness." Burrell's fellow seminarian Warren Moore enthusiastically urged those assembled to "get the church on the move."[2] All of the participants at the Prairie Street gathering spoke with passion, fervor, and clear vision. They evinced, in a word, charisma. Yet after African-American Mennonite pastor and activist Vincent Harding spoke, the direction of the conversation shifted. Largely on the basis of Harding's appeal, those attending the Prairie Street meeting agreed to break with the long-standing practice of the (Old) Mennonite Church and "influence legislation even as we do ... the [military] draft."[3] Although the four other African-American speakers had also proposed action plans with energy and passion, in the end—as was the case in scores of other Mennonite settings in the late 1950s and early 1960s—Harding's voice prevailed.

This chapter explores how Harding bridged the gap between the streets and Mennonite homes and sanctuaries. Unlike most other African-American civil rights leaders, Harding expended as much energy demonstrating for an end to segregation in the street as he did in his church. These dual demonstrations gave Harding a unique influence on Mennonite attitudes toward interacting with the state. Although a gifted and charismatic speaker, Harding's influence derived from his ability to straddle the border between traditional Mennonite quietism and civil rights activism. As he negotiated boundary lines, Harding connected the internal legacy of Rowena Lark, Fannie Swartzentruber, and Fresh Air children to the external action of Fannie Lou Hamer, Martin Luther King Jr., and other civil rights activists. More than any other Mennonite leader, white or African-American, Harding shaped the Mennonite church's response to the Second Reconstruction.

The narrative of Harding's straddling sojourn with the Mennonites from 1958 through 1966 challenges those historians who debate Martin Luther King Jr.'s role in terms of Weberian charisma.[4] Following the terms of this debate, historians have attempted to decide, for example, whether King created the civil rights movement or the civil rights movement created King.[5] Such debate tends to occlude the contributions of women, local communities, and faith-based change efforts. This chapter seeks to reframe bipolar charisma-centered inquiry not by expanding the field of scholarship to study gender, grassroots organizing, or belief but by analyzing those who straddled boundary lines.[6] From a bordered perspective, Harding's charisma appears less important than his position between a sectarian religious community and the civil rights movement. In the same way, King's personal charisma seems less salient when he is cast as a border dweller. King confounded the preconceptions of white people who expected buffoonery and servitude while also refusing to conform to the expectations of African Americans and white people who anticipated calls to violence. Like Harding, this nonviolent, well-educated African-American minister attracted the attention of the nation not only because his oratory proved arresting but also because he had a place in both African-American and white communities. Civil rights historians can thus use the study of borderers as presented in this chapter to analyze the movement anew.[7]

This study also repositions Mennonite historiography of the civil rights period. Perry Bush and Paul Toews acknowledge Harding's charisma but fail to ask why Mennonites centered on Harding in an era when several charismatic African-American men had risen to prominence.[8] Charismatic African Americans in the Mennonite church at the time included Bishop James Lark, James Harris, Ed Riddick, and others. Lark and Harris both led revivals and spoke at church meetings and, especially in the case of Lark, asked provocative questions of the church. Yet even the highly charismatic and widely respected Bishop Lark never reached the national and international prominence of Harding. Although Lark also moved between the church and the world, his evangelical mission was squarely lodged within the church. Harding, however, maintained equal footing in both the church and the movement. Whereas Lark worked from a church base to bring converts off the streets and into pews, Harding stood abreast both the church and the movement to get church members off pews and into the streets. This chapter suggests that Harding achieved greater attention not because he was more charismatic than Lark but because he was more evenly divided between two worlds.

Similarly, other treatments of Mennonite engagement with the civil rights movement have either ignored Harding's wide-reaching impact entirely or explained his intervention in terms of the growing influence of black power.[9] During Harding's most influential years, however, he moved in circles far more influenced by King than by the Student Nonviolent Coordinating Committee's Stokely Carmichael. In 1963, for example, John Lewis, just elected the committee's chairperson, actively promoted a Christian nonviolent agenda.[10] Carmichael's and Willie Ricks's call for black power would not enter the national scene until mid-1966.[11] Furthermore, a regional study of Camp Landon in Gulfport, Mississippi, puts far more emphasis on visits by white church administrators in 1963 than on a visit by the Hardings, though local staff referred to the latter visit more frequently and with deeper appreciation.[12] Harding, a Mennonite convert, challenged the church on its own terms even while gaining the trust of civil rights leaders. Setting a new direction in Anabaptist history, this chapter explains why Harding's border-straddling position as an African-American Mennonite allowed him to rise from a field of charismatic African-American male leaders to critique the church without relying on black power rhetoric.

The true measure of Harding's unique role at the border between the Mennonite and civil rights communities became most apparent in 1963. During that year, every aspect of the relationship between white and African-American Mennonites and of their engagement with the broader issues of the day became the focus of intense conversations. Mennonites debated what it meant to nonconform to the world in a time of social crisis. They explored the meaning of legislative advocacy for a more just society as cities erupted in racial tensions and violence. Discussions surfaced in church publications and denominational meetings about the sins of racism, the realities of Mennonite prejudice, and biblical passages that allegedly supported African-American servitude. Church leaders issued statements to their congregants and national political leaders. Although the years leading up to and following the momentous events of 1963 frame the story, this chapter focuses on Harding's words and actions during that year of "racial revolution."[13]

Harding's sojourn among the Mennonites, and his challenge to the church on issues of race, turned on his status as someone who could move with integrity between two very different communities. On the one hand, Harding brought sterling Mennonite credentials. He knew Mennonite history, led a Mennonite voluntary service unit, and had served as a Mennonite pastor. He embodied Mennonite virtues of humility, frugality, servanthood, and integrity. Harding did not just talk about the need for racial reconciliation; he and his wife Rosemarie demonstrated it through the integrated ministry they led at Mennonite House in Atlanta.[14] Harding also claimed full-fledged membership because he spoke like a Mennonite. His presentations appealed to love, long-suffering, and nonconformity. More forthright than Guy Hershberger, the leading Mennonite theologian and social ethicist of the time, Harding articulated a rationale for, and practical theology of, sustained social engagement that, he argued, would save the church from destruction. In his service, speech, humility, and theology, Harding thus could legitimately claim a Mennonite identity, even as he actively challenged Jim Crow practices, spent time in jail, and earned the respect of civil rights movement leaders. In the precarious posture of a carpenter straddling a roof crest, Harding kept one leg in the world of separation and another in that of engagement. Although his charisma prodded people to action, it was his ability to straddle two worlds that got their attention and kept it.

A Congregational Camelot

Harding was drawn to Mennonites by the witness of the early Anabaptist community. Born in 1931, he was raised by his mother in the West Indian community of New York City, where his mother worked in a variety of domestic jobs. In his youth, he attended the Victory Tabernacle Church in Harlem, "an offshoot of the Black Seventh-Day Adventist denomination," where his pastor made early reference to peace activists like Mahatma Gandhi but not to Mennonites.[15] Harding served in the Army at Fort Dix in New Jersey from 1953 through 1955, and his time in the armed service left him "deeply disturbed" by the dehumanizing power of the military.[16] Having developed a love of history while earning his bachelor's degree at City College of New York, he went on to pursue his master's in history at the University of Chicago, where he began to encounter the writings of sixteenth-century Anabaptists.[17] Harding was struck by "their discipline, self-sacrificing love, . . . [and] willingness to accept death rather than inflict suffering."[18]

While studying for his master's degree Harding encountered contemporary Mennonites at Woodlawn Mennonite Church on the south side of Chicago. In that congregation he also met his future wife, Rosemarie Freeney, a teacher in the Chicago public schools who had earned her degree from Goshen College, a Mennonite liberal arts school in northern Indiana.[19] By 1958, the Woodlawn congregation had called Harding to serve as its associate pastor while he worked toward a doctoral degree in American history at the University of Chicago. During those years, Harding and lead pastor Delton Franz received attention from the General Conference Mennonites for their integrated pastorate (see figure 4.1). Although by 1958 the (Old) Mennonite Church included more than two-dozen congregations with significant African-American memberships, none of those churches could boast such a high-profile integrated pastoral team.[20] What the General Conference lacked in African-American congregational membership it made up for in pastoral balance. Indeed, the two men captured the imagination of the church to such an extent that a Mennonite historian

Fig. 4.1 Vincent Harding and Delton Franz, Woodlawn Mennonite, Chicago, 1957
E. Neufeld, "That the World Might Recognize Christ," *The Mennonite* 72, no. 45 (November 12, 1957):
709. Photo courtesy of Mennonite Publishing Network, Scottdale, PA

later referred to Woodlawn as a "congregational Camelot."[21] Never before
had the General Conference denomination included an African-American leader.[22]

In the summer of 1958, Harding, fellow African-American Mennonite
Ed Riddick, and three of their white coreligionists—Franz, Glen Boese,
and Elmer Neufeld—traveled through the South in an effort to gain new
insight into the "Negro's demands" and the "white man's fear."[23] Unlike
most of the Mennonite groups who also toured the South to learn more
about racial issues during the latter half of the 1950s and the early 1960s,
the Woodlawn group connected southern segregation with northern separation.[24] Both Franz and Harding emphasized that white Mennonites
throughout the country had denied African Americans "a place in our fellowship" and, in so doing, had "denied Christ" as well.[25] The denominational editors and reporters who profiled much of the activity emerging
from Woodlawn at that time made no exception regarding this trip. The
men's visit to the South received significant public attention.

The five men also sought to connect Mennonite nonresistance to nonviolent strategies then gaining traction in the emerging civil rights movement. At the time, many church leaders felt that the doctrine of nonresistance entailed an absolute rejection of all coercive force—including nonviolent public protest. Guy F. Hershberger, the most vocal and informed proponent of a consistent Anabaptist approach to nonresistance at the time, applied that vision of noncoercive nonresistance to the civil rights agenda by promoting a middle road. Although Hershberger encouraged Mennonites to "take an open stand against segregation," advocated "a ministry of concern, of sympathy, and of love" to African Americans, and called for a "witness" to segregationist or unconcerned white people, he also criticized civil rights groups for promoting nonviolence as a tactic rather than a biblical principle.[26] Here, as elsewhere, Hershberger and his coreligionists used *witness* to indicate any morally substantive exchange with an outsider, not just evangelically specific interactions.

By contrast, the Woodlawn contingent called for direct action. Harding in particular urged Mennonites to protest publicly "the inaction of Congress and the President on the segregation controversy in the schools."[27] At least one other promising young church leader from the (Old) Mennonite community raised similar concerns. J. Lawrence Burkholder, a Princeton Theological Seminary doctoral student and future Goshen College president, also challenged the validity of Hershberger's position.[28] Nonviolent measures like street marches, Harding and Burkholder maintained, did not coerce, and, Christians concerned about racial oppression were therefore free to participate in nonviolent direct action.

Hershberger countered the young men's critique by returning to core Mennonite principles even while remaining open to further dialogue. In a chapter devoted to race relations in his 1958 text, *The Way of the Cross in Human Relations*, Hershberger made no mention of the 1954 *Brown v. Board of Education* Supreme Court desegregation decision, the subsequent Montgomery bus boycotts in 1955 and 1956, or the Reverend Martin Luther King Jr., who had long since entered the national and world stage.[29] Despite his somewhat inexplicable avoidance of these national events, Hershberger did evaluate the biblical basis for equality of the races and enjoined the Mennonite community to enact scriptural mandates in their daily lives. Although he unfailingly opposed racial subordination and dampened his public criticism of King so as not to encourage reactionaries in the church, Hershberger continued to critique the kind of direct, nonviolent action proposed by Harding. In light of conversations with Harding and other civil rights leaders like Fellowship of Reconciliation staffer and King confidant Bayard Rustin, Hershberger eventually expressed openness to nonviolent action taken in a spirit of suffering love rather than tactical coercion. In 1959, Hershberger even participated in a spontaneous sit-in of sorts, during which his integrated traveling party asked for and eventually received service at a segregated restaurant in the Atlanta airport.[30] Although Harding continued to disagree with Hershberger's theological opposition to coercive street demonstrations, the two men remained in conversation through the period of this study.

Following the group's sojourn through the South, Harding increasingly challenged Hershberger and the entire Mennonite community on the principle of integrity. In an essay titled "To My Fellow Christians: An Open Letter to Mennonites," Harding called upon his readers to bring such cherished Mennonite values as discipleship, nonresistance, and consistency of belief to bear on the urgent reality of racial oppression. "Can the voices which once sounded so loudly in opposition to warfare," Harding asked, " . . . now be silent when men are destroying other men (and themselves) with hatred?" He enjoined his co-believers to demonstrate the same integrity of "words and deeds" they had shown when Mennonite men faced mandatory military training.[31] In the past, leaders from the church had met with high-level governmental officials to negotiate nonviolent options like alternative service in Civilian Public Service during World War II and I-W service during the Korean and Vietnam conflicts. As Harding observed his coreligionists, they seemed far less eager to lobby on behalf of racial justice. Undaunted, he called white Mennonites to leave secluded communities and align themselves with African-American struggles as an expression of "the way of the disciple."[32] For the first time before a national Mennonite audience, Harding employed core Anabaptist concepts to support civil rights goals. He continued to focus the church's attention on civil rights issues in dozens of articles, hundreds of speeches, and countless conversations with white Mennonites through the next four years.

Eight months later, Harding and Franz hosted a seminar on race relations at which Harding stated his position squarely at the boundary between the Mennonite church and the civil rights movement. Held at Woodlawn from April 17 through 19, 1959, the conference drew leaders from the hosts' General Conference denomination but also from the Lancaster Conference, the Mennonite Brethren, and the (Old) Mennonite Church.[33] In a departure from other meetings on race relations held up to that point and, in many cases, subsequent to that point, nearly 30 percent of the approximately fifty participants were African Americans.[34] Harding addressed this diverse audience as a Mennonite but also spoke from his commitment as a movement activist. In a plenary address he questioned how Mennonites could profess nonconformity to a sinful world while "slavishly and silently" acquiescing to racial segregation. From his perspective, nonconformity should lead believers to oppose racially unjust laws and practices. Even as he called Mennonites to move forward into the world he also pointed back to the Mennonite church itself. Having noted how "the cultural stereotype of Mennonitism" excluded non-Europeans, he called his audience to bring African Americans "into the deep places" of Mennonite fellowship. In his most direct challenge to Hershberger's separatist nonresistance, Harding closed his speech with a series of laments that Mennonites had "too long" remained separate.[35] At the crest between separation and engagement, Harding directed Mennonites to demonstrate against segregation within and without the church.

Menno House in Atlanta

Harding's position at the boundary of the Mennonite church and the civil rights movement stabilized in the following years as he moved into leadership in both circles. In 1960 the Hardings celebrated their marriage at the Woodlawn congregation and, within a year, started a Mennonite Voluntary Service unit in Atlanta under the auspices of the Mennonite Central Committee's Peace Section, the peace advocacy arm of the Mennonite family of churches (see figure 4.2). Rosemarie resigned from her teaching post and Vincent took a leave from his dissertation project in order to direct a new voluntary service unit, which Vincent later described as "a combination residence for an interracial team of local Movement participants and social service volunteers, a house of refuge for field workers from the various Movement organizations, an ecumenical community, and a base of operations for our own ministry of reconciliation."[36] The Hardings located Mennonite House—as locals dubbed the unit—only a block away from Martin and Coretta Scott King's home. Harding had met King

Fig. 4.2 Vincent and Rosemarie Harding, 1962
V. Stoltzfus, "A Talk with Vincent Harding," *Christian Living* 9, no. 10 (October
1962): 11. Photo courtesy of Mennonite Publishing Network, Scottdale, PA

during his trip to the South three years earlier, and they soon developed a
close friendship. By moving to Atlanta, he solidified his relationship with
key civil rights leaders and established a base from which to become more
engaged with the activism he called on the church to embrace.

Soon after their arrival in Atlanta, King invited the Hardings to join
the Southern Christian Leadership Conference's protest work in Albany,
Georgia, to "help keep this a Christian movement."[37] From December
1961 well into 1962, the Hardings repeatedly traveled to Albany to hold
discussions with white and African-American community leaders about
"the way of reconciling love."[38] During one of their Albany sojourns in
1962, Vincent spent three days in jail for praying in public as part of a
demonstration at city hall, an action that blurred the boundaries between
Christian piety and social activism.[39] King and Albany sheriff Laurie
Pritchett then urged Harding to accept release so that he could help calm
anger roused in the local African-American community after police officers beat a prominent black lawyer.[40] Harding accepted their counsel and,

once Pritchett signed Harding's bond, visited "bars, pool halls, [and] bar-
bershops" to call "for a Christian response to violence."[41] Although the
Albany protests saw little success, the Hardings' efforts gained the trust
of civil rights movement leaders. Through the remainder of 1962 the
Hardings regularly hosted civil rights leaders at Mennonite House and
attended meetings to help craft movement strategy.

Harding brought the high drama of his Albany experiences to the Mennonite church. While in jail he considered his speaking assignment at the
Mennonite World Conference, less than two weeks away. He pondered
how to address a community still uncertain about involvement in worldly
pursuits of any kind, let alone political agitation. Despite the activist example of white Mennonites like Woodlawn co-pastor Delton Franz in the
General Conference denomination and Lee Heights (Cleveland) pastor
Vern Miller among (Old) Mennonites, most members of the community
viewed integrationist activity with suspicion and, in some cases, outright
antagonism. Harding knew his audience, however, and used biblical imagery to make his case, a strategy he had used many times before. He mulled
over the possibility of forgoing his speaking responsibilities because he
was "weary . . . of talking and talking and talking about the church and
race." He considered instead sending "a short, gracious note of invitation,
urging" Mennonites to join him in Albany in his jail cell. Although he left
his cell to maintain peace in Albany, Harding mentioned his weariness at
the Mennonite World Conference and concluded his talk with one of his
harshest indictments to date. Drawing on the prophetic imagery of the
book of Revelation, he said, "We . . . are insipidly lukewarm on the challenge of racial brotherhood and human justice."[42]

A Revolutionary Year, 1963

Vincent and Rosemarie, however, had not left the Mennonite world.
Early in 1963, they described their work among Mennonites as "meaningful, frustrating, and rewarding." Among the most meaningful of their
activities came the opportunity to act as "sympathetic confessors" to white
church leaders. In addition to writing for all of the publications in both
the General Conference and (Old) Mennonite Church denominations,
the Hardings listened to the "untold inner agonies" of white church leaders, tried to "understand them," and called them to costly response.[43] Al-

though their calls for public action clearly troubled those committed to separatist nonresistance, the Hardings' personal engagement also appealed to Mennonites committed to maintaining right relationships.

At the same time, Harding's impatience with the church became increasingly evident. On February 5, 1963, for example, he published an article in which he called on his readers to let go of their "Swiss-German Mennonite" identity. Unlike other featured writers, Harding also pressed the church to move beyond good intentions to interracial "fellowship, neighborhood life, school comradery [sic], and job relationships." Yet even here, Harding wrote as an insider. He used plural pronouns twenty times in the article, repeatedly referring to "our problem," "our captivity," "our life in one body," "our thinking."[44] Concurrent with such strong claims of membership, white church news reporter Daniel Hertzler lauded the Hardings for their courageous action in Atlanta.[45] Other editors had heaped praise on the Hardings in the previous year as well.[46] Although his claims of Mennonite identity would dissipate as the year progressed, Harding soon proved so influential that any Mennonite leader who hoped to speak about the racial tumult of 1963 had to address issues Harding raised.

At least one white Mennonite leader found Harding's growing influence objectionable. Following a visit by the Hardings to Eastern Mennonite College in Harrisonburg, Virginia, Mahlon Blosser, a local white Mennonite church executive, objected to Harding's observation that the Virginia Conference had acquiesced to Jim Crow practices. Blosser bristled at Harding's proposal that the conference host a race relations meeting to better equip Virginia Mennonites to oppose segregation.[47] "Can one person go into a [M]ennonite community of about 2000 members," Blosser queried, "and have one meeting with less than 200 present, then have a meeting with the student body at E.M.C. and then write an accurate evaluation of the race situation in the community?" He answered his own question by declaring that such a race relations gathering would prove harmful.[48]

Other white Mennonite leaders found Harding's words challenging but remained open to his activist message. For example, as Bishop Blosser penned his letter, Vincent, Rosemarie, and their infant daughter, Rachel, were spending time with the staff of Camp Landon in Gulfport, Mississippi, where General Conference church executives had asked them to assess the camp's twenty-year-old program. The conscientious objectors' work in constructing sanitary privies at Camp Landon during World War II had garnered local respect.[49] By 1950, church administrators had built on that respect to create a ministry to African Americans in the form of public school religious education, recreational leadership, and youth bible education.[50] By 1963, the voluntary service workers also administered rural visitation programs, staffed a weekly radio broadcast, ran a lending library, and served on a variety of local ministerial groups.

From all reports, long-term white staff members Edna and Orlo Kaufman and Harold and Rosella Regier nervously awaited the Hardings' visit. Orlo Kaufman had heard Harding speak at Woodlawn's 1959 race relations conference in Chicago and knew firsthand his ability to challenge the status quo. In response to a query about the Hardings coming to work at Camp Landon in 1960, Kaufman wrote that he would accept the idea only if they agreed to do "personal work"—by which he meant service rather than civil rights activism. Explaining his objections, Kaufman stated, "I'm not sure that Vincent fully understands [the southern reality], and being a Northerner could get into ... serious difficulty."[51] At that time, the local African-American community had begun to agitate for access to the Gulfport beaches.[52] Kaufman and other Camp Landon staff had sought to be mediators in the dispute by participating in an integrated ministerial alliance.[53]

For these efforts and their work with African-American children, staff faced local harassment in the form of name-calling, suspicion, and both overt and covert attention from the Mississippi State Sovereignty Commission, a state-sponsored vigilance committee tasked with identifying and intimidating supporters of integration.[54] Local tensions rose to new heights in advance of the Hardings' visit as white members of the Gulfport community expressed their support for Governor Ross Barnett's refusal to enroll James Meredith at the University of Mississippi.[55] In light of these prior exchanges and local conditions, Edna Kaufman requested prayer that the Hardings' visit would be "beneficial for all of us."[56]

Despite the collective nervousness and a full schedule—Orlo Kaufman scheduled Vincent to speak seven times and to visit numerous local leaders—the Hardings spent most of their four-day visit with Camp Landon members.[57] In three extended sessions, they discussed every aspect of the camp program. According to Kaufman, the exchanges made a profound impression. He later wrote that Vincent "never leaves one the same."[58] No wonder then that Kaufman wrote to the national offices on April 30 ex-pressing concern that the Hardings' report had not yet arrived.[59] In the interim, Orlo Kaufman wrote an article in which he described Harding's challenge to relate to white segregated churches, support civil rights activ-ity, and reconsider where staff lived and worshipped.[60]

When Harding's report did arrive, it gave Camp Landon administrators and staff much to consider. The recommendations touched on all the issues Kaufman had named in his article, but with greater intensity. The Camp Landon group, Harding wrote, needs "to resolve its schizophrenia of week day work with Negroes and Sunday worship where Negroes cannot go."[61] Although he recognized that Camp Landon staffers had mentored Afri-can-American children and young adults, Harding lamented the absence of a Mennonite church that would welcome them. The two Mennonite congregations in the area, Gulfport and Crossroads, practiced segregation and, in the latter case, did so vociferously. As in previous speeches and articles, Harding called the Camp Landon staff to pay attention to racial dynamics within their organization. Not surprisingly, he also called for greater involvement with civil rights groups outside the church. Admit-ting that the "swirling, often confused patterns" of civil rights changes made it difficult to know exactly how to become involved, Harding urged staff to "take our heritage seriously" and act on the belief that God would make it clear how to join in the racial "revolution."[62] Such an invitation contrasted with the gradualist, relationship-centered approach advocated by Kaufman.[63]

Yet the Hardings' visit clearly had an impact. On June 27, for example, Kaufman urged the Gulfport mayor to appoint a biracial committee as a proactive measure to avoid violence.[64] In that same month, Harold Regier broadcast a Sunday school lesson on the radio in which he discussed the murder of Medgar Evers and Governor George Wallace's refusal to admit African-American students to the University of Alabama.[65] Kaufman and Harold Regier's resolve was strengthened by their attendance, in Decem-ber 1963, at an NAACP dinner where a group of white protestors threw rocks and debris at the banquet hall.[66] These and other new initiatives continued, so that by March of 1964 the interracial activities of the Camp Landon staff brought them under renewed investigation by county and state officials.[67] Five years later, staff continued to reference Harding and seek his counsel.[68] Such public engagement represented a significant shift

for Kaufman and his staff as they began likewise to straddle the Mennonite church and the civil rights movement.

Almost immediately, the Hardings paired this Mennonite encounter
with another venture into civil rights activism. On the heels of their visit
to Camp Landon, they traveled to the Mississippi Delta to visit white
and African-American community leaders. Working from the home of
African-American activist Amzie Moore in Cleveland, the Hardings met
with a plantation owner, a white businessman, an Episcopalian minister,
an African-American businessman, and several Franciscan monks. Even
more notable than the breadth of their contacts was the manner of their
initial invitation. The Hardings refrained from identifying themselves as
African Americans when first requesting meetings over the phone. They
explained, "We decided to move about and converse with individuals just
as if Mississippi were well."[69]

Occasionally during these grassroots ventures, the two worlds the Hardings straddled overlapped. While on a similar trip to the Delta that same
year, the couple arranged to meet Titus Bender, a white Mennonite pastor
seeking to support civil rights activity in the town of Meridian. Given
the racial tension in the region, Bender told the Hardings not to ask locals
where he lived, since such a query could draw dangerous attention. Instead, they planned to rendezvous at a local gas station where, when he
saw them, Bender would start driving and the Hardings would follow.
When the Hardings approached the gas station, however, Bender got out
of his car in front of the older white men gathered at the station and gave
Vincent the Holy Kiss, a traditional Mennonite greeting. Harding later
recalled Bender's salutation as a bold "kind of risk-taking" at the juncture
of Mennonite identity and civil rights activism that encouraged him to
continue the difficult work of mediating between the two worlds.[70]

Such contact with grassroots civil rights activists influenced how Harding spoke when he returned to the Mennonite community. In April, following his travels during the previous month with Rosemarie and their
infant daughter, Rachel, he went to Broad Street Mennonite Church in
Harrisonburg, Virginia, where congregational leaders promoted him as
an evangelist.[71] He did not, however, act like one. Speaking at this small
church, the first racially integrated congregation in the Virginia Conference, Harding preached each evening for seven days on the "challenge of
the cross" (see figure 4.3).[72] Rather than direct his comments toward per-

Vincent Harding, Atlanta, Ga., in charge of The Mennonite House, MCC sponsored race relations project in the South, sees our job as calling men to reconciliation.

Rev. Vincent Harding

****

ALL ARE WELCOME !!!

Bring a FRIEND

BROAD STREET

SPIRITUAL LIFE CONFERENCE

March 31   to   April 7
           1963
Each evening   7:30 p.m.

Speaker -

Rev. VINCENT HARDING

The MENNONITE HOUSE

Atlanta, Georgia

****

Fig. 4.3 Flier for Broad Street Spiritual Life Conference, Harrisonburg, Virginia, 1963
Virginia Mennonite Archives, uncatalogued box, Broad Street 1936–1979, Richard & Virginia
Weaver, "Hear Vincent Harding . . . ," Broad Street Mennonite Church, 1963, March 31–April
7. Photo courtesy of Virginia Mennonite Conference, Harrisonburg, VA

sonal evangelism and end his sessions with an altar call, however, Harding
concluded each evening's service with open discussion, an unusual practice for an event billed as a "spiritual life conference."[73] Although interest in the tent revival ministries of charismatic evangelists like Virginia
Conference minister George R. Brunk II had passed its peak by the time
Harding traveled to Harrisonburg, audiences still expected to be called
forward to repentance, not invited into open conversation. Once again,
Harding created a new form of witness as he straddled two worlds.

Harrisonburg Mennonites continued to discuss Harding's challenges
after he left the area, especially the idea of hosting a meeting on race relations. On March 31, 1964, a year after the Broad Street meetings, ministers and lay members from the Virginia Conference gathered at Chicago
Avenue Church in Harrisonburg to discuss "the Christian and race."[74] Significantly, however, whites dominated the meeting, despite the fact that a
number of gifted African-American speakers served within the Virginia
Conference, including Billy Curry, an ordained deacon at Broad Street,
and Leslie Francisco, pastor of the Virginia Conference congregation in

Newport News. Both men had significant speaking experience within and beyond their congregations and regularly spoke to large audiences. Yet rather than invite either of these local charismatic African-American leaders, the Virginia Conference brought in Paul G. Landis, a white bishop from the Lancaster Conference. Ironically, only Landis mentioned Harding in public session.[75] The Virginia Conference leaders' refusal to invite or even refer to Harding—even though the meeting emerged from his earlier visit—suggests a fear that Harding would further disrupt their internally focused and nonconfrontational approach to racial integration. It also suggests that even those who opposed Harding's call for more involvement in social activism could not ignore his challenges.

Into the Battle

Rather than wait for the Virginia Conference to discuss race relations, the Hardings continued to deepen their civil rights work. With responsibilities complete in Harrisonburg, they returned to Atlanta on April 7 to attend a baptismal service led by Rev. Martin Luther King Jr. at Ebenezer Baptist, King's home congregation. At the end of the service, King contacted Rosemarie and requested that she and Vincent travel to Birmingham to act as intermediaries between civil rights demonstrators and white community leaders. After considering the request for several days, on April 10 the Harding family drove to Birmingham, where they played a critical mediating role with white "clergymen, lawyers, businessmen, [and] political leaders."[76] Behind the scenes, they helped keep communication channels open between Southern Christian Leadership Conference leaders and the local white establishment in the midst of violence, incrimination, and large-scale unrest.

In accepting this assignment, the Hardings drew on skills honed through their work at the border with the Mennonite church. In these engagements, however, they did not display the weariness that had begun to creep into their work with white Mennonites. Here, the drama and deep sense of engagement with matters of historical import proved invigorating. Owing to the sensitive nature of the contacts, for example, the Hardings often attended secret meetings and private negotiations.[77] And they willingly refrained from participating in the actual Birmingham demonstrations in order to better facilitate their negotiations between the white leaders and civil rights demonstrators, which lasted well past Easter. In Birmingham, the Hardings evinced a new level of sophistication and gravitas in their civil rights work. Working out of the public eye, they supported civil rights street activism with the Mennonite-modeled skills of daily demonstration.

These intense civil rights negotiations, in turn, led to new public appearances in the Mennonite church and beyond. After returning to Atlanta on April 20, Harding left for a speaking engagement in Connecticut followed by additional meetings in Nashville, Tennessee, and Akron, Pennsylvania, headquarters of the Mennonite Central Committee. He returned to Atlanta on April 25 and, by order of his doctor, went on bed rest from April 28 through May 5. The second day back on his feet, Harding traveled to Birmingham with Mennonite minister Paul Peachey, staff member for Church Peace Mission, an organization of Protestant peace groups. Peachey had come to Atlanta to meet with Harding, King, and other movement leaders, but upon his arrival he received a message from King that he should go to Birmingham and meet with committee members there.[78] Harding traveled with Peachey to participate in the ad hoc peace meeting but quickly entered into negotiations between demonstrators and city officials. At one point Harding went into the streets to "help stop the battle between the fire hoses and the Negro crowd."[79]

Through May 10 Harding stayed in the city to mediate between the two sides. Before he returned home, he drafted the press release King would read upon completion of the negotiations.[80] When bombs exploded the night of May 11 at the home of King's brother, the Reverend A. D. King, and at the Gaston Motel, where King had been staying, Harding got back on the phone with civil rights leaders and white officials, urging them to keep their agreement. Shuttling between activism in the streets and speeches in churches, Harding stayed connected to both Mennonites and movement leaders.

In events at Birmingham, Harding played a role that affected the nation. As reporters broadcast images of fire hoses, police dogs, and batons battering civil rights marchers, the rhetoric of democracy lost credibility. Although he had been hesitant to address previous civil rights campaigns, President Kennedy expressed outrage at the brutality in Birmingham and growing concern over increasing levels of violence.[81] In a nationally televised broadcast on June 11, Kennedy appealed to the nation's moral sensibility and asked American citizens to accept changes to the racial order.[82] The skills and experience Harding had gained working at the border between white Mennonites and civil rights leaders allowed him to play a significant role in this broader shift in national perception.

As the struggle for civil rights in Birmingham continued, Mennonites across the church began to pay new attention to racial oppression within their own communities. Incidents of overt racial discrimination came under new scrutiny and received swift, public condemnation. For example, Mae Schrag, a white staff member at Camp Landon, reported on conversations she had with five African-American girls who had attended Mennonite colleges. In May, she informed Camp Landon supporters that white Mennonites had used offensive racial epithets in front of the girls, denied the young women associate membership status in local congregations, and housed the girls in separate rooms by race.[83] News of these incidents spread far beyond Gulfport and eventually entered the national Mennonite press.[84] At a time when both the General Conference and (Old) Mennonite communities had begun to define their identity by emphasizing selfless service and the pursuit of social justice rather than visible marks of nonconformity, such overt evidence of racism inside the church proved troubling. Mennonite claims of racial egalitarianism weakened in the face of such reports and brought renewed attention to Harding's increasingly high-profile ministry.

At the same time, the growing visibility of national civil rights activism prompted Mennonite church officials to promote the Hardings' work. Mennonite leaders noted the rising intensity of racial struggle, marked by the June 12 murder of civil rights activist and NAACP field secretary Medgar Evers.[85] Five days later, Ed Metzler, executive secretary of the Peace Section of the Mennonite Central Committee (MCC) and the Hardings' supervisor, contacted every Mennonite peace committee in the country to inform them of the Hardings' work in Atlanta and to encourage lobbying for civil rights. Although he stopped short of calling for mass street action, Metzler nonetheless moved away from Guy Hershberger's posture of separatist nonresistance, thanks largely to the influence of the Hardings. Metzler knew his audience. Before suggesting a new departure he had to demonstrate the couple's integrity in word and deed. Thus in his appeals Metzler first described how the Hardings served "as a reconciling bridge between the white and Negro communities." Only after establishing their credibility in traditional Mennonite language did he advocate for "witness to government on civil rights legislation."[86]

As the year progressed, Harding spent less energy on Mennonite contacts while simultaneously moving ever closer to an embattled civil rights community. The summer of 1963 saw 1,122 civil rights demonstrations throughout the country and some twenty thousand arrests in the South.[87] White southerners responded by incarcerating and beating demonstrators. Police officials and other segregationists attacked women in the movement with particular intensity.[88] For example, Mississippi state police arrested Fannie Lou Hamer—the voting rights activist who would later captivate the attention of the nation at the 1964 Democratic National Convention— and a group of her co-workers from the Student Nonviolent Coordinating Committee while they traveled home from a June voter registration workshop.[89] During her time in jail, the police officers forced African-American inmates to beat Hamer with a blackjack. After her release, Hamer traveled to Atlanta to meet with staff members from the Southern Christian Leadership Conference and to recover from the brutal beatings. She stayed at Mennonite House while in Atlanta, where she spoke and laughed long with the Hardings.[90] Through such encounters, Vincent's commitment to the civil rights movement grew stronger.

Harding's increasing civil rights involvement drew even more attention from Mennonite church leaders as the summer months progressed. While on a tour of the South, Guy F. Hershberger met with Harding in late July. The two men spent less time on their theological differences than on the "urgency of the [civil rights] situation." Harding felt that the "integrity of the church" would be irreparably damaged if Mennonites did not act soon. Once again, he advocated for interracial bible schools and summer camps, vocal stands against public school segregation, and direct nonviolent action in support of civil rights.[91] Although Hershberger's own subsequent recommendations focused on matters of education, missions, and personal reconciliation rather than the public advocacy proposed by Harding, he nonetheless quoted Harding at length. Goshen College professor and theologian C. Norman Kraus also spent three weeks in Atlanta from mid-July through early August. Harding put Kraus in touch with a broad range of civil rights activists, including Southern Christian Leadership Conference executive Ralph Abernathy, Student Nonviolent Coordinating Committee communications director Julian Bond, Koinonia Farms founder and author Clarence Jordan, and leaders of the White Citizens Council.[92] Thanks to Harding's contacts, Kraus enjoyed a level of access unusual for a white northerner.

Ironically, the more Harding turned his face toward civil rights activism, the more leaders from both the General Conference and the (Old) Mennonite Church denominations regarded him as the church's spokesperson on race relations. By August of 1963, denominational officials regularly called on Harding to attend their meetings and to challenge Mennonite listeners. Early that same month, David Augsburger, the host of a nationally broadcast radio program known as the Mennonite Hour, interviewed Harding on air.[93] Several weeks later, (Old) Mennonite Church delegates passed a resolution on "reconciliation" at a national assembly where leaders challenged their constituents to follow the Hardings' example.[94] In correspondence with Guy Hershberger following the assembly, home missions secretary Nelson Kauffman proposed a meeting with African Americans, "in addition to Vince Harding," to instruct white church leaders in how to relate to civil rights groups.[95] Kauffman underlined Harding's prominence by referring to him repeatedly. Hershberger followed suit. When he released a report on his southern trip to more than thirty groups and individuals, Hershberger included only one African American, Vincent Harding, in the distribution list.[96]

Harding's profile rose even higher in the Mennonite press. On August 6, 1963, editors of both *The Mennonite* and the *Gospel Herald*—the weekly national publications of the General Conference and the (Old) Mennonite Church denominations, respectively—referred to Harding. On the General Conference side, Maynard Shelly quoted Harding's bracing speech at the 1962 Mennonite World Conference that challenged his audience to engage in civil disobedience. *Gospel Herald* editor John M. Drescher noted that Harding had influenced his thoughts on segregation. Drescher also printed an article by Harding challenging the church to be true to its calling of nonconformity to "prejudice and discrimination."[97] In the five months that followed, the editors of these two magazines included appeals to legislative action no less than five times, a significant departure from the relationally based efforts promoted by Hershberger and other supporters of a less politically engaged Anabaptism.[98] Once again, Harding's agenda guided the church's response.

Harding ended the summer at the center of national civil rights activity. On August 28 he joined a quarter of a million civil rights demonstrators at the March on Washington for Jobs and Freedom, where King gave his "I Have a Dream" speech.[99] Unlike their antagonists, the interracial demonstrators did not resort to violence.[100] In subsequent weeks, the Student Nonviolent Coordinating Committee and other civil rights groups built on the success of the national protest by conducting nonviolent voter registration drives in Mississippi and throughout the South.[101] Despite the tactical nature of the nonviolent action, the public, disciplined display of the peaceful protests drew the attention of the nation and challenged those Mennonite leaders who continued to criticize King and his associates for using nonviolence but not committing their lives to it. Nonetheless, the nonviolent discipline of the activists offered an implicit critique of Mennonites' quiet withdrawal.

In the face of such critique, Mennonite officials who had previously given scant notice to civil rights activity began to pay attention. On September 14, two weeks after the March on Washington, Harding attended the hastily organized meeting on civil rights at the Prairie Street Mennonite Church in Elkhart, Indiana, that opens this chapter. The meeting, originally proposed by Kauffman and supported by Hershberger, purported to "inquire of our colored brethren what in their mind should be the role of the Mennonite churches in the current racial revolution."[102] Twenty-five leaders gathered on that Saturday, all but two of whom were men.[103] At least seven of the twenty-five leaders were African Americans, and five of those "colored brethren," besides Harding, opened the meeting with statements of concern. Their comments encouraged dialogue, love, educational initiatives, interracial church fellowship, church-based evangelism, and interracial visitor and pulpit exchanges. Although the men spoke with passion and fluency akin to Harding's own, none of them advocated involvement in civil rights demonstrations.

Harding, by contrast, insisted on a more activist approach. Once the other speakers had concluded, Harding called for immediate, concrete political action. Rather than focusing on pulpit exchanges or generic admonitions to love, Harding turned his attention to employment, housing, and equality, topics central to the March on Washington. "It may be that God is ready to use revolution as a prelude to resurrection," he proclaimed. "Most of our people will never be ready for the requirements of the hour, and we cannot longer wait for them."[104] Harding's mention of "the requirements of the hour" appears prescient in retrospect. The next day four girls died from a bomb thrown into a crowd of African-American youth at the Sixteenth Street Baptist Church in Birmingham. Such horrific events only increased the frustration already evident in Harding's comments at the Woodlawn conference in 1959. Harding seemed to be on the verge of abandoning Mennonites if they could not at least join him in public demonstration, when he and his civil rights colleagues were considering even more revolutionary measures.

Ironically, even as Harding's frustration with Mennonite disengagement neared a breaking point, white Mennonites began to take tentative action. In northeast Indiana, Mennonites mobilized to write letters, lobby representatives, and distribute the church's race relations statement to every member of Congress.[105] Congressman John Brademas later said that Elkhart Mennonites gave more support to the 1964 Civil Rights Act than any other religious group.[106] Although they did not take to the streets, their legislative initiatives signaled a more profound shift toward engagement than Harding realized. As Harding himself often noted, white Mennonites had previously lobbied only for conscientious objector status in the military. By September of 1963, however, some church members had followed Harding across the boundary of Mennonite quietism toward civil rights activism.

The group gathered at the September 14 meeting at Prairie Street also moved closer to active engagement than perhaps even Harding had anticipated. Despite the participation of Guy Hershberger and other leaders who had opposed organized street protest, those present called for action that went beyond the standard emphasis on church constituent education. The group recorded their support of limited but definitive involvement in civil rights marches. An anonymous quote from the day's proceedings stated, "The disciple must be on the side of the oppressed, and this may have many ramifications, possibly even marching, sitting-in, and jail."[107] This succinct encapsulation of a position long advocated by Harding suggested an openness to new tactics. Later on that year, Hershberger drafted a widely distributed pamphlet on race relations in which he encouraged Mennonites to consider becoming involved with civil rights organizations, a significant shift in his position.[108] Although he stopped short of advocating for direct street action, Hershberger joined other white Mennonite leaders who moved closer to activism as a result of conversations with Harding. Across the church, members considered the new calls to action, and some responded by shifting their action to the streets. Many more, however, continued to focus on demonstrations inside their homes and sanctuaries.

In the wake of the limited Prairie Street shift toward public and confrontational forms of protest, Harding pressed his activist message throughout the church with even more zeal. A week after the event, Harding attended a regional gathering of the Indiana-Michigan Conference where, once again, he provided the only racial diversity. Guy F. Hershberger noted that "we had Vincent Harding there for these people to see and talk to."[109] Yet despite the awkward mix of deference and paternalism surrounding the event, Harding continued to challenge Mennonites with direct, uncompromising, and increasingly stark language.[110] At this point, he remained committed to bringing together his work with Mennonites suspicious of politically oriented, tactically nonviolent activists and his engagement with civil rights organizers wary of quietist, sectarian, religious communities. The balancing act continued.

Disengagement

Eventually, Harding's high-profile itinerancy elicited special scrutiny from church officials on the Mennonite Central Committee board responsible for Harding's work. From January through the end of September 1963, Harding had written or been cited in seventeen separate items in the national Mennonite church press in a spate of articles that looked surprisingly similar across both General Conference and (Old) Mennonite publications.[111] In light of this attention, Peace Section board members asked for more detail about Harding's day-to-day activity.[112] Given that other Mennonite Central Committee administrators, like voluntary service director Edgar Stoesz, had already relayed constituent concerns about Harding's civil rights involvement, it is likely that board members had begun to hear criticisms about Harding's activism.[113] Although Harding's supervisor, Ed Metzler, did not explain why board members made their request, Metzler's requirement that Harding keep a journal for the last three months of 1963 demonstrates an uncommon level of scrutiny of Harding's activity.[114]

From October through December, Harding met with Martin Luther

King Jr. and Southern Christian Leadership Conference associates such
as Andrew Young and Fred Shuttlesworth, hosted Ella Baker from the
Student Nonviolent Coordinating Committee, spent a day talking with
author James Baldwin, and visited with white civil rights activist and
Baptist pastor Will Campbell. During the same period, Harding met
with representatives from at least twelve additional groups, including the
Georgia and Alabama Councils on Human Relations, the National Council of Churches, the Anti-Defamation League, and a local White Citizen's
Council. This period of intense activity also included a keynote address
at a national conference on race and religion.[115] Board members concerned
that Harding had strayed too far into civil rights territory found little com-
fort in the report he offered on his high-profile straddling of church and
secular contacts.

Despite an increasingly demanding schedule, Harding continued to
speak with a broad range of Mennonites. On October 12, only a month
after he had declared his deep impatience with Mennonite passivity on
the question of racial justice, Harding agreed to meet with the leaders of a
Mennonite Voluntary Service unit in Atlanta, based in Berea Mennonite
Church, a congregation opposed to the "crusade for individual rights for
the Negro."[116] Unit leaders John and Beth Miller asked to discuss their
relationship with Mennonite House, the Mennonite Central Committee
service unit led by the Hardings, where unit members, by contrast, regularly participated in civil rights organizing and tested extant segregation
laws.[117] The Millers' request to meet with Harding and his subsequent
consultations with them show the extent of Harding's influence within
the church; both those who found his activist message suspect and those
who embraced it sought his counsel.

So influential had Harding become that he received speaking requests
from outside the United States. From late October into early November, Harding traveled to southern Ontario to speak to Mennonites in the
Kitchener-Waterloo area.[118] Consistent with his overall approach, he challenged Canadians as directly as U.S. citizens. In his writing, he returned
again to familiar theological territory of selflessness and discipleship by
calling on white Mennonite Canadians to surrender their lives and face
the prospect of "social ostracism and economic deprivation" in pursuit of
racial justice.[119] Upon completion of meetings at Sterling Avenue Mennonite Church, Harding traveled to Mennonite Central Committee head-

quarters in Pennsylvania, where he led multiple discussions for volunteers preparing to serve overseas and throughout North America. Unbeknown to those who sought his insight, such international influence and high-profile connection had already begun to sow the seeds of his departure.

While such seeds of discontent remained hidden, Harding's energetic and persistent appeal to the church began to show results. As the year progressed, Mennonite church leaders acknowledged the political, as well as personal, dimension of the racial problems inside the church and throughout American society. Within the General Conference denomination, for example, a November 1 staff report by administrator Vern Preheim summarized meetings held "to discuss Mennonite involvement in the social and racial revolution."[120] Toward the end of the year, members of the Mennonite Central Committee's Peace Section approved Hershberger's civil rights pamphlet, "From Words to Deeds in Race Relations," that listed twenty-eight concrete actions church members could take in "response to the challenge of the racial revolution."[121] Harding had long used such politically charged terms and continued to do so even with the most conservative of Mennonite church leaders. For instance, on November 22—the day of President Kennedy's assassination—Harding met with bishops and pastors from congregations sponsored by the Lancaster Conference in Alabama, Georgia, and Florida to discuss "our churches and the racial revolution."[122] Now, in the South and across the church, a few Mennonite leaders used political language strikingly similar to Harding's own.

Harding's tireless efforts to shape the church's racial agenda, however, came at a cost. During the past year, he had spent much of his time away from Rosemarie and their daughter, Rachel. In the month of December alone, Harding attended fifteen conferences and gave four plenary addresses, enjoying only four days free of meetings or speeches.[123] The strain of his schedule and on-going frustration with Mennonite reluctance to support visible and confrontational witness began to show itself in Harding's growing impatience. The benefit of his doctor-ordered bed rest earlier in the year had long since worn off. Harding needed rest but instead got more meetings.

Harding finally erupted at a national meeting in the Midwest. On December 4, leaders from the General Conference Board of Christian Service gathered in Newton, Kansas, for conversation with Harding and Hershberger. Harding sat yet again through a meeting dominated by white Mennonites. With growing impatience he listened to another round of talk about racial intermarriage, education, and the tension between non-resistance and demonstration. By the end of the afternoon, Harding had had enough. After Guy Hershberger described plans for yet another series of educational meetings on race, Harding let loose. In his longest speech of the day, he pled with his fellow Mennonites to speak to him directly, to even get "angry as hell" with him. He admitted to his own anger that Mennonites played "games with this issue so often." That anger then turned into biting critique as he lamented that God had to bring about change through the Supreme Court, the Communist Manifesto, and the NAACP rather than the church. In the depth of his lament, he asked his co-believers to become the "front light" to the world rather than the "rear light."[124] No one interrupted as he spoke.

Even in such passion Harding chose his closing words carefully. As in his essay in the February *Gospel Herald*, he consistently used plural pronouns when he spoke of Mennonites. "We," "our," "us," and "ourselves" appear more than one hundred times in his recorded comments. Clearly, Harding still considered himself a Mennonite. His relationship with the church, however, had become strained. Although he clarified that he was "not quite" ready to leave the Mennonite community, he nonetheless was "tempted pretty much when I hear us talking about so many things that seem so important to us and yet in terms of the living and the dying of the people in the world it seems so unimportant to me."[125] With that sobering comment still ringing in the room, Harding then challenged the church to embrace all people rather than give "preference to whites." The Mennonite community, in Harding's mind, had a particular responsibility to step into the racial revolution with the selfless courage shown by Mennonite martyrs in the sixteenth century. The Mennonite theological commitment to nonconformity, love, and selfless sacrifice, he argued, lost all its integrity if church members held back from a forceful engagement with the civil rights struggle. From his perspective, he had done nothing more than call upon his white co-believers to live out their professed commitment to join word and deed. Harding concluded with a challenge to the white male church leaders in the room: "This revolution will never be complete until the church does what it was called upon to do in the first place."[126]

The response to Harding's impassioned plea proved disheartening.

Chair Robert Kreider sidestepped Harding's criticisms and returned the discussion to educational initiatives by asking, "What about the joint secretariat idea?" Committee member David Habegger suggested that a few members of the group draft "some sort of statement" in response to the racial crisis.[127] No one leapt up and called for a march, a demonstration, or a letter-writing campaign. Even in the relatively more politically active General Conference environment, church officials suggested the same sort of educational and pronouncement-focused strategies promoted by their (Old) Mennonite cousins. The meeting concluded with a tentative commitment to appoint church staff to educate Mennonites on racial issues. Among this group of General Conference leaders—some of whom had personally lobbied politicians to obtain conscientious objector status for young white men—Harding's call for political advocacy on behalf of African Americans went unanswered.

Other Mennonites less entrenched in church institutions did move toward active political engagement by year's end. Harding again prompted their action. In his last formal interaction with Mennonites in 1963, Harding attended an all-day planning meeting on December 17 at Mennonite House to prepare for a conference on race and the Mennonite churches of the South, which would be held in Atlanta in the coming year. The initiative for the 1964 conference emerged from conversations the Hardings had with Orlo Kaufman during their visit to Camp Landon in March. Although Harding was again the only African-American Mennonite to speak at the February 25–26 conference, local African-American leaders including C. T. Vivian of the Southern Christian Leadership Conference and Charles Demere, an African Methodist Episcopal minister in Atlanta, also addressed the assembly.[128] The Atlanta meeting opened up space, perhaps for the first time among southern Mennonites, for members within the church to support a more activist response to the racial revolution. Although conference participants remained divided on the question of involvement in street marches, many made enthusiastic declarations of their commitment to boldly oppose segregation upon return to their home communities.[129]

The race-focused gathering in Atlanta marked the end of Harding's long effort to straddle the border between activism inside and outside the church. Following a trip to visit European Mennonites during the summer of 1964, the Hardings returned to Atlanta in August and requested a six-month leave of absence.[130] In the midst of the heavy travel schedule and rigorous public presentations Harding had, like his friend and mentor, Martin Luther King Jr., been unfaithful to his spouse. Unlike King, however, Harding took direct and immediate action to end his infidelity of "thoughts, words and deeds." He abruptly stepped aside from active involvement with civil rights organizing to salvage his marriage and "make as clear a break as possible with the duplicity of the past." At the end of the leave in early 1965, Harding gave frank witness to what he called "sexual undiscipline and lack of honesty," claimed cleansing and renewal, resigned his post with the Mennonite Central Committee, and accepted a teaching assignment at Spellman College.[131] Having cut institutional ties with the Mennonite church, Harding moved to further distance himself from the Mennonite community. He signaled his departure in 1966 by quoting colleagues who asked him, "Are you going to stay with those nice white Mennonites, Anabaptists, Christians? Are any of them going to join the fight, Vince? Where do they stand, Vince? Where do they stand?"[132] Other than a controversial address Harding gave at the Mennonite World Conference in 1967 and a few equally provocative articles he published in the Mennonite press that same year, Harding left the Mennonite world.[133]

The Dual Demonstration

Harding's abrupt departure reveals dynamics introduced by his dual demonstration. Harding resigned for a combination of reasons. He had clearly grown frustrated with the church's hesitant, half-hearted, and unenthusiastic response to his plea to join the movement. But behind the obvious frustrations with the church's response loomed other, more personal, reasons. The physical demands of an itinerant schedule left him exhausted. He and Rosemarie requested their six-month leave of absence "for purposes of personal spiritual rehabilitation and family reasons."[134] Although the couple used that time to restore their marriage, they did not seek to take up their previous leadership roles within the Mennonite community. Rather than follow a process of "confession and forgiveness" within the church, Harding chose to move away from the church. The language Harding used to explain his abrupt departure drew on a principle he learned from Mennonites. In his resignation statement, he confessed to inconsistency of "words and deeds" and expressed a desire for personal integrity. Although he did not include details of his "sinful past," he felt that he had been "unfaithful" to his religious community by not showing integrity in his personal and professional life.[135] In the end, regardless of his frustration with the apparent lack of integrity among white Mennonites in their response to the racial revolution, Harding could no longer tolerate personal inconsistencies in his own life. The desire for integrity that had attracted him to Mennonites had truly become his own.

Harding had proved attractive to Mennonites precisely because of that commitment to integrity. He called for sacrificial service while leading a voluntary service unit. He spoke about the values of nonviolence after personally helping to calm angry mobs in the streets. He demanded that Mennonites love their enemies at the same time that he counted a southern, white, prosegregationist sheriff as "a personal friend."[136] Given his high profile, Harding had little trouble attracting Mennonites' attention. During his sojourn among these daily demonstrators, he often acted more like a Mennonite than the Mennonites themselves.

Yet that same concern for integrity, when joined to the lessons he had learned from the civil rights community, kept Harding at the church's border. The civil rights community had taught him to embrace activism, exercise leadership, and claim his racial identity. Those lessons made Harding hard to describe. He served as a Mennonite minister, but he marched and spent time in jail. Neither birthright Mennonite nor child convert, he nonetheless spoke like other Mennonite leaders. Unlike other African Americans active within the Mennonite community in the late 1950s and early 1960s, Harding had not come into the church as a recipient of Mennonite missions or service outreach. Instead, he called Mennonites to include activism in their service in order to remain true to the Anabaptist values of discipleship and peacemaking. Thus Mennonites at the church's center could claim Harding as their own, even as his activist leadership and racial identity moved him to the periphery.

Harding's concern for integrity thus reconfigures the relationship of the church and the civil rights movement. As previously mentioned, many historians have identified how African-American congregations inspired activists, provided infrastructural support for demonstrations, and, at points, offered sanctuary from racial tumult. Other historians note that some white congregations provided similar support and many lobbied for civil rights legislation in 1963 and 1964. Still others remind us that many white churches distanced themselves from activism or opposed the civil rights agenda entirely. All these scholars assume that energy and resources flowed in one direction, from the church toward the streets. Harding's sojourn at the border of church and movement reveals a bidirectional exchange. Harding learned lessons from demonstrating in the streets that shaped how he demonstrated in the sanctuary. And lessons learned from his adopted church influenced how he participated in the movement. Harding's concern for integrity, for instance, showed up in his writing for King and other civil rights leaders. In short, the church conversed with the movement.

More important, Harding's story reveals civil rights struggles unfolding within the church. Not just a staging ground, the church was a battleground. Harding argued, cajoled, and agitated on a daily basis to get Mennonites to end segregation and discrimination inside the church. He never stopped pushing his co-believers to join social protests, but those calls to action emerged from his critique of Mennonite racism. Like Lark, Swartzentruber, and the Fresh Air children who entered Mennonite homes before Harding ever heard the word Mennonite, Harding challenged the church to act in keeping with its professed doctrine. Rather than a separate or ancillary tale, the narrative of such church struggles is central to civil rights history.

In the end, white Mennonites found Harding so attractive and so troublesome precisely because he attempted to hold together the stories of the church and the civil rights movement. His charisma helped bring those stories together, but his position as a Mennonite–African American, an insider-outsider, and a church leader–civil rights activist gained him an audience. Harding challenged the false divisions between church members and outsiders, between withdrawal and engagement, and between whites and blacks precisely because he himself straddled two communities. In some cases his actions and words successfully transcended these divisions in ways that led to new forms of action. Intense contact with Harding led Mennonite leaders like church theologian Guy Hershberger and Lancaster Conference bishop Paul Landis to modify their perspectives and to promote new strategies of social engagement.[137] In other instances, Harding's actions unnerved his fellow Mennonites. White leaders like Mahlon Blosser of the Virginia Conference and Orlo Kaufman of Camp Landon initially found Harding's activism threatening. As southerners,

Blosser and Kaufman feared shifts in the social order to a greater degree than did Hershberger and Landis in the North. Nonetheless, encounters with Harding unquestionably shaped Blosser's and Kaufman's responses. Although they disagreed with his new application of church doctrine, they could not ignore him. Ironically, they often enacted the initiatives Harding proposed.

Harding never entirely gave up his dual demonstration. He continued to contribute to the struggle for racial justice and, periodically, to the Mennonite church. In 1969, a *Newsweek* reporter dubbed him the "pope" of black studies in an article describing Harding's efforts to unify African-American scholars from his post as the director of the Institute of the Black World at the King Memorial Center in Atlanta.[138] Once again, Harding balanced between two worlds, this time between the academy and the activist community. Following his work at the King Center and several teaching posts, Harding went on to write an influential history of antebellum African-American resistance, served as senior adviser to the *Eyes on the Prize* civil rights documentary series, and, along with Rosemarie, moved freely between the academic and activist communities by leading workshops and giving speeches.[139] White and African-American Mennonites continued to seek out Harding for advice and counsel well into the 1970s and beyond.[140] In 1996 the Hardings and their daughter, Rachel, returned to Atlanta to celebrate thirty-five years of Mennonite Central Committee work in the city and to mark the formal closing of the service unit, a termination stirred in part by the same tensions between activism and withdrawal that Harding had brought together.[141] At the gathering, Harding offered words both pastoral and prophetic to the gathered administrators and former volunteers.[142] Once again he joined the sanctuary with the street.

Harding's struggles as a dual demonstrator parallel the difficulties faced by interracial couples in the Mennonite church. Like Harding, African-American men and white women who became romantically involved often straddled two worlds. Their perch was no less precarious than Harding's. Like him, they demonstrated on a daily basis to end segregation and racism among Mennonites. The chapter that follows shows how civil rights struggles about interracial marriage inside the church also brought about significant social change.

CHAPTER 5

The Wedding March

Once . . . we have come to know each other as brethren . . . even the bogey of
intermarriage begins to lose its meaning.
—H. Ralph Hernley and Guy F. Hershberger, white church leaders, 1955

Getting Beyond the Bogey

Annabelle and Gerald Hughes thought the worst was over. The pastor at Oak Grove Mennonite Church in Smithville, Ohio, had supported their interracial marriage, on November 21, 1954, despite objections from members of the all-white congregation.[1] The Hugheses had found a replacement for the men's quartet member who withdrew because of concerns about their union. The business meeting held to discuss whether they could be married on church property had gone in their favor. College friends, interested observers, and a returning missionary with no previous connection to the couple replaced those who shunned the celebration.[2] The Hugheses' ceremony went forward without visible interference.

The disruption came several days later. Rather than take a honeymoon, the couple returned to Cleveland. Gerald needed to return to his job at Hawthorne State Hospital, where he served as the only African-American conscientious objector in a group of Mennonite men completing alternative service terms. As the newlyweds traveled the fifty miles from Smithville to Hawthorne, they anticipated living in their own apartment on the hospital grounds. Annabelle looked forward to starting a new job at the facility as well. Soon after their arrival, however, hospital administrators dismissed Gerald without explanation. Only later did he discover that a leader from the Ohio Mennonite Conference, a regional governance body of the (Old) Mennonite Church, had protested the hospital's support of an interracial couple. Despite the objections raised by other alternative service workers and national church officials, Hawthorne administrators sided with the Ohio Conference leader. Gerald and Annabelle returned to Annabelle's mother's home until Gerald received word that he could serve out the remainder of his term at Gladstone Mennonite Church in Cleveland, where he and Annabelle first met.[3]

Thirteen years later, Annabelle's and Gerald's names again came to the attention of church officials. On August 28, 1967, Mennonite theologian and peace activist Guy F. Hershberger nominated Gerald and three other men for service on the (Old) Mennonite Church's Committee for Peace and Social Concerns. Annabelle's name appeared alongside her husband's in the nomination penned by Hershberger: "Gerald Hughes . . . Married to Anabelle [sic] Conrad (white)."[4] Although Hershberger described the pedigree of all four men in terms of their church involvements and commitment to racial justice, he identified the wife of only one other African-American nominee, Curtis Burrell. About a decade after church leaders had objected to Gerald's interracial marriage, different church leaders sought him out precisely because he had married a white woman. The reception given an African-American man who had married into the white Mennonite community had changed dramatically.

The white church leaders who expressed interest in Gerald contradicted earlier church claims. From the late nineteenth century forward, Mennonite writers supported racial equality and opposed interracial marriage, usually without specific scriptural reference. Between 1950 and 1955 alone, six Mennonite writers had taken that position in church publications.[5] By the time Hershberger nominated Gerald while referencing his marriage to Annabelle, however, a change had taken place. Rather than racial threats to the church, African-American men had become racial saviors. Those who married white women provided white church leaders with the means to counter a growing perception that the Mennonite community lacked integrity in their professed support of racial equality. This chapter explains how an interracial wedding march from 1930 through

1971 in homes and sanctuaries shifted Mennonites' opinion of African-American men from threats to prized participants and brought about significant changes alongside those realized by legislators and street demonstrators.

The story of Annabelle and Gerald Hughes challenges existing historical literature about interracial marriage by pointing past legality to internal church dynamics. The white Mennonites who wrote about interracial marriage in the twentieth century did not concern themselves with legislation. Although more than 180 Mennonite congregations sanctioned interracial marriages in states subject to antimiscegenation statutes, white Mennonite writers paid no attention to legal questions regarding interracial marriage.[6] Indeed, the only mention of antimiscegenation legislation through the period of study was in an article by an African-American writer, a reprint from a 1926 edition of a church periodical.[7] By contrast, historians writing about interracial marriage have focused first and foremost on legislative changes.[8] Those studies have, in turn, ignored the place where interracial marriages were conducted and the people conducting many of them—congregations and church officials.[9] Mennonites offer historians of interracial marriage a unique opportunity to study how a religious community unconcerned with legislative issues modified theological commitments, negotiated conflicting reactions, and responded to church leaders' tactics. This study thus opens up new lines of inquiry into interracial marriage absent from legislatively centered literature.

A narrative about Mennonite interracial marriage reveals historical dynamics obscured by more visible trends. For example, some scholars argue that, owing to biblical injunctions, the Christian community did not welcome interracial couples or promote the value of marriage across racial lines in the 1940s and '50s.[10] While this conclusion is borne out in the Mennonite community, scholars who promote this viewpoint miss the efforts of Mennonites and other Christians to hold together strong assertions of racial equality and repeated cautions against interracial marriage. Scholars likewise contend that legislative changes in the 1960s increased interracial socializing that, in turn, led to a new openness among white people toward interracial marriage.[11] Yet as early as the 1940s and '50s, white and African-American Mennonites socialized through church-planting efforts. Among Mennonites, theological contradiction and evangelical impulse brought about changes as dramatic as those precipitated by more overtly political forces.

Mennonite historians have largely ignored the topic of interracial marriage. Other than seminary students and the author of a history on the Camp Landon ministry in Gulfport, Mississippi, historians of the American Mennonite experience have written as if Mennonites never discussed the issue.[12] Yet every decade in the period of this study saw at least one and as many as twenty-four different published articles referring to interracial marriage. Similarly, fifteen years after (Old) Mennonite Church delegates stated in 1955 that the Bible did not forbid interracial marriage, activists in the church continued to report difficult conversations with congregants on the subject.[13] In comparison to other race-related issues, whether congregational integration, social equality, or civil rights legislation, the topic of interracial marriage troubled white Mennonites for a longer period, proved more difficult to discuss, and involved fewer appeals to scripture. Given the prominence of interracial marriage discourse, a complete history of Mennonite race relations requires an explanation of the manner in which white Mennonite leaders came to support interracial marriage by the end of the 1960s, even as congregational members continued to oppose the practice.

The lives of Annabelle and Gerald Hughes thus open a window onto changes in Mennonites' approach to interracial marriage. Alongside the record left by published writers and official church statements, the Hugheses' story reveals a church community conflicted over whether to follow social wisdom or biblical mandate.[14] White Mennonite leaders like Gerald's nominator, Guy F. Hershberger, advocated a response grounded in scripture. At the grass roots, a half century of church teaching on the foolishness of interracial marriage bore fruit as congregational members continued to raise grave concerns about unions like the Hugheses'. Only as Hershberger and other church leaders began to pay more attention to the broad justice concerns of the civil rights movement rather than to the narrow internal "bogey of intermarriage" did a measure of change begin to appear.[15] The story of how that change was brought about begins in the decade Annabelle and Gerald were born.

From Connection to Union

At the time Gerald Hughes and Annabelle Conrad entered the world, Mennonites were expressing their opposition to interracial marriage in terms supplied by eugenicists. Born in 1930 in Philadelphia to Vertell and

Henry Hughes, Gerald knew little of Mennonites or their opinions about interracial marriage during the first ten years of his life. Although white Mennonite missionaries labored to evangelize African Americans at the Philadelphia Colored Mission during the 1930s, the missionaries there did not encounter Gerald's family. Had they met, Gerald's Presbyterian grandfather might have pointed out that white Mennonites drew more from eugenic thought than from scripture to articulate their perspectives on interracial marriage. Eugenics, a highly influential social movement and academic pursuit in the first half of the twentieth century, sought to protect society from inferior "genetic stock" through forced sterilization, support of antimiscegenation laws, and immigration restrictions.[16] As Jacob and Sadie Conrad prepared for and then welcomed their daughter Annabelle in 1932, they surely encountered eugenics-influenced articles by Mennonite editors and writers arguing that interracial partners came from "entirely different race stock, habits and ways of thinking" and their children inherited "the worst qualities of their parents."[17] Rather than scriptural arguments, writers in these years accepted the stated scientific assumption that interbreeding between races would result in "foolish" and "backward" offspring.[18] Accepted scientific opinion discouraged even the thought of Annabelle's and Gerald's future union.

The Mennonites who opposed interracial marriage on scientific grounds in the 1930s followed in the tradition of Mennonite opinion before them. As early as 1889, Abram B. Kolb expressed his opposition to interracial marriage "for many reasons," none of them scriptural. Although he also maintained that people of all racial groups should "be equal and enjoy the same" God-ordained privileges, he articulated this egalitarian principle without appeal to scripture.[19] As assistant editor at the *Herald of Truth* and a leader in early Mennonite mission efforts, Kolb established an oft-repeated pattern: support for racial equality and opposition to interracial marriage.[20] More than thirty years later, in 1924, the Virginia Mennonite Conference, another regional governance body of the (Old) Mennonite Church, took a similar position when it accepted African Americans as members but opposed "close social relationships" and "marrying between the colored and white races."[21] Kolb and leaders from the Virginia Conference articulated a position the Mennonite church followed through the middle of the twentieth century.

Annabelle and Gerald came into closer proximity in the 1940s, when

Gerald and his three brothers relocated to Andrews Bridge, Pennsylvania, at the same time white Mennonites began to evangelize African Americans. After Gerald's parents separated, when he was about ten years old, Gerald and his three brothers joined the Thompson household in southern Lancaster County, where members of the Mellingers Mennonite congregation had held services since 1938 (see figure 5.1).[22] As he worshipped with the conservatively dressed Mennonites, Gerald soon realized that African-American converts came under greater scrutiny in their dress and demeanor than did white converts.[23] Yet he eventually joined the fledgling Andrews Bridge congregation, where his singing ability quickly gained attention. By 1948, eighteen-year-old Gerald had begun to lead songs at the Lancaster Conference gatherings of the Colored Workers Committee, a group dominated by white mission workers serving in African-American communities but also attended by African-American Mennonite proselytes.[24] Gerald had found a new home among the Mennonites.

Gerald thus became intimately involved with white Mennonites at a time when eugenics-driven arguments had begun to lose favor. The only instance of eugenic thought to relate to interracial marriage in the 1940s appeared in 1943, when church statesman Daniel Kauffman argued against birth control for white people because it could lead to "race suicide" and being "overwhelmed" by the "hordes of colored (and renegade white) races."[25] In light of his lament over low white reproduction rates, Kauffman saw no need to mention interracial marriage. As World War II ended and Nazi atrocities became public, however, white Mennonites followed the lead of scientific and political leaders around them by shedding vestiges of eugenic thought. They focused instead on "Negro Missions" as the solution to the "sin" of racial discrimination.[26] During these same years, Gerald and his brothers became ever more involved in a church that claimed unity of the human race as expressed in "one blood" and opposed "any practices which are based on an assumption of white superiority" and acknowledged that young white Mennonite men in rural communities sometimes harassed African-American pedestrians.[27] Amid such universal claims and prejudicial practice, Gerald worshipped with church leaders who had not yet considered that their evangelistic efforts might lead to interracial marriage.

The absence of attention to interracial marriage during the latter half

Fig. 5.1 Andrews Bridge Mennonite Church Sunday school classes with Gerald Hughes in second row on far left,
Andrews Bridge, Pennsylvania, circa 1940s

Lancaster Mennonite Historical Society, box Andrews Bridge Cong, unmarked green folder, A. Rohrer. Photo courtesy of
Lancaster Mennonite Historical Society, Lancaster, PA

of the 1940s comes as no surprise. Mennonites during this period placed great doctrinal weight on marrying within the faith community. From the turn of the century forward, Mennonite confessions of faith supported only unions between believers.[28] From the beginning of the twentieth century through the 1940s, confessional statements and Mennonite writers also opposed interdenominational marriages.[29] During a time of war, when Mennonites experienced persecution for their nonresistant belief, the prohibition against interfaith marriages kept young white Mennonites marrying within their religious community. As a result, Mennonite leaders offered scant commentary on interracial marriage. Even as Gerald traveled to Goshen College in northern Indiana in 1949, to study music education and live with more white Mennonites, the threat of African-American men marrying white Mennonite women seemed worthy of only minimal concern.

Annabelle and Gerald married in the early 1950s, a period of unprecedented attention to interracial unions. They first crossed paths in 1950, when Annabelle attended Goshen College for one year. Although they did not begin dating at that time, the two young people met again during the summer of 1951, when Gerald moved to Cleveland, Ohio, in hopes of working in the steel industry and serving Gladstone Mennonite Church during evenings and weekends. Because of a strike, however, Gerald ended up working for the Mennonite mission board as a staff member at Gladstone. Annabelle had accepted an assignment with the church as a voluntary service worker before Gerald's arrival. After Annabelle completed her assignment, she stayed on to support the Gladstone ministry while working in the offices of a local manufacturing company. In the pages of the national church news magazine, Annabelle avidly recruited young people to join her at Gladstone.[30] Although Gerald returned to Goshen College during the school year, he also served as leader of the congregation's voluntary service unit during the summers of 1952 and 1953.[31] Annabelle's and Gerald's courtship had begun.

The couple's mutual interest developed at a time when church leaders began again to publicly oppose such interracial attraction. In early 1951 Esko Loewen, editor of the youth section of the General Conference news magazine, The Mennonite, cautioned against racial intermarriage because it "is not generally wise" owing to "many barriers to be hurdled."[32] Although he chided church leaders for promoting racial inclusiveness while practicing racial prejudice, his opposition to interracial marriage remained. Like Abram Kolb in 1889, Loewen replicated a familiar formula: support for racial inclusion based on scriptural mandate combined with caution against interracial marriage based on social convention. Loewen offered no encouragement for the prospects of Annabelle and Gerald's budding romance.

Other leaders from the General Conference and the (Old) Mennonite denominations mounted stronger social arguments against interracial unions. At a 1951 churchwide conference, John R. Mumaw, president of Goshen College's sister school, Eastern Mennonite College, in Harrisonburg, Virginia, declared his opposition to interracial marriage without appealing to scripture.[33] Writing several months later, Mary Toews, a Mennonite missionary with ten years' experience "working side by side with the African," passionately objected to the idea of interracial marriage without giving the slightest nod toward the biblical text. She asked, "What has the colored family to contribute to my happy married life? One marries the family, Granny, Aunt Jemima and all." Toews also stressed that children of interracial unions should, like all Africans and African Americans, keep with "others of like skin and custom." Toews concluded that a white mother of a dark-skinned child would find her offspring so "strange" that she would then "divorce" her child.[34] In short, Toews offered commentary indistinguishable from that of an ardent segregationist. Despite subsequent efforts by editors at *The Mennonite* to distance themselves from her article, Toews took a position substantively similar to other Mennonite writers in the early 1950s.[35] Like Loewen and Mumaw, Toews favored equality for the African-American community while opposing interracial marriage. Toews simply delineated her opposition while trafficking in stereotypes avoided by more cautious authors. Such critique again did not bode well for Annabelle and Gerald's growing attraction.

Yet the young people's courtship did receive support from some of those involved in interracial ministry. Within the African-American neighborhood where Gladstone members ministered, church workers and community residents supported Annabelle and Gerald. As they made community visits, distributed evangelical tracts, and handed out church bulletins, Annabelle and Gerald encountered no local opposition. In the national Mennonite community, a white Mennonite writer associated with the integrated Woodlawn congregation in Chicago also expressed his support for interracial marriage.[36] Just over a month after Toews's article appeared, William Keeney wrote an article for *The Mennonite* that, for the first time in the Mennonite church's publication history, supported interracial marriage without reservation. Rather than withdraw from interracial contact for fear of negative reprisals, Keeney maintained, Christians should challenge the prejudicial attitudes that fostered such fears. Keeney called sinful those who opposed interracial marriage based on race prejudice. Quoting Colossians 3:9–11, Keeney enjoined Mennonites to become blind to color and so transcend the divisions of Jew and Greek, circumcised and uncircumcised, citizen and slave. Even more strikingly, Keeney brought core doctrine to bear by stating that some may be called to the "life of suffering love by intermarriage."[37] Mennonites committed to the church doctrine of pacifist nonresistance and patient love could not ignore such commentary. Although uncharacteristic of other white Mennonites at the time, Keeney and Gladstone members supported Annabelle and Gerald as their relationship matured.[38]

Other white Mennonite workers at African-American mission sites offered less support for interracial marriage. In July of 1952, from his mission station in Philadelphia, minister Luke G. Stoltzfus took up the question, Is Christianity a hindrance to race relations? After arguing strongly for congregational integration, racial equality, and just treatment for all, Stoltzfus asserted that African Americans' interest in marrying white people decreased as racial equality increased.[39] Four months later another writer queried, "Would you like for your daughter to marry a Negro?" Like Stoltzfus, this writer claimed that African Americans lost interest in marrying white people when their economic and social situations improved. He concluded that, despite those few individuals who married outside their group, fears about intermarriage were "imaginary."[40] By the end of 1952, however, Annabelle and Gerald had begun to show enough interest in each other that the prospect of their union became quite real.

In the fall of 1954 the couple announced their plans to marry. Despite decades of written opposition to interracial marriage in Mennonite church periodicals, Annabelle's only living parent, her mother Sadie Conrad, welcomed Gerald without concern. Conrad had met Gerald during a previous summer, when she lived and worked with the voluntary service workers in Cleveland. According to Annabelle, Conrad liked Gerald because of his education and his interest in teaching. Although Annabelle's mother had discouraged a previous suitor by telling him he was "too pushy," Conrad supported Annabelle's and Gerald's relationship. Early on, Conrad admitted that the church's past teachings had influenced her, applauding her daughter for doing something that she herself "couldn't do."[41] Gerald's family also supported his relationship with Annabelle. Two of his brothers later married women from other racial groups. Although some of Annabelle's relatives expressed initial reservations, Gerald won them over through conversation and, in one instance, the shared task of cutting wood "with a cross-cut saw."[42] The opposition Annabelle and Gerald encountered came from the church at large, not their families.

Annabelle and Gerald's mutual attraction fit a consistent trend in American history. Despite periodic setbacks and laws in twenty-two states in both the North and the South outlawing interracial marriage into the 1960s, African-American and white partners continued to marry.[43] Following a brief period of relative support for interracial marriages during the Reconstruction era in the South, the odds of a couple marrying across racial lines decreased between 1880 and 1930. The likelihood then increased through 1940, held steady through the 1960s, and then increased precipitously from the 1970s forward.[44] By 1970, more than three hundred thousand couples had entered into interracial marriages, a number that more than doubled by 1980.[45] A significant portion of those unions had joined African-American and white partners. As of the 1960 census, 148,000 couples had married across racial lines, with black-white unions numbering 51,000 of the total. Of the latter couples, about 26,000 involved black women marrying white men, and 25,000, white women marrying black men.[46] Such gender parity countered the norm. From 1960 forward, the period during the twentieth century when most of those unions were celebrated, black male–white female marriages predominated.[47] Although church statisticians never compiled data on interracial marriage within the Mennonite church, anecdotal evidence suggests that, of the interracial unions celebrated in Mennonite congregations, estimated at fewer than one hundred, a substantial majority involved African-American men and white women.[48] Annabelle and Gerald heralded this trend.

On one point, however, Annabelle and Gerald proved an exception. As they prepared for their wedding in the company of thousands of other interracial couples across the country, they sought recognition of both the state and the church. Period evidence suggests that, at least through the 1960s, interracial couples sought out civil ceremonies but less commonly celebrated church weddings.[49] The social and ecclesial reservations present in the church at the time deterred many couples from seeking the blessing of clergy and faith communities. By choosing to celebrate their wedding in a sanctuary, Annabelle and Gerald forced a discussion that would not have taken place in the same way had they chosen to exchange vows before a justice of the peace. They took the sanctioning of their relationship into the one place where many similar couples refused to go. In so doing, they participated in yet another demonstration.

Exile

Annabelle and Gerald enjoyed their wedding despite the controversy. Although Annabelle's home congregation met separately, and without the couple's knowledge, to vote on whether they could be married in the church building, with the support of their pastor the ceremony went forward as planned. Although some refused to take part in preparing the wedding meal and others voiced their disapproval, still other church members volunteered to prepare food for the reception and blessed the union.[50] A large crowd gathered to witness Annabelle and Gerald exchange vows on November 21, 1954 (see figure 5.2). The couple felt far more supported and encouraged by those who came to wish them well than discouraged by those who chose to stay away.[51]

The large turnout and attendant controversy is not surprising, given that the wedding took place only six months after the Supreme Court's May 17, 1954, *Brown v. Board of Education* decision. Following *Brown*, a flurry of articles, all written by white men, took up the problem of racial prejudice in the church and presented theological arguments for racial equality and inclusion.[52] Although no one articulated a new position on interracial marriage, the issue remained current. A group of Mennonite students participating in a Chicago-based study program on industry discussed, for example, whether "intermarriage" solved "the race problem."[53] As Annabelle and Gerald returned to Cleveland after their wedding, in anticipation of several years' work at Hawthorne State Hospital, they had gained a level of notoriety that would only increase in the following year.

Annabelle and Gerald first gained wide attention as church leaders

Fig. 5.2 Gerald and Annabelle Hughes, Oak Grove Mennonite Church,
Smithville, Ohio, 1954
Tobin Miller Shearer, "Laws of Attraction vs. Sentiments of Separation,"
Mennonite Historical Bulletin 68, no. 4 (2007): 3. Photo courtesy of Gerald and
Annabelle Hughes

decided how to respond to the Hawthorne administrators' decision to
fire Gerald. A church official from the Ohio Conference contacted Hawthorne administrators to object to Gerald's placement, even though he

had worked successfully at the hospital before his and Annabelle's wedding. After deciding not to invite the local chapter of the activist group Congress of Racial Equality to advocate on their behalf, the Hugheses returned to the Conrad homestead in Smithville, Ohio, to await the decision of mission board executives and Selective Service personnel. Shortly thereafter, the couple received word that Gerald had been transferred to the Gladstone congregation. The Hugheses gladly returned to the congregation that had brought them together.[54] They would never again leave.

The Hugheses began to participate in the life of the broader church from their base at Gladstone. In a year that began with yet another white Mennonite editor raising social objections to interracial marriage, the young couple took part in a conference that would come to define the church's official position on interracial marriage.[55] From April 22 to 24, 1955, the Hugheses joined more than one hundred church leaders and congregants on the Goshen College campus for a meeting planned by the (Old) Mennonite Church's Committee on Economic and Social Relations, an education and advocacy group led by the same Guy F. Hershberger who would come to nominate Gerald at a later date.

Two presentations established the central role interracial marriage would play at the conference. The Hugheses and other attendees listened to two plenary addresses on interracial marriage. Conference organizer Guy Hershberger and H. Ralph Hernley, chair of the social relations committee, raised the topic of interracial marriage in their introduction to the assembly proceedings. The two men said that through mutual acquaintance and brotherhood across racial lines, "the bogey of intermarriage" would lose "its meaning."[56] Conference planners did not, however, leave participants with only this assurance. The Hugheses also listened to a lengthy and exhaustive exegesis of key Old Testament and New Testament passages by church theologian C. Norman Kraus, noting that Moses married outside his group and had not broken any biblical commands by doing so. Kraus's call for unity based on Pauline texts also addressed concerns about the mixing of the races.[57] Kraus first established the biblical basis of his argument before suggesting any application. Indeed, Kraus left it to subsequent speakers to comment on practical matters regarding marriage across racial lines. Yet he brought specific scriptural texts into a conversation long dominated by social arguments.

The Hugheses also heard an official report about their wedding. Although he did not mention their names, conference attendee D. Richard Miller, from Smithville, Ohio, supplied sufficient detail to make clear about whom he was speaking. In his report about "the incident which has attracted the most attention" in his area, Miller identified the Hugheses' congregation, the debate over whether to allow them to marry in the Oak Grove church building, and the church they attended (Gladstone). Miller closed his report by mentioning that the groom had led music at Oak Grove Mennonite following their wedding but that many members continued to express concern about "the welfare of the couple and the problems which confront them and will confront them as they take their place in society."[58] If the Hugheses had not previously captured the attention of the participants at the Goshen conference, they had done so by the end of Miller's presentation.

Toward the end of the gathering, the Hugheses and the rest of the conference participants had the opportunity to respond to a new race relations statement. Paul Peachey, a sociologist and incoming pastor at Broad Street Mennonite, the African-American congregation in Harrisonburg, Virginia, where Rowena Lark and Fannie Swartzentruber labored together, presented a statement that undermined scriptural objections to interracial marriages.[59] Although he earlier had objected to mixed race marriages, citing their "foolish" and "inadvisable" nature, Peachey put scripture before social objections in the official document.[60] In "The Way of Christian Love in Race Relations," Peachey took a small but significant shift away from past writing. Giving more attention to this topic than to any other specific point of application, Peachey wrote, "On the question of interracial marriage we [will] help our people to understand that the only Scriptural requirement for marriage is that it be 'in the Lord'; that there is no valid biological objection to interracial marriage." This clear statement of support did come with a caveat. The clause ended with the caution that "as in all marriages, the social implications of any proposed union should receive careful consideration."[61] As thus amended, the 1955 document pointed to social considerations but placed interracial unions on equal footing with all marriages. With little debate, conference participants approved the document in Goshen, and churchwide delegates did the same four months later in Hesston, Kansas. Unlike several mainline Protestant groups at the time, the (Old) Mennonite Church removed explicit scriptural barriers to marriage across racial lines.[62]

Couples like the Hugheses thus made concrete a previously intangible issue. Having participated in the 1955 race relations conference, other attendees could not ignore the flesh-and-blood presence of interracial couples within their churches. The newlyweds from Cleveland made clear that the church would have to deal with marriage across racial lines. Leaders responded quickly. Less than a month after the release of an initial draft of "The Way of Christian Love in Race Relations," administrators at Bluffton College, a Mennonite college in northwestern Ohio, issued a statement on race relations that encouraged racial equality but discouraged interracial dating.[63] Hershberger received several letters suggesting changes to the statement's marriage clause. One correspondent advocated stronger wording in support of interracial couples; others expressed caution.[64] The section on interracial marriage received far more attention than any other portion of the document. Regardless of where they stood on the issue, white Mennonite church leaders could not ignore the fact that more than a decade of church evangelism among African Americans had led to unexpected results.

Some church leaders did not agree with the direction taken by Hershberger, Peachey, and others at the race relations conference. When Vern Miller, the Hugheses' pastor and co-worker, prepared to request ministerial credentials for Gerald from the Ohio Conference in 1955, conference leaders told him not to proceed. They made clear that because he had married a white woman, Gerald could not be considered.[65] As a woman, Annabelle had not even been considered as a recipient of ministerial credentials. Although the couple did not learn of the blocked request until much later, their lives had again been pushed in a different direction by those opposed to their union. The couple continued in ministry at Gladstone but without official recognition by the Ohio Conference.

The Hugheses' marriage and reactions from members of their religious cohort marked the end of a six-year period, from 1950 to 1955, notable for at least three transitions. First, leaders of the (Old) Mennonite Church reversed a fifty-year tradition and gave priority to scriptural support for interracial marriage over social objection. After relying on secular rationales for fifty years, the church put scripture first. With the passage of the 1955 "Way of Christian Love in Race Relations" document, the (Old) Mennonite Church went on record in support of interracial marriage. Second, this shift highlighted a new fissure between (Old) Mennonites and their

General Conference denominational cousins. The silence of the (Old) Mennonite Church's sister denomination, which did not act on interracial marriage until 1962, emerged from different congregational demographics. Leaders of the General Conference Mennonite Church hesitated to speak on interracial marriage in part because their membership included few couples like the Hugheses. Finally, a gap widened between church leaders and grassroots members on the question of interracial marriage. Although few voiced public opposition to marriage across racial lines, many white Mennonites raised private objections at the local level when interracial couples announced their wedding plans.

Only two of these three transitions stabilized during the next seven years, from 1956 through 1962. The denominational divide continued in place as the General Conference delegates debated the question of interracial marriage but passed a race relations document in 1959 that made no mention of the issue. The gap between lay members and denominational leaders remained, even as church leaders and activists attempted to educate their constituencies. Following official approval of the 1955 race relations document, however, the first transition noted above reverted to its prior state as social objections to interracial marriage again dominated church press articles. Members of both denominations returned repeatedly to the question of interracial marriage, even as they began to address a wider range of racial issues.

As the Hugheses settled into their lives and work in Cleveland, they continued to read articles debating their union. A writer in 1956 stated that the "Bogey of Intermarriage" broke no religious laws but nonetheless led to persecution and was therefore "unwise."[66] The following year a voluntary service worker in Chicago penned a cautionary tale about the hard life of a child of an interracial union whose mother would not let him live with her.[67] In 1958 a Mennonite editor again commented that those who married across racial lines lacked wisdom.[68] Yet the Hugheses continued to live, work, and worship in a community that welcomed them and other interracial couples. When they read articles opposing their marriage, they responded as they had to those who expressed disapproval at the time of their wedding. In Annabelle's words, "I never paid [them] too much attention."[69] She and Gerald claimed the church as their own despite such judgments.

That same forbearance manifested in comments Gerald made at another major conference where interracial marriage received fresh attention. During a gathering hosted by the Woodlawn Mennonite congregation in Chicago from April 17 to 19, 1959, Gerald reflected on his experience at Goshen College and noted that, with time, his classmates came to see him as an individual (see figure 5.3).[70] That individual recognition, however, still had not resolved white Mennonites' concerns about marriages across racial lines. Rev. Vincent Harding, at that time Woodlawn's associate pastor and a doctoral student at the University of Chicago, gave a plenary address in which he introduced the topic of interracial marriage. For a leader who would soon express exasperation at being called constantly to address the issue, Harding conceded a surprising point. After expressing disappointment in white Christians who had not yet overcome their prejudices, Harding allowed that one could engage in "the ministry of reconciliation" without "full-hearted approval of interracial marriage." Harding also argued that most African Americans did not seek to become "part of our blood families" because, employing a phrase that had been used by other African Americans in the period, "Negroes generally seek to be Christian brothers rather than brothers-in-law."[71] Gerald's presence in the audience suggested otherwise.

Neither Hughes nor Harding successfully prompted the General Conference members at the Woodlawn conference to rally their denomination on the question of interracial marriage. Although the topic of interracial marriage attracted the attention of delegates at the General Conference national assembly in August of 1959, the delegates took no action. After heated and substantial debate, church leaders presented a draft of "A Christian Declaration on Race Relations" to the delegate body gathered in Bluffton, Ohio.[72] Delegates read a shorter, more circumspect document than the (Old) Mennonite Church analogue.[73] The document's authors offered only tentative confession and presented shorter, less encompassing suggestions for action. Most notably, the General Conference position paper passed on August 17 made no mention of interracial marriage. The General Conference writers simply lapsed into a silence on the matter that would last for three more years.[74] Without the high-profile, concrete witness of a couple like Annabelle and Gerald Hughes, the General Conference Church set the matter aside.

In the following year Gerald joined a host of other Mennonite writers who focused on interracial marriage. Unlike many, however, Gerald

Fig. 5.3 Participants in the Mennonite Churches and Race seminar, Gerald Hughes in second row, fifth from the right; Vincent Harding in first row, fourth from right; and Delton Franz in first row, third from right, Woodlawn Mennonite Church, Chicago, 1959

Peace Section Photographs of the Mennonite Central Committee Photograph Collection, IX-13-2.4, box 2, folder 108, file Race Relations, Seminar 1959, Conference 1964. Mennonite Church USA Archives. Photo courtesy of Mennonite Church USA Archives, Goshen, IN

spoke from firsthand experience. In a January 28 reply to a white Mennonite pastor from Chicago who supported racial segregation and opposed
interracial unions, Gerald wrote that he and Annabelle were "deeply disturbed" by the pastor's commentary and referred him to official church
statements on the matter.[75] After rebutting the author's segregationist
arguments, Hughes closed by expressing his gratitude for "those in our
brotherhood who have given a positive Christ-inspired witness in this
area."[76] His reply typified the gentle forbearance typical of his and Annabelle's engagement with their fellow church members. Others followed
Hughes's lead by stating that ongoing debates about integration stemmed
from white evangelicals' and Mennonites' fear of interracial marriage.[77]
Although they and their allies had not convinced the entire church of the
value of their union, many began to listen to the Hugheses with new attention.

The Hugheses also helped build a congregation where other interracial
couples felt welcome. In 1961 a young white Mennonite woman studying
at the Carnegie Institute in Cleveland met and began dating an African-
American man. Because interracial couples like the Hugheses belonged
to the Cleveland congregation, then known as Lee Heights, the young
woman and her boyfriend began attending there as well. When the woman's parents received word of their daughter's interracial relationship,
they became "very much upset" and urged her to withdraw from classes
at Carnegie and end the relationship.[78] Following an intervention by Guy
Hershberger and Vern Miller, the pastor at Lee Heights, the young woman's parents calmed down considerably and tried "to take a constructive
attitude" toward the pairing.[79] Based on his long-term relationship with
the Hugheses, Miller had earlier assured Hershberger that interracial
unions were "not that bad."[80] Thus through their witness to Miller and
others at Lee Heights, the Hugheses quietly calmed the "unnecessary fears
concerning interracial marriage" that, according to Hershberger, hampered
Mennonites' ministry.[81] Although by 1961 Gerald had still not received
ministerial credentials, he continued to lead choirs and preach in Miller's
absence and, with Annabelle, to support a church community that loved
and respected them.[82]

Other than members of integrated congregations and the denominational executives who supported them, many Mennonites continued to
oppose interracial marriages during this period. By 1962 more than fifty

(Old) Mennonite churches reported African-American membership.[83] In
these settings, interracial couples often found a home. The white Mennonites involved in integrated congregations like Lee Heights faced their
fears of interracial marriage and came to cherish couples, like the Hugheses, who made the idea concrete. The General Conference congregants
had far fewer opportunities to learn to know integrated couples. Only a
handful of congregations from the General Conference reported African-
American membership in 1962.[84] The white majority from both denominations rarely had contact with African-American Mennonites or those
who married them. Although church leaders and administrators learned
to drop their social objections after 1955 and, as in the case of Hershberger,
actively worked to educate white constituents, grassroots members' fears
increased as they learned of interracial marriages come to pass. In the General Conference setting, where fewer African-American members had
joined the church, the issue remained present but somewhat less urgent.
For many (Old) Mennonite congregants, interracial marriage continued as
the primary threat associated with accelerated integration.

The period from 1963 through 1965 nonetheless began with an ex-
plosive turn away from the issue of interracial marriage by leaders in both
the (Old) Mennonite and the General Conference Mennonite denominations. The Hugheses found themselves temporarily out of the spotlight as
attention turned from interracial marriage to the civil rights movement
with a deluge of writing on the topic. The number of articles on race-related themes published by the Mennonite press in 1963 exceeded that
published in the previous five years and nearly tripled the previous high
set in 1953.[85] More than one hundred writers in eighty-eight different
articles addressed various civil rights questions, many of them focusing on
Mennonite integrity. Delton Franz, the white pastor of Woodlawn Mennonite Church in Chicago, captured this latter concern when he suggested
that white Mennonites unable to demonstrate peacemaking should stop
calling themselves a "peace church and hand the title over to our Negro
Christian brothers who have surely earned it."[86] Only one article, by a
writer from outside the Mennonite church, took up the question of interracial marriage.[87] A second article, published first in an (Old) Mennonite
Church magazine and then a General Conference publication a few days
later, reported on a meeting in which participants reiterated the church's
1955 position on interracial marriage but offered no new commentary.[88]

As was the case in other denominations during this period, civil rights issues displaced concern about interracial marriage.[89]

Return

Church leaders' attention thus turned away from Annabelle and Gerald Hughes, the interracial couple, and toward Gerald Hughes, the African-American Mennonite. Although Mennonite church leaders had prompted Hughes's dismissal from his alternative service assignment and refused to give him ministerial credentials, from 1963 forward church leaders recruited Hughes and other African-American men married to white women for churchwide leadership positions. On August 6, 1963, the General Mission Board of the (Old) Mennonite Church elected Hughes as secretary of an urban pastors' subcommittee.[90] A month later, Hughes offered one of the opening statements at a September 1963 meeting held to discuss the church's response to "racial and civil rights tension."[91] The meeting, held at Prairie Street Mennonite Church in Elkhart, Indiana, featured Curtis Burrell, another African-American man married to a white woman, whom Hershberger would later nominate, along with Hughes, for a national church position.[92] During their opening statements, Hughes and Burrell spoke at greater length than the other three speakers combined and displayed a more nuanced understanding of the white Mennonite community. Other participants appear to have noticed the difference. Soon leaders from both the (Old) Mennonite and the General Conference denominations began to ask African-American men married to white women to fill church leadership positions. Hughes and Burrell had set a trend.

The very men feared by a majority of the Mennonite community thus entered church leadership circles, a trend that continued on into 1971. Hughes in particular rose to new prominence. On December 4, 1963, Hershberger referred to Hughes as "the music secretary of the Christian Education Cabinet of the Ohio conference" and mentioned that he, Annabelle, and "their three little chocolate girls" gave music programs throughout the Ohio Conference.[93] The 1963 proceedings of the annual conference of the (Old) Mennonite Church also referred to Hughes alongside early church pioneers James and Rowena Lark.[94] By July 29, 1968, Hughes, Lee Heights pastor Vern Miller, and Lee Roy Berry, another African-

American man who would soon marry a white woman, agreed to convene
a meeting of the church's first interracial council.[95] Hughes came to that
assignment as the only African-American man serving on the church's
national church mission board.[96] In 1969 Hughes chaired the executive
committee of the Urban Racial Council, the predecessor to the Minority
Ministries Council that figures prominently in the narrative in chapter
7.[97] Three of the four African-American members of that committee had
also married white women.[98] Hughes also chaired the first annual meeting of the Minority Ministries Council in 1970.[99] In (Old) Mennonite
Church leadership circles, the threat posed by Hughes and others like him
had diminished by the end of the 1960s.[100]

Yet white church leaders continued to confront grassroots sentiment
opposing mixed marriages. Articles in 1964, 1967, 1968, and 1970 mentioned interracial marriage as an ongoing concern among Mennonite
church members.[101] Members of the Colored Workers Committee of the
Lancaster Conference discussed "The Bible and Interracial Marriage" in
1969.[102] White church activists and leaders in 1968, 1970, and 1971
also complained about white constituents' frequent mention of the issue.[103] One of those activists, Lynford Hershey of the Minority Ministries
Council, reported on March 23, 1971, on a race relations survey of 2,694
Mennonites. A majority of the respondents did not support the church's
official position on interracial marriage. Some respondents asserted, "Even
the blackbirds and robins know better and do not cross-mate."[104] Hershey
replied, "I . . . hope we can think on a much higher plane than of animals"
and noted that the more apt analogy within the animal kingdom was that
cows and dogs mated without regard to color.[105] Leaders from the Lancaster Conference tried to educate their constituents on the matter by
publicly confessing in July of 1971 that they had not "been supportive
and accepting of interracial marriage."[106] Leaders in the (Old) Mennonite
Church came to recognize that simply including African Americans like
Hughes on church committees would not change the opinions of all their
constituents.

The shift to embrace African-American men bonded to the church by
marriage most clearly marked the division between the (Old) Mennonite
and the General Conference denominations. African-American leadership
on a national scale failed to materialize within the General Conference
following the departure of Vincent Harding in the mid-1960s. Owing

primarily to a paucity of African-American congregations, leaders in the
General Conference had a smaller pool from which to draw.[107] Although
they might have developed leaders from the dually affiliated Woodlawn
Mennonite Church in Chicago, the General Conference leaders distanced
themselves from the congregation and its pastor, Curtis Burrell, following
a series of "disruptive actions against the church" described at length in
the next chapter.[108] The decision to limit the General Conference's Camp
Landon ministry in Gulfport, Mississippi, to service rather than evangelism likewise forestalled the possibility of bringing in African-American leadership through church planting.[109] Without leaders like Gerald
Hughes to prod the church forward, the General Conference leaders lost
interest, and by 1971 only a handful of articles addressed race relations
issues.

The transitions regarding interracial marriage that had been made evident sixteen years earlier came to fruition by 1971. Leaders from the General Conference and the (Old) Mennonite Church took different paths
toward race relations in general and interracial marriage in particular. The
former group opted for a more proactive engagement with legislative issues and a decidedly less proactive stance regarding evangelism within
African-American communities. The (Old) Mennonite Church remained
more committed to evangelism within the African-American community,
which led to increased African-American membership in the church and,
eventually, to a greater incidence of interracial marriages. Although (Old)
Mennonites' evangelistic efforts did not usually lead to legislative action,
the cross-racial exchange did prompt some white Mennonite leaders to
support interracial couples.[110] Such support helped ameliorate discomfort
with racially mixed marriages. As Hershey's 1971 survey made clear, sentiment against interracial unions predominated in the (Old) Mennonite
Church at the grassroots level, despite education by white leaders and activists. Even as Annabelle sent Gerald off to chair churchwide committees
and sit on national boards, she and Gerald continued to face negative reactions to their interracial marriage.

The March Continued

As 1971 came to a close, the Hugheses traveled through a church that they
had helped change. Through their persistence and willingness to relate

to those who found their union objectionable, the Hugheses altered the (Old) Mennonite white community. While this change was realized most clearly at the leadership level, the Hugheses also transformed the perspectives of Annabelle's extended family and white congregants at Oak Grove in Smithville, Ohio. Furthermore, even General Conference members had to debate interracial marriage, with the knowledge that their sister denomination supported reputable couples like the Hugheses. Simply by showing up, the Hugheses brought the Mennonite community to a new understanding of the theological concerns and social realities surrounding interracial marriage.

The Hugheses and other couples like them did not, however, shift the church's approach to mixed marriages by themselves. The marked difference in opinion between leaders and constituents stemmed from four other influences: church doctrine, secular rationale, evangelism, and civil rights debate. Each influence shaped the church, alongside the quotidian efforts of interracial couples like the Hugheses.

The first historical theme shaping change in Mennonites' approach to interracial marriage carried the greatest weight. A biblically centered people rarely based their objections to interracial marriage on scriptural passages. Even the most vocal opponents of interracial marriage shied away from mounting theologically grounded objections. An editorial by Levi C. Hartzler in 1955 came closest to arguing that scripture forbade interracial marriage, but even he referred only to the tepid declaration that God intended for there to be distinct races and humans should not interfere with that plan.[111] Otherwise, Mennonite writers did not rely on scripture to oppose interracial marriage in any of the periods outlined here. Although male church leaders used scriptural dictates to keep women out of church leadership positions, they seldom relied on biblical mandates to prohibit interracial unions.

The same church leaders who refrained from mounting scriptural objections to interracial marriage offered little scriptural support for those who married across racial lines. Only one writer discovered in the course of this study applied core Mennonite theological values to the issue of interracial marriage. William Keeney's 1952 article paired the call to interracial marriage with the value of "suffering love."[112] He took what he had been taught as an adult convert to the Mennonite community and applied it to a pressing issue of his day, though longtime members did not find the need to do so. Beginning in the first half of the 1950s, writers in the church press instead noted that the scriptures posed no specific barriers to marriage across racial lines, a tack taken in the 1955 race relations statement and echoed in church press documents through the 1960s. With the exception of Keeney, church leaders turned away from scripture in both opposing and supporting interracial marriage, a tactic that often left them in a defensive position within a biblically centered community.

The second theme flowed from the first as post-1955 church leaders and activists spent much of their energy refuting the social objections raised by their predecessors. Because biblically based objections had never been a consistent part of the discussion, the resulting dialogue about interracial marriage centered on social arguments. Church members had listened well to the writers who claimed that the children of interracial marriages would live troubled lives, that such unions invariably ended in divorce, that African-American men did not desire to marry white women, and, by implication, that only aberrant individuals did.[113] Though most church leaders stopped emphasizing secular rationales in the wake of the 1955 (Old) Mennonite Church race relations statement, grassroots church members continued to employ the same set of social objections taught to them by church leaders for more than fifty years.

Those who debated social objections to interracial marriage also had to reckon with the influence of evangelism. The (Old) Mennonite Church invested more resources in African-American evangelism than did their General Conference counterparts, which led to an increase in interracial marriages in the 1950s and '60s. Those couples, in turn, intensified the debate. The Goshen College students and overseas mission workers who filled the pews at the Hugheses' 1954 wedding demonstrated their support to Oak Grove congregants still uncertain about their decision to host the celebration.[114] The concrete circumstance of a specific interracial marriage called congregants and leaders alike to define their positions. Corresponding to a less proactive record of evangelism in African-American communities, leaders in the General Conference backed away from claiming a public position on interracial marriage in 1959 and seldom took up the topic through the subsequent years of this study. Evangelism thus shaped discussions about interracial marriage in both communities.

Finally, civil rights debate changed the church. After 1963 leaders from the General Conference and their colleagues in the (Old) Mennonite

Church both shifted their attention to nonresistance and the civil rights movement. Debates over the problem of how best to respond to civil rights leaders' challenges pushed discussion of interracial marriage to the side as fewer and fewer writers addressed the topic. Although congregational members continued to express fears of African-American encroachment through interracial marriage, church leaders turned their attention elsewhere. A torrent of more than 250 articles, editorials, news reports, and official church statements between 1963 and 1971 focused on the civil rights movement, while only six mentioned interracial marriage. A new threat had drawn the attention of white Mennonite leaders in the United States. They did not want to be seen as lacking in integrity on the question of nonresistance. Concerns about interracial marriage seemed less urgent by comparison.

Forces internal to the Mennonite community thus played a greater role than did outside influences. First, the wedding march beat the law. On the topic of this study, church leaders and grassroots members paid far more attention to theology than to legal precedent. The 1955 (Old) Mennonite race relations statement on interracial marriage challenged many more white Mennonites than did the 1967 Supreme Court ruling that struck down antimiscegenation legislation. Second, the wedding march overcame popular opinion. Mennonites supported the principle of racial equality independent of shifts in broader social thought. From the nineteenth century forward, church leaders had written about the importance of racial equality before such egalitarian measures found wide purchase across the country. Finally, within the context of the Mennonite community, the wedding march trumped the street march. Mennonites socialized interracially as a result of church-based evangelism rather than civil rights activism. Those Mennonites who crossed racial lines did so most consistently in congregations integrated by evangelical efforts rather than in schools or neighborhoods integrated by marches and demonstrations. Although the civil rights movement did help turn Mennonites' attention away from interracial marriage, the intensity of subsequent discussions about nonresistance arose from within the community. White Mennonites articulated positions about interracial marriage while discussing church doctrine, promoting racial equality, and worshipping across racial lines rather than while marching in the streets.

Internal demonstrators like the Hugheses and other interracial couples influenced the church to such an extent because they challenged a central symbol of Mennonites' separation from society. White Mennonite women such as Annabelle Hughes and Fannie Swartzentruber came to represent Mennonites' separatist status through their attire and social position, an association that reached its height at the time of the Hugheses' wedding. Women who wore prayer coverings symbolized the manner in which the church defined itself as separated, sanctified, and free of contagion from the outside world. The virginal status of unmarried white Mennonite women intensified their symbolic role.[115] As this narrative makes clear, church leaders and congregants identified men like Hughes as the most persistent threat to the symbolic status of white Mennonite women. Although other interracial pairings also took place during the 1950s and '60s, the union of an African-American man and a white woman received the most attention. Church leaders and grassroots members alike felt threatened by African-American men who, from their perspective, would sully white Mennonite women and, through them, the entire church community. Couples like the Hugheses nonetheless refused to be bound by such assumptions. Every time an interracial couple walked down the wedding aisle, they called into question the church's association of separation from the world with the attire, sexual activity, and racial relationships of young white women.

Through the wedding marches led by interracial couples, the threat of racial contact represented by African-American men morphed into the promise of restored integrity. This study of white Mennonite responses to interracial marriages shows that a man like Gerald Hughes, formerly feared as a threat to white Mennonite women, came to be seen as a valued resource for restoring ethical integrity to the church's race relations record. Church leaders across denominations, but most actively in the (Old) Mennonite Church, employed those they had previously rejected. In the course of four decades, a racialized menace had become a welcome asset. The specter of African-American males sullying the church by marrying the community's white daughters diminished as the former black encroachers deepened relationships, served in leadership roles, and would not leave. Annabelle, Gerald, their children, and other integrated families transformed a threat into a resource by unremittingly promoting and embodying the racial reconciliation that had become a central symbol of Anabaptist integrity.

The wedding marchers thus encouraged substantive changes. To be sure, the few assimilated African-American men who joined church-wide committees did not overthrow the ecclesiastical structures that gave power and privilege to white Mennonites. Furthermore, white church leaders readily referred to the African-American men who joined their committees as evidence that they had begun, as enjoined by their critics, to "do something to stop this present system of racism!"[116] Neither the men who joined the committees nor their wives, who made it possible for them to serve, allowed others to use them so easily. The Hugheses, for example, continued to attend church conventions, visit other congregations, and remain active in the church well past the period of this study. Along with other interracial couples and members of the Minority Ministries Council featured in chapter 7, they defied the label of threat, critiqued ongoing racism in the church, and, for at least a season, created an arm of the church where interracial unions mattered less. Through their challenges and persistent presence, the Hugheses changed what it meant to be a Mennonite.

Nonetheless, the Mennonite church as a whole had not yet fully recognized the contributions made by interracial couples at the end of the 1960s. At the same church in Smithville, Ohio, where the Hugheses exchanged their vows in 1954, a second interracial couple celebrated their wedding in 1969. Like the Hugheses before them, Beth Hostetler and Lee Roy Berry also had the support of the pastor of Oak Grove Mennonite Church, even though a different man held the position. During the fifteen years between the two weddings, most of those who had opposed the Hugheses' wedding, including Hostetler's father, had learned to accept the couple and ceased their opposition.[117] Not everyone had. One of Hostetler's cousins continued to oppose interracial marriages, as did the person who placed an anonymous phone call to Hostetler's brother-in-law warning him that "something bad was going to happen at that wedding." Berry recalled, "I got on my knees at the altar [and] I kept one eye opened to see if someone was going to come into the church to shoot me."[118] Although no one opened fire or even disrupted the wedding, the threat remained real as the couple entered into marriage that day.

Such threats took many forms. The following chapter chronicles how two congregations in and near Chicago dealt with threats found within neighborhoods transitioning from white to African-American. External racial threats again figured prominently in the stories of Community Mennonite Church in Markham, Illinois, and Woodlawn Mennonite Church in Chicago as did painful and tumultuous years of transformation. The question before those congregations was not, however, how to gain integrity. Members of Community Mennonite and Woodlawn Mennonite wanted their beloved fellowships to survive. Rather, the congregations dealt with a volatile mix of politics, racial tension, and, in one case, interracial marriage as they struggled to stay alive. Racial threats and the internal marchers who confronted them emerged afresh when internal racial turmoil threatened the lives of these two cherished congregations.

CHAPTER 6

Congregational Campaign

It has been nearly two years since our church had its first Negro visitors . . . The persons who made up our congregation at that time had mixed feelings about having Negroes coming to our church—some had moved to Markham from Chicago for the express purpose of getting away from Negroes.
—Larry Voth, pastor of Community Mennonite Church, Markham, Illinois, 1963

Community Mennonite: A Congregational Convulsion

Community Mennonite convulsed the first time a black preacher stood behind the pulpit. In early 1959 pastor Ron Krehbiel invited Vincent Harding to speak to his congregation in Markham, a suburb just south of Chicago. Soon after the African-American Mennonite pastor and activist finished preaching, members of the small, all-white church inundated Krehbiel with objections. They declared, "If you're going to do this, then we're going to leave." At meetings in Kansas City the following day, Krehbiel told colleagues that he "didn't know how much of a church" would remain upon his return.[1]

Six years later another Mennonite congregation hosted an African-American pastor and activist. In September of 1965, Pastor Delton Franz welcomed Martin Luther King Jr. and his colleagues from Operation Breadbasket to a fried-chicken lunch meeting.[2] As they ate their meal at Woodlawn Mennonite on the south side of Chicago, a dozen police officers kept crowds of curious onlookers from gaining entrance.[3] Unlike

their co-believers in Markham, members of the racially integrated congregation in North Kenwood did not raise a ruckus in response to King's
visit. Instead, they opened their building to weekly "civil rights training
sessions."[4] With the support of his congregation, Franz called on Mennonites across the country to "thank God for the protest" movement led by
King.[5]

Although these two Mennonite congregations reacted differently toward African Americans in their midst, the pastors who invited Harding
and King to visit their congregations shared King's assumption that integrated churches would support the civil rights movement. A year before
Harding preached at Community Mennonite, King observed that Sunday at 11:00 a.m. was the "most segregated hour of Christian America."[6]
In his struggle to end Jim Crow segregation, King gave little attention to
the implications of his critique. He simply assumed that those involved in
integrated churches would be effective in their "attack on outside evils."[7]
From King's perspective, attendance at an integrated congregation led to
civil rights activism. Clergy from the liberal, white church community
joined King in holding up a vision of congregational integration as the
most desirable of the civil rights movement's various ends.[8]

This chapter complicates that assumption by examining how two Chicago area congregations integrated their pews and served in their streets.
Between 1956 and 1971, the leaders and congregants of Woodlawn and
Community Mennonite churches tried to move past discussion of mere
integration and live out "total acceptance."[9] The stories of these two rare
integration attempts demonstrate the manner in which congregational integration supported and detracted from the goals of the civil rights movement.[10] For both congregations, the internal march toward integration
encouraged social ministry. At the same time, the external resources and
internal commitment necessary to sustain integration discouraged long-
term activism. As black nationalists equated integration with oppression,
Mennonites at Community and Woodlawn faced new challenges that led
to the demise of one congregation and the continuation of the other.[11] The
following narrative highlights the primary historical factors behind those
two outcomes and explains how they challenge King's assumption about
the beloved community.

Historians of the civil rights and black power movements have rarely
taken up questions about change and longevity in racially integrated

congregations. Most often, they have accepted Martin Luther King Jr.'s statement about the "most segregated hour" and ignored a less well known passage of his 1958 text, in which he conceded that a small number of Protestant congregations were "actually integrating their congregations."[12] Historians have avoided studying such integrated groups and only glanced at the assumption behind King's critique of segregated churches.[13] Although several historical works have interrogated the assumptions behind integrationist ethics in studies of education, housing, government, and the military, they have let stand King's assumption that integrated churches would lead to integrated society.[14] Lacking a thorough understanding of congregations that worshipped across racial lines, they fail to note the fragility of the vision of the "beloved community" and the effect of integrated congregations on the struggle for civil rights and black power.[15]

Nestled in the narrative of racially integrated churches sit Mennonite stories in need of retelling. Mennonite historians have told the stories of racially integrated congregations in much the same way. Of the two congregations featured here, Woodlawn has received by far the greater historical attention. No less than six different historians refer to portions of Woodlawn's story.[16] All these writers correlate conflict at Woodlawn with the rise of the black power movement. I suggest that a range of religious convictions proved more influential than black power rhetoric in shaping the resolution of that conflict. Advocates of black power at Woodlawn remained in conversation with the larger Mennonite community for far longer and with greater deliberation than previously assumed, but they eventually found their dialogue disrupted by ongoing concerns about Mennonite doctrine. Furthermore, the few historians who have attended to Community Mennonite have told the story as the effort of one man, Larry Voth.[17] To be certain, Voth shaped the congregation. Yet the arc of Community Mennonite's congregational life includes the contributions of African-American and white members who weathered significant controversy. Together, these retold stories challenge the assumption that the failure or success of integrated congregations in this era turned on the influence of black power alone. In the end, they also signify the influence of passionate commitment, poor judgment, and collective perseverance.

Woodlawn: Happening upon Integration

The story of Woodlawn Mennonite's integration opens on the campus of Mennonite Biblical Seminary in late 1957. Delton Franz, only twenty-five at the time and with fewer than two years of pastoral experience, wrote an impassioned appeal to the General Conference constituency to support the six-year-old Woodlawn Mennonite Church.[18] He feared that the impending exodus of the seminary from the Southside Chicago neighborhood of Woodlawn to the city of Elkhart, located in rural north central Indiana, would lead to the demise of his congregation.[19] Franz challenged the broader church to support Woodlawn as he and his congregation faced a "decision between life or death."[20]

Franz wrote his appeal to a denomination that by the end of the 1950s had become increasingly acculturated. As noted in chapter 1, the polity of the General Conference allowed for greater congregational autonomy that, in turn, mediated against the stricter dress and lifestyle dictates of the (Old) Mennonite community. While (Old) Mennonite leaders fretted over prayer coverings, jewelry, plain coats, and cut hair well into the 1960s, General Conference staff at Camp Landon in Mississippi, for example, stepped out for a night on the town in 1960 bedecked in pearls and bowties, coifed and covering free.[21] Along with loosening sartorial guidelines, leaders of the General Conference remained generally more open than their (Old) Mennonite cousins to political entanglements. As we have already seen, however, that relatively more politically engaged stance did not always translate into more racially egalitarian action. Franz wrote with clear knowledge that in the constituency he addressed, stated commitments did not always guide their actions, however acculturated they might have become.

A brief account of the congregation's relationship to the departing seminary explains Franz's anxiety. When Woodlawn began, white Mennonite missionaries in Chicago paid little attention to race relations. Of the eleven Chicago mission sites active in 1953, only one—Bethel Mennonite Community Church—served African Americans.[22] A second congregation served Mexican migrants, but members there had little contact with other Mennonites in the city.[23] The remaining nine mission sites, sponsored by both the General Conference and (Old) Mennonite mission boards, ministered to church members who did not come from traditional Mennonite backgrounds but shared a common white racial profile.[24] Although church leaders hinted at demographic changes affecting congregations in Chicago, few yet spoke of those shifts in racial terms.[25] Those who did mention race took no clear position on whether churches should leave, stay, or embrace the impending change.[26] The national General Conference denomination likewise offered little in the way of incentive to evangelize African Americans. Denomination-sponsored mission efforts focused on service to African Americans rather than evangelism.[27] In 1953 most Mennonites in Chicago expressed little interest in racial integration.

The seminary students who ran the Woodlawn congregation in 1953 likewise had few questions about integration. As they studied in a neighborhood that one long-time African-American resident described as "rather rough," the students responded to the growing needs of the increasingly crowded, poor, and African-American community around them.[28] For example, having purchased an entire city block worth of real estate for $200,000 in the wake of white flight, the seminary had plenty of property. Seminary leaders shared that space with neighborhood children through church programs.[29] In connection with this programming, adults began to participate as well.[30] Woodlawn's 1954 vacation bible school attracted more than thirteen white and fifty-five African-American children and was led by eight white and two African-American adults.[31] Without having set out to do so, the seminary students stumbled unwittingly into racial integration.

In 1957 Delton Franz thus feared losing a practice of racial integration and a cohort of seminary students committed to Woodlawn. A native Kansan and graduate of Bethel College and Mennonite Biblical Seminary, Franz had little experience in urban communities before coming to Woodlawn.[32] Yet serving as he did in a neighborhood troubled by crime, overcrowding, and property abandonment, he quickly gained a passion for urban ministry. Franz feared the seminary's departure because Woodlawn had depended on the institution for both members and facilities. Ministry in a demanding neighborhood like Woodlawn already taxed the congregation. Franz sent a plea to the General Conference constituency because he needed outside help to continue work inside the neighborhood.

Franz felt the crisis keenly because he believed the seminary's leaders had abandoned their interracial ministry. Already in 1953, rumors spread among church leaders that the African Americans entering the formerly all-white Woodlawn area would "slowly crowd Mennonite Biblical Seminary out of the neighborhood."[33] Seminarians experienced theft and vandalism that, at least in the minds of some, came to be associated with integration.[34] Although administrators cited changes in leadership, a developing relationship with Goshen Biblical Seminary, and city officials' interest in their property as reasons for relocating, those who stayed felt that seminary leaders had fled because of the neighborhood's racial composition.[35] In his 1957 appeal to the broader church, Franz declared that the seminary's move put the Mennonite church "on trial."[36] From where Franz stood, the future of race relations in the church seemed to ride on Woodlawn's success or failure.

The broader church met Franz's challenge with a steady gaze during the following decade. For the three years following Franz's 1957 appeal, church reporters showered attention on Franz and his co-pastor, Vincent Harding, in more than thirty articles. During the years of their integrated partnership, Franz and Harding toured the South, became ever more involved with the civil rights movement, and hosted a 1959 conference on race relations attended by representatives from the General Conference, (Old) Mennonite, and Mennonite Brethren denominations.[37] In addition to contributing to a dozen church press articles as writers or interviewees during their joint tenure, Franz and Harding spoke throughout the church and served on denominational committees. Church leaders highlighted this "congregational Camelot" as proof of their collective racial egalitarianism.[38]

Attention to Woodlawn Church meant attention to the North Kenwood neighborhood. Under Franz and Harding's leadership, Woodlawn members and voluntary service workers posted at the congregation wrote articles and spoke about the difficulties of serving an urban environment, using phrases such as "overcrowded jungle," "dirt and filth," and "a world of dark strangers."[39] If white Mennonite readers knew anything about North Kenwood, they knew that dangerous African Americans surrounded earnest white workers there.

Heightening the rhetoric of racial contrast, African-American leaders at Woodlawn praised white Mennonite volunteers. Although more than thirty local African-American members served under Harding and Franz's leadership, white outsiders received disproportionate attention.[40]

For example, Harding lauded the self-sacrifice of two Mennonites who left jobs in Mountain Lake, Minnesota, to serve the Woodlawn congregation. According to Harding, Arthur and Helen Ross felt they could no longer discuss voluntary service in Sunday school unless they "were willing to offer their own lives."[41] The Rosses expressed that self-sacrificial spirit by moving to Chicago. To be certain, such praiseworthy examples showed Woodlawn's white members as exemplifying the best of Mennonite self-sacrifice. Yet the equally courageous efforts of African-American Mennonite members received scant attention. With the exception of Harding, Woodlawn's African-American members took second place behind the white Mennonites who had relocated to North Kenwood.

Community Mennonite: Deliberate Distance

Another congregation marched toward integration from deliberate segregation. In 1956, the same year that Delton Franz began pastoring at Woodlawn, a group of Mennonites purchased property in the white Chicago suburb of Markham. Led by John T. Neufeld, longtime pastor of Grace Mennonite Church in Chicago, and supported by local and national mission commissions, the group sought to evangelize new converts and reach Chicago Mennonites who had moved to the suburbs.[42] As they purchased property for a new church building, Neufeld and his associates agreed to exclude "any one who is not a Caucasian" from the premises.[43] Although unenforceable under United States law following the 1948 Supreme Court ruling *Shelley v. Kraemer*, the restrictive covenant drew the group's attention. Neufeld wrote to the sale agent that the clause would "cause no difficulty."[44] Although several months later Neufeld asked whether there was "anything we should or can do about" the clause, the congregation's leaders signed the contract without addenda.[45] Regardless of the legal issues involved, the congregation's founding members accepted the covenant as necessary.[46] From the beginning, the leaders of Community Mennonite intended to serve only white people.

The emerging church at Markham then turned its attention to more pressing issues. Between 1956 and 1960, board members struggled to pay a pastor, build a sanctuary, and administer programs. At the same time, congregants contributed to overseas mission projects in Paraguay and the Belgian Congo but paid less attention to domestic outreach.[47] By 1959 the congregation had dedicated a new church building in a public ceremony attended by local Markham officials.[48] Members invited newcomers to join their "active and energetic group" (see figure 6.1).[49] Charter members recall the early years as a time of warm fellowship, strong family bonds, and great appreciation for children in a church where "we were all close ... [We trusted one another so much that] my kids are your kids."[50]

That friendly congregation, however, soon gave a chilly reception to an African-American guest. As noted above, shortly after the congregation dedicated their new church building pastor Ron Krehbiel invited Vincent Harding to speak. Krehbiel had met Harding while taking classes at Mennonite Biblical Seminary in the North Kenwood neighborhood. Assuming that his congregants would welcome an African-American speaker as readily as had the white Mennonites at the congregations Krehbiel attended as a child, Krehbiel invited Harding to speak without consulting congregational leaders. Although he did not notice rejection during the service, Krehbiel observed "very disturbed" expressions as he shook people's hands afterward. Later on that afternoon, Krehbiel's phone began to ring. Many of the congregants who had been raised in the South called Krehbiel to inform him, "If this ever happens again, we cannot come to your church anymore."[51] Rather than wait for further dissension to build, Krehbiel organized a congregational meeting that evening.

The meeting set a decade-long course. Despite short notice, most of the church's sixty-five congregants attended. Those who had voiced their objections on the phone again threatened to leave the congregation if African Americans were invited back to the church. Following the gathering, church council members prayed, discussed, and arrived at a decision. In particular, council member Al Levreau lobbied for not placing "restrictions" on visitors or new members. The council concurred and passed an "open door policy" by unanimous vote.[52] Krehbiel's example, denominational teaching, and the council members' personal experiences trumped the restrictive covenant. In response to the leaders' decision, nearly a third of the congregation left. Most of those who departed had been raised in the South outside of white Mennonite enclaves and, although active participants, had not officially joined the congregation.[53]

Community's open-door policy came to the test a few years later as the neighborhood around the church began to change. Between 1950 and 1960 Markham's African-American population had grown from 67 to

Fig. 6.1 Community Mennonite Church members, Markham, Illinois, circa 1959
Photo by Don Burklow. Photo courtesy of Community Mennonite Church, Markham, IL

2,524, accounting for more than 25 percent of the suburb's census.[54] By 1964 the African-American cohort in Markham had expanded to nearly 30 percent of the population and ballooned to 45 percent by 1969.[55] At the outset of that burgeoning change, pastor Krehbiel completed his tenure and the church welcomed a new pastor, Larry Voth.

Voth invigorated the fledgling group. He came to the congregation in December 1960 while still a student at the Mennonite seminary in Elkhart, formed in 1958 when Mennonite Biblical Seminary left the Woodlawn community.[56] Like Franz, Voth hailed from Kansas and had little prior urban pastoral experience.[57] Yet he dove into the work. Beginning in January of 1961, Voth commuted between the seminary and the church for the next six months until he, his wife Jane, and daughters Laurie and Leslie moved to Markham in June.[58] From the start, Voth brought abundant energy and a vision for new initiatives even as the congregation at times struggled to meet payroll.[59] Despite a small building, membership rolls counting no more than thirty-two, and Sunday morning worship census in the forties, Voth aimed to involve lay members in community service.[60] Congregants realized they had hired a visionary.

Voth soon faced a significant challenge to his leadership. In response to Voth's initiative, Markham residents took notice of the small church on Kedzie Avenue. Some who visited were white. Others were members of the growing African-American population. On a Sunday in 1961, only a few months after Voth's arrival, three African-American women entered the brick-walled sanctuary and sat down in a pew.[61] They came because Voth had stopped by their homes and invited them to church. Faye Mitchell, Ola Mae Smith, and Johnetta Wooden, who arrived "well-dressed and well-mannered," drew the attention of the entire congregation.[62] Despite the church's open-door policy, real African Americans in the sanctuary proved threatening. As a result, Voth soon faced a congregational crisis.

Racial tensions at Community stemmed from Markham's demographics. Although by 1961 many African Americans had moved to Markham in pursuit of better schools and housing, the neighborhood around Community remained white.[63] Several miles away, the Kingston Green subdivision included many African-American homeowners, but Canterbury Gardens, directly across from the church, had none.[64] Streets, toll roads, and industrial sites demarcated the two subdivisions.[65] Despite such geographical boundaries, dozens of white families had already left Canterbury Gardens. But Canterbury's local property manager refused to sell the vacant homes to African-American buyers.[66] The three women who entered the congregation thus represented the potential for racial change within both the congregation and the surrounding neighborhood.

Voth witnessed his congregation waver in their commitment to welcome all people. In response to the women's stated intention to return, some members declared that they had moved to Markham because they did not want to live near African Americans.[67] Others expressed concerns about interracial marriage.[68] Some claimed the congregation would soon become all African American if the three women continued to attend.[69] The congregation's theoretical commitment to inclusion had become real in a way that made many white congregants uneasy. In response to the tumult, Voth visited with members to articulate his belief in the importance of a church open to members of all races. As threats to leave mounted, Voth called a congregational meeting to discuss how church members could help African Americans "feel a part of our fellowship."[70]

The subsequent meeting led to new action and unsettled emotion. By all accounts, members made their perspectives known without apology.[71] Following an intense round of discussion and scripture study, a majority of the congregation voted to welcome any African American who professed Christian belief and desired to become a part of their fellowship.[72] Jerry Mares, a charter member and church leader, summed up his reasons for supporting racial integration with a heavenly reference. He said, "God wasn't going to create two heavens, one for the blacks and one for the whites, so we better deal with [integration] right now."[73] Yet the congregation had not settled the issue. Many white members remained unconvinced that Community Mennonite had chosen the correct path. Some searched for a new congregation even as African Americans asserted that Community belonged to them.

Tension thus roiled through the church and surrounding neighborhood. Following President John F. Kennedy's November 1962 Executive Order 11063 outlawing discrimination in the sale of federal property, some African-American families expressed interest in Canterbury Gardens properties, more than thirty of which had been repossessed by the Veterans Administration.[74] Less than a year after Kennedy's intervention an African-American family purchased a home in Canterbury Gardens, but unidentified arsonists set it on fire before the family moved in.[75] Other

African Americans succeeded in integrating the surrounding neighborhood, however, and at the invitation of pastor Voth they began to attend
Community. By the end of 1962, African Americans participated in all
aspects of church life. William Smith, husband to one of the first three
African-American women to attend the congregation the previous year,
was proud to serve on the board.[76] Other African Americans participated
in the youth group, women's fellowship, and Sunday school classes.[77]

Not all Community members welcomed the change, however. Such
rapid integration fostered conflict even as it strengthened relationships.
Youth group members fought.[78] White adults accused an African-American
Sunday school instructor of teaching false doctrine.[79] During one church
board meeting, a white member started the racially offensive rhyme, "Ee-
nie, Meenie, Miney, Moe . . . ," only to hear an African-American member
reply, "Finish your thought."[80] Although board members laughed about
the exchange, tension hummed in the room. Amid such tension, African
Americans nonetheless developed strong relationships with the pastor
and other white members.[81] The relationships made church attendance
worthwhile.

Such congregational tension prompted Voth to seek external support.
The men who counseled him on September 24, 1963, came from outside
Markham. Like Voth, they carried a passion for racial integration. Del-
ton Franz brought seven years' experience pastoring Woodlawn.[82] Peter
Ediger came as field secretary for city churches on behalf of the General
Conference Home Missions Commission.[83] Pastor Harry Spaeth hailed
from First Mennonite in the Southside Chicago neighborhood of Engle-
wood, another community facing rapid racial transition. Like Voth, these
General Conference leaders reflected their denomination's politically informed approach as together they laid plans for a "Mennonite strategy for
Chicago."[84] These acculturated pastors employed the militarily derived
terms of strategy and tactics then popular among civil rights movement
leaders.[85] Rather than travel alone, Voth sought like-minded partners who
would counter congregational and conference leaders' cautionary appeals.
Although he invited William Smith, Community's sole African-American
board member, to report on African-American recruitment, Voth relied on
white men to integrate his church.

Crisis finally erupted at Christmas time. In December of 1963, about
three months after Ediger, Franz, and Spaeth met with Voth, Commu-

nity Mennonite staged a Christmas pageant featuring an interracial holy couple.[86] Less than a month later, on January 17, 1964, the church board listened as Ediger affirmed their integration efforts. In response to Ediger's comments and the Christmas pageant, board chair Al Levreau—the same council member who had supported the church's open-door policy—stated his objection to interracial marriage. As would become increasingly the case from the mid-1960s forward, the gap between Levreau and Ediger reflected the ever-wider disparity between church leadership and grassroots members in both the General Conference and (Old) Mennonite communities on the question of interracial marriage. The ensuing debate ended when Levreau resigned from the council and declared he would no longer attend worship services.[87] A few other white congregants followed suit.[88] The departures this time, although fewer in number than after Harding's sermon, stemmed from greater acrimony. One departing member told a fellow congregant who was also his employee that he would "go to hell" for worshipping with African Americans. The employee retorted, "You're going to go to hell because you left."[89] As such exchanges made evident, feelings remained raw in the aftermath of Levreau's resignation, and some wondered whether Ediger believed interracial marriage would solve racial strife.

Voth responded by drawing the larger church into Community's crisis. This time he invited his denomination's president to meet with him. During that meeting, on February 17, 1964, another member of the congregation, Margaret Carr, threatened to leave because she thought integration would lead "to inter-marriage." In response, President Walter Gering asked African-American board member Smith to comment. Smith explained that the African-American members of the congregation did not want to marry across racial lines. He and other African-American members found the discussion puzzling. They had joined the church to worship, not to intermarry.[90] Apparently intending to deflect criticism of national staff, Gering stressed that the General Conference's personnel had never encouraged "intermarriage."[91] When apprised of Gering's statements, former chair Levreau refused to rejoin the congregation owing to continued fears about "who and what kind of people" might come to Community as a result of integration.[92] By March the board accepted Levreau's resignation and declared, "The church body welcomes continued growth on a racially integrated basis."[93] Voth then asked every pastor in the Central District

Conference to pray for the white members of his congregation who found it "hard to accept people of a different color."[94] Like the voter registration drives and school integration efforts then captivating the nation, the integration process at Community captivated a denomination.

Congregational Comparison: Two Paths Emergent

Through articles and personal contact, members from both congregations challenged the church to support integration. By 1963 Franz and his congregants had written about racial integration and their ministry at Woodlawn a dozen times.[95] At national church meetings that year, Voth asked denominational leaders what "total acceptance" would entail.[96] In the same way, Franz prodded church leaders to "become true peacemakers in this revolution against the evil of segregation."[97] Franz believed that integration could not be sustained without civil rights activism. Unlike activists who questioned the viability of racial integration in 1963, Voth and Franz promoted the ideal even as they tested its limits.[98] Given that most white Mennonites found discussions of integration at best foreign and at worst threatening, the two men and the congregations they represented walked a lonely path. Yet both Voth and Franz tirelessly invited members of their denomination to join them.

For the following three years, these two white Mennonite pastors balanced denominational contact with congregational outreach. From 1963 through 1965, Franz and Voth developed interracial service opportunities. Although the two congregations had only sporadic contact with each other through their pastors, both groups poured their energies into voluntary service, youth programming, and various neighborhood services. Woodlawn and Community supported the civil rights movement during this era, but efforts to develop local ministry gained the most attention. As in the early years of both communities, mission and service came first.

Community Mennonite served the surrounding neighborhood through a children's day-care center. To build this program, Voth turned again to the broader Mennonite church. Rather than draw on local resources, Voth invited Mennonite education students to move to Markham, find local teaching jobs, and develop the center in their spare time. Nearly a dozen teachers responded to this charismatic and demanding vision.[99] The congregation founded the center in 1964 with the teachers' help, the assistance of Mennonite Voluntary Service workers, and the leadership of the center's first director, Carol Selman, a local church member.[100] Although the ministry introduced new frustrations as congregants shared the building with day-care staff, it also encouraged church growth.[101] African-American members such as Ivorie Lowe and Mary Ann Woods, who would later emerge as pivotal leaders, joined after having made use of the day-care facilities. White congregants like R. A. and Florence Ekstrom did the same.[102] Service raised the congregation's profile.

In the same way, Woodlawn built relationships in their neighborhood through creative service. In 1963 Franz initiated a new ministry that captured the imaginations of workers and community members alike.[103] Replicating a model developed by the Church of the Savior in Washington, D.C., the congregation opened a coffeehouse in a former family-owned laundry.[104] Known as the "Quiet Place," the combination coffeehouse and bookstore offered coffee, donuts, and reading material to all who entered.[105] Franz described it as an effort to share "faith in a way that is not repugnant" to the "man on the street."[106] Like Community Mennonite's day-care center, Woodlawn's coffeehouse increased the congregation's neighborhood profile. Relationships built over coffee and donuts fostered bible study and small support groups.[107] Likewise, the Quiet Place and other Woodlawn ministries relied on voluntary service workers from across the country.[108]

Volunteers from afar also staffed youth programs at both congregations. From its start, Woodlawn sponsored Sunday school and vacation bible school programs attended by local African-American youth.[109] The congregation's Fresh Air program sent hundreds of children from Woodlawn, Markham, and other Chicago neighborhoods for short stays in Mennonite country homes.[110] As of 1964, Mennonite voluntary service workers continued to staff summer youth programs at Woodlawn.[111] In addition to running Sunday schools and participating in Woodlawn's Fresh Air venture, Community Mennonite initiated new youth ministries. In October of 1965, Voth helped found Markham's Youth Services Council, in concert with local African-American churches, to reduce youth violence and gang activity.[112] Community Mennonite then obtained a grant of $2,500 from the regional Mennonite conference to staff the council with a volunteer.[113] Throughout the period of this study, outside resources fueled integration efforts at Community and Woodlawn.

From late 1965 forward, Community and Woodlawn took different paths as Martin Luther King Jr. focused on Chicago. At Community, civil rights activism drew less attention than neighborhood service.[114] Voth participated in the occasional demonstration but spent more time inviting African-American residents from nearby Canterbury Gardens and other parts of Markham to join the congregation.[115] During a time of racial unrest, members of Community thus practiced integration without agitating for it.[116] At Community, both white and African-American members kept integration and civil rights activism separate.

Woodlawn members, however, linked integration and civil rights. As noted above, in September of 1965 Franz hosted Martin Luther King Jr. at the Woodlawn Mennonite Church (see figure 6.2). In addition to writing about Mennonites' racial prejudices, dozens of church members participated in protests.[117] At one point the Woodlawn congregation, along with Voth and a few members from Community Mennonite, took part in a nonviolence workshop led by Jesse Jackson.[118] Later they marched with King into a white, segregated neighborhood.[119] Such high-profile activism attracted press attention. Reporters covering Woodlawn's involvement in civil rights activities quoted both white and African-American leaders and mentioned local church members and external volunteers.[120] Woodlawn members promoted the nonviolent tactics that other Mennonites found problematic.

The reports that highlighted Woodlawn's integrated activism also introduced Woodlawn's summer pastor, Curtis Burrell. Although as a younger man Burrell had assured Mennonites that salvation took priority over integration, by 1965 Burrell advocated for racial justice.[121] Like many of the white church leaders around him, Burrell had been radicalized by the street activism of the 1960s. He defended his arrest during an early summer demonstration in Chicago in forthright biblical terms. Casting himself and his codefendants in the role of Old Testament prophets, Burrell stated, "Like Jeremiah who had a burning message in his heart and could not help but shout, we too have to shout our message."[122] The cautious integrationist had become a passionate activist. Burrell's high-profile activism signaled a change that would soon transform Woodlawn.

That change had not yet come about as fall turned into the winter of 1965. The three years from 1963 through 1965 had been good ones for both congregations. New programs turned local neighbors into commit-

Fig. 6.2 Martin Luther King Jr., center, and Delton Franz, standing, Woodlawn
Mennonite Church, Chicago, 1965

D. Franz, "King Comes to Woodlawn," *The Mennonite* 80, no. 35 (September 28, 1965): 607.
Photo courtesy of Mennonite Publishing Network, Scottdale, PA

ted members. Strong leaders emphasized traditional Mennonite service, publicized their ministries, and gathered human and financial resources for their neighborhoods. The two churches demonstrated to Mennonites throughout the United States that racial integration could be achieved. After long absence, the presence of African Americans at the two churches assured members of the General Conference church that they might indeed be able to keep pace with their (Old) Mennonite cousins in the racial arena. As Burrell prepared to minister at Woodlawn and new African-American members joined Community, the future looked bright for both groups.

Woodlawn: Departures

In particular, Curtis Burrell made that future shine. He came to Woodlawn in the summer of 1966 with widely respected Mennonite credentials.[123] He earned those credentials after having contacted respected Mennonite pastor Hubert Schwartzentruber in early 1958 while yet incarcerated in the Missouri state penitentiary.[124] Upon his release, Burrell plunged into the life of the Mennonite community. He attended the Ontario Mennonite Bible Institute in 1959 and continued his Mennonite school education at Hesston College (Kansas), Goshen College, and Goshen Seminary.[125] In addition to contributing articles to various Mennonite church publications, he spoke at numerous church events and served for a short while with the Hardings in Atlanta.[126] By 1963 church officials ranked him alongside the Hardings and longtime African-American church leaders James and Rowena Lark as exemplars of the church's race relations ministry.[127] With Burrell's arrival, some hoped that a second era of interracial leadership had come to Woodlawn.

The integrated leadership that had worked so well in 1959 could not, however, be transplanted to 1966. In inner-city Chicago, as throughout much of the nation, black power had arrived. In the summer of 1966, Burrell and other African-American church leaders listened closely as Stokely Carmichael urged African Americans to seize power. Soon Burrell was promoting black self-determination. Like his predecessor Vincent Harding, Burrell confronted Mennonite racism. Unlike Harding, however, Burrell questioned the value of integration. As he embraced black nationalism, Burrell challenged the precept that racial integration supported racial justice.

Although his partnership with Franz did not usher in another era of robust integrated leadership, Burrell nonetheless remained in conversation with white Mennonites throughout his tenure at Woodlawn. In the fall of 1966 he declared freedom from white norms but proclaimed that all believers, white and African-American alike, could be transformed in Christ.[128] One month later he emphasized both "black political representation" and traditional Mennonite values of "love, courage, peace, tolerance, faith, spiritual . . . good deeds, redemptive suffering."[129] By the middle of the following year, Burrell lauded Muhammad Ali's conscientious objection to war.[130] White Mennonite readers did not appreciate Burrell's perspective on Ali, an outspoken prizefighter who explained his refusal to bear arms in a manner antithetical to Mennonite humility.[131] When faced with Burrell's wholehearted embrace of Ali, one white Mennonite responded, "I am disgusted."[132] She could not countenance how any Mennonite could support such a controversial figure. Despite such reaction, Burrell continued to engage white Mennonite audiences.

In his critique and conversation, Burrell followed Franz's example. Burrell's co-pastor had long advocated for more active involvement in the civil rights movement. Franz called on Anabaptist values, quoted Karl Marx, and urged Mennonites to offer their bodies as a "living sacrifice" to the cause of justice.[133] In 1959 Franz prodded the church to fulfill its "duty to work against social injustice."[134] His message had sharpened by 1966. He accused the church of stalling in order "to think out pious religious answers to ugly and practical problems."[135] Franz had criticized Mennonites for their inaction and acquiescence to the status quo far earlier than Burrell.

Despite his radical rhetoric, Franz nonetheless anchored Woodlawn to the broader church. He first drew on a racially homogeneous network of family and friends to support the North Kenwood ministry. Likewise, as the examples above suggest, Franz used Mennonite theological terms with ease. He drew on traditional values of nonconformity and separation from the world to urge sacrificial action. He also demonstrated integrity, another value important to Mennonites, by living in a racially oppressed community. These social, theological, and personal values connected Franz and his congregation to the national denomination even as he criticized and cajoled church leaders.

The same church officials who tolerated Franz ostracized Burrell. In December 1967 the congregation decided to remain integrated and support black power, an approach rare among integrated congregations at the time and suggestive of the Anabaptist value of reconciliation.[136] Although they expressed scant awareness of the unique path they blazed, Woodlawn members committed themselves to an integrated ministry while professing black nationalist values, a tack that even as experienced a group as the Student Nonviolent Coordinating Committee could not sustain. Six months later, Franz resigned to accept a position with the Mennonite Central Committee in Washington, D.C.[137] After Franz departed, national white church leaders scrutinized Woodlawn, and white congregational members reconsidered their participation. Questions were raised about Burrell's viability as a pastor of an integrated congregation. The same leaders who rewarded Franz's critique with a national leadership post rejected Burrell's prophetic words. Denominational leaders grew uncomfortable with Burrell's black power rhetoric and apparent disavowal of nonviolence.[138] Soon after Franz's departure, a regional Mennonite reporter described Burrell as an ineffective leader of a "puzzled, uneasy congregation." By contrast, despite his theologically suspect alliances with local political officials in Markham, Voth received accolades from the same writer.[139] In her review of four Chicago congregations and their pastors, the reporter criticized Burrell alone. Burrell found himself on the church's margins.

Burrell nonetheless continued to be a voice in the Mennonite church. Concurrent with Franz's summer 1968 departure, Burrell called white Christians to "repent of their racism" and declared that "America" needed to follow "bold black leadership."[140] At the national General Conference assembly that same year, he challenged white Mennonites to convert to "blackness" and pronounced, "The black man is better equipped [than white people] to lead mankind morally."[141] Although he no longer appealed to Christian unity, Burrell persisted in his correspondence with white co-believers.

Burrell's hesitancy to promote racial unity stemmed from his growing commitment to the North Kenwood community. Although the Mennonite press described Woodlawn's neighborhood as a mission site, Burrell eschewed a traditional service model.[142] To begin, Burrell transformed the Quiet Place coffeehouse into a restaurant training program for African-American young adults known as the Palace Restaurant. Rather than relying on white voluntary service workers for staff needs, Burrell brought in local neighborhood members so that they could gain skills in restaurant management, cooking, bookkeeping, and hosting.[143] Building on the success of local initiatives, Burrell moved in circles outside the confines of Woodlawn Mennonite. Through his elected position as president of a powerful neighborhood association, the Kenwood Oaklawn Community Organization, Burrell laid plans in 1969 to improve housing, schools, and medical facilities through African-American leadership.[144] He also confronted leaders of the Blackstone Rangers, a youth gang that had intimidated the neighborhood through violence, petty theft, and burglary.[145] Burrell poured his energy into meeting the needs of the African-American community where he lived (see figure 6.3). Union with white Christians continued to be important but only insofar as those relationships helped support his Woodlawn-based ministry.

Of all the problems he addressed, gang violence presented Burrell with his most daunting and irresistible challenge. From their start in 1966, the Blackstone Rangers had galvanized the attention of police, church, and community organizations.[146] After white officials removed African-American police officers from the North Kenwood community, gang-related

Fig. 6.3 Curtis Burrell, Chicago, 1971

J. Fairfield, "Curtis Burrell: A Bullet Hole in the Window," *Christian Living* 18, no. 5 (May 1971): 21.

Photo courtesy of Mennonite Publishing Network, Scottdale, PA

crime increased.[147] In the absence of black police officers, the Rangers recruited new members until they counted more than two thousand youth in their "super gang."[148] In response, community-based groups like the Woodlawn Organization offered job-training programs, and Woodlawn's First Presbyterian Church opened up their building to Rangers parties and meetings.[149] These positive efforts notwithstanding, numbers of both African-American and white congregants from Woodlawn Mennonite left the area because of the gang-related violence.[150] Burrell, however, felt called to work directly with "the hard core" youth like the Rangers.[151]

Burrell's vision, passion, and ability to articulate the need for African-American self-determination lifted him to citywide leadership. In 1969 Burrell hired several Blackstone Rangers, by that point known as the Black P Stone Nation, to work for the Kenwood Oaklawn Community Organization.[152] That same year Burrell resigned his position as cochair of Mayor Richard J. Daley's Model Area Planning Council because he claimed it was "stacked against the interests of the people."[153] With this bold action Burrell attracted the attention of Jesse Jackson and other political leaders.[154] At the same time, Burrell's political work further estranged him from most white Mennonites.

Yet Burrell sought Mennonite support in the midst of tensions in his congregation. Even as he entered ever more dangerous and controversial territory, Burrell kept Mennonites abreast of his activity. In early 1969 Burrell spoke with a reporter from the Central District Conference, Woodlawn's conference body, about his vision for a black-led ministry. Four months later, a second account described his congregants' concern and unease.[155] Although Burrell gained citywide attention as he hired gang leaders to staff his community organization, members of his congregation expressed discomfort with his organizing efforts. They disapproved of his scheduling meetings at the church with men who did not have "the best reputations."[156] Though he based his activism on the Mennonite theology espoused by Franz, Schwartzentruber, and seminary professor John Howard Yoder, Burrell's relationship with his own congregation showed signs of stress. The merger of integrationist and black power perspectives had begun to come apart.

Eventually his connections with the Mennonite world would attenuate and snap. His final demise came through his work with gangs. Unlike Franz or Voth, Burrell related to the most dangerous members of his church's neighborhood. Such gang ministry proved volatile when he held the young men accountable for their work assignments. He subsequently fired three gang members, and the Rangers responded with violence. On June 10, 1970, Burrell put his family in hiding. Shortly thereafter unknown assailants bombed his offices, and on June 22 gang members shot nine times into his home.[157] As Burrell rallied community support through neighborhood marches, the harassment increased. Following gunfire exchange at Woodlawn Church between the Rangers and Burrell's bodyguard, on July 30, 1970, an arsonist set fire to the church.[158]

The Rangers chose a target that should have unified Burrell and his Mennonite sponsors.[159] At first both the Mennonite community and the local Woodlawn neighborhood rallied around Burrell and his congregation. Four days after the fire, Burrell organized an outdoor worship service before an audience of five hundred that included an address by civil rights activist Jesse Jackson.[160] Delton Franz returned from Washington, D.C., and sat on the outdoor platform along with Burrell and other community leaders.[161] Franz's inclusion on the makeshift dais symbolized Mennonite support, as did the presence of white Mennonite church leaders, including future Bluffton College president Elmer Neufeld, incoming Central District Conference minister Jacob T. Friesen, General Conference Commission on Home Ministries chair David Habegger, community activist and academic Don Schierling, and Mennonite Central Committee Peace Section executive secretary John Lapp.[162] The entire Mennonite community appeared to support Burrell's efforts to rebuild his church.

Burrell remained in the public eye during the next two years. Mennonite reporters covered Burrell's appearance before the Senate Subcommittee on Permanent Investigations on August 4, 1970, where he testified about confronting the Black P Stone Nation.[163] Another writer highlighted Burrell's efforts to "apply the historic Mennonite faith" to a "poor black community" and noted that Burrell and his wife Lois often hosted white Mennonites.[164] In May of the following year, a reporter referred to Burrell's interracial marriage, a point made salient by the Mennonite church's turn toward embracing marriage between African-American men and white women.[165] The article also mentioned Burrell's ongoing appreciation of white Mennonites like Franz, Yoder, and Schwartzentruber. More so than Mennonite connections, however, the reporter focused on Burrell's black power rhetoric and his willingness to use violence in self-defense.[166] According to this reporter, Burrell carried a handgun in his briefcase.

These denominational reporters underplayed Burrell's political and ecclesiastical struggles. One writer claimed that in Chicago's African-American community, only Jesse Jackson held more power than Burrell.[167] The assertion, however, rang hollow. By the end of 1971, the board of the Kenwood Oaklawn Community Organization dismissed Burrell from his position as executive secretary, the remaining members of the Woodlawn church—both African-American and white—raised questions about his leadership, and Central District mission board members fretted about his theology.[168] In particular, reports about Burrell's possession of a handgun alarmed mission board members. Despite Burrell's protests that the General Conference denomination made no effort to "understand the theology we express," the Central District mission board cut off his salary in August of 1971.[169] Lacking support from the conference and without a director's income, Burrell could not keep the church open. Woodlawn Mennonite closed its doors.

Community Mennonite: Introductions

Community Mennonite took a different path. Free of the scrutiny focused on Woodlawn, Community's members promoted racial integration rather than black self-determination through the 1960s. By 1965 Markham had become 30 percent African-American, and community leaders, including pastor Larry Voth, expressed concern that Canterbury Gardens across the street from Community would become a "Negro ghetto."[170] Leaders feared that such a concentration would lead "to political and economic exploitation."[171] Voth served on the town's Human Relations Commission and joined in efforts to pursue a "dream of integration" through education, personal contact, and response to acts of violence and intimidation toward African-American families.[172] Community Mennonite lived that same dream on a weekly basis as the congregation's African-American membership rose from five in May of 1964 to thirty-three of seventy-nine members by 1969.[173] Sunday mornings found both white members and African Americans scattered through the pews (see figure 6.4).

African-American members came to the church on Kedzie Avenue despite its white majority and white pastor. Mary Ann Woods joined because members welcomed her and offered their support during a financial crisis. Mertis Odom appreciated receiving meal invitations from white congregants like Dave and Marlene Suter.[174] Such individual experiences reflected a congregation-wide commitment to interracial ministry. Having weathered significant controversy, the congregation claimed its integrated status.[175] African-American members continued to join the congregation through 1971.[176] Other African-American residents of Markham, such as Lee King, attended church services but never became members.[177] In a community known for its racial balance and relative lack of public unrest, no singular African-American voice rose from within the congregation calling for black self-determination. The African-American members in attendance focused instead on making the church their own.

The congregation worshiped across racial lines even while supporting ministries dominated by white volunteers. White church members Jerry and Dolores Mares attested to a communal spirit evident in the congre-

Fig. 6.4 Larry Voth, standing, and Community Mennonite Church members, Markham,
Illinois, circa late 1960s

CMC pastor's office, large black binder with eight-by-ten-inch black-and-white photos.

Photo courtesy of Community Mennonite Church, Markham, IL

gation's worship and outreach ministry.[178] That communal spirit did not,
however, translate into fully integrated programs. A white pastor led the
integrated congregation; white volunteers carried out much of the congregation's day-care programming; and a white Mennonite volunteer staffed
the Markham Youth Committee, an employment program for troubled
youth.[179] Yet the congregation did develop some local leadership. In 1970
the church hired African American Phyllis McKemey, a local resident, as
the day-care center's first paid staff person. She went on to become the
facility's director.[180]

In both service and worship Community Mennonite thus navigated racial tensions in the community and the congregation. By 1970 the nearby
Canterbury elementary school had become 60 percent African-American,
an indication of demographic changes throughout Markham.[181] Although
public reports touted successful integration in the police force, schools,
and Community Mennonite itself, a different story emerged in daily interactions.[182] For example, a Markham housing activist accused the city
council of disbanding the Human Relations Commission on which Voth
served because the commission confronted racial inequity. The activist also

noted a "militant trend" among students and teachers that foreshadowed future difficulties.[183] Such citywide tensions surfaced in the congregation. Some white congregants objected to African Americans' serving in leadership roles. A few more white members left the congregation because of the recurring controversy.[184] African-American members like Odom and Woods nevertheless made the congregation their home, and Voth and other white members like Grace and Don Burklow and Jerry and Dolores Mares joined them. By the early 1970s, Sunday mornings at Community Mennonite countered King's claim of ecclesiastical segregation.

As 1971 closed, the legacies of integration at Community and Woodlawn contrasted sharply. The congregation at Woodlawn Mennonite no longer met. Burrell's efforts to begin a new congregation known as the First Church of MAN (Making a Nation) bore little fruit.[185] Conference officials sold the Woodlawn church building to a Baptist group the following year.[186] Although no longer in Chicago, Franz brought his Woodlawn experience into the federal arena as he represented Mennonites in Washington, D. C.[187] Other white church members who had passed through Woodlawn also held influential positions in the denomination.[188] By contrast, African-American members from Woodlawn departed the church. As already noted, by 1971 Vincent and Rosemarie Harding no longer claimed Mennonite membership. Curtis Burrell likewise ended his affiliation. Although former Woodlawn member Ed Riddick spoke at a cross-cultural consultation sponsored by the Minority Ministries Council of the (Old) Mennonite Church in 1973, few other African-American members from Woodlawn moved in church leadership circles.[189]

By contrast, Community Mennonite sponsored vibrant ministries and launched members to national church positions. Under Voth's leadership, the congregation founded a sheltered care workshop for mentally challenged adults in addition to their ongoing day-care and youth ministries.[190] Neighborhood residents joined the church in such numbers that within four years the church swelled to a ninety-member congregation equally divided between African-American and white Mennonites.[191] Voth's influence grew as well. In addition to earning the respect of the local Markham community for his record of community outreach, Voth served on the church's national race relations committee and went on to direct development at Bethel College in Newton, Kansas.[192] African-American members from Community attracted churchwide attention at a later date. For example, in 1977 the congregation supported Ivorie Lowe's candidacy on a national church committee. Her election opened the way for others, such as Mertis Odom, to follow.[193]

Beloved Communities: Confirmation and Challenge

These narratives of Burrell, Franz, Voth, and their congregations confirm and challenge the assumption behind Martin Luther King Jr.'s 1958 critique of segregated churches. King suggested that integrated worship would confront social segregation by motivating the "beloved community" to enter the streets.[194] For a period, Woodlawn embodied that assumption. As a result of worshipping across racial lines, Woodlawn members joined marches, participated in demonstrations, and supported the civil rights movement. Members of Community Mennonite also marched on occasion. Nevertheless, activism at both churches did not endure. Over time, the process of maintaining an interracial congregation could as easily work against street activism as support it. The practice of integration proved more complex, contradictory, and messy than King's rhetoric suggested.

King promoted integrated churches for good reason. Relationships, service, and doctrine prompted members from both congregations to support the movement. From an existential perspective, white and African-American members found meaning at integrated churches. That purpose, often renewed in interracial worship, motivated some to seek an integrated society through street action. For example, relationships nurtured on Sunday mornings led an integrated group from Community, including Larry and Jane Voth, to march with King in Chicago.[195] Service activity radicalized others. Delton Franz supported the civil rights movement because he witnessed the effects of poverty and racism while ministering to the North Kenwood neighborhood.[196] Scripture urged yet others into the streets. A white member from Woodlawn defended her participation in marches by noting that "Jesus provoke[d] . . . Jewish leaders."[197] These examples confirm King's assumption. As African-American and white believers worshipped and worked together, they found reason to protest. In this, King was correct.

Other influences, however, mediated against civil rights activism. An activist path put Woodlawn members at odds with their sponsoring denomination. As long as a trusted white pastor led the church, denominational tensions did not block financial and human resources. When a black pastor exercised sole leadership, tensions over activism increased, and external resources dried up. Activism and the church itself then met their demise. At Community, Markham's relatively slower demographic shift led to a more stable integration process that, in turn, reduced the urgency to join marches. At both churches, African-American and white styles often clashed. As a result, the tasks of choosing worship songs, teaching Sunday school classes, and holding meetings required careful attention. Sometimes little energy remained for marching in the streets because demonstrating in the sanctuary took so much time.

More than any other factor, service stymied external activism. Admittedly, African-American members joined after visiting Woodlawn's coffeehouse or enrolling their children in Community's day-care center. In this regard, service fueled integration that, in turn, prompted activism. Yet that same service ethic created problems. When Burrell requested financial resources after the Woodlawn fire, white Mennonites did not know how to respond. Rather than money, they offered Mennonite Disaster Service.[198] White Mennonites knew how to serve and volunteer in poor and African-American communities. They knew less well how to respond to political and social changes that drew white-led service into question. Marching was even more foreign. Because both congregations relied on denominational support, they needed service more than activism. Woodlawn never regrouped after white voluntary service workers left. Community survived because fewer members challenged white-led service. Ironically, the same service that made integration possible made activism difficult to sustain.

The growing presence of the black power movement also hovers over the two stories. After the assassinations of Malcolm X and Martin Luther King Jr., black power advocates denounced integration. Where black and white integrationists saw the promise of vibrant community and engaging fellowship, black power activists saw stifling control and oppressive racism. Most fundamental, Stokely Carmichael, Willie Ricks, and other black power promoters sought space to "think without constant reference to what pleased whites."[199] Such intellectual freedom required distance from white people. Historic black congregations like the African Methodist Episcopal Church had long provided social and cognitive escape to its members. Integrated congregations offered no such freedom.

Yet historians too often assume that black power advocates stopped communicating with white people.[200] Burrell's example suggests otherwise. As this study shows, Burrell found great legitimacy in the movement for black self-determination. His writings and speeches from 1966 forward bristle with references to black power. Throughout the period of his ministry at Woodlawn, precisely when black power rhetoric peppered his speeches, Burrell nonetheless remained in regular contact with Mennonite leaders. He kept in touch with Voth, for example, at least through March of 1972.[201] In all these interactions, Burrell engaged black power from a Mennonite frame. Even when he appeared before the Senate Subcommittee on Permanent Investigations, Burrell claimed his Mennonite identity: "As a minister, and as a Mennonite minister especially, we don't usually turn our backs on anyone needing help."[202] Those who promoted black power did not always eschew white contact.

All these factors—pastoral identities, denominational tensions, demographic shifts, worship styles, service programs, and black power ideologies—complicated the ideal outcomes sought by King. To clarify one of those dynamics, not every congregation dissolved when pastored by an African American. As of 1970, African Americans successfully led five racially integrated congregations and twelve predominantly African-American congregations in the Mennonite church.[203] Local politics and personal misjudgment widened the disjuncture between Burrell's world and the world of his conference sponsors. By comparison, leaders from the Central District Conference connected to Voth's service ethic, familiar last name, and white identity. Although both pastors made misjudgments and pushed their denomination past quietism into the streets, Voth encountered less backlash in response to his errors and criticism.[204] When promoting integrated congregations like Community and Woodlawn, King failed to consider practical issues such as the racial identity of church pastors.

The stories of Community and Woodlawn suggest that, in the end, King was more right than wrong. As noted above, a less well known passage follows King's 1958 statement that Sunday at 11:00 a.m. was the "most segregated hour of Christian America." King also asserted that a small number of Protestant congregations were "actually integrating their congregations."[205] Although he did not emphasize it in this latter statement, King left open the possibility that integrating a congregation intrinsically attacked segregation. Burrell, Franz, Krehbiel, Voth, and their congregants proved that the movement to end segregation inside the church demanded as much courage, energy, strategy, and support as any street march.

Those who integrated Community and Woodlawn prepared the way for new efforts to address segregation and prejudice throughout the denomination. John Powell and the Minority Ministries Council, the subjects of the next chapter, intensified the inside movement begun in these and other integrated Mennonite churches. Most of the leaders of the Minority Ministries Council came from congregations that welcomed African-American and white worshippers. They knew firsthand how much energy integration required. The chapter that follows traces the broadening of the inside movement from the sanctuary to the church at large.

CHAPTER 7

The Manifesto Movement

We confess that we have accepted a "false kind of integration" in which all power remained in the hands of white brothers.
—Minority Ministries Council statement to the church, 1971

Introducing the Black Manifesto

On April 26, 1969, black power activist James Forman presented the "Black Manifesto to the White Christian Church and the Jewish Synagogues in the United States of America and All Other Racist Institutions" at the National Black Economic Development Conference in Detroit. With the backing of the Detroit conference delegates, Forman demanded an initial payment of $500 million for Christian and Jewish participation in slavery and the ongoing oppression of African Americans. Although Forman was not the first African American to call for reparations, the former Student Nonviolent Coordinating Committee executive secretary seized the attention of the white community when he carried out his threat to disrupt worship services. Within a month of releasing his manifesto, Forman marched up the aisle of the Riverside Church in Morningside Heights, New York, and took over the pulpit to restate his demands. As the national press followed Forman's ecclesiastical disruptions, opposition to his actions grew. A Gallup poll revealed that only 2 percent of the white community and only 21 percent of African Americans supported the Black Manifesto.[1] With his controversial manifesto, Forman and his colleagues challenged white Christians throughout the nation and in the rural communities of southeastern Pennsylvania, where many Mennonites worshipped.

The white Mennonites who paid attention to the Black Manifesto belonged to the Lancaster Conference, a regional governing body of the (Old) Mennonite denomination that gave oversight to more than three hundred Mennonite congregations along the eastern seaboard. More so than most other (Old) Mennonite regional members, Lancaster Conference Mennonites maintained a robust commitment to hierarchy. Despite a doctrine that valued collective discernment, a group of powerful bishops set and enforced policy for the conference and its members. By the end of the 1960s, rural representatives continued to dominate the bishop board. Centered in a rural farming community two hours northwest of Philadelphia, the Lancaster Conference supported Mennonite pastors in rural Pennsylvania towns, like Mount Joy and Menges Mills, who led services more likely to be interrupted by roving livestock than reparations requirements.

This chapter chronicles how white rural Mennonites from the Lancaster Conference came to have a conversation about the Black Manifesto with leaders from the Minority Ministries Council, the most outspoken African-American church body in Mennonite history. During the four years leading up to the 1969 manifesto, leaders from the Lancaster Conference helped initiate programs to address racial inequities in the church. Those programs proved largely ineffective until new leadership emerged in 1968 with the birth of the Urban Racial Council. Under the guidance of African-American pastor John Powell, the Minority Ministries Council emerged from the Urban Racial Council as the preeminent Mennonite voice for racial justice in the aftermath of the Black Manifesto. Paul G. Landis, a young white bishop from the Lancaster Conference then serving in the powerful position of conference secretary, shaped much of the conference's response to the manifesto in the ensuing years. Like many other leaders of white Christian groups faced with the dramatic prospect of congregational takeovers, Landis and his colleagues focused first on the manifesto's assertive methods. As Powell reinterpreted the manifesto in Mennonite terms, however, Landis and other white leaders entered into intense and previously rare conversations about racism in the Mennonite church.[2]

Those rural Mennonites and their African-American interlocutors offer
new insight into the history of the civil rights movement. Most historians
emphasize the growing gap between African Americans and whites by
the end of the 1960s. Rather than conversation, historical accounts highlight miscommunication, division, and failure.[3] Mennonites' intense exchange about the Black Manifesto reveals a different story. The daily demonstrations led by Vincent Harding, Curtis Burrell, Rowena Lark, Fannie
Swartzentruber, and Gerald and Annabelle Hughes fostered an environment in which Mennonites talked across racial lines. Although nonviolent
Mennonites had little apparent reason to be threatened by Black Manifesto emissaries and even less reason to engage in dialogue about black nationalism, the topic of reparations and black power galvanized the church.
Five years after Forman presented his demands in Detroit, Mennonites
continued their conversation. The evidence of Mennonites' response to
the manifesto suggests that people within and without the church held
interracial discussions for far longer than previously thought.

This study also reinterprets the Black Manifesto by demonstrating a diversity of theologically sophisticated responses within the Christian community. To begin, the story of Powell and Landis counters the finding that
white respondents avoided theological questions about reparations. For
example, an influential legal analyst has claimed that white church leaders
who responded affirmatively to Forman's demands either admitted guilt
or endorsed repentance but did not articulate theological arguments for
the payment of reparations.[4] Other scholars have noted that white opponents tended to focus on the manifesto's ideology, its apparent support of
violence, and the methods used to promote it and failed to mount a rigorous theology of refusal.[5] Yet Mennonite responses to the manifesto reveal
a different story. White Mennonites presented finely honed theological
and ethical arguments for both the payment and denial of reparations. For
historians of the Black Manifesto and the civil rights movement, Mennonites thus offer insight into the manner in which one religious community
employed sacred texts to disparate ends when faced with unequivocal demands.

This record of Mennonite conversations about reparations furthermore
reframes civil rights movement historiography by paying more attention
to unintended consequences than to the success or failure of movement
initiatives.[6] Other demands-focused studies have taken up the question of

whether the Black Manifesto succeeded or failed in meeting its stated goal of black self-determination.[7] By evaluating success or failure, such treatments often miss the unsought changes stemming from the manifesto. This chapter follows the Mennonite response for the two and a half years after Forman's intervention in order to explore the intended and unintended consequences that resulted from this uniquely ecclesiastical crisis.

The historiography of Mennonites during the late 1960s and early 1970s likewise requires reexamination in light of the Black Manifesto. Historians tasked with describing the period act as though Mennonites had no knowledge of this assertive movement.[8] In fact, many national bodies, church agencies, regional conferences, and congregations discussed the manifesto and took positions on the manner in which Mennonites should respond. Individuals in the church also struggled with both the content of the manifesto and its method. For the better part of five years, the Minority Ministries Council, the advocacy program led by John Powell that most actively worked to advance manifesto aims within the Mennonite community, captured the attention of Mennonites at all levels. Church leaders traveled to converse with council staff, individuals corresponded with Powell and other council leaders, and congregations hosted council speakers despite significant reservations about Minority Ministries' methods and their association with the Black Manifesto. As violence and money fused in the aftermath of urban rebellions triggered by Martin Luther King Jr.'s assassination and the subsequent Black Manifesto, these conversations between white and African-American Mennonites achieved their highest level of honesty. The previous seven decades since African Americans first entered the Mennonite church saw a few periods of forthright discussion across racial lines, but none offered as sustained, focused, and intense an exchange as that which took place when white Mennonites worried that African-American men might disrupt the order of their worship services.

Building Black Power

The route to those forthright conversations began at a meeting dominated by white men. Bishop Paul G. Landis and the other white Lancaster Conference leaders traveled to Youngstown, Ohio, in early March 1965 to take part in the first of two Urban Racial Conferences planned by the

Home Missions Committee of the (Old) Mennonite Church's Board of Missions and Charities.[9] At that time Landis worked as both associate director of the Lancaster Conference's Voluntary Service Program and as the conference's secretary (see figure 7.1). Since working alongside a Jamaican pastor in ministry to migrants in Homestead, Florida, in the 1950s, Landis had expressed a keen interest in race relations.[10]

Landis brought that interest to his oversight of the Lancaster Conference congregations in New York City. His familiarity with the issues faced by racially integrated New York congregations prompted him to join a delegation of sixteen leaders from the Lancaster Conference who traveled to Youngstown, Ohio, for the March 4 through 5 meeting.[11] Only the white men's names appeared on the official delegation list from the Lancaster Conference, even though the Reverend James Harris, an African-American pastor from a Lancaster Conference mission outpost in Anderson, North Carolina, was also in attendance.[12] Indeed, Harris was the only African American who spoke from the platform.[13] Given the gathering's emphasis on "integrating our total denominational life," Harris's lone billing is significant. Although at least two other African Americans were in attendance, Landis and his colleagues heard far fewer African-American voices than those present at the second conference in the Urban Racial series, held in St. Louis a few days later.[14]

The men who gathered at the Youngstown meeting nonetheless envisioned new possibilities even while failing to institute them. Although one reporter described a mood of "impending doom" hanging over the meeting, the delegates imagined new initiatives.[15] The Lancaster Conference delegates, like other white participants, supported a call for new race-based programs. Their vision for the future included cautious engagement with nonviolent civil rights activities, integrated fellowship, housing, employment, and "an office or agency to work in the area of race relations."[16] In response to this vision, Landis and his colleagues at the Board of Missions and Charities distributed findings from the meeting throughout the Lancaster Conference. They did not, however, act on the suggestion to develop a new race relations program. Instead, the Lancaster Conference leaders relied on individuals in attendance to take their "improved understandings and relationships" into the church as a whole.[17] At the beginning of 1965, Landis and his colleagues balked at committing the finances necessary for a new program initiative.

Fig. 7.1 Paul G. Landis, Salunga, Pennsylvania, 1964
"Behind the Scenes," *Volunteer* 7, no. 7 (July 1964): 4. Photo courtesy of Lancaster Mennonite
Historical Society, Lancaster, PA

During the next two years, white leaders throughout the church displayed a similar hesitancy to support emerging African-American leaders.
In particular, from 1966 through 1967 white Mennonite writers voiced
objections to black power ideology. For example, based on two years' experience in an African-American community, one white Mennonite voluntary service worker declared that the black power movement could not
succeed because "Negroes simply will not truly commit themselves to an
all-Negro organization or institution."[18] Another argued that black power
appeals undermined the broad base achieved by civil rights leaders.[19]
Even those sympathetic to black power initiatives did not call for race-
based programs.[20] The focus stayed on individual conversion and general
corporate responses. Money had not yet been put on the table.

Publications from the Lancaster Conference followed suit. Those who reported on evangelism, service, and rebellion within the African-American community did not invite specific corporate response.[21] White writer Arden Almquist warned readers in the Lancaster Conference, "Whitey, your time is running out." Almquist called for love and mutual understanding to replace "a legacy of suspicion and fear, hesitation and distrust, distance, resentment, guilt, doubt, continued segregation and discrimination."[22] Although Almquist explained why African Americans pursued self-determination, like most Mennonite writers in 1966 and 1967 he stopped short of calling for church programs to support black power.

As 1968 opened, Bishop Paul Landis supported racial activism in the Lancaster Conference and the larger church. For example, the day after he returned from April 4–6, 1968, meetings of a national Mennonite mission board, Landis preached a sermon lamenting King's death. In front of his home congregation, the predominantly white and conservative Mellingers Mennonite, Landis thanked God "for one who had attempted to direct the flood tide of deep hurt, hate, and revenge into positive, nonviolent efforts."[23] As had been the case between General Conference leaders like Peter Ediger and congregational members like Al Levreau at Community Mennonite, the gap between Landis and his congregation remained wide. Although members of his congregation objected to his racial advocacy, Landis continued to bring a racial agenda to the church's attention. By the end of the year, at least twenty-three Mennonite writers had joined Landis in raising their lament over King's assassination.[24] Having met with King to discuss Mennonite nonresistance, Landis felt King's loss keenly and, despite criticism that he preached too often on "race and Bible," joined other Mennonite leaders from across the country in calling for increased involvement with civil rights activities.[25]

Few of those who called for civil rights action anticipated what form the response would take or who would lead it. At a time when leaders in both denominations remained focused on finding ways to restore racial integrity in the face of conflicted response to the civil rights movement, Landis and other white church officials sympathetic to civil rights measures focused on secular race problems. Few white leaders thought to direct their energies toward racial inequities inside the church before turning their attention to the streets. Nevertheless, a group of twenty-five urban pastors who gathered in Elkhart, Indiana, took the discussion in another direction. At meetings on June 3 and 4, 1968, the pastors focused on the Mennonite church.[26] John Powell, an African-American assistant pastor in Detroit, spoke for the first time in the Mennonite press to report on the June gathering. Powell called white Mennonites "passivists [rather] than pacifists" because he felt that his white co-believers pronounced their nonresistance but refused to join the nonviolent civil rights movement.[27] Using terms a step more assertive and blunt than had been expressed by either Curtis Burrell or Vincent Harding before him, Powell gave notice that change had come to the Mennonite church.

The June meetings heralded a summer during which Landis and other leaders from the Lancaster Conference would distance themselves from urgent appeals to civil rights action. In the aftermath of King's assassination, between June and September 1968 more than forty-five articles in the national church press called for legislative and direct street action in response to racial unrest.[28] By contrast, writers in the Lancaster Conference cautiously advocated for Mennonite service through Fresh Air exchange programs, educational initiatives, health care, and youth work.[29] Despite Paul Landis's continued interest in racial justice, he and his colleagues waited rather than act upon the agenda articulated by Powell at the Elkhart meetings.

The Lancaster Conference thus played the part of observer at the founding meeting of the group that would come to embody the interests of the Black Manifesto in the Mennonite church. Gene Shelly, a white pastor from New York under Landis's authority, attended meetings in Chicago on October 4 and 5, 1968, and reported that they marked "a milestone in the history of the Mennonite Church in America."[30] The urban pastors at the Chicago meeting elected five men, four of them African-American, to constitute the steering committee of a new advocacy group, the Urban Racial Council.[31] Shelly's enthusiastic report reflected the influence of the black power movement within the steering committee. He wrote, "We can neither dictate power nor use [African Americans] as puppets in a basically white controlled power structure." In keeping with this emphasis on self-determination, the council aimed to give African-American church leaders the right to "make decisions which directly involve them." Shelly encouraged the Lancaster Conference leaders to sponsor a similar African American–led body in their region.[32]

Landis's failure to act on Shelly's suggestion typified a critical shift in Mennonite race relations. From the late nineteenth century forward, the Lancaster Conference had led race relations efforts in the Mennonite church. They ran the largest Fresh Air exchange program, had more African-American congregations, and placed more voluntary service workers in racially integrated communities than any other part of the church. Their Colored Workers Committee had brought together white and African-American church workers for fellowship and instruction for the better part of twenty years. Yet the Lancaster Conference leaders pulled back from actively supporting the first minority-led churchwide committee in any American Mennonite denomination. Serving alongside Latino representative John Ventura and vocal white activist and Bethesda Mennonite Church pastor Hubert Schwartzentruber, the three African-American steering committee members—Lee Roy Berry, Gerald Hughes, and Powell—hailed from Goshen, Cleveland, Denver, Detroit, and St. Louis.[33] Only one member, Gerald Hughes, had direct connections to the Lancaster Conference. Hughes had grown up at the Andrews Bridge congregation in southern Lancaster County. As an adult, however, he worked alongside pastor Vern Miller and other members of Lee Heights Community Church in Cleveland.[34] Although the Lancaster Conference counted several capable African-American leaders in their number at that time, including Macon Gwinn, James Harris, and Richard Pannell, no one in the conference's leadership structure sponsored their membership on the council's executive group. Most notably, then, the Lancaster Conference bishops pulled back at the very point when an assertive African-American majority committee emerged.

It thus fell to those outside the bishops' inner circle to explore new areas of race relations. Notably, those who publicly addressed racial concerns came from a generation not yet represented on the bishop board. Merle Good, a young white entrepreneur and dramatist already making waves in the Lancaster Conference because of his presentation of the Mennonite experience through public theatre, explored racial tensions in fictional form in the pages of one national Mennonite weekly in early February 1969, although he crossed over to a General Conference publication to do so.[35] Closer to home, Leon Stauffer, the youthful director of the Lancaster Conference's Voluntary Service and 1-W programs, enjoined Mennonite leaders in March 1969 to leave behind a legacy of paternalism and begin to trust African-American "brethren with dollars . . . leadership . . . personnel. . . organization [and] . . . goal-setting."[36] Stauffer's experience as a voluntary service worker in New York City had convinced him of the need to let go of control. Unlike Landis and other bishops who remained focused on maintaining control of the conference's doctrinal and financial resources, Stauffer understood that organizational change would require significant financial redistribution. Money, in short, mattered.

Forman's Manifesto

More than any other document at the end of the 1960s, James Forman's Black Manifesto changed the way leaders of the Mennonite church and wider Christendom approached racial issues. Ironically, Forman brought about that change after disowning the church. Forman came to the Detroit meeting of the National Black Economic Development Conference with a distinguished record as a civil rights activist. After he left his administrative post with the Student Nonviolent Coordinating Committee, Forman marched at Selma and garnered the respect of African-American clergymen.[37] Despite positive relationships with black church leaders, Forman had long denounced Christianity for its collusion with slavery and support of economic inequity. His personal experience in both Protestant and Roman Catholic churches and schools had led him to become an atheist by his midtwenties.[38] Forman thus presented his Black Manifesto with all the passion of a preacher but none of the belief.

Nonetheless, Forman focused his reparations demands on Christian churches. The manifesto presented to the Detroit gathering called for $500 million in reparations for Christianity's and Judaism's part in exploiting the "resources, . . . minds, . . . bodies, [and] . . . labor" of the African-American community.[39] Although he named the Jewish community in the document, his subsequent efforts were concentrated on Christians.[40] Addressing Catholics and Protestants, Forman pointed to the churches' involvement in racial subordination long after slavery's demise. Contrary to subsequent misinterpretation, Forman demanded reparations to African Americans for a history of having been "degraded, brutalized, killed and persecuted" that extended well past emancipation.[41] Forman proposed to use reparations to purchase land, develop media outlets, start black-led businesses, found a southern black-led university, and organize black welfare recipients and laborers. Forman exhorted members of white churches and synagogues to send payment to the National Black Economic

Development Conference. If Christians did not meet Forman's demands, they risked having their offices seized and worship services interrupted.

Only after Forman made good his threat to disrupt worship services did Mennonites and the rest of the white community pay attention. The day after Forman took over the worship service at the interdenominational Riverside Church in Morningside Heights, New York, on May 4, 1969, Mennonites read of Forman's intervention on the front page of their local newspapers.[42] They were not presented with the content of the Black Manifesto, however; rather, they encountered descriptions of Forman's rush down the sanctuary aisle as he "pushed his way past two elderly ushers."[43] More than the monetary demands, the manner of the message received the most public attention. As they read the coverage, Mennonites began to talk.

Mennonites in the Lancaster area and along the East Coast continued to read about Forman's activities during the following months. He and his colleagues took over worship services, occupied denominational offices, and faced backlash from church officials, all of which received prominent press coverage.[44] Reporters emphasized the disruption caused by Forman and his associates and the forceful responses by white Presbyterian, Southern Baptist, United Church of Christ, and United Methodist leaders. Several church officials had not hesitated to call the police, and in at least one instance, officers removed a woman who interrupted a Catholic service to protest racial discrimination.[45] Activists in nearby Philadelphia took even bolder action and appropriated an electric typewriter from the Presbyterian Church headquarters.[46] Although the activists later returned the typewriter, they had demonstrated their ability to disrupt the workplace as well as the sanctuary.

The threat of takeovers arrested white Mennonites' attention and opened discussions of reparations. In response to Forman's demands, Mennonite church leaders and program administrators called for increased giving to denominational urban mission programs, an approach Presbyterians and United Methodists also chose when they channeled funds internally rather than through Forman's organization.[47] In church board meetings, congregational gatherings, and Sunday school classes, white Mennonites began to talk about the Black Manifesto as they received appeals to increase their giving. At this early stage, however, conversations in the Mennonite church took place among white people. Although Powell and his allies had begun to lay the organizational groundwork necessary for sustained dialogue, they had not yet initiated a conversation about the manifesto.

Even as national Mennonite organizations struggled to respond to the Black Manifesto, Forman intensified his demands. Given that some black nationalist leaders criticized Forman for having requested insufficient funds, his next move does not surprise.[48] On June 13 and again on July 6, Forman raised the reparations demand to $3 billion. He indicated that the additional funds would support a southern black college independent of white control.[49] Financial response to the manifesto became even more important.

Mennonites in the Lancaster Conference noted a new threat in the extensive press coverage and increasing attention to reparations. Never before had the prospect that strangers would disrupt worship services seemed so immediate. Even during World Wars I and II, when Mennonites' commitment to their nonviolent doctrine of nonresistance drew public harassment, they experienced little or no disruption when gathered together on a Sunday morning.[50] The simple, unadorned Mennonite meetinghouses offered sanctuary from a world that some believers continued to find alien and suspect. From the perspective of many white Mennonites, emissaries of that foreign world stood ready to violate the sanctity of their worship space. White Mennonites in Lancaster Conference expected that the threat they feared would come wrapped in dark skin.

Don't Call the Police

Bishop Paul Landis was ready to talk about the manifesto. Landis felt, however, that Lancaster Mennonites had to deal first with the possibility of violence before discussing reparations. Rather than approach the Black Manifesto as a document fundamentally concerned with money, on July 10, 1969, Landis and other conference leaders sent a letter to every Lancaster Conference minister that focused on the doctrine of nonresistance. As encouraged by the doctrine, many Mennonite young men in the Lancaster Conference refused to participate in the military, opting instead for alternative service. Nonresistance called its adherents to a greater commitment, however, than the refusal to bear arms. Mennonites also made careful distinctions between Christian nonresistance and secular nonviolence. Like theologian Guy F. Hershberger and other traditional Mennonite leaders, Lancaster Conference officials opposed "strikes, boycotts, and organized pressures of any kind" because such tactics used coercion rather than pacifist testimony to bring about change.[51] Furthermore, a 1940 nonresistance statement asserted that "even if the Christian is the victim of injustice or crime, he cannot violate Bible principles to avenge himself or to punish the wrongdoer."[52] By 1969, Lancaster Conference leaders continued to oppose civil rights tactics, even though some members questioned whether church doctrines actually prohibited street marches.[53]

Landis and his colleagues then used the familiar theological language of nonresistance to interpret the Black Manifesto. To be certain, they asked the more than three hundred pastors in the conference to repent of "racial prejudice" and to make "financial resources available" where needed.[54] Landis did so, however, only after focusing on nonviolence. He and his colleagues wrote nearly three times as much about nonviolence as about reparations or race relations.[55] Lancaster Conference leaders asked their pastors to "be willing to have our services disrupted" and stressed the "way of love."[56] Before responding to the Black Manifesto, the Lancaster Conference leaders had not even considered that a Mennonite minister might contact police to restore order to a worship service. Yet reports published in the local papers made evident that some Christian communities had called law enforcement officers into their sanctuaries.[57] Spurred by such examples, Landis and his fellow committee members then cautioned pastors against "calling the police" or restraining "those who would enter our services," though caution against physical restraint had not previously been necessary.[58] Landis clearly warned pastors not to pummel intruders.

This surprising fear of violence from ordained leaders of a nonviolent church reveals an eroding commitment to nonresistance within the denomination. During World War II, Mennonite men enlisted in the military in far greater numbers than hoped for by church leaders. Thirty percent of the church members drafted in 1942 chose a form of military service. Likewise, from 1940 through 1947, more Mennonite men served in the military than in the wartime Civilian Public Service camps. The divisions evident in these disparate rates of military service reflected harsh disagreements among Mennonites over how best to live a nonresistant life.[59] That members of a nonresistant church would accept violence had become a new possibility.

In light of these internal divisions about nonresistance, Landis and other committee members directed attention even further away from reparations to undergird nonviolence with service. From the mid-twentieth century forward, Mennonites across the country had begun to emphasize selfless service as a core identity. Lancaster Conference leaders did the same. In the penultimate paragraph of their statement to conference ministers, Landis and his colleagues wrote, "Recently a black member of the Mennonite Church stated that the Mennonite Church has much more than money to give to the black people in our society."[60] They made their point clear. Although African Americans in the secular world asked for money, African Americans in the Mennonite community asked for love, equality, and access to employment. Mennonite ministers knew how to respond to these needs. A service-based record of African-American evangelism had prepared the pastors to tend to the disadvantaged on a case-by-case basis. Tithes from congregations located in one of the "wealthiest farming counties in the nation" supported service, poverty relief, and evangelism rather than the publishing houses, black-led academies, and training centers proposed by Forman.[61] Landis proposed that, instead of responding violently to intruders, the ministers offer selfless service to the Black Manifesto emissaries. Through his letter, Landis prepared ministers in the Lancaster Conference to talk about the manifesto in terms of the doctrine of nonresistance and its supporting service ethic rather than discuss financial reparations.

At least one Lancaster Conference member offered an alternative to Landis's nonviolence-focused response. Mahlon Hess, an ordained minister with a long record of evangelism in Alabama, Virginia, and Tanganyika, supported reparations.[62] Hess used his position as editor of the conference's mission magazine to caution his readers against dismissing activists who delivered reparations demands in a "provocative way."[63] In contrast to the many Christian responses that made no mention of scripture, Hess invoked the biblical precedent in Exodus 12:35–36, where Israelites demanded gold and jewelry from the Egyptians before fleeing to the desert. Hess had found a theological metaphor that encouraged his readers to answer the call to conversation and dialogue at the heart of the Black Manifesto. Although he also urged readers to contact legislators, develop job-training programs, and enter into equal relationships, Hess focused on finances. He wrote that Christians needed to take "the lead in making financial resources available" through sacrificial giving.[64] Even as the Peace Committee's nonresistance-focused response gained national attention, Hess's editorial sounded a counter call to pay financial reparations.[65]

Three months after Forman's initial intervention, leaders from the Lancaster Conference remained unsettled in their response to the Black Manifesto. Landis used the doctrine of nonresistance to discourage Mennonites from paying reparations. Hess promoted a financial response based on sacred scripture. Both men started with core Mennonite values but arrived at different interpretations. Which perspective would sway the greatest number of church members was unclear. The response to their respective appeals eventually turned on a common though unexamined aspect of their approaches: neither leader had directed his comments to people of color within the church. Although Mennonite doctrine gave them terms to talk about the Black Manifesto, those beliefs had not encouraged the white conference leaders to hear African-American perspectives. Only after leaders from the African-American community approached Hess and Landis would they begin to talk across racial lines.

Money Matters

John Powell was ready to talk about the Black Manifesto. As the twenty-eight-year-old African-American Mennonite pastor from Detroit strode to the podium before an audience of a thousand Mennonites, Powell prepared himself to speak frankly. He came to the 1969 biennial assembly of Mennonites in Turner, Oregon, as newly appointed secretary of the Urban Racial Council (see figure 7.2).[66] Although church officials had invited Powell to speak and sent out copies of the Black Manifesto to each delegate in advance of his talk, those gathered before him worried that he would disrupt the assembly as Forman had upset other denominations' gatherings.[67] The delegates knew of Powell's penchant for prophetic critique. To the surprise of many, by the time he finished speaking, Powell and his audience had begun a conversation that would continue for half a decade.

The young up-and-coming preacher brought his black power—infused message to a historic gathering. In addition to the issue of reparations, delegates at the Oregon gathering also witnessed a group of young draft resisters confront the church and request support for their version

Fig. 7.2 John Powell, 1969
"Powell Joins Board Staff," *Gospel Herald* 62, no. 45 (November
18, 1969): 1017. Photo courtesy of Mennonite Publishing
Network, Scottdale, PA

of nonresistant witness. Although at least one delegate was offended by
the young people's unkempt appearance, the delegate and the draft resisters eventually clarified their positions and expressed mutual forgiveness.[68] In the midst of the dramatic exchanges, delegates drafted and then
passed a position in support of the young people. The delegates thus departed from more typically quietist forms of nonresistance witness while
also reordering church governance and inviting women to take on formal
decision-making roles. The entire denomination had begun to step out

of old theological and organizational structures into fresh forms. Few at the conference anticipated, however, that this departure would also involve much more intense conversations about racial disparity inside the church.

Powell started the dialogue by plunging forward into controversy. The church's executive secretary later referred to Powell's speech and the resulting discussion as "almost traumatic."[69] Another white delegate recalled that Powell "sent shock waves" through the assembly.[70] Such collective distress arose more from the tenor of Powell's comments than from the content of his proposal. Powell stated that Mennonites would have "tarred and feathered" James Forman if he had addressed the crowd.[71] Mennonites found such an accusation particularly irksome because they cherished the memory of forebears who had been tarred and feathered for their refusal to go to war. Powell's race also added to the controversy. He spoke with pride of his racial identity to an audience that remained uncomfortable with racial discussions, despite the ongoing efforts of Fresh Air children and leaders like Harding.[72] Rather than a thankful recipient of the church's largesse, Powell came as an outspoken critic of the church's integrity. In response to Powell's blunt commentary, one white delegate stood up in the assembly and pronounced, "If we do what John Powell tells us, they'll have me out of my pulpit and a nigger in there."[73]

Such vociferous response masks the care Powell took to use audience-appropriate terms. He and his colleagues on the Urban Racial Council set aside Forman's demands- and disruption-centered rhetoric. Demands did not sit well within a church community known for congregational autonomy. Rather than demands, Powell presented seventeen "recommendations," the first of which called on white Mennonites to confess to "sins committed against black people."[74] In addition to using terms attuned to Mennonite polity and theology, Powell proposed that the executive committee of the church's mission board oversee gathered funds. By ceding authority to the denomination's largest program board, Powell sidestepped objections about financial accountability common in other denominations' discussions of the Black Manifesto.[75] In this moment of high drama, Powell and his colleagues had chosen language intended to invite conversation rather than shut it down.

Although they had adapted the language of their proposal, Urban Racial Council leaders had not lost sight of the financial focus of the Black

Manifesto. Powell asked the delegates to commit themselves to $500,000 above an already ambitious $4 million budget.[76] He explained that the Urban Racial Council would use the money to provide African Americans and Latinos/as with jobs and education.[77] In addition to funding empowerment projects, the money would serve a second purpose. Before the Turner gathering, the council lacked an official budget, a staff, a clear mandate, and authority over other church bodies. Only the urgency of a roiling racial revolution channeled through a few determined African-American leaders like Powell opened space for the group in church structures. By raising funds independent of existing church structures, Powell and his colleagues sought to solidify their position and increase respect. In concert with "racial sensitivity" training for white Mennonites, funds given to the council would encourage equal, interracial conversation among church leaders.[78]

Despite attendees' initial negative reaction to Powell's comments, white delegates like Landis supported Powell and pushed hard for a positive vote. After two days of executive negotiation, a six-point motion was presented to the delegates for their consideration.[79] The motion confessed racial wrongdoing and called for above-budget giving of $6 per member.[80] Although he had pushed members of the Lancaster Conference to avoid monetary contributions in response to Forman's external demands, Bishop Landis took a different response to Powell's internal recommendations. The young preacher's impassioned appeal had moved Landis as much as it had riled others. Representing two national committees, Landis supported Powell's presentation on Monday, August 18, and moved to accept the financial proposal the following day.[81] The motion carried.

Initial reaction to the vote seemed positive. The delegates passed a second motion to collect an offering in support of "urban and minority crisis projects."[82] Delegates contributed $5,000 that evening to the Urban Racial Council, a sum that more than quadrupled the previous evening's offering.[83] Back in the Lancaster Conference, Mahlon Hess penned a September editorial on reparations and published an article in which Powell challenged the church to share power and move beyond parochial isolation.[84] In his new capacity as the executive director of the Urban Racial Council, now faced with the prospect of $500 million in funding for each of the next five years, Powell enjoined the church to talk frankly about race.

Delegates from the Lancaster Conference returned home from Turner, Oregon, in late August of 1969 uncertain of the gathering's racial legacy. The church had encountered, debated, and then come to support a disruptive emissary of the Black Manifesto message. The very threat that Landis and his colleagues feared would materialize in Lancaster County appeared on the other side of the country. Powell's intervention, however, took an unexpected form. Powell disrupted the church not by rushing uninvited down the center aisle of a somber Mennonite meetinghouse but by pointing to inconsistencies in core church doctrines and inviting financial response. Members of the Lancaster Conference now faced the threat of ongoing internal disruption. Unlike external Black Manifesto emissaries, the internal Urban Racial Council members appeared ready to stay and talk. The prospect of that dialogue changed the direction of the Lancaster Conference leaders. Rather than prepare ministers and congregants to respond nonviolently to forceful pulpit takeovers, Landis and his colleagues began to prepare themselves for conversations about racism inside their own community. Although they weathered the Oregon intervention, they did not know how new conversations would change their service models and ways of talking across racial lines.

As a result of Powell's intervention, the Urban Racial Council and the Lancaster Conference moved closer together. Powell softened Forman's assertive language and proposed internal mechanisms for financial accountability, a process missing in the Black Manifesto. Rather than initiate an independent black-led group, Powell recommended creation of a body lodged within a white-led denomination. In so doing, he launched a conversation that invited white church leaders and grassroots members alike to examine internal racial disparities and fund nonpaternalistic programs to restore doctrinal integrity. Landis accepted Powell's invitation to self-scrutiny and proclaimed his support for the Urban Racial Council's initiative, even though he had previously turned attention away from reparations demands. With a forthrightness often lacking in prior attempts at interracial dialogue, both groups appeared ready to discuss the state of Mennonite race relations.

Continuing the Conversation

Members of the Lancaster Conference nonetheless gave the Urban Racial Council's conversational initiative a mixed reception. Despite both groups'

modified positions, Paul Landis and other members of the Lancaster Conference's Peace Committee discussed the Urban Racial statement at length
in early October but took no common action.[85] The Lancaster Conference's Colored Workers Committee addressed Black Manifesto themes
more directly during their November meeting at Bowmansville Mennonite Church. Although white men dominated the leadership structures
and facilitated worship, small groups of African-American and white participants discussed how the Bible related to poverty, interracial marriage,
and Christian unity, topics central to calls for economic reparations and
black separatism.[86] Likewise, on January 4, 1970, Tom Skinner, a charismatic African-American evangelist from New York City, spoke before a
crowd of six hundred people at Paradise Mennonite Church, a Lancaster
Conference congregation. Having read about ongoing racial turmoil in the
newspapers and heard of Powell's intervention in Turner, Oregon, local
Mennonites filled the sanctuary to listen to Skinner comment on a variety
of racial topics, including the Black Manifesto. During his presentation,
Skinner stated that the "problem with the Black Manifesto is not James
Foreman [sic], but the people and the conditions that make a Foreman necessary."[87] Although he did not offer a ringing endorsement, Skinner nonetheless supported the manifesto. His large Mennonite audience listened
with rapt attention. In the five months following Powell's proposal, lay
members of the conference seemed more interested than ordained leaders
in conversation about the manifesto.

Landis and other Lancaster Conference leaders initially seemed unresponsive to grassroots members' growing interest in speakers like Skinner
and others who promoted the Urban Racial Council agenda. In lieu of
direct support, the conference's leadership employed the same strategy in
private that they used when faced with the prospect of worship takeovers:
they prepared for conversation with potentially hostile outsiders, in this
case Powell and members of the Urban Racial Council, but gave no money.
In public, the leaders seemed to have turned their attention elsewhere.
Rather than discuss how the conference could become involved in the service and fund-raising initiatives proposed by the Urban Racial Council,
Landis and his colleagues used the pages of the conference newsletter to
interpret church doctrines of nonconformity and submission to authority.[88] At the end of the 1960s, the same issues—how to maintain and promote nonconformist doctrine—that had proved so problematic for women
like Broad Street matron Fannie Swartzentruber back in the 1940s con-

tinued to command the attention of clergy and lay leaders alike. Members of the bishop board invested far more energy in figuring out how to keep women's hair uncut and covered up than in deciding how to pay for the legacy of slavery. Although Landis had backed Powell's recommendations in Turner, Oregon, he generated little interest in Black Manifesto conversation among his fellow bishops and ordained clergy.

African-American Mennonites quickly grew frustrated with the lack of financial support from Landis, other Lancaster Conference leaders, and white Mennonites across the country. In March of 1970, Powell reported that the newly named Compassion Fund of the Minority Ministries Council, successor to the Urban Racial Council, had raised only $38,075, far below the $250,000 necessary to reach the $500,000 mark within a year.[89] Despite the early indication of support from delegates at the Oregon gathering, congregational members did not follow their representatives' example. Without a personal connection to Powell or the experience of having debated the Urban Racial Council's proposal, grassroots members felt little of the urgency so palpable in Oregon. Powell and his colleagues quickly realized that raising the promised funds would take more than one speech at a national gathering.

Members of the council nonetheless remained in conversation with the white church. Perhaps in response to the disappointing giving rate, Powell made some effort to distance the council's appeal from the Black Manifesto but wrote glowingly about the manifesto just one week later.[90] In the wake of diminished giving, exasperation mounted. African-American Mennonite minister and council associate Hubert Brown, for example, reported on the "Bullshit" he encountered among white Mennonites "all 'decked out' like gods who come to do 'blackie' a favor" in the inner city.[91] Yet the frustration itself indicates that Brown, Powell, and their associates continued to talk with white church leaders. At this point those conversations took time and energy but seldom led to increased giving. Even as they dialogued, they failed to generate the expected funds.[92]

In response to the council members' notable frustration, Landis and his colleagues sought out new conversation partners. Instead of waiting for a Minority Ministries Council preacher to show up unannounced, Lancaster Conference administrators urged local pastors to invite "minority" speakers to preach from their pulpits.[93] More than a year after Powell's dramatic intervention in Oregon, Lancaster Conference ministers began to invite recognized African-American and Latino/a leaders into their congregations, chosen from a list of pastors who had been noticeably absent from the activities of the increasingly bold Minority Ministries Council.[94] Rather than choosing outsiders like Powell, over whom the conference had no authority, conference leaders brought in trusted converts accountable to Landis and the other bishops.

Powell and the Minority Ministries Council, however, wanted more from the Lancaster Conference than a list of tame speakers. In early fall of 1970, council staff approached Landis about setting up a time to discuss "racist attitudes among" the Lancaster Conference constituency.[95] On November 13, Lynford Hershey, a white Minority Ministries Council staff person hired by Powell to educate white Mennonites, met with nine Lancaster Conference bishops and staff members. Hershey came to the meeting with close family ties to the Lancaster Conference, a long record of civil rights activism, and a strong personal relationship with Powell.[96] He used the meeting to describe the "indirect and direct" ways he encouraged white people to move aside so that African Americans could help themselves.[97] Landis and other bishops in attendance told Hershey about their forthcoming race relations statement, but little else seemed to emerge from the meeting. Longer-term outcomes of the conversation would not appear for several months.

As he traveled from one congregation to another, Hershey found lay members willing to talk about racial inequities. In late November he commented on the "almost unbelievable" gap between white rural Mennonites, like most Lancaster Conference members, and Mennonites, both white and from communities of color, who worshipped and worked in the city.[98] Despite that divide, white lay members welcomed Hershey's efforts to "deal with white racism" more readily than did church leaders.[99] At least in terms of Hershey's experience, those least threatened by calls to redistribute power remained most open to discuss race relations.

Those grassroots conversations came about through a distant and unlikely source. Given that Hershey received funding from Powell based on an appeal prompted by Forman, ultimately it was the Black Manifesto that got Mennonites talking about race. The line connecting the National Black Economic Development Conference in Detroit to rural Mennonite congregations in Lancaster ran through a document often thought to have cut off such contact. Rather than stifling conversation, as claimed by period pundits, the Black Manifesto fostered dialogue and contact with an intensity white people in the church rarely encountered. Although few lay members made the same connection, Powell and his colleagues recognized the antecedent to their efforts and made no subsequent attempt to distance themselves from Black Manifesto promoters.

In the aftermath of the Black Manifesto, conversations at the leadership level continued after a slow start. On July 14, 1971, Leon Stauffer, a colleague of Landis, assured Hershey that the conference's subcommittee on race relations was hard at work.[100] Minority Ministries Council members also continued to push forward. The day after Stauffer penned his report, Powell and Hubert Brown traveled to Atlanta to meet with Vincent Harding, whom Forman had nominated to serve on the Black Manifesto's steering committee, to discuss "methods . . . to liberate blacks in the church."[101] Following these meetings, council staff challenged the Lancaster Conference leaders to match public statements about racism with bold action and to refrain from hiring "non-whites that we have taught to act white."[102] Lancaster Conference staff responded by recommending that pastors bring white council staff member Lynford Hershey into their congregations.[103] As they prepared for Hershey's itinerancy, Landis and other leaders from the conference kept on talking about a subject that few had anticipated would still hold the church's attention more than two years after Forman spoke in Detroit.

The Minority Ministries Council built on the ongoing interest by holding an annual meeting in October 1971 that marked the apex of their influence in the white world. As council members gathered in Detroit, where Forman had first presented the Black Manifesto, Powell highlighted a host of new activities. Mirroring the practice of other racial minority caucus groups lodged within majority-white denominations, Powell and other council members had disbursed more than $75,000 and laid plans for disbursing $95,000 more. A new alliance between Latino/a and African-American Mennonites had grown. Outspoken council members held influential positions within existing church structures.[104] A few white Mennonite executives even expressed support for the council. The secretary of information services for a national Mennonite mission agency supported the Compassion Fund as a means to "recognize our participation as white anglo Mennonites in the overall racist and discriminatory and insensitive patterns in our society."[105] In public, the Minority Ministries Council looked like a healthy, powerful conversation partner with church leaders.

During the meeting, council members demonstrated their interest in continuing to talk with white Mennonites by rejecting a statement that would have strained relationships within the church. Their decision took on additional significance in light of the financial constraints facing the council. The Compassion Fund's first-year receipts reached only $100,000 of its $500,000 goal. Receipts in the second year dropped to $60,000.[106] Powell asserted that denominational officials' requirement that council staff submit more detailed financial reports than other departments, a requirement indicative of the church's distrust of council staff, had, in turn, slowed the pace of giving.[107] As funds failed to materialize, Powell tried to achieve self-sufficiency by proposing that the council foster credit unions and small businesses in racially oppressed communities.[108] At the same time, council caucuses reviewed a statement that rejected integration based on Mennonite paternalism and renewed the call for financial support of council initiatives.[109] In light of the already greatly diminished financial response, numerous Black Caucus members and even more Hispanic Caucus participants objected to the document because "it may hurt the very whites who were friends and were concerned."[110] Despite their reputation as angry, demanding agitators, council members remained invested in relationships with white Mennonites.

Such investment bore fruit in the Lancaster Conference. Although discussions about a proposed Minority Ministries cross-cultural seminar never got beyond the planning stages, Landis and his fellow bishops fostered conversations through a variety of actions in the following years.[111] In 1972 the conference published a race relations study guide that, for the first time in the group's history, confessed to racism in the church and lamented a lack of support for "housing, education, employment, and leadership" for racially oppressed communities.[112] Building on other themes prominent in the Black Manifesto, the statement also called on Mennonites in the Lancaster Conference to grant "equal power to racially oppressed people" and to distribute "economic resources."[113] One year later, the conference appointed African-American leaders like Harold Davenport to significant leadership positions.[114] The conversation continued through 1974, a full five years after the Black Manifesto was issued, when Raymond Jackson, an African-American Mennonite minister from Philadelphia, traveled to Kenya to take part in a conference sponsored by the Minority Ministries Council.[115] Influenced by Jackson and subsequent reporting, leaders and lay members in the conference discussed racial inequities in Forman's terms.[116] Even as late as 1976, a group of Mennonites and their denominational cousins gathered in New Jersey to examine racism in the church using concepts made popular through the Black Manifesto.[117] Although by 1976 he received little attention, Forman's controversial document continued to influence Mennonites and other white-majority denominations through groups like the Minority Ministries Council.

Conversation as Counterdemonstration

The Mennonites who talked about the Black Manifesto complicate the traditional timeline of the civil rights movement. At a point where many had already written the movement's eulogy, African-American and white Mennonites held their most intense conversations about race. Rather than denouement, the discussions among Powell, Landis, and their contemporaries appear as climax. At least in many white-majority religious communities, the civil rights movement did not peak during the three-year period from 1963 through 1965, when marchers descended on Washington and congressional representatives passed civil and voting rights legislation. The movement culminated, instead, in the period from 1969 through 1971, as churches distributed funds, examined service programs, and discussed racism within their communities. Only by looking beyond the streets to the homes and sanctuaries where members of the Minority Ministries Council and the Lancaster Conference spent so much time talking does the story shift forward six years.

That story also reveals that the Black Manifesto fostered more conversations than it quelled. Because Forman and his emissaries interrupted work and worship, white Mennonites and other northern Christian groups talked about ecclesiastical racism with African-American leaders. Had the manifesto been a one-sided, unresponsive monologue, such direct exchange could not have followed. The frank and sustained interracial discussion also generated new outcomes. Conversation between the Minority Ministries Council and the Lancaster Conference exposed racial inequities, challenged urban missions, and birthed fresh programs. Instead of encouraging churchly strife, the radical document invited careful conversation and measured change.

At the same time, miscommunication and strife hampered these ecclesi-astical conversations. In the process of tailoring their comments for Chris-tian—and initially Jewish—audiences, the religious writings of Forman and his emissaries invoked countervailing forces. For example, theological commitments among Mennonites grounded conversation about the Black Manifesto even while fostering misinterpretation. Because Powell and Landis held Christian faith and doctrine in common, they had reason to talk. The two men shared confessional commitments to "faith and belief," "the Cross," and "the words of the prophets" as used by Forman in the manifesto. At the same time, terms like "revolution," "demands," and "col-onization" fit Powell's theology but clashed with Landis's.[118] Leaders of the Lancaster Conference preferred to emphasize "the redemptive love of Christ," while Minority Ministries staff focused instead on "paternalism in our churches."[119] Even on the most central of Mennonite doctrines, the two groups differed. Leaders from the Lancaster Conference eschewed any association with the military.[120] Powell and other council staff used military idioms to describe their plans for a "war against prejudice and discrimination" in which they would become "the 'generals' of our troops" and appoint white Mennonites as "foot soldiers."[121] As Christian commit-ment brought the groups together, theological interpretations pulled them apart.

A second often-obscured tension became evident as the two groups narrated contrasting racial histories. The white Mennonite community in Lancaster thought they had managed race relations rather well. They remembered that the first baptism of African-American Mennonites had occurred in a Lancaster Conference congregation and felt confident that they knew better than civil rights leaders how to improve racial condi-tions within their church. A Lancaster Conference member claimed, for example, that a predominantly white Mennonite church in Harlem of-fered "potentially greater gains for the claims of Christ than . . . ten civil-rights marches led by Rev. M. L. King, Jr."[122] John Powell and the Minor-ity Ministries Council told another story. In Powell's tale, the Lancaster Conference leaders, pastors, and lay members—from Paul Landis to el-derly, covering-clad grandmothers—promoted paternalism. Powell and members of the Minority Ministries Council faulted white Mennonites in the Lancaster Conference and throughout the church for calling on peo-ple of color to be more like them than like Christ. Rather than continue to participate in a "false kind of integration," Powell and his associates sought

to write a new history in which they developed "indigenous congregations" and confronted their "white Christian brothers."[123] This new history upended and revised the earlier tale told among the white Lancaster
Conference Mennonites. The contrasting stories became apparent in the
conversation generated by the manifesto. Without that conversation, the
tensions may have led to even greater disruption.

Contrasting approaches to systemic injustice also intensified interracial
conversation among Mennonites. Like many evangelical communities in
the twentieth century, white Mennonites from the Lancaster Conference
had little experience in responding to systemic inequities. From long practice and theological preference, they knew how to administer service programs based on interpersonal relationships.[124] They knew much less about
responding to systemwide impersonal forces like those identified in the
Black Manifesto. Members of the Minority Ministries Council, however,
initiated new programs that addressed institutional injustice by channeling financial resources to oppressed communities. Both groups stated their
intention to right racial wrongs, but they disagreed on the most effective
means to do so. In particular, Mennonites in the Lancaster Conference felt
threatened by the council's proposed changes. When Mennonites in the
Lancaster Conference heard Powell propose shifting relation-based service to institution-based advocacy, many felt slighted. Such redirection
ignored their sacrifice and commitment to interracial ministry. Although
the two groups kept talking, the conversation became strained as interpersonal and institutional visions for service clashed.

In the end, the conversations collapsed because the money stopped. By
the time educational resources on racism reached past the church elite to
congregants, Minority Ministries Council staff were discouraged by administrative restrictions placed on promotion of the Compassion Fund,
their fiduciary lifeline. When the money dried up, so did much of their
influence. Although council members had once been able to demand
that functionaries travel to meet with them, Powell and others soon had
to travel to gain a hearing. Already in 1972, church administrators cut
funds for Lynford Hershey's education program.[125] By September 1973,
John Powell talked about feeling isolated.[126] Soon afterward, Mennonite
church leaders structured the Minority Ministries Council out of existence.[127] In its place, African-American and Latino/a leaders gained a
few leadership posts, but the institution that had once advocated on their

behalf no longer functioned. The existing theological, narrative, and pro-grammatic tensions identified in this chapter proved overwhelming. Less than a year later, Powell resigned.[128] When the money left the table, the interracial conversation died.

Other conversations, however, continued. Within the ethnically spe-cific caucus groups that developed out of the ashes of the council, African-American and Latino/a Mennonites continued to talk among themselves. Those conversations led to new ways of defining identity based on both racial pride and religious affiliation.[129] Although council members no lon-ger received the same kind of churchwide attention that they had at the end of the 1960s, some stayed within the denomination and eventually resurfaced in otherwise white leadership circles. In 1979, for example, a group of Black Caucus members, several of whom had been involved in the Minority Ministries Council, met with leaders of the Mennonite Central Committee, the leading relief and development organization of the Mennonite family of churches. The caucus members called the com-mittee "a racist institution which believes in equality but does not practice it" and challenged the organization's executives to change their policies and behaviors.[130] Like prior exchanges, the conversations remained tense but also led to identifiable change.

As interracial conversations at the leadership level dwindled, so too did race-focused action within the white community. Soon after Powell resigned, white Mennonite leaders across the church turned their atten-tion elsewhere. Even before Powell's resignation, race had fallen from the agenda of the Lancaster Conference. During the decade following 1972, bishops from the Lancaster Conference discussed its race-related agenda twice, once to deny funding for an African-American youth ministry team and once to inquire about a local meeting of the Mennonite Church Black Caucus.[131] Without the Minority Ministries Council to initiate dialogue, white leaders in the Lancaster Conference focused on other pressing mat-ters. They turned their attention to structural reorganization, church dis-cipline, overseas missions, and controversies over charismatic worship.[132] In essence, having recognized the disjuncture between their racial self-assessment and that of people of color, leaders in the Lancaster Conference withdrew.

Before its demise, the five-year dialogue initiated by the Black Mani-festo nevertheless led to specific, tangible, and at times unexpected outcomes. Within the Lancaster Conference, leaders used the occasion of the Black Manifesto to strengthen the core doctrine of nonresistance, a move that corresponded with unexpected support for young draft resisters and increased opposition to the Vietnam War.[133] Additionally, administrators from the conference supported an initiative to hire African-American and Latino/a youth from Philadelphia and other urban centers for summer service programs in their home neighborhoods.[134] White rural Mennonite youth had formerly dominated summer service ventures. Without Powell and others agitating on behalf of such initiatives, urban youth would not likely have gained such opportunities. Fresh Air programs also received new attention from council members. Lancaster Conference leaders discontinued their Fresh Air program in a slow and attenuated process that began in 1971. At that time, Powell criticized paternalism in Fresh Air ventures and called for "stale-air" exchanges that would bring white Mennonite children into African-American urban homes.[135] Changes, even those not sought by promoters of the manifesto, came about because Minority Ministries Council staff members and Lancaster Conference leaders talked with each other for months on end.

Those conversations led to three different kinds of counterdemonstrations. First, the conversations between council and conference leaders served as a counterdemonstration against black nationalist separatism. By talking about the Black Manifesto, Powell, Landis, and their colleagues demonstrated that African Americans and whites had something left to discuss. They countered the assumption that integrated communities had become irrelevant after the ousting of white members from the Student Nonviolent Coordinating Committee in 1966. Ironically, a document based on black nationalist ideology brought white and black Christians into close contact. Second, the conversations led by Powell and Landis countered street demonstrations. To be certain, Lancaster Conference members had long censured political action. Aware of this history, Powell and other council members invited Lancaster Mennonites to discuss internal issues rather than legislative ones. Those Black Manifesto discussions, in turn, brought about change independent of street action. The new urban programs and Fresh Air criticism emerging from these conversations necessitated no marches and thereby encouraged white Mennonite involvement in a dimension of the civil rights movement. In essence, it became clear that public demonstrations are not the only route to change. Finally,

Black Manifesto conversations stopped because many white Mennonites countered daily demonstrators. Although they recognized positive outcomes from the conversations with white Mennonites, Powell and his colleagues also remembered the reluctance, opposition, and outright antagonism shown to them by leaders from the Lancaster Conference and the church at large.[136] Such backlash pushed donors away from the council and prompted conversational collapse. In the midst of dialogue, counterdemonstrators helped bring the exchange to an end.

Their fizzled conclusion should not detract from the conversations' significance. A conservative, white religious group discussed a divisive, racial agenda. Leaders examined racial inequities in financial appropriation, resource control, and committee appointment. In addition, the conversation initiated by the Black Manifesto lasted longer within the Mennonite church than in most secular settings and, following the ten-year hiatus noted above, reemerged. In time, Powell returned to the church and by the early 1990s held a leadership post at the denominational level.[137] As part of that appointment, he helped reopen conversation about the Black Manifesto's financial and political themes.[138] A new generation of leaders in the Lancaster Conference and throughout the church talked about racial inequities in their religious community. Although still one of the whitest and most conservative bodies within the Mennonite church, the Lancaster Conference once again entered a conversation prompted by the Black Manifesto.

The manifesto invoked a remarkable response. Forman opened conversations of surprising longevity among Mennonites and other Christian groups. A challenge directed at secular groups would most likely not have lasted so long. In the absence of Mennonites' commitment to repair broken relationships, for example, civic leaders might have summarily dismissed reparations demands. As a result, a shorter, less intense conversation seems almost certain. Yet Forman chose the church. Because of that choice, Mennonites and other religious groups like them explored the way racial identities fostered financial and institutional inequities. At a time when many white people assumed that the racial revolution had died with Martin Luther King Jr., interracial conversation thrived, and concrete changes coalesced.

This chapter chronicles daily but reluctant demonstrators. Although they ultimately changed the church by conversing with Minority Ministries Council members, many white Mennonites from the Lancaster Conference would have preferred to avoid racial conversation. They kept talking only because their faith mandated reconciled relationship. They wanted to maintain open communication with African-American co-believers but were offended that former converts now expected equal status. Many white members of the Lancaster Conference expressed discomfort at taking leadership from those they thought should just be grateful. Nonetheless, white Mennonites demonstrated on a daily basis to bring an end to segregation in the church. They did so for many reasons—because they genuinely believed in racial justice, because Fresh Air children had made them aware of their prejudices, and because Gerald Hughes, Rowena Lark, Vincent Harding, and many others had made themselves Mennonites. They also wanted to avoid the public derision that would ensue if a Mennonite pastor were to slug a Black Manifesto emissary on a Sunday morning.

The chapter that follows turns to another group of Mennonites who, like the reluctant participants from the Lancaster Conference, also demonstrated for a variety of reasons. It provides an ending where this narrative began, with members of Bethesda Mennonite in St. Louis bringing together the street and the sanctuary. On the steps of their church, these unexamined Mennonites tell a new story of the civil rights movement, one that builds on the work of John Powell, Paul Landis, and many other daily demonstrators.

CHAPTER 8

A New Civil Rights Story

The nonviolent movement is telling us, by its philosophy and ritualistic acts, that change comes not only by a few external acts but by a great many internal acts.
—Lillian Smith, white southern writer and social critic, 1963

A Sunday Morning Demonstration

Members of Bethesda Mennonite gathered for a Sunday morning demonstration in 1961. Two children offered impish grins to an unnamed photographer (see figure 8.1). Perhaps they had recently returned from a Fresh Air vacation in the country. The other demonstrators from this St. Louis congregation paid no heed to the photographer as they conversed after worship. At the top of the steps, two women—one white, one black—wore prayer coverings at a church where evangelist Rowena Lark once wore hers. Like Lark, they demonstrated their claim to church membership through sacred dress. Farther to the left, pastor Hubert Schwartzentruber held one of his children while he spoke with his wife, June, and another churchgoer. Perhaps they discussed Curtis Burrell, an African-American member of their congregation away at seminary. They may have commented on Burrell's marriage to Lois Headings, a white Mennonite from Hutchinson, Kansas, whom he met through church connections. The two men standing below them might have been discussing the sermon, local politics, or street marches through the Pruitt-Igoe Housing development. On this Sunday morning in St. Louis, these dozen Mennonites demonstrated while talking after church.

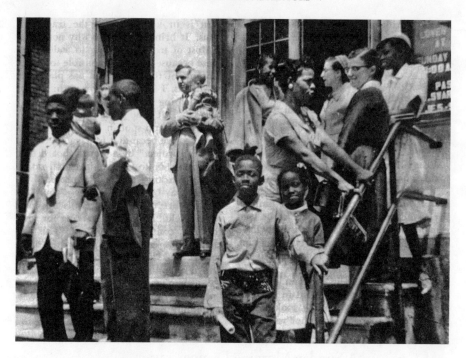

Fig. 8.1 Bethesda Mennonite Church members, St. Louis, 1961
N. E. Kauffman, "Light Shines Out from the Inner City," *Gospel Herald* 54, no. 23 (June 6, 1961): 517.
Photo courtesy of Mennonite Publishing Network, Scottdale, PA

The Bethesda members transformed their informal gathering into a demonstration by holding interracial conversations. Within a housing project segregated from white St. Louis, Bethesda members sent a message. They evinced—as had Louis Gray, Rowena Lark, Nettie Taylor, June Schwartzentruber, and Susie Smith when they first posed for an integrated Sunday school photo in 1957—the possibility of integrated worship. They stood on the steps of their church having worshiped together, now visiting together, and in so doing, they challenged segregation. At this intersection between home and sanctuary, Bethesda members organized yet another daily demonstration of segregation's demise. Some members joined street marches to further challenge the color line. Many chose to demonstrate in their living rooms. All took considerable social risks to support the goals of the civil rights movement.

Bethesda's history speaks of a congregation well prepared to demonstrate across racial lines. Church planters Rowena and James Lark came to the city in 1956 at the invitation of local church federation leaders interested in encouraging "wholesome evangelism" in urban St. Louis.[1] The Larks chose to locate their ministry efforts in the Pruitt-Igoe housing project, a federally funded development built to stem the spread of substandard housing and so protect downtown property values. The massive facility covered more than fifty acres and offered 2,870 apartments for up to fifteen thousand inhabitants, a higher density than that in the residences it replaced. Although originally conceived as a segregated housing site—planners had designated Pruitt project for African Americans, Igoe for whites—the Supreme Court's *Brown v. Board of Education* decision forced city supervisors to declare the project integrated when it opened in 1954. By the time the Larks arrived, however, demand for urban housing had begun to decline, and de facto segregation followed.[2] Only African Americans lived at Pruitt-Igoe.

By 1957 a young couple from southern Ontario, Hubert and June Schwartzentruber, arrived in St. Louis to take over leadership at Bethesda. The couple had been wed only six weeks before their arrival at Bethesda, and they brought with them even less ministerial than marital experience. By the time they set foot in Pruitt-Igoe, the development already showed signs of deterioration from poor construction, inadequate maintenance, and bureaucratic neglect. The Schwartzentrubers nonetheless moved into a project apartment and, according to a mocking letter sent to them by a white resident of the city, became "the first-and-only white tenants" of the housing project.[3]

During their fifteen-year tenure at Bethesda, the Schwartzentrubers helped build a congregation known for its interracial ministry. Although the congregation comprised mostly Pruitt-Igoe residents like Louis Gray, Susie Smith, and Nettie Taylor, who appeared in the *St. Louis Argus* photo that opens this volume (figure P.1), the congregation also attracted white Mennonite volunteers who moved to St. Louis to join the Schwartzentrubers in ministry. Church members supported efforts to address housing, education, and employment needs in the Pruitt-Igoe community and, in the process, merged demonstrations of the home and sanctuary with those in the street.[4] Hubert, in particular, challenged the church to become more active in the cause of racial justice lest blood from the "ghetto . . . flow in Menno Simons country, to shoofly-pie village," a reference to rural and racially homogenous Mennonite enclaves.[5] Under his and June's leadership, the congregation embodied interracial fellowship within and without the sanctuary.

Bethesda members thus represent the primary themes of this book. *Daily Demonstrators* has explored the deep texture of the civil rights movement, the often obscured actions taken by African-American and white churchgoers in their homes and sanctuaries. Only by examining the intimate spaces where women, children, border straddlers, interracial couples, integrated congregations, and black power advocates struggled and survived do the mechanisms of social change during the Second Reconstruction become evident. Alongside street marches and mass protests, another kind of demonstration brought an end to de jure segregation. In this kind of demonstration, Vincent Harding challenged his co-believers to move outside segregated communities, Annabelle Conrad married Gerald Hughes, and Larry Voth kept the doors of Community Mennonite open to all. If nothing else, Bethesda members and their co-believers manifested the integrated future sought by marchers in Birmingham, Chicago, and Selma.

The stories of those who stood on Bethesda's church steps also confirm, challenge, and offer new insight into the civil rights movement. Like other evangelical groups, Bethesda congregants favored service and interpersonal initiatives over organized political action; they proposed relational rather than political solutions to racial inequality.[6] Nettie Taylor, a founding member and matriarch of Bethesda, underscored this relational sentiment when she invited other African Americans from Pruitt-Igoe to "come and learn to love white people."[7] Leaders from Community and Woodlawn likewise discovered that Mennonites would support integrated congregations only as long as they focused on service. Attempts to organize political action rarely drew the broader church into the street.

The Bethesda members featured in figure 8.1 also confirm other historical findings. Note the ratio of seven women to three men. On the steps of Bethesda, as in the broader civil rights movement, women played a central role in ending segregation.[8] At Bethesda, Taylor, Smith, Schwartzentruber, and their contemporaries—both those who wore plain clothes and those who did not—led Sunday school classes, organized integrated social activities, and offered sage counsel. In Virginia and elsewhere, Lark exercised new leadership roles, Broad Street matron Fannie Swartzentruber protested Jim Crow communion practices, and Fresh Air participant Margie Middleton challenged her hosts' racial prejudices. The stories of African-American activist and teacher Rosemarie Harding in Atlanta, of white urban missionary Jane Voth in Markham, and of African-American church administrator Joy Lovett await exploration. Throughout these stories, women often led when men hesitated.

Bethesda's pastor Hubert Schwartzentruber and the children who shared the steps with him furthermore confirm church-based legislative advocacy. Schwartzentruber challenged white churchgoers to "support legislation that will help to remove some of the causes" of racial injustice.[9] In particular, churches lobbied hard for the 1964 Civil Rights Act and the Voting Rights Act that became law the following year.[10] Individual church members wrote their senators and representatives for many reasons. The children from Bethesda who stared boldly at the camera represent one of them. Although the children and their parents focused more on obtaining country vacations than politicizing their hosts, they nonetheless profoundly affected those who invited them to the country. In a few significant instances, Fresh Air participants prompted their hosts to enter the political realm by exposing racial prejudice in Mennonite communities. Because pastors like Schwartzentruber and participants like the two children from Bethesda ventured into unknown theological and relational territory, Mennonites and other Christian believers helped overturn legalized disfranchisement.

As the Mennonite experience illustrates, organizers staged civil rights actions in church sanctuaries. Congregations like Bethesda provided space, infrastructural resources, and emotional encouragement for marchers.[11] Schwartzentruber offered additional support by joining public demonstrations. The first time he marched, a bystander called out, "Come and see the stupid preacher marching with them today."[12] By marching and opening their sanctuaries to organizers, pastors like Schwartzentruber invited taunts and physical harassment. Although few Mennonites participated in demonstrations, some joined Schwartzentruber in the streets. Minority Ministries Council member Lynford Hershey frequently demonstrated, as did those who responded to Vincent Harding's 1963 challenge at Prairie Street Mennonite Church in Elkhart, Indiana. Even in a quietist community, some congregations supported civil rights activism by sending church members to take public action.

In addition to confirming evangelical withdrawal, female leadership, and congregational activism, the Mennonites featured in this book demonstrate that activists within congregations and homes need to be treated as part of the civil rights narrative but on their own terms. The church was not just a staging ground for civil rights activity; it was also a site of civil rights activity. To be certain, leaders of an organizing effort like the Montgomery bus boycott depended heavily on churches to house the mass gatherings that offered hope and succor to those who refused to ride segregated public transportation. Yet congregations like Bethesda and other integrated worshipping communities fought their own battles against segregation inside church walls. Although Bethesda members appeared relaxed as they stood on the steps of their church, they struggled to worship across racial lines. The effort to do so could leave leaders discouraged and all too cognizant of the limits of interracial ministry. Reflecting on his years in St. Louis that ended in the uncertainty and tumult of black nationalist calls for racial separation, pastor Hubert Schwartzentruber later recalled, "We tried integration and of course integration didn't work."[13]

Members at Community and Woodlawn also grappled with ecclesiastical integration. By trial and error, they tried to master interracial worship. As they stumbled forward, members of Bethesda, Community, and Woodlawn revealed integration's fault lines. Like leaders of street-based demonstrations, pastors of integrated churches did not always succeed. Just as civil rights movement historians have studied both the failed Albany campaign and the more successful Birmingham venture, scholars have much to learn from the failed Woodlawn and the more successful Community Mennonite congregations. Both of the latter sites reveal concentrated efforts to overturn sectors of a racially segregated society.

This story also challenges the primacy of legislative strategies. Although evangelical groups placed relationships before civil rights action, they sometimes led where public officials followed. At Bethesda, for example, church members welcomed interracial unions. Burrell's marriage to Lois Headings received little comment.[14] By supporting such unions, members from Bethesda, Lee Heights, Woodlawn, and other churches forced their co-believers to reexamine racial assumptions. These congregations fostered intimate contact across racial lines well before the Supreme Court's 1967 *Loving* ruling overturned antimiscegenation laws. At many Mennonite congregations located in African-American neighborhoods, white people came to worship, fell in love with the community, married locally , and, like Annabelle Conrad, never left. Although not comparable in scope to a national Supreme Court ruling, the interracial relationships of all kinds that emerged from congregations like Bethesda were accepted by members of those churches in advance of judiciary action. Members of interracial churches lived in different neighborhoods, ate with differ-ent families, spent money at different businesses, and married different partners than they would have had they belonged to segregated churches. *Loving* may have changed the law, but integrated churches had long before changed people's lives.

The histories of Bethesda and other Mennonite churches also call into question the idea that black nationalists terminated contact with whites. In the main, historians have pointed to the separatist impulse promoted by leaders of the Student Nonviolent Coordinating Committee and other less well known groups like the Revolutionary Action Movement.[15] Many of those same scholars portray the willingness of a group like the Black Pan-thers to ally with white radicals as an exception to the historical norm.[16] On the contrary, the story told in this volume points to ongoing contact between members of the white community and black nationalist groups. Rather than end all dialogue, black nationalists kept talking to the very people they claimed to disown. Schwartzentruber again provides an ex-ample. In 1967 "the most militant black power leader" in Pruitt-Igoe asked Schwartzentruber for "a meeting place for youth."[17] The local leader kept talking with Schwartzentruber even though the pastor remained ambiva-lent about the request. Similarly, Student Nonviolent Coordinating Com-mittee chairman Stokely Carmichael, his successor H. Rap Brown, and Black Panther Eldridge Cleaver frequently spoke before white audiences. In the Mennonite church, leaders of the Minority Ministries Council also conversed with white people. John Powell and his contemporaries asked for reparations and stayed to talk about it. James Forman and his Black Manifesto emissaries did the same. Woodlawn pastor Curtis Burrell dia-logued with white Mennonites well past the point when Mennonite offi-cials cut ties with him. Rather than voicing a one-sided demand, the black power movement looks like a pointed call for conversation.

Evidence of such sustained contact points to a broader interpretation of the civil rights movement. Rather than an increasingly segregated and splintered movement that ended in a collapse upon the assassination of

Martin Luther King Jr. in 1968, the movement in support of racial justice continued to attract white and black members alike. Although the nature of the contact had changed, the presence of ongoing conversations, however strained and contentious, provides evidence of an interracial network that had not disintegrated as much as contemporary accounts and later historians have suggested.[18] The beloved community praised by King may not have come to fruition in the way he envisioned, but an interracial network nonetheless emerged out of the public purview that fostered contact and conversation across racial lines.

The Mennonites studied in this work also provide new insight into the inner workings of the civil rights movement. Children, for example, appear more central to civil rights initiatives. The grinning children on Bethesda's steps represent the thousands of Fresh Air participants who challenged racism in white homes during the 1950s and '60s. Because they entered foreign territory, they prompted their hosts to take new action. Such action, however, came at a cost. For all the courage and determination displayed by the Fresh Air children, their stories also reveal an unsettling strand of paternalism and misuse. Some adults hosted children to establish their credentials as racial egalitarians at a time when critics labeled them racists. Others forced their relatively powerless charges to conform to standards of belief and social practice that did not make sense in the children's home communities. Still other Fresh Air providers assumed the worst of the children and claimed that the white, rural way of life was superior to the children's African-American, urban existence. Such actions did significant harm. At the same time, the children found creative ways to resist their hosts' paternalism by acting boisterous, building friendships, and connecting with their peers from home. The stories of Margie Middleton, Albert Potts, Sammy, Jerry Smith, and their contemporaries reveal that children brought the movement to communities untouched by adult organizers.

Likewise, Fresh Air hosts, white missionaries, and African-American converts maintained strong social networks. June and Hubert Schwartzentruber stayed in touch with Curtis Burrell for many years.[19] A young woman who taught Sunday school in Bethesda in St. Louis also worked at an integrated mission church in Reading, Pennsylvania.[20] A volunteer from Andrews Bridge in southern Lancaster County later served at Glad Tidings in New York City.[21] As church members nurtured friendships and workers volunteered at multiple mission stations, connections among race workers flourished. The missionaries and converts relied on friends and acquaintances from this network to challenge racism among Mennonites. This informal social network sustained efforts to end segregation in the church in the same way that intergenerational contacts between older and younger activists supported street action.[22]

In addition to insight into children's activism and social networks, this study of Anabaptists also reveals that church doctrine both undermined and supported efforts to end ecclesiastical Jim Crow practices. Hubert Schwartzentruber, for example, articulated well the danger of Mennonite theology. He noted that anemic interpretations of discipleship repulsed African Americans who ventured into the church when "fine words about conscientious objection and nonresistance" did not translate into tangible action for racial justice.[23] As a result, he excoriated "the mickey mouse stuff" taught by some Mennonite leaders.[24] Schwartzentruber may have been referring to executives from the Lancaster Conference who responded to the Black Manifesto by steering attention away from reparations. In this instance and elsewhere, the bishops claimed separation from the sinful world and thus obscured the church's participation in worldly racism.

Along with Lancaster bishops, others across the church found their integrity reduced by the separatist doctrine of nonconformity. Although church leaders from the (Old) Mennonite Church side of the community struggled to promote commitments to separatist belief while leaders on the General Conference side spent less time defining nonconformity in terms of dress and other distinctive practices, members from both denominations continued to articulate an identity defined by collective separation. When that nonconformist perspective combined with racial prejudice, many white Mennonites came to view African-American converts with intense suspicion. Those who inhabited the pristine terrain of nonconformed Christianity from birth viewed those who came from the former sinful world as alien and different, an otherness compounded by white Mennonites' unexamined racial prejudice. To say the least, the juxtaposition of doctrine and racial ideology proved volatile.

At the same time, many African Americans joined the church because of doctrine and, following their entry, confounded white Mennonites' expectations. The Anabaptist vision of social justice and spiritual atone-

ment attracted Curtis Burrell, Betty Gwinn, Vincent Harding, Gerald
Hughes, Rowena Lark, Margie Middleton, and other African-American
converts.[25] Once in the Mennonite church, they refused to accept sub-
ordinate status. They led, demanded full membership, and claimed both
black and Mennonite identities. In response, some of their white co-believers rejected stereotypes that depicted African Americans as inferior,
second-class believers. Other white Mennonites rejected the challenges
brought by African-American converts. In 1952 a church member in Chicago rebuffed the Larks' leadership by claiming that "lassitude, and im-
morality" defined the African-American community.[26] Three years later
officials from the Ohio Conference denied ministerial credentials to Gerald Hughes because he had married a white woman.[27] In the 1970s white
Mennonites in Atlanta forced African-American pastoral leaders Betty
and Macon Gwinn to step down from their leadership at Berea Mennonite during a time of church growth. The white leaders "of Mennonite
origin" had registered their complaints with leaders from the sponsoring
conference body because they felt "there shouldn't be change."[28] Despite
such evidence of racism in the church, many African-American Mennonites continued to promote and claim church doctrine as their own. Others found the inconsistencies overwhelming and left. Mennonite church
doctrine thus both repelled and attracted African Americans.

Study of the civil rights movement has already shown that Christian
doctrine could support activism as easily as the status quo. This study
adds nuance to that insight by directing attention inside the church.
Other historians have claimed that church doctrine pushed believers into
the street to either end segregation or support it. *Daily Demonstrators* argues that church doctrine also pushed believers into the church to either
end segregation or support it. Of course, some churchgoers found ways
to remain active in both the street and the church. Regardless of where
church members became involved, their actions suggest that church doctrine was neither one-directional nor one-dimensional. The faith commitments affirmed by believers pushed and pulled for better and for worse.
In short, belief balanced. For every doctrinal commitment that attracted
an African-American convert, another blocked his or her entry. For every
statement of belief prompting a white Mennonite to welcome a visitor
regardless of skin color, another encouraged suspicion and cold distance.

A New Civil Rights Story

Although its focus has been on the Mennonite church, this narrative as-
sumes that most white-majority religious groups during the 1940s, '50s,
and '60s crossed the color line in a similar manner. Like Mennonites, Protestant and Catholic groups also practiced paternalism, struggled to integrate their services, and hesitated to take part in street-based civil rights
activism. The divide between church leaders who urgently pursued racial
justice and grassroots members who remained skeptical of such action also
tied Mennonites to other Christian communities. Although the Mennonite story bristles with details often missing from larger and less contentious communities, the story told here parallels other plots.

This story unearths a number of new insights about the civil rights
movement. One is that children played a significant part in the daily
demonstrations for racial justice. The record of Fresh Air children who
challenged their hosts' political commitments reveals the young people's
frontline activism. Rather than a controversial exception in the annals of
street action, the children's march during the 1963 Birmingham campaign becomes a public representation of a common though less dramatic
exchange between African-American children and white adults. African-
American children also encountered white adults through Sunday school
programs, widely popular vacation bible schools during the 1950s and
early 1960s, and recreational summer programs. Although the children
held significantly less power than the adults with whom they came in
contact, they nonetheless attracted the attention, time, and resources of
the white church members simply by attending such programs in large
numbers. When situated as an essential part of the civil rights movement,
children emerge as first responders to the paternalism of the white church.
African-American children encountered—and were frequently damaged
by—the kind of white, paternalistic action African-American adults
sought to eradicate.

The civil rights movement is also revealed as encompassing a greater
variety of resistance activity than previously thought. No cameras rolled as
Fannie Swartzentruber marched out of Broad Street Mennonite in 1944
to protest segregated communion services, but every member of that congregation and those they told about the disturbance paid close attention
nonetheless. Although reporters failed to cover Faye Mitchell, Ola Mae

Smith, and Johnetta Wooden when they integrated Community Mennonite Church in 1961, the women influenced those around them as much
as the Little Rock Nine influenced the students, faculty and staff at Central High. Rowena Lark's long-term commitment to asserting her church
membership by wearing Mennonite attire also drew little public comment but made a strong impression on members of her church community.
When Lynford Hershey set up weekend seminars to bring members of
the Minority Ministries Council into contact with white rural pastors,
the national press did not send reporters to cover the events; nonetheless,
the encounters changed lives. In addition to street marches, boycotts, sit-
ins, and picketing, the civil rights movement also involved congregational
walkouts, integration visitations, distinctive attire, and structured seminars within religious groups.

In the story told in *Daily Demonstrators*, the movement was more contradictory and less defined by moral contrasts than is usually suggested.
Within the Mennonite community, racial oppressors were also racial egalitarians: The Mennonites who segregated church sacraments in Virginia
also integrated an institution of higher education before other colleges in
the commonwealth.[29] The Lancaster Conference leaders who baptized the
first African-American Mennonites segregated their worship services before their southern counterparts. The mission board that challenged segregation in Gulfport, Mississippi, addressed racial prejudice in their home
base of Newton, Kansas, with much less enthusiasm. Rather than a story
defined by faultless street marchers and evil segregationist mobs, this new
story of the civil rights movement follows individuals and institutions re-
plete with multiple commitments, contradictory impulses, and unpredict-
able allegiances.

Significantly, the story told in *Daily Demonstrators* paints a civil rights
movement less dependent on charismatic heroes than traditional scholarship has suggested. Long before I conceived this project, southern white
writer and racial progressive Lillian Smith observed that a "great many
internal acts" changed the racial order.[30] Those internal acts required
less dramatic heroism and more quotidian determination. The bravery
of Medgar Evers, Fannie Lou Hamer, Martin Luther King Jr., and other
street marchers should not overshadow the courage displayed by Gerald
Hughes, Rowena Lark, Nettie Taylor, and other internal actors. Although
the latter group did not endure police brutality, death threats, or mob re-

prisals, they faced antagonists in the intimate spaces of home and congregation on a recurring basis. Instead of tear gas, nightsticks, and police dogs, they faced groping hands, demeaning names, and slammed doors. As Lillian Smith suggested, these daily acts of resistance proved as necessary as street mobilization.

The "internal acts" mentioned by Smith depended on much the same kind of character and insight as street action. When Bethesda pastor Hubert Schwartzentruber advised Minority Ministries Council staffer Lynford Hershey to "absorb the hostility" directed at African Americans and other people of color, he pointed to a strategy that required repeated exposure to emotional aggression.[31] When Vincent Harding and Lancaster Conference secretary Paul Landis held frank discussions about their working relationship, they disrupted a pattern of paternalism common among Mennonites.[32] As Rosella Regier, a white staffer of Camp Landon in Gulfport, Mississippi, and Lizzy Barnett, an African-American resident from the area, prodded the local bookstore to sell John Howard Giffin's Black Like Me by organizing residents to request it, they adapted to local conditions.[33] These internal acts required the same kind of long-term commitment, relational depth, and strategic creativity displayed in the most successful public campaigns of the civil rights movement.

This new story of the Second Reconstruction flattens out the civil rights timeline. The popular narrative of the freedom struggle starts in Montgomery with the boycotting of buses, rises to Birmingham with encounters with fire hoses, and collapses in Memphis with the killing of King. When sanctuaries and living rooms take their place alongside streets and sidewalks, the storyline evens out across time. Rowena Lark and Fannie Swartzentruber nourished their friendship from 1937 through 1970. Fresh Air children clamored for rural vacations throughout the 1950s and 1960s. African-American and white Mennonites kept worshipping together long past King's assassination. The relationships, programs, and worship spaces that emerge from study of internal acts appear less vulnerable to dramatic crescendo and collapse.

The narratives contained in this volume ultimately reposition the role of religion in the civil rights movement. As noted in the preface, much has already been made of the Mennonite church's role in both supporting and impeding efforts to overturn segregation and secure civil rights. Scholars have capably demonstrated the ways in which the church provided motivation, infrastructural resources, and rhetorical power to movement participants.[34] Another body of scholarship documents the church's role in fostering positions opposed to racial justice.[35] The contribution offered through this text notes that religious community in the era of the civil rights movement was a part of that movement, not just its ground or a means of contributing to it. Racial freedom is incomplete unless it extends to religious groups. James Forman recognized the importance of the religious community to full freedom when he addressed his Black Manifesto to sanctuaries and synagogues rather than civic groups and business associations. To analyze the period effectively, historians also need to include religious actors.

Finally, the new story explored among Mennonites suggests fruitful research opportunities for other religious communities as well. Existing studies usually ask how the church became involved in movement sites rather than how the church became a site of the movement. Nancy Ammerman's treatment of Baptists, John McGreevy's exploration of northern Catholics, and Peter Murray's work on the Methodists, while rich and worthy of attention on their own merits, nonetheless underemphasize the centrality of the church as a civil rights arena.[36] Even David L. Chappell, whose masterful text *Inside Agitators: White Southerners in the Civil Rights Movement* reveals the breadth of and divisions within white southern thought, focuses on the streets and sidewalks and treats action inside sanctuaries as a staging ground for public organizing.[37] Scholars of other religious communities, including Jewish, Islamic, Bahá'í, and other groups outside the Protestant majority, can approach their subjects with full confidence that they study the very center of the civil rights story.

A New Mennonite Story

This volume tells not only a new story of civil rights but also a new Mennonite story. The race relations narrative chronicled within the Mennonite community has been typified by a mixture of self-congratulation and unease. Leaders from the church have made note of Mennonite involvement in the first written protest against slavery in the British colonies.[38] Members of the church community have also pointed to the record of the early inclusion of African Americans in Mennonite communities beginning in 1897 in the Lancaster Conference.[39] Indeed, the community received encomiums from external sources as well. The passage of the 1955 (Old) Mennonite Church statement, "The Way of Christian Love in Race Relations," drew the praise of other denominational groups for its clarity and grounding in the biblical text.[40] African-American residents from the mountains of southeastern Pennsylvania stated in 1963 that Mennonite mission workers were "more helpful than any other single church group."[41] Members of the 1967 U.S. Congress heard about Mennonites' good works in places like Harlem.[42]

Yet leaders also noted the underside of Mennonite race relations from the 1940s forward. Mennonites from the General Conference community, like Peace and Social Concerns secretary Leo Driedger, opposed their co-believers' "hesitancy to receive Negroes into our brotherhood" in 1960.[43] Already in 1952, Guy Hershberger, the secretary of the Mennonite Church's version of the General Conference's social issues committee, drew attention to Mennonites' "condescending attitudes" toward African Americans.[44] Those who praised and those who critiqued the church's race relations record treated the problems as anomalies and the successes as the norm.[45] In the main, Mennonites told a story in which racism came from the outside world into the church but never the reverse.

The narrative presented here suggests that the relationship between white Mennonites and African Americans within and without the church emerged from the church's core convictions. Racial problems and successes both came from within the church community. Social practice and acculturation likewise played important roles in shaping how African-American and white Mennonites interacted, but convictions about nonresistance, humility, community, and, most important, nonconformity proved central. As noted in chapter 1, the Mennonite commitment to separate from a sinful world both attracted and repelled African Americans. Similarly, the belief that the community had successfully separated itself from sinful influences made it difficult to uproot racial prejudice. Few white Mennonites recognized that their cherished beliefs helped sustain proscribed actions.

From this perspective, the story of Mennonite race relations requires careful retelling. Racial intolerance and overt oppression need to be framed as common practice rather than as exceptions. Racial prejudices need to be assessed as present within the church, not merely as contagion from outside. Historians and theologians alike can gain from reappraising doctrines that were as likely to exclude as include. The church looks different when redemptive words are shown to augment exclusionary deeds. Mennonites have a story to tell that is no less essential for being filled with as much racial animus as egalitarianism.

More specifically, the evidence presented in this volume suggests that the civil rights movement chapter of the Mennonite race relations story can no longer be told as a distant and somewhat irrelevant tale. Those same living room and sanctuary settings that prove integral to a complete telling of the Second Reconstruction also fill in narrative cracks in the Mennonite history of that time. The relationship between Rowena Lark and Fannie Swartzentruber not only underlines the importance of long-term relationships in the civil rights movement but also shows that Mennonite nonconformist symbols like prayer coverings held many more meanings than were recognized by church leaders. Vincent Harding's ability to straddle borders and the Mennonite response to his activity across region and internal division reveal one way that movement leaders changed social segregation. The story of John Powell and other members of the Minority Ministries Council shows that interracial dialogue about reparations continued far longer than suggested by street-based activity and also illustrates how Mennonite leaders and grassroots members alike hesitated to support racially egalitarian commitments with financial resources. The meaning of religious symbols, the consistency of racial response, and the integrity of verbal commitments constitute the heart, rather than the extremities, of Mennonite history.

Others joined the daily demonstrators who operated within Mennonite settings. We already know that Southern Baptists clashed over whether to engage in evangelism or activism in the same way Mennonites struggled over quietism and public witness.[46] Like Rowena Lark and Fannie Swartzentruber, women in the Methodist community fought long and hard to change their denomination's discriminatory practices.[47] Episcopalians, Presbyterians, and Roman Catholics also debated the Black Manifesto.[48] Within their homes and sanctuaries, members of these religious communities held many of the same sorts of conversations, developed similarly lasting relationships, and participated in programs like Fresh Air exchanges that brought African-American and white children and adults into intimate contact.

These stories are integral chapters of the civil rights narrative. Some of those accounts have already been told and need only new frames to place them at the center of the Second Reconstruction. Others need fresh attention to bring them out of obscurity. This volume suggests some of the more fruitful avenues of research to make that retelling possible. Within the Mennonite community, study of interracial marriage has revealed especially intense discussions of the most intimate of encounters across racial lines. The records of racial caucuses have surfaced unexpected conversations about black nationalism. The evidence from times and locations where interracial encounters took place—whether through hosting programs, urban missions, or integrated congregations—has pointed to stories that deepen and enrich our understanding of organized struggles for racial justice in the middle of the twentieth century. Only when researchers in other religious communities start at similar locations and follow the evidence will a more complete telling of the civil rights story be possible.

From the City to the Sacred

In 1944 Virginia, African Americans still sat at the back of the bus. In at least one instance, so did a white Mennonite. Harry A. Brunk had traveled from Harrisonburg, a Mennonite enclave nestled in the Shenandoah Valley, to Staunton, about thirty miles to the southwest. A teacher of history at Eastern Mennonite College, which at that point restricted membership to white students, Brunk also ran a small farm and wrote Mennonite histories. He spent the day of July 25 examining probate records in the Augusta County clerk's office. By four o'clock, he had completed his research and struck out for the bus station. Evidently, the Staunton-Harrisonburg route drew numerous commuters, both white and black. Brunk could find a seat only in the "colored apartment" in the "very back seat of the bus." Reflecting later on his ride home, he commented, "My but it was hot."[49]

Approximately six years later, another white Mennonite from Virginia rode a segregated bus. In the early 1950s, Goldie Hummel boarded a bus for Delaware along with two daughters of Roberta Webb, one of the first African Americans to become a member at the Gay Street Mission in Harrisonburg, where Rowena Lark and Fannie Swartzentruber worked together. Hummel, who would later marry and take the surname Hostetler, had served in India with the Mennonite Board of Missions since 1948. While studying at Eastern Mennonite College before beginning her service overseas, she and her friend Tillie Yoder had met with college president John Stauffer to protest the school's segregationist policy. Stauffer explained that, despite his sympathy for the young women's position, objections from local Virginia Mennonites made change impractical.[50] Yet the year after Hummel left for India, administrators at her alma mater defied local custom and admitted Ada Webb. As Hummel and the Webb sisters settled in for the bus trip that would take them to summer jobs in a seafood restaurant, the three young women brought with them that history of activism within the Mennonite church. Unlike Professor Brunk, they did not sit quietly in the back. Hummel explained, "I could have sat on a seat by myself so that white folks could sit by me. Instead I sat with one of the girls and the other sat in the seat before me. No one sat by her." She concluded, "We were a little bit ornery. On the way up we sang that song 'There's Plenty Good Room in my Father's Kingdom.'"[51]

These two stories raise the question, How do we best describe the race relations efforts of white and African-American Mennonites? This book has used the trope of daily demonstration to describe interracial off-street action. But is that description ultimately sufficient? Does it capture the full breadth of Mennonite racial exchange during the 1940s, '50s, and '60s? Does it limit Mennonites' ability to speak beyond sectarian confines? Harry Brunk, Goldie Hummel, and the Webb sisters suggest that the daily demonstrators label fosters new inquiry into the civil rights movement even while limiting analysis of city-country, church-state, and sacred-secular relationships.

The two bus sojourns described here—one short, one long—delineate the classic signs of racial resistance. Although not an activist by any means, Brunk nonetheless opposed the racial order by sitting at the back of the bus without complaint. He was discomforted more by the temperature than by the racial company. During their much longer trip, Hummel and the Webb sisters arranged themselves to point out the contradictions of segregated seating. As they sang hymns laced with sacred irony, they challenged other passengers to recognize that Jim Crow custom alone kept a seat unfilled on a crowded bus. All involved knowingly crossed boundaries maintained by the state. All did so in light of their faith commitments. Hummel came to know the Webb sisters through her involvement at Gay Street. Brunk commented on race relations during the semidevotional act of writing diary entries. While they would not have described themselves in those terms at the time, Brunk, Hummel, and the Webb sisters were demonstrators of the most daily variety and, like the other Mennonites chronicled in this text, acted up in off-street venues.

At the same time, the label of daily demonstrator may obscure other traits of Mennonite action. Most immediately, these and other stories reveal previously unexplored connections between city and country. Brunk makes the case. He both taught and farmed. Besides setting up classroom debates about slavery, he tended produce, coaxed reluctant machinery into action, and marketed greenhouse flowers. For him, going to the city meant going to Harrisonburg, a town that by 1970 claimed fewer than twenty thousand residents. Although he kept track of current events, eventually by acquiring a radio, and commented on the passage of the 1964 Civil Rights Act, he focused first and foremost on his Mennonite and agrarian worlds.

The observations of this rural scholar were more about cities than about color. His diaries mention only a few other encounters with African Americans. At one point he asked for directions to the Norfolk courthouse from a "portly colored man."[52] On a long train trip, he bought pictures of Harper's Ferry from a "colored porter."[53] He described such encounters only in passing. More typically, trips to urban centers like Norfolk or Staunton received more attention. In Brunk's world, city sojourns trumped daily demonstrations. He spent more time writing about the weather or his purchase of a radio than about encounters with African Americans. Brunk was, in short, a country man, centered on farm life and sectarian scholarship rather than racial agitation on the streets or sidewalks.

Many of Brunk's students had similar worldviews. The youthful evangelists who ventured into the African-American section of Harrisonburg in the 1930s and '40s did so under the umbrella of the Young Peoples Christian Association's "City Workers Band."[54] Local reports referred to the African-American Broad Street congregation and its segregated Chicago Avenue white counterpart as the "City Missions."[55] The mission workers not only commented about "gross sin and vice" among "colored people in Harrisonburg," they also defined the objects of their evangelism in urban terms.[56] Their reports are filled with references to streets and sidewalks, alcoholism, and imprisonment, terms identical to those used by urban reformers from the turn of the century forward. In a country that by 1920 had become more urban than rural, the Mennonites of Virginia—

like most of their coreligionists in the period of this study—saw themselves as visitors and outsiders to the city. Given the forces that led to the
Great Migrations of the early twentieth century beginning around 1915,
many African Americans had begun to see themselves as urban insiders.
The white Mennonites who evangelized African Americans came as rural
representatives to a city setting.

Mennonite debates over street protest arose in part from rural distrust
of the city. Mennonite bishops approved the involvement of Rowena Lark
in the Gay Street summer vacation bible school program, but they called
her "a colored sister of Washington, D.C.," the biggest city in the area.[57]
At the time, Rowena, James, and their children lived on a farm in rural
Pennsylvania; she only worked in the city.[58] Those who opposed Vincent
Harding knew that he came from a definitively urban background, having
grown up in New York City, and that he served the highest-profile urban
ministry at the time, Woodlawn Mennonite. Throughout their involvement with the Fresh Air programs, Mennonite hosts and promoters used
labels like "city children" more often than "Negro," "colored," or "Spanish"
to describe their young guests.[59] Church planters in Chicago, Cleveland,
New York, and Philadelphia ran afoul of dress and lifestyle dictates that
originated in rural ecclesiastic power centers. One minister in New York
City complained to his bishop that plain clothes undermined "the work
and witness of the church," since urbanites viewed plain suits, prayer
veils, and cape dresses as symbols of "a cult."[60] As these various references
suggest, when Mennonites crossed racial lines, they also traversed urban
and rural boundaries.

Such a dual crossing of both race and city points to larger questions
beyond civil rights. The first of those asks whether the city has always
initiated change. Popular assumptions and many a formal history trace a
trajectory of innovation starting in the city and moving to the country.
Breakthroughs in transportation, manufacturing, governance, and entertainment have frequently followed this vector. In the 1940s, '50s, and
'60s, however, Mennonites made clear that change could also initiate in
the country and move toward the city. Fresh Air children demonstrated
on the front lines of the civil rights movement in white rural homes and
brought perspectives from their time in the country back to the city. Vincent Harding immersed himself in the theology of peace and nonresistance
that had been treasured and cared for by rural Mennonites and brought

those doctrines to the city. Rural Mennonite pastors feared interruption from urban Black Manifesto emissaries, but they also asked their urban counterparts to think of the manifesto as a document about nonviolence rather than racial reparations. In so doing, they shifted attention from racial inequities in their own church, but the shift nonetheless began in rural Lancaster County and moved on to Philadelphia and New York.

In short, Mennonites raised questions about the relationship of city and country. Although the sheer size and demographic weight of urban complexes favored city dominance, the country also played a role. Rather than simply reacting to their urban cousins, the rural Mennonites featured in this book initiated substantive changes. From Fresh Air hosts to nonresistant bishops, Mennonites from the country did not wait upon the city before acting. When white Kansan Mennonite and General Conference Church executive Henry A. Fast personally applauded President Johnson for passage of the 1964 Civil Rights Act, he lent the support of a rural people who championed civil rights legislation in part because they brought city children into their rural homes. Rather than waiting for the city to creep up to their doorstep, they sought the city on their own terms.

Fast's proactive initiative engenders multiple queries. Although complete answers require fuller treatment than this study allows, the questions themselves deserve attention. The Mennonite story of action in both city and country asks, How did rural and urban denizens influence each other during the middle three decades of the twentieth century? Which metaphors best describe their interaction? Has the city's size obscured rural action in the same way that street action has obscured daily demonstrations? Did rural or urban labels ever mask racial dynamics? Did racial labels ever conceal demographic exchange?

Such questions suggest additional research projects worthy of future attention, but a few observations may offer initial insight. During the period of this study the city and the country seemed to have depended upon mutual innovation and challenge. As *Daily Demonstrators* has shown, sanctuary-centered action supported street-based agitation. Together, they altered the nation's racial order. Although street action often prompted living room efforts, those who demonstrated in less public locations brought civil rights initiatives to otherwise untouched venues. In the same way, the city transformed the country by rendering sectarian dress dictates irrelevant, by making mass-produced mechanical innovations like the tractor widely available, and by providing a home—albeit often a hostile and aggressive one—to African Americans oppressed in southern segregated hamlets and excluded from northern sundown towns. At the same time, the country changed the city as it sent its youth to proselytize urban neighborhoods, uprooted tens of thousands of city children each summer for two-week stays in rural locales, and provided figures like Harding and King with theological grounding for their nonviolent initiatives.[61] In the pockets and places where city and country collided, no one left unchanged.

The civil rights movement thus tells an urban and a rural tale. We already know that the Southern Christian Leadership Conference conducted high-profile campaigns in the cities of Albany, Birmingham, and Chicago. Alongside those urban-centered ventures, Student Nonviolent Coordinating Committee workers organized effectively in rural locations like Lowndes County, Mississippi. Fannie Lou Hamer hailed from the Mississippi delta and, with uncommon courage, registered African-American voters in rural settings. Activists like Septima Clark, Medgar Evers, Amzie Moore, and Bob and Dottie Zellner likewise worked primarily in rural settings. Mennonites like Curtis Burrell, Lynford Hershey, Gerald and Annabelle Hughes, and Orlo Kaufman either came from or worked predominantly in the country to change the church's attitude and actions about race relations. Albany, Birmingham, Chicago, and Montgomery may have garnered headlines, but Americus, Georgia; Blue Ball, Pennsylvania; Goshen, Indiana; and Macon, Mississippi, fostered change. In these latter, smaller, rural locales, activists took risks equal to those that journalists wrote about in urban centers. Klansmen murdered student voter registration activists James Chaney, Andrew Goodman, and Michael Schwerner near the rural town of Philadelphia, Mississippi, not the major urban center of Philadelphia, Pennsylvania. Rural workers formed the backbone of the civil rights movement.

The stories of white and African-American Mennonites that raise questions about urban-centered innovation also generate queries into the relationship of church and state. Popular narratives again provide a starting point. School children learn that the United States' most treasured documents mandate church-state separation. At the same time, by the 1940s politicians—with a few notable exceptions—had accepted that they had to evoke religious affiliation to gain office. While state bodies held no authority over religious communities, membership in a mainline Protestant group offered political legitimacy as no civic membership could. Politicians who claimed Jewish, Hindu, Muslim, Bahá'í, or even Catholic affiliation, however, saw election bids fizzle. The separation of church and state, whether or not one takes Mennonites into account, was, at best, complicated.

Such an involved relationship demands even more thorough analysis when viewed from the perspective of the Mennonite story. Mennonites witnessed to government officials with new deliberation during World War II when they lobbied for conscientious objector status and alternative service options on behalf of their young men. In the 1950s and '60s, Vincent Harding and white allies like Delton Franz, Marie Regier, and Hubert Schwartzentruber insisted that their co-believers show integrity by lobbying for racial justice as actively as they had pursued conscientious objector status. As a result of their advocacy, a number of Mennonites from both the (Old) and General Conference communities contacted their elected representatives in support of civil rights legislation. Although other historians have pointed out the importance of church-based advocacy in the passage of the 1964 civil rights bill, few have noted the involvement of a sectarian group that had previously refrained from calling its members to political action.[62] The relationship between Mennonites and the state had changed.[63] The question is not whether the change took place but how best to describe it.

One approach posits that Mennonites in the (Old) and General Conference denominations became skeptical observers. Even if they did not shift from writing letters to marching in the streets, some monitored state action with new attention. Mennonites like historian and farmer Harry A. Brunk began to keep closer tabs on the government. The day after President Johnson signed the 1964 Civil Rights Act into law, Brunk noted the occasion of its passing and the limits of its reach. Although a "very important piece of legislation," he wrote, it would take "some thing more than law" to bring about substantive change.[64] Perhaps he knew that members of Lee Heights Church in Cleveland had already begun to change attitudes in their neighborhood and church by embracing the interracial marriage of Annabelle Conrad and Gerald Hughes long before the legislature or judiciary ended miscegenation laws in 1967. His diary confirms that he knew African-American Mennonite Roberta Webb. Almost certainly he knew of African-American church planter and preacher Rowena Lark. In a close-knit community like Harrisonburg, he also would most likely have known of the friendships between Webb, Lark, and Fannie Swartzen-truber and their common challenge to the church's segregation practice. He had witnessed Eastern Mennonite College open its doors to African-American students like Webb's daughter Ada six years before the 1954 *Brown v. Board of Education* ruling. As Brunk monitored the government's actions in the 1950s, '60s, and '70s, he did so with a skeptical eye, informed by the actions of daily demonstrations all around him.

The skeptical observer role that Mennonites like Brunk defined for themselves calls for new interpretive schemes. Spatial metaphors, those that define church-state relationships in terms of distance, prove less help-ful in illuminating history than do those of content and dynamic. A spatial metaphor would suggest that Brunk and his Mennonite contemporaries moved closer to the state in the same way that spies creep forward seeking unobstructed sight lines or neighbors bend over backyard fences strain-ing to eavesdrop. By contrast, rather than evaluating the relative distance between church and state, interpretive metaphors focus on content and dynamic to assess the nature of the relationship.

For instance, an alternate way to describe Brunk's relationship to the state suggests that, by observing state action, he picked up a new garden-ing tool, the hoe of observation and advocacy. Such an instrument had long been available. Other gardeners outside the Mennonite church regularly used such an implement. But by tradition, few Mennonites had. They pre-ferred to garden by hand, to avoid both observation and advocacy. Only after outsiders pointed to the inconsistency in public witness did Menno-nites seek new tools. By the beginning of the 1970s, some Mennonites had begun to use observation and advocacy in earnest. Many would continue to use traditional forms, of evangelism and daily demonstration. But some Mennonites had chosen advocacy and, in some settings, received church blessing for doing so. Although such proactive implements would long feel uncomfortable in the hands of many church members, more so among (Old) Mennonites than their General Conference cousins, that church members had picked them up and not been disowned made future use inevitable.

Thus even as the city and the country intertwine, so too do the church and state. Historians of this period need to set aside questions that interrogate the distance between the two entities. They can instead ask, How did already intertwined relationships change? How long did these last? Who shaped them? In what order did they develop? How frequently did they develop? Such questions change not only the metaphors employed to explain the past but also the avenues of inquiry down which historians travel. In the case of Mennonites, interpersonal exchange at the grassroots level again took priority over public action. The full interweaving of church and state relationships manifested in the midst of those quotidian interactions.

Finally, this chronicle raises questions about the division between the secular and sacred during the middle three decades of the twentieth century. In the past, scholars of religion divided religious practice and worldly engagement into separate spheres. More recent scholarship, especially in studies of the African-American religious experience, has challenged such rigid boundary setting. In contemporary studies, religious adherents appear as highly engaged citizens who connect individual salvation to collective action, bring political leaders into worship spaces, and claim divine prompting in the midst of specific historical stimuli.[65] More than anything, scholars argue that the sacred and the secular interpenetrate.[66] This study does not challenge that basic observation but does raise questions about its applicability across time. In the 1940s, Goldie Hummel and the Webb sisters would have had few opportunities to travel from sacred space into the secular world as equals. In the 1950s, they challenged secular Jim Crow bus regulations with sacred tools: church hymns and interracial fellowship. By the 1960s, they might have responded differently, perhaps by both praying and writing letters to local state representatives. The walls between the secular and the sacred may have been exceedingly thin; that is not in question. But the manner of their relating across the sacred-secular divide changed over time.

How does this basic observation about diachronic change in the relationship of the sacred and the secular shape our understanding of the civil rights movement? Some have claimed that, as a revival, the movement surpassed the Great Awakenings in scope and impact.[67] Others, that charismatic leaders like King and Ralph Abernathy clothed a political campaign in religious rhetoric but ultimately based their campaign outside the church.[68] This narrative asks whether the fundamental observation beneath those claims—that civil rights participants chose between the secular and the sacred—assists in the interpretive work of history. Are there more effective framing devices than secular-sacred dichotomies? Can students of the civil rights movement and U.S. history adopt analytical frameworks that acknowledge religious practitioners' deep engagement with all aspects of society and pay attention to how their actions change over time? How can historians craft narratives about periods of significant change that do not separate the streets and sidewalks from the pulpit, bimah, altar, or prayer rug? Humans practice religion. They appear resolute in this pursuit. How can scholars describe religious practice with precision and nuance without replicating past interpretive errors? This study suggests one approach, deliberately setting aside questions of distance between street and sanctuary, city and country, church and state, and the sacred and secular. Other approaches remain to be discovered. By paying attention to shifts over time, setting aside clear demarcation between religious and secular pursuits, and discarding spatial metaphors, clearer more definitive understandings of the civil rights movement may yet emerge.

And so we come back to buses. Civil rights movement narratives have frequently featured buses: those that Bayard Rustin and others rode in 1947 in a failed attempt to enforce integrated interstate travel, those that ran empty because of boycotts in Baton Rouge in 1953 and in Montgomery two years later, and those that burned because Freedom Riders integrated them in 1961. Although the bus that Goldie Hummel and the Webb sisters rode to Delaware and the one that carried Harry A. Brunk home to Harrisonburg never appeared on the nightly news, they lumber through history carrying new insight. These lesser-known buses, like those examined by Robin Kelley in his study of working-class commuters who protested maltreatment by spitting in the faces of bus drivers, open new lines of inquiry into where change came about, how religious commitments and orientations shaped that change, and the manner in which both state and church responded.[69] We understand the civil rights movement better because we now also know of buses on which Goldie Hummel and the Webb sisters acted ornery while singing sacred hymns and where Harry A. Brunk willingly wedged himself into the back seat and so into integration.

Heirs of an Inside Movement

For four days in August 1976 a small group of Mennonites came together to focus on racism. As participants in a seminar sponsored by a group of evangelical Christians committed to putting their faith into action, the integrated group joined Baptists, Brethren in Christ, and about two hundred other Christian practitioners in a "last-ditch effort to catalyze action to attack racism in church and social institutions." Planners brought in secular speakers like Lerone Bennett, a historian and *Ebony* senior editor, and members of the religious community like Vernon Grounds, president of the Conservative Baptist Seminary in Denver. In addition to listening to plenary talks, seminar participants joined task forces, where they laid plans to "confront racism" in local congregations, at church-sponsored schools, throughout denominational boards, and in the arts and media.[70]

The group met in Newark, New Jersey. Nine years earlier, that city had been the site of a racial uprising triggered by an instance of police brutality and quelled by even more violent law enforcement action. Soon after the violent street activity, more than a thousand African Americans traveled to Newark to participate in the Black Power Conference, the second national gathering of African-American politicians and activists focused on bringing the black power agenda into the political realm. Although the two conferences held little in common other than locale—the 1967 conference was political, the 1976 group, religious—participants in both gatherings planned how to confront racism. Their strategies, however, differed. The 1967 conference encouraged "economic development, community control, armed self-defense, and black identity."[71] Eleven years later, the church group focused on education of people in the pew. Yet the two groups shared an underlying analysis of the problem they sought to overcome. Participants at both conferences sought ways to end what the later group referred to as the "racist system of society."[72]

At the end of the 1976 meeting, the five Mennonite participants joined seven of their religious cousins from the Brethren in Christ and Mennonite Brethren communities in drafting a statement. They called on their coreligionists to end racist practices in church and society through education, relationship building, and institutional transformation. Notably, the Anabaptist workshop participants drew on the distinction between individual and institutional racism that black nationalist activists Stokely

Carmichael and Charles Hamilton had articulated scant months after the
1967 Newark conference.[73] In calling their religious community to elimi-
nate "subtly racist practices within structures of the church," the group
noted the difference between individual and "corporate/institutional"
racism.[74] Although the black nationalists who attended the first conference
did not concern themselves with majority-white Christian denominations
as they sought to achieve racial autonomy, echoes of their discussions continued to reverberate throughout the sectarian meetings held nine years
later.

Mennonite participants in the second conference were not, however,
religious mimics of secular agitators. They brought with them the legacy of decades of daily demonstration. Among the dozen signers of the
1976 Statement on Racism by Concerned Anabaptists, two individuals
make the case. The last name listed was Hubert Schwartzentruber. The
former pastor of Bethesda Mennonite in St. Louis at that point worked
for a Mennonite mission agency, the Mennonite Board of Congregational
Ministries. He brought nearly two decades' experience gained from prod-
ding individuals and organizations to serve African Americans and other
people of color as well as they served white people. During those years,
Schwartzentruber had learned to push for racial justice by appealing to
community values. Rather than simply regurgitating the rhetoric of black
nationalism, Schwartzentruber and his colleagues called the church to
"a renewed commitment to nonconformity" to racial prejudices of the
world.[75] The practice of talking in vestibules and at dinner tables about
racism in the church had taught them to ground racial advocacy in ecclesial commitments.

Dwight McFadden also built on daily demonstrators' actions. McFadden, an African-American Mennonite hailing from New Holland, Pennsylvania, had been introduced the previous fall as the associate general
secretary of the Mennonite Church.[76] McFadden represented the denomination's newly formed Black Caucus, the group that had risen from the
ashes of the Minority Ministries Council. As he attended conferences like
the one in Newark, agitated for change in denominational and parachurch
organizations, and organized Black Caucus members to ensure fair representation on church boards and committees, McFadden followed in the
footsteps of Minority Ministries Council executive secretary John Powell, Atlanta service unit leader Vincent Harding, and early church founder

Rowena Lark. McFadden and his colleagues were able to call for an end to "subtly racist practices" within the church because Powell, Harding, Lark, and others before them had spent years identifying those practices for removal.[77]

The effect of a document like the 1976 Statement on Racism by Concerned Anabaptists remains unclear. Schwartzentruber released the statement through the Mennonite Board of Congregational Ministries, and it subsequently appeared in the church press.[78] The historical record has left no overwhelming evidence that church members read the document and then began speaking "in a prophetic and redemptive manner."[79] We do know that through the 1990s, staff from the Mennonite Board of Congregational Ministries continued to call on Mennonites in their homes and sanctuaries to resist racism.[80] Although Schwartzentruber and his cosigners may not have catalyzed as much action "to attack racism" as they had hoped, they nonetheless established a foundation that made future action possible.

We also know that in the summer of 1997, Dwight McFadden became the first African-American moderator of the (Old) Mennonite Church. The Mennonites who supported McFadden's nomination had been visited by many a daily demonstrator. Those delegates, like most members of religious communities, had also been influenced by street-based agitation. The racial order shifted—an African-American Mennonite entered high church office—because both sets of civil rights movement actors demonstrated. Although African-American Mennonites continued to attest to the presence of racism within the church well after McFadden's term ended, his installation nonetheless tied together two streams of history.[81] On that hot summer day in 1997, the street and the sanctuary merged.

Such a confluence completes the movement narrative. Church, home, street, and sidewalk combine to tell a story that deepens our understanding of the Second Reconstruction. Although every bit as complex as the waters that ran together in the nomination of a black man to lead a white church, such narratives await further retelling. Once told, stories from the sanctuary and living room place Vincent Harding, Rowena Lark, and Fannie Swartzentruber alongside public agitators like Martin Luther King Jr., Fannie Lou Hamer, and Anne Braden. In this new, more complete story of the civil rights movement, the Mennonites featured here take no minor part. Like Dwight McFadden on the dais the day that he accepted his nomination, they stand at the center of the story. By so enriching the civil rights narrative, Fresh Air children, interracial couples, and all those who took risks outside the public purview finally get their due. Their names become known and their internal actions receive validation. The narratives of these actors' lives in turn reveal an important historical insight. From perhaps the most unexpected of religious communities—a quietist, white-dominated, marginal group of Mennonites—we learn that mobilized marchers did not walk alone as they overturned de jure segregation. Daily demonstrators walked alongside them.

APPENDIX

Interview Subjects

All interviews conducted by author.

Berry, Lee Roy, and Beth Berry, Goshen, Ind. / Evanston, Ill., August 29, 2006;
   60 minutes; phone.
Brock, Thomas W., Harrisonburg, Va. / Evanston, Ill., May 17, 2005; 45 minutes;
   phone.
Burklow, Don, and Grace Burklow, Markham, Ill., April 15, 2005; 60 minutes; in
   person.
Curry, Peggy, Harrisonburg, Va., March 29, 2005; 60 minutes; in person.
Dagan, Paul L., Lancaster, Pa. / Evanston, Ill., March 15, 2003; 60 minutes;
   phone.
Douple, Betty, Long Beach, Miss., May 25, 2005; 75 minutes; in person.
Eby, John, Philadelphia / Evanston, Ill., February 28, 2003; 60 minutes; phone.
Geil, Libby, Gulfport, Miss., May 25, 2005; 60 minutes; in person.
Gwinn, Betty, Atlanta / Evanston, Ill., April 26, 2008; 30 minutes; phone.
Hershey, Lynford, Payette, Id. / Evanston, Ill., March 2, 2003; 90 minutes;
   phone.
———, Payette, Id. / Evanston, Ill., March 6, 2004; 30 minutes; phone.
Horst, Barbara, Ephrata, Pa. / Evanston, Ill., April 22, 2003; 10 minutes; phone.
Horst, Samuel, Harrisonburg, Va., March 31, 2005; 60 minutes; in person.
Hostetler, Goldie, Goshen, Ind. / Lancaster, Pa., March 14, 2002; 30 minutes,
   phone.
Huber, Harold, Harrisonburg, Va. / Evanston, Ill., February 26, 2005; 30 min-
   utes; phone.
Huber, Harold, and Vida Huber, Harrisonburg, Va., March 29, 2005; 60 minutes;
   in person.

Hughes, Annabelle, and Gerald Hughes, Cleveland Heights, Ohio / Evanston, Ill., August 29, 2006; 60 minutes; phone.

Kennel, Ron, Goshen, Ind. / Evanston, Ill., February 26, 2004; 20 minutes; phone.

Krehbiel, Ronald, Hesston, Kans. / Evanston, Ill., April 25, 2007; 20 minutes; phone.

Landis, Paul G., Lancaster, Pa. / Evanston, Ill., March 8, 2003; 70 minutes; phone.

——, Lancaster, Pa. / Evanston, Ill., April 28, 2005; 80 minutes; phone.

Mares, Gerald, and Dolores Mares, Markham, Ill., September 17, 2006; 40 minutes; in person.

Miller, Oren, and Dorothy Miller, Gulfport, Miss., May 26, 2005; 60 minutes; in person.

Moran, Edna, Gulfport, Miss., May 24, 2005; 60 minutes; in person.

Odom, Mertis, Markham, Ill., July 3, 2005; 60 minutes; in person.

Peachey, Paul, and Ellen Peachey, Harrisonburg, Va., April 1, 2005; 75 minutes; in person.

Powell, John, Buffalo, New York / Evanston, Ill., March 16, 2003; 60 minutes; phone.

Redekop, Calvin, Harrisonburg, Va. / Evanston, Ill., April 27, 2004; 20 minutes; phone.

Regier, Harold, and Rosella Wiens Regier, Newton, Kans. / Evanston, Ill., July 12, 2005; 90 minutes; phone.

Shenk, Michael, Harrisonburg, Va. / Evanston, Ill., March 19, 2003; 20 minutes; phone.

Shenk, Norman G., Salunga, Pa. / Evanston, Ill., March 22, 2005; 60 minutes; phone.

Stoltzfus, Miriam, Lancaster, Pa. / Evanston, Ill., March 15, 2003; 60 minutes; phone.

Swartzentruber, Homer, Shipshewanna, Ind. / Evanston, Ill., May 19, 2005; 60 minutes; phone.

——, Shipshewanna, Ind. / Evanston, Ill., February 24, 2007; 15 minutes; phone.

Vogt, Virgil, Evanston, Ill., May 6, 2004; 20 minutes; phone.

Weaver, Dave, and Sue Weaver, Gulfport, Miss., May 26, 2005; 90 minutes; in person.

Weaver, Richard, and Virginia Weaver, Harrisonburg, Va., March 30, 2005, 2005; 60 minutes; in person.

Williams, Sue, Gulfport, Miss., May 25, 2005; 60 minutes; in person.

Woods, Mary Ann, Markham, Ill., April 29, 2005; 60 minutes; in person.

Zehr, Paul, Lancaster, Pa. / Evanston, Ill., March 1, 2003; 30 minutes; phone.

Notes

Abbreviations

AMC — Archives of the Mennonite Church USA, located on the campus of Goshen College, Goshen, Indiana

CCM — Central Conference Missions, a missions body of the Central Conference of the General Conference Mennonite Church

CESR — Committee on Economic and Social Relations, a national committee of the (Old) Mennonite Church

CHM — Commission on Home Ministries, the domestic service board of the General Conference Mennonite Church

CMC — Community Mennonite Church, Markham, Illinois

CPSC — Committee on Peace and Social Concerns, a committee of the (Old) Mennonite Church

EMBMC — Eastern Mennonite Board of Missions and Charities, the Lancaster Conference's mission agency

EMM — Eastern Mennonite Missions (www.emm.org), the mission agency of the Lancaster Conference of Mennonite Church USA, located in Salunga, Pennsylvania

EMU — Eastern Mennonite University archives, located in Harrisonburg, Virginia

GC — General Conference Mennonite Church denomination

LMHS — Lancaster Mennonite Historical Society, located in Lancaster, Pennsylvania

MB — Mennonite Brethren denomination

MBM — Mennonite Board of Missions, the former mission board of the (Old) Mennonite Church

MBMC — Mennonite Board of Missions and Charities, an older name of MBM

MC   Mennonite Church denomination; also known as the (Old) Mennonite Church

MCA   Mennonite Church Archives

MCC   Mennonite Central Committee, the relief and development organization of the Mennonite family of churches, located in Akron, Pennsylvania

MDS   Mennonite Disaster Service, a disaster response organization of the Mennonite family of churches

MHLVA   Mennonite Historical Library, located on the campus of Eastern Mennonite University, Harrisonburg, Virginia

MLA   Mennonite Library and Archives of the Mennonite Church USA, located on the campus of Bethel College, Newton, Kansas

NCC   National Council of Churches

OMC   (Old) Mennonite Church denomination (also MC)

PSC   Peace and Social Concerns, a shortened form of CPSC

SCCO   Study Commission on Church Organization, a committee tasked with examining (Old) Mennonite Church organizational issues in the early 1970s

VAMC   Virginia Mennonite Conference Archives, located on the campus of Eastern Mennonite University, Harrisonburg, VA

VS   Voluntary Service

Preface

1. Quoted by Paul G. Landis, interview with author, April 28, 2005.

2. For examples of street-focused historical works, see Andrews, *Freedom Is a Constant Struggle*; Findlay, "Churches Join"; Greene, *Our Separate Ways*; Lewis, *Massive Resistance*; Verney, *Debate on Black Civil Rights*.

3. For a discussion of the need to reframe the study of the long civil rights movement to include its roots in the 1940s and '50s and its continuation into the '70s, see Biondi, *To Stand and Fight*; Hall, "Long Civil Rights Movement"; Joseph, introduction to *The Black Power Movement*.

4. Kelley, *Race Rebels*, 2–10, 19–20, 68.

5. Orsi, "Everyday Miracles," 7.

6. See, for example, "The Way of the Cross in Race Relations" (statement presented at the meeting of the Committee on Economic and Social Relations of the Mennonite Church, Mennonite Community Association, Goshen, Indiana, April 22–24, 1955).

7. Peggy Curry, interview with author, March 29, 2005; Annabelle Hughes and Gerald Hughes, interview with author, August 29, 2006.

8. To unify home and sanctuary, I have for purposes of this study rejected philosopher Jürgen Habermas's division between public and private spheres. For a more extended examination of Habermas's theories see Habermas, *Public Sphere.*

9. Zook, *Mennonite Yearbook and Directory,* vol. 62, 42; Presbyterian Church (U.S.A), "Membership for the Presbyterian Church (U.S.A.): 1960 to 2005," Presbyterian Church, www.pcusa.org/research/reports/trends.htm (accessed January 22, 2009).

10. Chappell, *A Stone of Hope,* 97; Harrison, "Women's and Girls' Activism," 244–45.

11. For examples of those who have, in various degrees, glossed over intimate encounters across racial lines, see Collier-Thomas and Franklin, *Sisters in the Struggle;* Greene, *Our Separate Ways;* McGreevy, *Parish Boundaries;* Payne, *I've Got the Light.*

12. Stories from other racial and ethnic communities—especially the Latino/a, Native American, and Asian American Mennonite groups—also require retelling.

13. The designation "Old," which I put in parenthesis throughout this text, refers to a mid-nineteenth-century schism over matters of church discipline and organization that led to the formation of the General Conference denomination. Hence the (Old) Mennonite Church was literally older than the General Conference Mennonite Church.

14. Toews, *Mennonites in American Society,* 149–50.

15. Shetler, "A Prophetic Voice," 14.

16. In the main, Mennonites have claimed credit for the Germantown antislavery statement of 1688, the first written antislavery statement drafted in North America. See MacMaster, *Land, Piety, Peoplehood,* 43; Smith, *Story of the Mennonites,* 540. The document was written, however, by practicing Quakers to a Quaker assembly, a fact duly noted by scholars outside the Mennonite community. See Cone, *Black Theology,* 77; Raboteau, *Slave Religion,* 111. Although Mennonites chose not to own slaves, scholarship suggests that, at least in southeastern Pennsylvania, where Mennonites were most highly concentrated during the colonial and antebellum periods, the use of slaves was more a matter of conspicuous consumption than economic necessity. See Tully, "Patterns of Slaveholding." The claims of racial egalitarian status from the seventeenth century forward thus need to be held in tension with the historical situation of Mennonites who, in both the North and the South, generally did not need slaves to achieve economic sufficiency. See Longenecker, "Antislavery and Otherworldliness."

17. "Mennonite Race Relations: Still at a Low Point," news release, August 7, 1970, folder 77, Race—Articles/reports, box 6, MCA, I.Z.1, Peace and Social Concerns Committee of the General Conference Mennonite Church, MLA.

18. Bechler, *Black Mennonite Church,* 57–76; Schlabach, *Gospel versus Gospel,* 247–48.

19. Schlabach, *Gospel versus Gospel*, 255–57.

20. Throughout this study, *Mennonite church*—with a lowercase *c*—refers jointly to the (Old) Mennonite Church and the General Conference Mennonite denominations. Quotations that mention *Mennonite Church*—with an uppercase *C*—reference the (Old) Mennonite Church denomination. Bechler, "Facts, Considerations, and Membership," 1.

21. Harold S. Bender et al., eds., Global Anabaptist Mennonite Encyclopedia Online, s.v. "Nonconformity," www.gameo.org/encyclopedia/contents/n651me .html (accessed September 18, 2007).

22. Authors of the 1955 (Old) Mennonite Church race relations statement connected nonconformity with racial exclusion when they confessed, "We have failed to see that acceptance of the social patterns of segregation and discrimination is a violation of the command to be 'not conformed to this world.'" They continued their confession by noting that "attitudes of exclusiveness" had likewise blocked African Americans from joining the church. Throughout this book I note myriad ways in which the doctrine of nonconformity led directly to those attitudes of exclusion based on fears of contagion from the outside world. See Mennonite General Conference, "The Way of Christian Love in Race Relations," (statement passed at Mennonite General Conference, Hesston, Kansas, August 24, 1955), 4.

23. Murray, *Methodists and the Crucible*.

24. Ibid., 26; Schlabach, *Gospel versus Gospel*, 42.

25. Alvis, "A Presbyterian Dilemma"; McGreevy, *Parish Boundaries*, 101; Murray, *Methodists and the Crucible*, 200–201.

26. Findlay, "Religion and Politics," 66–67; Loescher, *The Protestant Church*.

27. Chrisman, "The Price of Moderation," 161–62; Findlay, "Religion and Politics"; Findlay, *Church People in the Struggle*, 3; McGreevy, *Parish Boundaries*, 221.

28. Loren Lind, "400 'Heroes' A Day," *Christian Living*, January 1967, 1, 3–5.

29. Paul G. Landis, interviews with author, March 8, 2003, April 28, 2005.

30. Andrew Schulze to Guy F. Hershberger, July 22 1955, St. Louis, Missouri, CESR papers I-3-7, box 6, folder 14, AMC; Grant M. Stoltzfus to Guy F. Hershberger, May 31, 1955, CESR papers, box 5, folder 99, AMC.

31. Jim Banman, "Integration Comes to Central Kansas as Mennonites Are Hosts to Negroes" (1961), VII.R GC Voluntary Service, Series 11 Gulfport VS Unit, box 4, folder 123, Fresh Air, 1961, MLA; Milo Dailey, "Mississippi Negro Boy Is Enjoying Life from Farm Family near Freeman," *Yankton Press and Dakotan*, Friday, August 1, 1969; Marvin Miller, "Churches and Social Agencies Work in Slum Area with Little Success," *New Era*, October 16, 1963.

32. David Chidester explicates the negative effects of religious boundaries when he writes, "Since being a person also requires being in a place, religion entails discourses and practices for creating sacred space, as a zone of inclusion but also as a

boundary for excluding others. Accordingly, religion, in my definition, is the activity of being human in relation to superhuman transcendence and sacred inclusion, which inevitably involves dehumanization and exclusion. Religion, therefore, contains an inherent ambiguity." See Chidester, *Authentic Fakes*, viii. See also Arthur, *Religion, Dress and the Body*; Gjerde, *Minds of the West*; Loewen, *Family, Church, and Market*; Tweed, *Retelling U.S. Religious History*.

33. Payne, *I've Got the Light*, 457.

34. I am indebted to the following scholars for their thoughtful commentary on the use of photographs as historical evidence: McDannell, *Picturing Faith*; Rose, *Visual Methodologies*; Schmeisser, "Camera at the Grassroots"; Williams, *Framing the West*.

35. The work of the following scholars has guided my interpretation of material cultural objects like the Mennonite prayer veil: Buckridge, *The Language of Dress*; Graybill, "Mennonite Women and Their Bishops"; Hawes, Schulz, and Hiner, "The United States"; Klassen, "Practicing Conflict."

36. Historians of the American Mennonite experience have paid little attention to white Mennonites' interaction with African Americans. Other than Le Roy Bechler's statistically sound but interpretively thin history of the African-American Mennonite church and Theron Schlabach's exploration of Mennonite missions and attitudes toward African Americans, the field remains relatively unexplored. In addition to presenting a new periodization of Mennonite engagement with African Americans in chapter 1, I argue throughout this work that white Mennonites were more aware of, engaged by, and focused on race relations than has been previously suggested by other scholars and that the particular history of relations with African Americans reveals a more unified approach to race relations by white Christians than what appears in the work of David Swartz and John McGreevy. See Bechler, *Black Mennonite Church*; McGreevy, *Parish Boundaries*; Schlabach, *Gospel versus Gospel*; Swartz, "Mista Mid-Nights"; Weaver, "The Mennonite Church."

Chapter 1. A Separated History

1. Quoted in Guy F. Hershberger, "Report of the Chicago Race Relations Seminar," memorandum, July 16, 1959, 8, CESR papers I-3-7, box 7, folder 58, AMC.

2. "The Mennonite Churches and Race," *Gospel Herald*, May 19, 1959, 460.

3. Hershberger, "Report of the Chicago Race Relations Seminar."

4. Bechler, *Black Mennonite Church*, 38.

5. Ibid., 39–41.

6. The periodization I offer here leans heavily on the work originally developed by J. Denny Weaver in his insightful treatment of Mennonite written materials on race. See Weaver, "The Mennonite Church." Although I have renamed and ex-

panded the evidentiary base for each of the periods and made slight adjustments to some of the beginning and ending dates, the basic framework comes from Weaver's work.

7. Gingerich, "Sharing the Faith"; Hinojosa, "Making Noise."

8. Bechler, *Black Mennonite Church*, 41.

9. Merle W. Eshleman, "Mission for Colored, Philadelphia," *Missionary Messenger*, February 16, 1936, 11.

10. Shenk, *By Faith They Went Out*, 40.

11. Ibid.

12. Peggy Curry, interview with author, March 29, 2005.

13. Weaver, "The Mennonite Church," 19.

14. Exact membership numbers are not available before 1950, but an estimate of 150 or fewer is consistent with the statistical data included in Le Roy Bechler's foundational text. See Bechler, *Black Mennonite Church*, 172. Awareness of disparate racial experience emerges from numerous oral histories conducted for this project. See, in particular, Curry, interview.

15. Daniel Kauffman, editorial, *Gospel Herald*, January 7, 1943, 865.

16. Schlabach, *Gospel versus Gospel*, 259.

17. Orie O. Miller, minutes of the Sixty-Third Quarterly Meeting of E.M.B. Of M. & C. And Lancaster Conference Board of Bishops, January 2, 1943, LMHS.

18. Shenk, *By Faith They Went Out*, 76.

19. Ibid.

20. Bechler, *Black Mennonite Church*, 172.

21. Melvin Gingerich, "Negroes and the Mennonites," *The Mennonite*, June 14, 1949, 4.

22. Haury, *Quiet Demonstration*, 22.

23. Lois Barrett Janzen, "Gulfport: Discovering What It Means to Be White among Blacks," memorandum, November 9, 1973, 2, VII.R GC Voluntary Service, Series 11 Gulfport VS Unit, box 6, folder 214, Reports, misc., MLA; Edna Moran, interview with author, May 24, 2005; Sue Williams, interview with author, May 25, 2005.

24. The (Old) Mennonite Church consisted of regional governing bodies such as the Lancaster and Virginia Conferences. The Lancaster Conference, the largest of the conferences, did not officially join the (Old) Mennonite denomination until 1971, although it did maintain a number of fraternal ties before that date. The Lancaster Conference extended its reach up and down the East Coast from New England to Florida. The vast majority of the Lancaster Conference congregations, however, clustered in and around Lancaster County in southeastern Pennsylvania.

25. Guy F. Hershberger, "Race Prejudice in America Today," memorandum, March 8, 1944, CESR papers I-3-7, box 7, folder 55, AMC; Schlabach, "Race, and Another Look," 3.

26. Reynold Weinbrenner, "Right Race Relations," *The Mennonite*, February 6, 1945, 3.

27. Irvin B. Horst, "Mennonites and the Race Question," *Gospel Herald*, July 13, 1945, 284–85; Dale M. Stucky, "Science Also Says, 'All of One Blood,'" *The Mennonite*, February 5, 1946, 4.

28. Horst, "Mennonites and the Race Question," 285.

29. On September 14, 1948, at the suggestion of the Colored Workers Committee, the Eastern Board decided to recommend to the joint board that "the care of our aged members in our several institutions be without race discrimination." See minutes of the Eastern Mennonite Board of Missions and Charities Executive Committee Meeting, September 14, 1948, 1, LMHS.

30. Minutes of Eastern Mennonite College Administration Committee, September 20, 1948, box II-B-4, John R. Mumaw Collection, box 27, EMU.

31. Reimers, *White Protestantism*, 111.

32. On this point, I disagree with J. Denny Weaver's finding. He notes that during the period from 1945 to 1949, church press reports gave only low-profile attention to African-American missions. (Note slight difference in periodization. I begin this period in 1944, with the founding of Bethel Mennonite in Chicago.) See Weaver, "The Mennonite Church," 23. Examination of regional press reports shows, however, that African-American Mennonites like James Lark were already receiving significant attention from church leaders and mission boards during these five years.

33. Daniel D. West, "What About Our Negro Missions?" *Missionary Messenger*, January 1946, 1; Zook, *Mennonite Yearbook and Directory 1946*. The practice of designating congregations as "Colored" had begun to dissipate by 1950 and was discontinued entirely by 1956. See Zook, *Mennonite Yearbook and Directory 1956*.

34. Stanley Shenk, "A Mennonite Colored Wedding," *Gospel Herald*, December 2, 1947, 782; "Zealous Larks," *Missionary Guide*, ca. 1947, 16; Turkey Creek Bible School, photo, Gulfport, Miss., *The Mennonite*, February 24, 1948, 15.

35. Toews, *Mennonites in American Society*, 76.

36. James M. Lapp, "Conferences and Congregations: A Review of Mennonite Church Polity," Historical Committee and Archives of the Mennonite Church, www.mcusa-archives.org/MHB/Lapp.html (accessed March 10, 2009).

37. Emma H. Rudy, Abraham L. Gehman, and Esther K. Lehman, "From Our Negro Stations," *Missionary Messenger*, January 1946, 5, 7.

38. John L. Stauffer, Introductory to Non-Conformity Conference, Chicago, Illinois, memorandum, Oct. 19–20, 1948, box I-MS-17, John L. Stauffer Collection, Misc. folders of Notes and Outlines, etc., box 8, VAMC.

39. Curry, interview.

40. Hershberger, "Race Prejudice in America Today."

41. Weaver, "The Mennonite Church," 31.

42. Bechler, *Black Mennonite Church*, 172. The figure of 150 African-American church members did not include infants, children, youth not yet baptized, or regular participants who had not yet officially joined the church. Actual African-American participation was most probably in the neighborhood of a thousand on a given Sunday during this period.

43. Shenk, *By Faith They Went Out*, 79.

44. On October 26, 1950, the Lancaster Conferences' Eastern Board and Bishop Board discussed the executive committee's "concern for counsel and advice on how to expand our witness and service in the work to the colored and for colored members" and referred the action to subcommittee. See Orie O. Miller, minutes of the Eastern Mennonite Board of Missions and Charities and Lancaster Conference Bishop Board, October 26, 1950, 1, LMHS. On March 8, 1954, the Lancaster Conference's Eastern Board established the Philadelphia home for the aged and declared that it was open to "male and female guests irrespective of race." See minutes of the Eastern Mennonite Board Executive Committee, March 6, 1954, LMHS; Good, "Forty Years," 21.

45. "Statement of Concerns of the Study Conference on Christian Community Relations," memorandum, July 24–27, 1951, 4, CESR papers I-3-7, box 2, folder 35, AMC.

46. Schlabach, "Race, and Another Look," 4.

47. William Yovanovich, "Leah Risser, Ahead of Her Time," *WMSC Voice*, November 1990, 5–7.

48. Le Roy Bechler, "Meeting the Challenge of the American Negro," *Missionary Messenger*, February 1952, 2; J. Lester Brubaker, editorial, *Missionary Messenger*, October 1950, 3; J. D. Graber, "An Open Letter to Ministers and Christian Workers of the Mennonite Church," *Gospel Herald*, January 12, 1954, 40; Robert Stoltzfus, "A Short History of Mennonite Work among the American Negro," *Missionary Messenger*, October 1950, 12.

49. Robert M. Labaree, "Can Christianity Solve the Race Problem," *Gospel Herald*, May 13, 1952, 473; Carl M. Saunders, "There's No White Blood," *Gospel Herald*, November 3, 1953, 1060.

50. Grant M. Stoltzfus, "Biological, Social, and Spiritual Aspects of the Race Problem," *Christian Monitor*, 1951, 14.

51. See the following articles in the *The Mennonite*: "A Primer on Race," February 6, 1951, 94–96; D. W. B., "Do You Want Your Daughter to Marry a Negro?" October 28, 1952, 684; William Keeney, "Reborn Color-Blind," January 8, 1952, 22, 25; Olin A. Krehbiel, "The Ministry of Reconciliation," April 4, 1950, 220, 24; Esko Loewen, "What Do You Want to Do, Marry a Negro?" February 6, 1951, 95; J. N. Smucker, "Mennonites and the Race Question," January 8, 1952, 19; Esther Soderholm, "White Supremacy," October 6, 1953, 618.

52. Schlabach, "Race, and Another Look," 6.

53. Ibid.

54. "Christian Race Relations" (proceedings of the Committee on Economic and Social Relations of the Mennonite Church, Mennonite Community Association, Goshen, Indiana, April 22—24, 1955).

55. Mennonite General Conference, "The Way of Christian Love in Race Relations" (statement passed at Mennonite General Conference, Hesston, Kansas, August 24, 1955).

56. MacMaster and Jacobs, *A Gentle Wind of God*, 90—91, 98, 186.

57. Although the objections to moustaches in this era arose from a concern about the association of this grooming choice with the military, the bishops' rigorous enforcement appears to have been racially triggered.

58. References to this instance at Newtown Gospel Chapel, Sarasota, Florida, appear in three separate oral history interviews with the author: Michael Shenk, March 19, 2003; Dave Weaver and Sue Weaver, May 26, 2005; Paul Zehr, March 1, 2003.

59. Notes of the Colored Workers Committee, 1953—57, 1—4, file cabinets far wall, first cabinet, top drawer, drawer marked Home Missions Locations and Other General 1956—1964, four numbered notebooks, EMM record room.

60. Ibid.

61. Bechler, *Facts, Considerations, and Membership*.

62. White converts also received instruction in the importance of wearing nonconformist dress. As the sources cited here demonstrate, however, white mission workers enforced those requirements for African-American converts with a relatively greater degree of intensity. Other examples of enforced dress and grooming requirements are cited in Curry, interview; Norman Derstine, "Dear Brothers and Sisters in the Lord," memorandum, Trissels Mennonite Church, 1955, box I-MS-17, John L. Stauffer collection, General Files H—Z, box 6, folder Nonconformity, VAMC; William M. Weaver, e-mail messages to author, January 30, 2003.

63. Romano, *Race Mixing*, 45, 83—84, 107—8.

64. See, for example, D. W. B., "Do You Want Your Daughter to Marry a Negro?"; Paul Erb, "Interracial Marriage," *Gospel Herald*, June 24, 1952, 611; Levi C. Hartzler, "Race Problem Unnecessary," *Gospel Herald*, February 8, 1955, 137, 40. As discussed at length in chapter 6, even the 1955 (Old) Mennonite Church statement on race relations hedged support of interracial marriage with social rather than theological references: "The social implications of any proposed union should receive careful attention." See Mennonite General Conference, "The Way of Christian Love in Race Relations," 6.

65. D. W. B., "Do You Want Your Daughter to Marry a Negro?"

66. I am here indebted to the work of Ann Taves for her insightful exploration of

the sexual body in the American religious tradition. See, especially, Taves, "Sexuality," 28, 41, 56.

67. D'Emilio and Freedman, *Intimate Matters*, 14; Romano, "Race Mixing," 5.

68. Thanks to Christina Traina, of Northwestern University, for adding this insight.

69. Annabelle Hughes and Gerald Hughes, interview with author, August 29, 2006; Gerald Hughes, e-mail message to author, January 19, 2007; Miller, "Building Anew in Cleveland," 84.

70. Shenk, *By Faith They Went Out*, 78–81.

71. Lancaster Mennonite Conference, "Statement on Race Relations," *Pastoral Messenger*, April 1960, 5.

72. Bechler, *Black Mennonite Church*, 174–77.

73. Weaver, "The Mennonite Church," 33.

74. Hinojosa, "Making Noise," 121.

75. L. C. Hartzler, "Looking at Race Relations," *Gospel Herald*, December 31, 1957, 1145.

76. Guy F. Hershberger, "Nonresistance, the Mennonite Church, and the Race Question," *Gospel Herald*, June 28, 1960, 577, 578, 581–82.

77. C. Norman Kraus, "Report from Durham," *Gospel Herald*, June 7, 1960, 509–10, 525.

78. Vincent Harding, "The Christian and the Race Question" (address to Mennonite World Conference, August 6, 1962), 3, IX-7-12, no. 2, box 6, Race Relations 1955–70, AMC.

79. Vincent Harding, "The Task of the Mennonite Church in Establishing Racial Unity," (address to Seminar on Christ, the Mennonite Churches, and Race, Woodlawn Mennonite Church, April 17–19, 1959), Hist. Mss. 1-48, box 60, John H. Yoder (1927–1997) Collection Race / Urban issues, file 60/1, AMC.

80. Eugene Stoltzfus, "Which Side of the Road?" *Gospel Herald*, May 26, 1959, 485.

81. Harding, "The Christian and the Race Question," 3.

82. "Segregated geographically, socially and matrimonially, defining their boundries [*sic*] and habitations, (surely he did not give all them that which he had taken away from them possibly none of them, for he gave some more talents than others, and never under heaven has he claimed that all are equal, he gave some one pigment of hair, skin etc. . . . and bade each to occupy what he had given them (KNOWING that that was the only way to keep them pure, Christ loves purity and Christ wants all his creatures to remain pure, for he loves all with the same pure love) until he comes." See J. Gordon Simpson to Guy F. Hershberger, n.d., 1960, I-3-7 CESR 7/39, Martin Luther King—(Guy F. Hershberger's evaluation of MLK), AMC.

83. Minutes of Summer Bible School, South Seventh Street Mennonite Church,

1954–1966, 55–56, box South Seventh Street, Reading, Summer Bible School Records 1954–66, gray-and-red bound notebook, LMHS.

84. In 1963 the ratio of African American to white service recipients pictured in the *Volunteer* was 2 to 13. By 1965 it had switched to 9 to 5. In the following years, through 1969, the ratio stayed at or about four photos of African-American service recipients for every one photo of a white service recipient, and in 1966 the ratio reached its highest, at 6 to 1.

85. Eby, *Fifty Years, Fifty Stories*, 32–37; Shenk, *By Faith They Went Out*, 80–81.

86. Maynard Shelly, a frequent editorialist on race issues, traveled to support the movement in the summer of 1964, along with Lynford Hershey. See "Northern Ministers Work for Southern Civil Rights," *The Mennonite*, March 24, 1964, 182–83. He later wrote proudly about the experience. See Maynard Shelly, editorial, *The Mennonite*, March 24, 1964, 196.

87. "List of Participants South-Wide Mennonite Conference on Race Relations, February 25–26, 1964," memorandum, I-3-7, Committee on Economic and Social Relations, Guy F. Hershberger File, Correspondence with Individuals, II, Ki–Z, correspondence with individuals, III, Miscellaneous, II, Race, to Race—Misc. box 5, folder CESR, 5/174, Race, Race—Miscellaneous, AMC; "Mennonite Churches in South Hold Conference on Race," *The Mennonite*, March 31, 1964, 203–4; Edgar Metzler to Orlo Kaufman and Harold Regier, January 17, 1964, VII.R GC Voluntary Service, Series 11 Gulfport VS Unit, box 5, folder 173, Mennonite Churches, Southern, MLA.

88. Eli Hochstedler, "I Went to Jail," *The Mennonite*, June 30, 1964, 433–34. Surprisingly, Hochstedler's experience received only scant attention in the church press and was not referred to by church leaders in any of the meetings held that year or in subsequent years.

89. Sanford G. Shetler, "Is This Our Task?" *Gospel Herald*, July 20, 1965, 629–30.

90. Schlabach, "Race, and Another Look," 34.

91. "Seventh Avenue Mennonite Church: Self-Analysis of Congregation in Response to Questionnaire Titled 'Some Questions to Ask When Describing a Church,'" memorandum, September 10, 1965, 10, Paul G. Landis, New York—Seventh Ave., LMHS.

92. Murray, *Methodists and the Crucible*, 212–14; Shattuck, *Episcopalians and Race*, 169–86.

93. Stanley Bohn, "Black Power and Nonviolence," *The Mennonite*, September 13, 1966, 557; Curtis Burrell, "Response to Black Power," *The Mennonite*, October 11, 1966, 620–21; John A. Lapp, "The Coming of Black Power," *Christian Living*, October 1966, 18–19.

94. Lynford Hershey, "Report #5 To: Counsel Reference Committee for Minority Ministries Education Program," memorandum, 1971, 3, fourth cabinet of row on far left wall upon entering room, second drawer, unmarked, folder Minority Ministry Council 1970–71, EMM record room.

95. Vincent Harding, "The Peace Witness and Revolutionary Movements," *Mennonite Life*, October 1967, 161–65.

96. Simon Gingerich and Lynford Hershey, "Minutes Counsel and Reference Committee for Minority Ministries Education," memorandum, March 5, 1971, IV-21-4 box 1, MBM, Minority Ministries Council, Data Files 1, A–K, folder Cross Cultural Relations 1971–1972, Lyn Hershey, AMC.

97. Historian Felipe Hinojosa notes that, despite the organizational collapse of the Minority Ministries Council, the ethnic caucuses developed from the ashes of the multiethnic-multiracial organization went on to serve an important function in developing distinct group identities and organizing foundations for the Latino and African-American Mennonite communities. See Hinojosa, "Making Noise."

98. Before codification of the nonconformity doctrine around the turn of the century, many Mennonite communities dressed like their neighbors. Plain, distinct dress was largely a twentieth- rather than a nineteenth-century phenomenon. See Hostetler, *American Mennonites and Protestant Movements*, 246.

99. Lancaster Conference bishops, "Statement on Racism," memorandum, July 23, 1971, Lancaster Conference, Statements, LMHS.

Chapter 2. Prayer-Covered Protest

1. Brian Kelly and others have identified, for example, interracial collaboration in labor unions. See Kelly, *Race, Class, and Power*.

2. Hollenweger, *Pentecost between Black and White*; K'Meyer, *Interracialism and Christian Community*; Sensbach, *A Separate Canaan*.

3. See, for instance, the history of women in the civil rights movement in the following texts: Collier-Thomas and Franklin, *Sisters in the Struggle*; Fosl, *Subversive Southerner*; Height, "We Wanted the Voice of a Woman to Be Heard"; Jones, *Labor of Love*; Kirk, "Daisy Bates"; Knotts, "Bound by the Spirit"; Ling and Monteith, "Gender and the Civil Rights Movement"; Robnett, "Women in the Student Non-Violent Coordinating Committee"; Stanton, *Journey toward Justice*.

4. Paul Toews's description of Mennonites and the civil rights movement, for example, foregrounds key male figures such as Vincent Harding, Guy Hershberger, and Martin Luther King Jr. but leaves out the witness and contributions of the women featured in this chapter. See Toews, *Mennonites in American Society*, 256–61. Similarly, Le Roy Bechler places far greater emphasis on James Lark than on Rowena. See Bechler, *Black Mennonite Church*, 49–54. One exception to this male-

dominated historiography is found in the work of Louise Stoltzfus. See Stoltzfus, *Quiet Shouts*. She gives voice to the experience of women in the Lancaster Conference and highlights the contributions of African-American leaders such as Mattie Cooper Nikiema of Diamond Street Mennonite Church in Philadelphia.

5. This chapter's focus on two women in an interracial relationship is not meant to negate men's sustained and deeply felt relationships. Figures featured in later chapters, such as Curtis Burrell and Hubert Schwartzentruber (no relation to Fannie Swartzentruber), John Powell and Lynford Hershey, and Vincent Harding and Delton Franz, represent interracial relationships between men that were sustained over time and mutually supportive. Fannie Swartzentruber and Rowena Lark's relationship is, however, representative of a depth of relationship and mutual appreciation that was atypical among men in the Mennonite church particularly during the late 1930s and through the 1940s.

6. This chapter about Lark and Swartzentruber centers on the (Old) Mennonite Church rather than the second largest Mennonite denomination in the United States, the General Conference Mennonite Church, because the first denomination was far more active in its evangelism of African Americans than was the second, especially during the 1930s and '40s. General Conference race relations efforts figure more prominently in later chapters of this work.

7. Gingerich, *Mennonite Attire*, 123; John A. Hostetler, "The Historical Development of the Devotional Covering in the Mennonite Church," term paper, 1956, 5–8, Hist. Mss. I-172, box 5, H. Ralph Hernley Collection, Data, Menn. M.–Z. Misc., folder 5/3, Papers re the Devotional Covering, AMC; John C. Wenger and Elmer S. Yoder, "Prayer Veil," Global Anabaptist Mennonite Encyclopedia Online, www.gameo.org/encyclopedia/contents/p739me.html (accessed May 8, 2007).

8. Kraybill, "Mennonite Woman's Veiling," 303.

9. Gingerich, *Mennonite Attire*, 131.

10. Graybill, "To Remind Us of Who We Are," 64–65; Klassen, "The Robes of Womanhood," 49.

11. Epp, "Carrying the Banner of Nonconformity," 26; Gingerich, *Mennonite Attire*, 119, 130; Regier, "Revising the Plainness of Whiteness." Marlene Epp's paper was the 1991 winner of the James Horsch Memorial Mennonite Historical Contest.

12. Bechler, *Black Mennonite Church*, 50.

13. Mahmood, *Politics of Piety*, 31.

14. O'Neal, "The African American Church," 127, 129.

15. Cunningham and Marberry, *Crowns*, 4.

16. On a related point, Pamela Klassen makes a convincing argument that nineteenth-century African-American women in the African Methodist Episcopal Church used dress standards nurtured in the church to establish their authority

and significance in the racist world outside the church. Although I pay attention to the manner in which African-American women used dress to establish their belonging inside the church, the underlying strategy remains the same. See Klassen, "Robes of Womanhood."

17. Homer Swartzentruber, interview with author, May 19, 2005.

18. Ernest L. Swartzentruber and Fannie Swartzentruber to the *Gospel Fellowship*, March 13, 1941, box I-MS-13, Harry A. Brunk Collection, Materials related to Virginia Menn. Conf., box 1, folder 8, Colored Work Broad Street Mennonite Church, VAMC.

19. Minutes of the executive committee of the Virginia Mennonite Board of Missions and Charities, December 19, 1938, box I-D-1, box 1, Board/Executive Minutes 1904–1969 Restricted, folder Board/Executive Committee Minutes 1931–1949 complete, VAMC.

20. Weber, "The History of Broad Street," 13.

21. Rosa Mae Mullet, "Broad Street Church in Review, Part IV," *Missionary Light*, July–August 1961, 8–10.

22. J. Eby Leaman, "YPCA Report, Missions," memorandum, October 31, 1937, box II-G-1e, box 1, YPCA Inclus. Dates 1926–42, folders A–Z, folder Missions 1926–1942, EMU; Weber, "The History of Broad Street," 11.

23. Brown, "The Larks," 9.

24. Bechler, *Black Mennonite Church*, 50; Lyons, "A Mother's Love," 5.

25. Cunningham and Marberry, *Crowns*, 4; O'Neal, "The African American Church," 117.

26. A primary exception to the pattern of integration followed by segregation occurred in the Welsh Mountain region, where Lancaster Conference leaders focused on African Americans from the beginning and kept that focus through most of their involvement there. See Ruth, *The Earth Is the Lord's*, 722.

27. Erb, *Studies in Mennonite City Missions*, 44.

28. Merle W. Eshleman, "Mission for Colored, Philadelphia," *Missionary Messenger*, February 16, 1936, 11.

29. Brunk, *History of Mennonites in Virginia*, 103–4.

30. Weber, "The History of Broad Street," 15–16.

31. Ibid., 13.

32. Ernest L. Swartzentruber to *Missionary Light*, December 18, 1941, box I-MS-13, Harry A. Brunk Collection Materials related to Virginia Menn. Conf., box 1, folder 8, Colored Work Broad Street Mennonite Church, VAMC.

33. Minutes of the Annual Meeting of the Virginia Mennonite Board of Missions and Charities, August 1, 1939, 66, box I-D-1, box 1, Board/Executive Minutes 1904–1969 Restricted, folder Board/Executive Committee Minutes 1931–1949 complete, VAMC.

34. Hall, "The Long Civil Rights Movement," paragraph 31.

35. Virginia Mennonite Board of Missions and Charities, "Policy Governing the Organization of a Mennonite Colored Organization," memorandum, November 11, 1940, box I-D-1, box 1, Board/Executive Minutes 1904–1969 Restricted, folder Board / Executive Committee Minutes (retyped) 1931–1947, VAMC.

36. Ibid.

37. Harold Huber and Vida Huber, interview with author, March 29, 2005; Paul Peachey and Ellen Peachey, interview with author, April 1, 2005; Weber, "The History of Broad Street," 17.

38. Virginia Mennonite Board of Missions and Charities, "Policy Governing the Organization."

39. Homer Swartzentruber, interview with author, February 24, 2007.

40. Rowena Lark to Fannie Swartzentruber, June 5, 1941, Hist. Mss. 1-738, Fannie Yoder Swartzentruber Collection, Rowena Lark Letters 1941–1967, folder SC, AMC.

41. Ernest L. Swartzentruber, "Harrisonburg Colored Mission," memorandum, 1942, box I-MS-13, Harry A. Brunk Collection Materials related to Virginia Menn Conf box 1, folder 8, Colored Work Broad Street Mennonite Church, VAMC.

42. Regier, "Revising the Plainness."

43. Many Mennonite groups at the time forbade the purchase of life insurance because it indicated a lack of reliance on God's providence. In 1941, for example, leaders at Gay Street requested prayer for "one woman that she may be willing to give up her life insurance." See Ernest L. Swartzentruber, "For Missionary Light Harrisonburg Colored Mission," memorandum, 1941, box I-MS-13, Harry A. Brunk Collection Materials related to Virginia Menn Conf, box 1, folder 8, Colored Work Broad Street Mennonite Church, VAMC.

44. Fannie Swartzentruber to Sewing Circle, January 9, 1942, box I-MS-13, Harry A. Brunk Collection Materials related to Virginia Menn Conf, box 1, folder 8, Colored Work Broad Street Mennonite Church, VAMC.

45. Ernest L. Swartzentruber, "Harrisonburg Colored Mission," memorandum, 1943, box I-MS-13, Harry A. Brunk Collection, Materials related to Virginia Menn Conf, box 1, folder 8, Colored Work Broad Street Mennonite Church, VAMC.

46. Minutes of the Virginia Mennonite Board of Missions and Charities Annual Meeting, June 8, 1943, box I-D-1, box 1, Board/Executive Minutes 1904–1969 Restricted, folder Board / Executive Committee Minutes 1931–1949 complete, VAMC; Roberta W. Webb to Rosalie Wyse, December 5, 1947, Papers of Va. Menn. Bd. of Missions and Charities, box Harold Huber's Papers, Broad Street Mennonite Church Materials (History, etc.), folder Broad Street—General History, VAMC.

47. "Chicago Bethel Church Development 1944–1953: Housing Project in

Mission Area Makes New Church Building Necessary and Enlarges Witnessing Opportunities," memorandum, 1953, 9, Rudy, Mass Emma, Diaries—1953, 1963, 1966, 1974, Historical & Commemorative notes, programs & periodicals, LMHS.

48. One account indicates that Lark continued her involvement at the Harrisonburg vacation bible school program through 1950. See Mullet, "Broad Street Church in Review." She makes few appearances in the mission's reports or articles, however, past 1944.

49. John L. Stauffer to Milo Kauffman, April 16, 1945, box II-B3-2, John L. Stauffer Collection, Correspondence, folder College Corres., Miscell. 1943–1946, EMU.

50. Roberta Webb and Janet Eaton, "Personal Copy of Mrs. Roberta Webb's Story," memorandum, September 7–9, 1981, 26, H B W38n, MHLVA.

51. Milo Kauffman to John L. Stauffer, April 9, 1945, box II-B3-2, John L. Stauffer Collection Correspondence, folder College Corres., Miscell. 1943–1946, EMU; Webb to Wyse, 1947.

52. I have settled on 1944 as the date of Swartzentruber's protest after discussions with her eldest son and the author of a 1971 paper that cites the date as 1941. The earlier date, based on notes of a conversation between Ernest Swartzentruber and an undergraduate at Eastern Mennonite College in 1971, does not concur with Fannie's statement, "God, you've put these men in charge of us. We're going to obey them until you show us otherwise." See Homer Swartzentruber, interview, 2007. As is evident here, Fannie left the communion service only after several years of building frustration with the segregationist dictate, not immediately after the dictate, as the 1971 account suggests.

53. Huber and Huber, interview.

54. Klarman, From Jim Crow to Civil Rights, 288–89.

55. Minutes of Virginia Mennonite Board of Missions and Charities executive committee meeting, January 5, 1945, 112, Papers of Va. Menn. Bd. of Missions and Charities, box I-D-1, box 1, Board/Executive Minutes 1904–1969 Restricted, folder Board/Executive Committee Minutes (retyped) 1931–1947, VAMC; Weber, "The History of Broad Street," 17–18.

56. Huber and Huber, interview.

57. Swartzentruber, interview, 2005.

58. Ibid.

59. Horst, Mennonites in the Confederacy, 9–10; Juhnke, Vision, Doctrine, War, 218.

60. "Eight Arrive at Grottoes Camp," Daily News Record, May 23, 1941.

61. Virginia Mennonite Board of Missions and Charities, "Policy Governing the Organization."

62. White Protestant groups in the North generally did not go on record against

segregation until after the March 1946 Federal Council of Churches declaration that "the pattern of segregation in race relations is unnecessary and undesirable and a violation of the Gospel of love and human brotherhood." See Wills, "An Enduring Distance," 172. After the Southwestern Pennsylvania Conference went on record against "prejudices and discrimination against minority groups" in 1948 and Mennonites gathered in Laurelville, Pennsylvania, expressed their opposition to racial segregation and discrimination in 1951, the (Old) Mennonite Church passed its first major statement against racial segregation in 1955. See "The Way of Christian Love in Race Relations," statement passed by Mennonite General Conference, August 24, 1955, Mennonite General Conference, 1898–1971, Constitutions, Minutes, Programs, etc., 1890–1971, I-1-1, box 6 (gray), Statements, 1917–1971, 6/14, AMC; "Statement of Concerns of the Study Conference on Christian Community Relations," memorandum, July 24–27, 1951, CESR papers I-3-7, box 2, folder 35, AMC; Weaver, "The Mennonite Church."

63. MacMaster and Jacobs, *A Gentle Wind*, 136, 60.

64. Hostetler, *American Mennonites*, 263–64.

65. Ibid., 265–66.

66. Swartzentruber, interview, 2005.

67. Stanley Shenk, "A Mennonite Colored Wedding," *Gospel Herald*, December 2, 1947, 782; William Gering, "A Negro Mennonite Minister," *The Mennonite*, March 25, 1952, 197; Robert Stoltzfus, "The Lord Made Room," *Christian Living*, August 1956, 24–25; Ernest Swartzentruber, "History of the Colored Mission of Harrisonburg, Virginia," *Missionary Light*, April 1943, 1, 3.

68. Rowena Lark, "The History of Bethel Mennonite Church," *Our Journal*, May 1950, 1–3.

69. Kauffman to Stauffer, 1945.

70. Lark, "The History of Bethel."

71. Minutes of the Lancaster Conference Bishop Board, June 16, 1948, LMHS.

72. The previous year, African-American student Willis Johnson was admitted on a part-time basis. See minutes of the Eastern Mennonite College administration committee, September 20, 1948, and January 26, 1949, 1, box II-B-4, John R. Mumaw Collection, box 27, EMU; Virginia Mennonite Conference, *Minutes of the Virginia Mennonite Conference 1938*, 303.

73. Newman, *Getting Right with God*, 180.

74. Jackson, *Crabgrass Frontier*, 234–44; Rowena Lark to Fannie Swartzentruber, December 25, 1945, Hist. Mss. 1-738, Fannie Yoder Swartzentruber Collection, Rowena Lark Letters 1941–1967, folder SC, AMC.

75. Bechler, *Black Mennonite Church*, 172; Melvin Gingerich, "Negroes and the Mennonites," *The Mennonite*, June 14, 1949, 4.

76. Lark, "The History of Bethel."

77. Ibid.

78. Ann Jennings Brunk to Guy F. Hershberger, June 10, 1952, Lombard, Illinois, I-3-7 CESR papers, 7/33 entitled "Race Relations Island of Sanity," AMC.

79. Miriam Stoltzfus, interview with author, March 15, 2003.

80. Byrd and Tharps, Hair Story, 47; Rooks, Hair Raising, 75.

81. Byrd and Tharps, Hair Story, 2, 13, 30; Graybill, "Mennonite Women and Their Bishops," 256–57; Paul G. Landis, interview with author, March 8, 2003.

82. "Negro Membership in Mennonite Church," memorandum, September 1, 1953, Hist. Mss. 1-566, James and Rowena Lark Collection, Negro Membership, Menn. Church, 1953, folder 1/5, AMC.

83. Wills, "An Enduring Distance," 169.

84. Congregational record book, Broad Street Mennonite Church, 1954–1956, box Broad Street Mennonite Church (deposited by Harold and Vida Huber on April 4, 1998), box 2, VAMC; "Chicago Bethel Church Development 1944–1953."

85. "Chicago Bethel Church Development 1944–1953"; photo, "Paul King in the Pulpit at Bethel Mennonite Community Church in West Side Chicago," photo collection, folder Churches—Illinois, MLA; photo by Anna Rohrer, reproduced as figure 5.1 in this volume.

86. "Chicago Bethel Church Development 1944–1953."

87. Weaver, "The Mennonite Church," 31.

88. Minutes of the Colored Workers Committee 1953–1957, 104, file cabinets far wall, first cabinet, top drawer, drawer marked Home Missions Locations and Other General 1956–1964, four numbered notebooks, EMM record room.

89. Norman Derstine, memorandum regarding Trissels Mennonite Church, 1955, 13–15, box I-MS-17, John L. Stauffer collection, General Files H–Z, box 6, folder Nonconformity, VAMC; Paul G. Landis, interview with author, April 28, 2005.

90. Ira J. Buckwalter, minutes of the Colored Workers Committee Notes 1947–1953, 88, file cabinets far wall, first cabinet, top drawer, drawer marked Home Missions Locations and Other General 1956–1964, four numbered notebooks, EMM record room.

91. Colored Workers Committee Notes 1953–1957, 125, file cabinets far wall, first cabinet, top drawer, drawer marked Home Missions Locations and Other General 1956–1964, four numbered notebooks, EMM record room.

92. "Christian Race Relations" (paper presented at the Conference on Christian Community Relations, Goshen, Indiana, April 22–24, 1955).

93. "The Way of Christian Love in Race Relations," 5.

94. Ruth, The Earth Is the Lord's, 922, 1052–64; Schlabach, Gospel versus Gospel, 13.

95. Shenk, *By Faith They Went Out*, 78—79.

96. Peggy Curry, interview with author, March 29, 2005. In addition to anecdotal evidence from Broad Street in Harrisonburg, Virginia, church records list the following overseas missionaries as having first been involved at Andrews Bridge, an African-American mission post in Lancaster County: Miriam Buckwalter, Rebecca Herr, Hershey Lehman, Elsie Groff Shirk, and Marie Shenk. See Bernard Kautz, "Mellinger Church 250th Anniversary Home Coming Andrew's Bridge," memorandum, 1967, box Andrews Bridge Cong., unmarked red folder, LMHS; Edwin Ranck, "Report Given at Mellingers 250 Anniversary," memorandum, 1967, box Andrews Bridge Cong., unmarked red folder, LMHS. Note also that Lancaster Mennonite Conference missionary Elam Stauffer preached one of the first sermons at an African-American mission in Lancaster City just a week before leaving for Africa. See Ruth, *The Earth Is the Lord's*, 922. Evidently the use of domestic mission outposts to prepare missionaries for overseas ministry was not limited to African-American congregations. An informal history of the Steelton Mennonite congregation includes mention of a Samuel Miller, who developed a "special concern for the Spanish-speaking peoples of South America through his work with the Spanish-speaking Mexicans at Steelton." See Reed, "A History of Steelton Mennonite Gospel Mission," 6—7.

97. "Cash Views African Work," *Gospel Herald*, July 17, 1962, 633.

98. Bechler, *Black Mennonite Church*, 172—77; Levi C. Hartzler, "Mennonite Board of Missions (Mennonite Church)," Global Anabaptist Mennonite Encyclopedia Online, www.gameo.org/encyclopedia/contents/M463734.html (accessed March 12, 2008).

99. Dudziak, *Cold War Civil Rights*, 132; J. N. Smucker, "Who Is My Brother," *The Mennonite*, February 21, 1956, 123; Eugene Stoltzfus, "Which Side of the Road?" *Gospel Herald*, May 26, 1959, 485. The critique of domestic missions to African Americans in comparison with African missions continued at least through the latter part of the 1960s. See Arden Almquist, "Whitey, Your Time Is Running Out," *Missionary Messenger*, November 1967, 12—15.

100. Robert J. McCracken, "Actions Always Speak Louder than Words," *Gospel Herald*, February 13, 1962, 137—38, 58—59.

101. Bechler, *Black Mennonite Church*, 174—77; Reimers, *White Protestantism and the Negro*, 178; Zook, *Mennonite Yearbook and Directory*, vol. 56, 62.

102. Rowena Lark to Fannie Swartzentruber, November 16, 1959, Hist. Mss. 1-738, Fannie Yoder Swartzentruber Collection, Rowena Lark Letters 1941—1967, folder SC, AMC.

103. Kathryn Aschliman, "Living Family Worship," *Gospel Herald*, June 12, 1962, 538—39, 50; photo of Billy and Peggy Curry and family, 1961, reproduced in this volume as figure 2.7; photo, "Mrs. Lewis, Mrs. Webb, Nancy, Frank &

Earl F. Lewis," 1961, box Broad Street 1936–1979 Richard & Virginia Weaver, VAMC; Virgil Vogt, "Emergent Church in Cleveland," *Christian Living*, October, 1961, 14–17, 34–35.

104. Lark, "The History of Bethel."

105. Minutes of the Colored Workers Committee, 1958–1963, 192, record room file cabinets, far wall, first cabinet, top drawer, drawer marked Home Missions Locations and Other General 1956–1964, four numbered notebooks, EMM.

106. Curry, interview; Stoltzfus, *Quiet Shouts*, 162.

107. Rowena Lark to Fannie Swartzentruber, February 5, 1963, Hist. Mss. 1-738, Fannie Yoder Swartzentruber Collection, Rowena Lark Letters 1941–1967, folder SC, AMC.

108. Ibid.

109. Ibid.

110. Swartzentruber, interview, 2005.

111. Amos S. Horst, "A Query," *Pastoral Messenger*, July 1962, 7.

112. Wenger, *The Prayer Veil*, 25.

113. Good, "Forty Years," 22–23.

114. Gingerich, "Sharing the Faith," 55.

115. Lynford Hershey, interview with author, March 2, 2003.

116. Lancaster Conference Board of Lancaster Conference Board of Bishops, "Cut Hair," *Pastoral Messenger*, October 1964, 8.

117. Ruth, *The Earth Is the Lord's*, 1077.

118. Kraybill, "Mennonite Woman's Veiling," 301.

119. Strikingly, editors of the *Gospel Messenger*, a publication of the Church of the Brethren denomination, an Anabaptist group with strong pietist roots, had also airbrushed hair coverings on white women, three years earlier, in 1963. See Bowman, *Brethren Society*, 369.

120. Gary Martin, "Countian Pulled Down Atlanta's Racial Bars," *Intelligencer Journal*, March 19, 1970, 30.

121. Betty Gwinn, interview with author, April 26, 2008.

122. Martin, "Countian Pulled Down."

123. Gwinn, interview.

124. Robert J. Baker, "Mennonite Church in Atlanta," *Gospel Herald*, November 26, 1968, 1056–57; Gwinn, interview.

125. As other studies of the prayer veil have found, small, seemingly insignificant changes to the covering and how it is worn hold great significance to religious insiders. See Reynolds and Bronner, *Plain Women*, 76; Schmidt, "'Sacred Farming' or 'Working Out'?" 86.

126. Bulletin from funeral of Rowena L. Lark, 1970, Accession Record 3421, Hist. Mss. 1-566, James and Rowena Lark, AMC.

127. Huber and Huber, interview.

128. Swartzentruber, interview, 2007.

129. David Chappell shows how African-American churches in the South rallied around civil rights leaders with the urgency and passion of a religious revival. African Americans in white churches were cut off from that emotional support. See Chappell, *A Stone of Hope*, 87–96.

130. Thomas, Witherspoon, and Speight, "Toward the Development of the Stereotypic Roles," 428–29.

131. Byrd and Tharps, *Hair Story*, 57–59; Rooks, *Hair Raising*, 6. A parallel to Gwinn's black covering can be found in the Kente cloth and other African-themed stoles worn by Roman Catholic and Episcopalian priests and some Protestant ministers. The stoles, however, appear only during formal worship services. Gwinn wore her covering inside and outside of church services.

132. In response to the convert's request for "pretty" ribbons for her prayer veil, Bishop Luke Stoltzfus removed the covering string requirement. Good, "Forty Years," 22–23.

133. I here quote the title of a text by African-American Mennonite pastor and author Hubert Brown. See Brown, *Black and Mennonite*.

134. Chappell, *Inside Agitators*, 108.

135. This chapter's focus on relationships and religious conviction as primary motivating forces for resistance to racial oppression adds to the rich documentation of other motivations for women's resistance such as the importance of community, the desire to break free of gender hierarchy, concern for family, integration of the private and public, and political commitments. The following authors have contributed significantly to that documentation: Greene, *Our Separate Ways*; Hine, *Hine Sight*; Jones, *Labor of Love*; Kirk, "Daisy Bates"; Schultz, *Going South*; West, *Disruptive Christian Ethics*.

136. Marathana Prothro, "Racial / Ethnic People's Event Draws Cultures Together," Mennonite Church USA, www.mennoniteusa.org/news/news/july-sept06/08_29_06.htm (accessed March 7, 2008).

137. Laurie L. Oswald, "Teams Strive to Dismantle Racism, Heal Hearts in Mennonite Church USA," Mennonite Church USA, www.mennoniteusa.org/news/news/april-june04/06_02_04.htm#5 (accessed March 12, 2008).

Chapter 3. Fresh Air Disruption

1. Margie Middleton and Ruth Y. Wenger, "Fresh Air Reminiscences," *Missionary Messenger*, July 1977, 12–13, 21.

2. Extant records do not mention Jerry's last name. For the sake of clarity and uniform reference, I have assigned him the last name of Smith.

3. Otto Voth and Marietta Voth to Orlo Kaufman, August 6, 1969, VII.R GC Voluntary Service, Series 11 Gulfport VS Unit, box 4, folder 130, Fresh Air, 1969, MLA.

4. I am in debt to the following authors for modeling how to write histories that treat children as agents of change rather than passive respondents to adult action: Gilfoyle, "Street-Rats and Gutter-Snipes"; Nasaw, *Children of the City.*

5. Harold Regier and Rosella Wiens Regier, interview with author, July 12, 2005.

6. For evidence of other mutually shaping evangelical exchanges, see Veer, *Imperial Encounters.*

7. By coming to treat African-American Fresh Air participants as innocents, the white Mennonite hosts adapted a theological assumption long made about their own children. Mennonites traditionally promoted an ideal of "complex innocence" that recognized the presence of original sin in children that was nonetheless covered over by grace until the child reached the age of accountability in his or her early to late teens. See Miller, "Complex Innocence," 194, 201–3. White Mennonites thus eventually came to see African-American Fresh Air children as holding the same sort of theological innocence as their own children, in addition to a racial innocence potent enough to counter racial strife.

8. The experience of the Fresh Air participants featured in this chapter suggests that children played a greater role in the civil rights movement than previously understood. Despite the excellent, children-centered work of Robert Coles and the work of Wilma King on children's participation in the Birmingham crusade, few texts examine children's participation in the civil rights movement. David Garrow's work on Martin Luther King addresses children mostly in passing. Barbara Ransby's biography of Ella Baker talks about Baker's focus on older youth movements and the formation of the Student Nonviolent Coordinating Committee. Charles Payne and Aldon Morris also speak of the prominent role teenagers played in local struggles, as does Anne Moody's autobiography. There is, however, no singular study of the role of preadolescent children in the movement. This chapter on Fresh Air children and their hosts picks up on these existing strands of thought and seriously considers the role of children and childhood in reconceptualizing the civil rights movement as a series of daily demonstrations. For further reading, see Coles, *Children of Crisis,* vii, 336–37; King, *African American Childhoods;* Moody, *Coming of Age in Mississippi;* Morris, *The Origins of the Civil Rights Movement;* Payne, *I've Got the Light;* Ransby, *Ella Baker and the Black Freedom Movement.*

9. Bains, "Birmingham, 1963," 180–81.

10. Van Slyck, *A Manufactured Wilderness,* 98–99.

11. Freed, "Mennonites in the Fresh Air Program," 10.

12. Schlabach, *Gospel versus Gospel,* 73.

13. Dorothy Bean, "The Value of Fresh Air Work," memorandum, April 3, ca. 1951, third cabinet of second set in on right side, bottom unmarked drawer, folder Testimonies and misc., EMM record room; "Whoso Shall Receive One Such Little Child . . . Receiveth Me," memorandum, 1951, third cabinet of second set in on right side, bottom unmarked drawer, folder Forms 1950–1952, EMM record room.

14. Ira J. Buckwalter, minutes of the Colored Workers Committee, 1947–1953, file cabinets far wall, first cabinet, top drawer, drawer marked Home Missions Locations and Other General 1956–1964, four numbered notebooks, EMM record room.

15. Despite the intentions of the Colored Workers Committee in 1949 to serve only African-American children, for the first three years of the Fresh Air program white children nearly equaled and in some cases actually outnumbered African-American and "Spanish" children in the program. See Paul N. Kraybill, "Report of Mennonite Mission Children Visitation Program," memorandum, 1953, third cabinet of second set in on right side, bottom unmarked drawer, folder Committee Action, EMM record room. Within ten years, white participation dropped dramatically and then disappeared almost entirely owing to white flight from the inner city. I focus here on the African-American children participants because of the program's original intent and the interracial environment created by their visits to white Mennonite homes.

16. J. Lester Brubaker, "Colored Missions," Missionary Messenger, May 1950, 11.

17. Minutes of the joint meeting of the Eastern Mennonite Board of Missions and Charities and the Bishop Board of the Lancaster Conference District, January 14, 1929, 2, LMHS.

18. Ruth Garman and Virginia Weaver, "History of South Christian," memorandum, 1970, 1, box South Christian Street, Now Crossroads Cong., folder History, LMHS.

19. Merle W. Eshleman, "Mission for Colored, Philadelphia," Missionary Messenger, February 16, 1936, 11.

20. Buckwalter, minutes of Colored Workers Committee; Melvin Gingerich, "Negroes and the Mennonites," The Mennonite, June 14, 1949, 4; "This Group of Urban Negro Children," Missionary Messenger, January 1946, 5; C. F. Yake, "A Sunday Morning after Dismissal at Lancaster Colored Mission, Lancaster, Pa.," Gospel Herald, March 4, 1947, 1069.

21. My initial inquiry suggests that white Mennonites' exposure to African-American children through Fresh Air programs was not unique. Although little scholarly work has been written about the Fresh Air programs, I surmise that a northern or midwestern white rural Protestant family in the 1950s, 1960s, or early 1970s was also far more likely to have come into close contact with an African American through a Fresh Air exchange program than through any social program,

government initiative, or church mission. I project that during the period of my study approximately 2 million host families and 2 million to 3 million guest children participated in Fresh Air programs.

22. Middleton and Wenger, "Fresh Air Reminiscences."

23. Ibid.

24. Mennonites opposed the practice of slavery and cherished the memory of having done so, even though those who signed the document were at the time not Mennonite but rather Quaker. See Bechler, *Black Mennonite Church*, 37; Drake, *Quakers and Slavery in America*, 11; Irvin B. Horst, "Mennonites and the Race Question," *Gospel Herald*, July 13, 1945, 284–85; Smith, "Mennonites in America," 92; Smith, *The Story of the Mennonites*, 540.

25. Gingerich, "Negroes and the Mennonites"; Rowena Lark, "The History of Bethel Mennonite Church," *Our Journal*, May 1950, 1–3; "Response to Leroy Bechler Survey," memorandum, 1954, Hist. Mss. 1-723, Le Roy Bechler Coll., Questionnaire on Race attitude, 1951–1954, AMC.

26. Sonencker to Paul N. Kraybill, August 1951, third cabinet of second set in on right side, bottom unmarked drawer, folder F–J, EMM record room.

27. E. G. Horst, memorandum, untitled collection of host testimonies, ca. 1951, third cabinet of second set in on right side, bottom unmarked drawer, folder Testimonies and misc., EMM record room.

28. "Testimonies: Mission Children Visitation Program of Lancaster Conference," *Missionary Messenger*, May 1951, 11.

29. Rosella Regier, "Fourth Successful 'Fresh Air' Year Completed," *Gulfbreeze*, September–October 1963, 6.

30. "St. Ann's Mennonite Church VSBS," memorandum, 1952, box I.S. Pictures Home Ministries, found on cabinets on far left wall when entering room, folder Archives—Home Missions—1940s and 1950s, EMM record room.

31. Middleton and Wenger, "Fresh Air Reminiscences."

32. Ibid.

33. Ibid.

34. Mary Rohrer and Anna Rohrer, "Mennonite Mission Children's Visitation Program, Visitation Record," memorandum, 1951, third cabinet of second set in on right side, bottom unmarked drawer, folder F–J, EMM record room.

35. Ibid.

36. S. L. Longenecker to *Missionary Messenger*, March 26, 1951, third cabinet of second set in on right side, bottom unmarked drawer, folder Testimonies and misc., EMM record room; "Whoso Shall Receive One Such Little Child."

37. Middleton and Wenger, "Fresh Air Reminiscences."

38. Paul N. Kraybill, "Mennonite Mission Children Visitation Program," memorandum, 1952, 5, third cabinet of second set in on right side, bottom unmarked

drawer, folder Committee Action, EMM record room. Often conducted in public, lice checks humiliated the children and enforced the administrators' power, a process replicated in many other parts of the country during this period. See, for example, Hunter, *To 'Joy My Freedom*, 212; Rivera, . . . *And the Earth Did Not Devour Him*, 92−93.

39. Ira J. Buckwalter to Allen Hoffnagle, August 14, 1956, third cabinet in on right side, bottom drawer, folder Mission Children's visitation Program−1957, EMM record room.

40. Paul N. Kraybill to Frederick Howell Lewis, June 25, 1952, third cabinet of second set in on right side, bottom unmarked drawer, folder F−J, EMM record room.

41. Middleton and Wenger, "Fresh Air Reminiscences."

42. Ibid.

43. Ibid. Note also that Middleton and her friend Pat were separated from each other as girls who made different decisions about the covering. Boys did not experience this kind of gender-based trauma.

44. Mennonite General Conference, *The Nurture and Evangelism of Children*.

45. Haury, *Quiet Demonstration*, 16.

46. Ibid., 22−23, 26.

47. Orlo Kaufman, "Go South for Service," *The Mennonite*, March 19, 1957, 186−88.

48. Martha, "Praise and Prayer," *Gulfbreeze*, November−December 1959.

49. Dozens of church press articles featured Camp Landon workers in the 1940s, '50s, and beyond. See, for example, J. Winfield Fretz, "The Community at Gulfport, Mississippi," *Mennonite Community*, January, 1949, 18−23; and from *The Mennonite*, "A Welcome and a Blessing Awaits Us," June 29, 1954, 407; "A Witness against Race Prejudice," October 14, 1947, 15; T. B. Brown, "Observations of Retreat," August 4, 1953, 477; "Center Program Expands," May 24, 1955, 333; Elmer Ediger, "Racial Tensions and Gulfport," January 11, 1949, 14; "Gulfport Dream Comes True," June 19, 1956, 404; Kaufman, "Go South for Service"; Orlo Kaufman, "Racial Tensions," May 5, 1959, 278; Orlo Kaufman, "Retreat for Gulfport Negro Youth," August 4, 1953, 477; Orlo Kaufman and Elmer Ediger, "Evangelical Work at Camp Landon," May 2, 1955, 280; Milton I. Lee, "Feeling the Difference," October 16, 1956, 664; "Race Barriers in the South," August 12, 1947, 11; Harold Regier, "Camp Landon—What Are Our Objectives," May 24, 1955, 333; Harold Regier, "Why a Camp Landon," July 28, 1953, 462; Turkey Creek Bible School, Gulfport, Miss., photo, February 24, 1948, 15; Don Yoder, Esther Schmidt, and Muriel Thiessen, "When You Pray Remember Nolan and Johnnie and Evelyn," May 5, 1959, 282.

50. Delton Franz to Orlo Kaufman, February 1, 1960, VII.R GC Voluntary

Service, Series 11 Gulfport VS Unit, box 1, folder 4, Correspondence—General Conf 1960, MLA.

51. "Goessel Group," photo, 1960, Photo collection, folder Mississippi—Gulfport, MLA; "Moundridge Group," photo, 1960, Photo collection, folder Mississippi—Gulfport, MLA.

52. Elmer Voth and Linda Voth to Orlo Kaufman, September 5, 1961, VII.R GC Voluntary Service, Series 11 Gulfport VS Unit, box 4, folder 123, Fresh Air, 1961, MLA.

53. Haury, *The Quiet Demonstration*, 46.

54. Although girls were generally relegated to more domestic tasks like washing laundry and preparing meals, many still were taught how to drive a tractor.

55. Orlo Kaufman to Andrew Shelly, August 10, 1960, VII.R GC Voluntary Service, Series 11 Gulfport VS Unit, box 1, folder 4, Correspondence—General Conf. 1960, MLA.

56. Voth and Voth to Kaufman, 1961.

57. Ibid.

58. "Host Parents Summary," memorandum, 1960, VII.R GC Voluntary Service, Series 11 Gulfport VS Unit, box 4, folder 122, Fresh Air, 1960, MLA.

59. Ibid.

60. Orlo Kaufman, "A New Venture," *Gulfbreeze*, July–August 1960, 1.

61. "Host Parents Summary."

62. Ibid.; Mrs. Dwight Stucky to Orlo Kaufman, August 14, 1961, VII.R GC Voluntary Service, Series 11 Gulfport VS Unit, box 4, folder 123, Fresh Air, 1961, MLA.

63. Stucky to Kaufman, August 14, 1961.

64. Ibid.

65. Mrs. Winton Stucky to Orlo Kaufman, August 12, 1961, VII.R GC Voluntary Service, Series 11 Gulfport VS Unit, box 4, folder 123, Fresh Air, 1961, MLA.

66. Marjorie Graber to Orlo Kaufman and Edna Kaufman, August 29, 1961, VII.R GC Voluntary Service, Series 11 Gulfport VS Unit, box 4, folder 123, Fresh Air, 1961, MLA; Ernie Hiedebrecht and Mrs. Ernie Hiedebrecht to Orlo Kaufman, 1961, VII.R GC Voluntary Service, Series 11 Gulfport VS Unit, box 4, folder 123, Fresh Air, 1961, MLA.

67. Voth and Voth to Kaufman, 1961.

68. Jim Banman, "Integration Comes to Central Kansas as Mennonites Are Hosts to Negroes," memorandum, 1961, VII.R GC Voluntary Service, Series 11 Gulfport VS Unit, box 4, folder 123, Fresh Air, 1961, MLA.

69. Rev. Arnold Nickel to Orlo Kaufman, February 27, 1961, VII.R GC Voluntary Service, Series 11 Gulfport VS Unit, box 2, folder 32, Correspondence—nonconf, 1961, MLA.

70. In 1961 at least one host couple was somewhat more forthcoming. They thought it would "be wise if the older boys could be placed in homes where there are no girls their age." The fears Nickel refers to may have centered on discipline concerns or relational intimacy, but at least some of his local contemporaries feared the possibility of interracial sexual intimacy between African-American boys and white Mennonite girls. See George E. Kroecker and Mrs. George E. Kroecker to Orlo Kaufman, August 20, 1961, VII.R GC Voluntary Service, Series 11 Gulfport VS Unit, box 4, folder 123, Fresh Air, 1961, MLA.

71. Richard F. Graber, "The Christian's Approach to the Problem of Prejudice," *The Mennonite*, April 28, 1964, 288; Esther Groves, "Gulfport at the Crossroads," *The Mennonite*, November 19, 1963, 697–99; Harold Regier, editorial, February 12, 1963, 112.

72. Carson, *In Struggle*, 2–3.

73. Mrs. Clayton Shaub, "An Unfinished Story," *Missionary Messenger*, June 1965, 14–15.

74. Countryman, *Up South*, 2.

75. Marsh, *God's Long Summer*, 8; Steinhorn and Diggs-Brown, *By the Color of Our Skin*, 116; Weisbrot, *Freedom Bound*, 222.

76. "Why Do White Folks Hate Us? Urban-Racial Meetings, Youngstown, Ohio, March 4, 5, St. Louis, Missouri, March 11, 12," *Mission Service Newsletter*, May 9, 1965, 1–4.

77. Lynford Hershey, "Souls and Civil Rights," *Gospel Herald*, July 6, 1965, 581–82; Sanford G. Shetler, "Is This Our Task?" *Gospel Herald*, July 20, 1965, 629–30.

78. John M. Drescher, "Race Relations Responsibility," *Gospel Herald*, August 11, 1964, 683, 701; Shetler, "Is This Our Task?"

79. Ira J. Buckwalter, "Report of the Chairman Mennonite Mission Children's Visitation Program," memorandum, January 9, 1951, 3, third cabinet of second set in on right side, bottom unmarked drawer, folder Committee Action, EMM record room.

80. Shaub, "An Unfinished Story."

81. Available records from the Children Visitation program suggest a rise in host involvement from the mid-1960s forward. Author's tabulation.

82. Kroecker and Kroecker to Kaufman, 1961.

83. Peggy Curry, interview with author, March 29, 2005.

84. Older teens had stopped participating in many white-led city missions by the mid-1960s. See, for example, the ineffective efforts of South Christian Street mission workers in Lancaster, Pennsylvania, to recruit teens to their services: Dale L. Weaver, "Annual Christian Worker Group Report," memorandum, 1964, 3, box South Christian Street, Now Crossroads Cong, folder S. Christian Street, LMHS.

85. Paul N. Kraybill, "Notes from Visit to Steelton," memorandum, 1963, first

cabinet of row on far left wall upon entering room, third drawer, Home Ministries, Locations New York City, City Wisconsin 1964–1975 (1961), folder Pennsylvania Steelton, EMM record room.

86. Shaub, "An Unfinished Story."

87. Norman G. Shenk, interview with author, March 22, 2005.

88. Shaub, "An Unfinished Story."

89. Paul G. Burkholder, "Glad Tidings Mennonite Church Herald Tribune Fresh Air Fund Agency Report 1966," memorandum, March 17, 1967, box Glad Tidings, folder Glad Tidings, LMHS.

90. John Eby, interview with author, February 28, 2003.

91. "Special Funds for Summer City Needs," *The Mennonite*, June 10, 1969, 390.

92. Shenk, *By Faith They Went Out*, 81.

93. Orlo Kaufman to C. D. Kaufman, August 7, 1968, and Harold Regier, "Harassment by County Patrolman," memorandum, August 9, 1968, VII.R GC Voluntary Service, Series 11 Gulfport VS Unit, box 2, folder 45, Correspondence—nonconf, June–Dec., 1968, MLA.

94. Note that Smith stayed with Marietta and Otto Voth in Newton. Albert Potts was hosted by Elmer and Linda Voth in Inman. Voth is a common Mennonite surname in eastern Kansas.

95. Voth and Voth to Kaufman, 1961.

96. Ibid.

97. Haury, *The Quiet Demonstration*, 49.

98. Milo Dailey, "Mississippi Negro Boy Is Enjoying Life with Farm Family near Freeman," *Yankton Press and Dakotan*, Friday, August 1, 1969; Delmer Hofer, "Towards Better Understanding between Races," *Northern Light*, September 1969, 2; "Local Farm Families Host Mississippi Children during Week-Long, 'Fresh-Air Program,'" newspaper clipping, VII.R GC Voluntary Service, Series 11 Gulfport VS Unit, box 4, folder 130, Fresh Air, 1969, MLA.

99. M. Arlene Mellinger, "200 Children Are Hoping . . . ," *Missionary Messenger*, May 1972, 12–13.

100. Paul N. Kraybill, "Mennonite Mission Children Visitation Program, Report of the Director," memorandum, 1951, 1, third cabinet of second set in on right side, bottom unmarked drawer, folder Committee Action, EMM record room; Mellinger, "200 Children Are Hoping . . ."

101. Nelson Good et al., "Racism Is a Primary Concern," memorandum, March 8, 1971, 3, Statements, Lancaster Mennonite Conference Race Relations Study Committee, LMHS.

102. Voth and Voth to Kaufman, 1961.

103. Haury, *The Quiet Demonstration*, 49; Barbara Horst, interview with author, April 22, 2003.

104. Middleton and Wenger, "Fresh Air Reminiscences"; Haury, *The Quiet Demonstration*, 49.

105. Edith Tschetter and Larry Tscheter, "Who Profited More?" *Gulfbreeze*, July–October 1970, 4.

106. Groves, "Gulfport at the Crossroads"; Harold Regier and Rosella Regier to Gary Stenson, April 11, 1963, VII.R GC Voluntary Service, Series 11 Gulfport VS Unit, box 2, folder 34, Correspondence—non-conf, Jan.–July 1963, MLA; Regier and Regier, interview.

107. Regier and Regier, interview.

108. Mae Schrag, "Mennonite Prejudice," *Gulfbreeze*, May–June 1963, 5.

109. Ardie Goering, "Friends for Life: Four African-American Men and Bethel College," Bethel College, www.bethelks.edu/mennonitelife/2008spring/friends _for_life.php (accessed July 9, 2008).

110. Minutes of South Seventh St. Workers' meeting, 1956, box South Seventh Street, Reading, Minute/Record Books, tan ring-bound notebook, LMHS; Leon Stauffer to J. Lester Brubaker, July 14, 1971, Lancaster, Pennsylvania, author's personal collection; Amos W. Weaver, "Response to Leroy Bechler Survey," memorandum, 1954, Hist. Mss. 1-723, Le Roy Bechler Coll., Questionnaire on Race attitude, 1951–1954, AMC.

111. Orlo Kaufman, "Bethel Graduates," *Gulfbreeze*, May–June, 1961, 4; Paul G. Landis, interview with author, March 8, 2003; John Powell, "Hesston College Visit," memorandum, April 16, 1970, Hist. Mss. 1-784, box 1, Hubert Schwartzentruber Collection, Miscellaneous, folder Minority Ministries Council, 1970, AMC.

112. Kaufman, "Bethel Graduates."

113. Orlo Kaufman to Harold Schrag et al., March 7, 1961, VII.R GC Voluntary Service, Series 11 Gulfport VS Unit, box 2, folder 32, Correspondence—non-conf, 1961, MLA; Harold Regier to Ervin Krehbiel and Mrs., Ervin Krehbiel, March 3, 1964, VII.R GC Voluntary Service, Series 11 Gulfport VS Unit, box 2, folder 36, Correspondence—non-conf, 1964, MLA.

114. Kaufman, "Bethel Graduates"; Orlo Kaufman to Harold Schrag et al., March 7, 1961, VII.R GC Voluntary Service, Series 11 Gulfport VS Unit, box 2, folder 32, Correspondence—non-conf, 1961, MLA; Harold Regier to Ervin Krehbiel and Mrs. Ervin Krehbiel, March 3, 1964, VII.R GC Voluntary Service, Series 11 Gulfport VS Unit, box 2, folder 36, Correspondence—non-conf, 1964, MLA; Regier and Regier, interview.

115. Betty Douple, interview with author, May 25, 2005; Libby Geil, interview with author, May 25, 2005; Orlo Kaufman to Roger Krehbiel and Judy Krehbiel, October 29, 1968, VII.R GC Voluntary Service, Series 11 Gulfport VS Unit, box 2, folder 45, Correspondence—non-conf, June–Dec., 1968, MLA.

116. Voth and Voth to Kaufman, 1961.

117. Moran, *Interracial Intimacy*.

118. Newman, *Getting Right with God*, 20; Sitkoff, *The Struggle for Black Equality*, 222; Sokol, *There Goes My Everything*, 237.

119. Although he uses the metaphor of an underlying stream bursting to the surface, Perry Bush captures a similar tension in his description of Mennonite separation and "missionary fervor" in the middle of the twentieth century. See Bush, *Two Kingdoms, Two Loyalties*, 11.

120. Matthew 25:45 quotes Jesus's description of final judgment in which those who have served "one of the least of these" receive the reward of "eternal life." White Mennonites, like many Christians, knew and frequently quoted the verse when speaking of all their mission efforts, including Fresh Air ventures. See, for example, Shaub, "An Unfinished Story."

121. "Why Do White Folks Hate Us?"

122. Bechler, *Black Mennonite Church*, 177.

123. Middleton and Wenger, "Fresh Air Reminiscences"; Voth and Voth to Kaufman, 1961.

124. Esther Eby Glass, "Report of Mission Fresh Air Sponsors' Meeting," memorandum, March 27, 1962, third cabinet in on right side, bottom drawer, folder Eastern Mennonite Board, Fresh Air Program 1962—1963, EMM record room; Harold Regier and Orlo Kaufman to Prospective Fresh Air Host Parents, April 9, 1962, VII.R GC Voluntary Service, Series 11 Gulfport VS Unit, box 4, folder 124, Fresh Air, 1962, MLA; Voth and Voth to Kaufman, 1961.

125. Although most of those in attendance at the 1963 Board of Christian Service meeting held General Conference membership, (Old) Mennonite leaders like Guy Hershberger also participated. Vincent Harding, then working for the inter-Mennonite organization Mennonite Central Committee, also participated and communicated regularly with both denominations.

126. "The Church Facing the Race Crisis," memorandum, December 4, 1963, 3, CESR papers I-3-7, box 5, folder 168, AMC.

127. Henry A. Fast, "Vigil for Rights Bill Begins," *The Mennonite*, May 19, 1964, 334.

Chapter 4. Vincent Harding's Dual Demonstration

1. "Record of the Meeting of Church Leaders for a Discussion on Racial and Civil Rights Problems to Discover Which Course Should Be Followed by the Mennonite Church in This Time of Social Revolution," memorandum, September 14, 1963, MCC Peace Section, Conjoint and Related Minutes, box I, file 1, Reports, 1952—68, AMC.

2. Ibid.

3. C. J. Dyck, "Dialogue on Race," *The Mennonite*, October 29, 1963, 648–49; "Record of the Meeting of Church Leaders."

4. For discussion of Weber's articulation of charismatic leadership, see Weber, *Sociology of Religion*.

5. Historian Adam Fairclough resolves the debate by suggesting that organizations like the Southern Christian Leadership Conference influenced King as much as King influenced those organizations and the entire civil rights movement. See Fairclough, *To Redeem the Soul of America*.

6. A group of scholars have already done an excellent job of expanding civil rights movement scholarship into previously neglected fields. For a treatment of gender, see Collier-Thomas and Franklin, *Sisters in the Struggle*; Ling and Monteith, "Gender and the Civil Rights Movement." For an exploration of Christian belief within the civil rights movement, see Marsh, *God's Long Summer*; Marsh, *Beloved Community*. For a particularly engaging treatment of grassroots organizing, see Payne, *I've Got the Light*.

7. Harding's story likewise challenges the argument that white Christian consensus splintered in the face of civil rights initiatives. In his influential treatment of Roman Catholic reaction to racial change in the urban north, John T. McGreevy argues that white racism takes multiple and contradictory forms that change over time. See McGreevy, *Parish Boundaries*, 3–4. David Swartz makes a similar argument about varied responses to the civil rights movement among Mennonites in Mississippi. See Swartz, "Mista Mid-Nights." Both McGreevy and Swartz offer convincing evidence for the particular stories they tell. Yet they miss how white church functionaries responded to civil rights leaders such as Harding with remarkably consistent terms of engagement. Harding met with many church leaders during his Mennonite sojourn, but he also engaged with local pastors, college students, voluntary service workers, and lay congregational members from across the country. Those diverse groups responded to Harding with a similar set of objections, questions, and unsettled emotion. Discrete Mennonite groups may have each engaged in particular ways with the civil rights movement, but their struggle to arrive at a response looked very similar in Goshen, Lancaster, and Gulfport. At the same time, I am particularly grateful for Swartz's treatment of the varied and contested responses of Mennonites to the civil rights movement. He successfully argues for a reconsideration of Leo Driedger's and Donald Kraybill's thesis that Mennonites in North America became increasingly engaged in activist pursuits and left behind a more quietist withdrawal over the course of the twentieth century. While I agree with Swartz that Driedger, Kraybill, and to a degree Perry Bush focus on church leadership at the expense of highly contested and often turbulent congregation-level engagement with race relations questions, the story I tell in this

chapter demonstrates that an individual like Vincent Harding had far-reaching influence among various Mennonite communities and at multiple levels of church life. In short, Harding was influential in circles far wider than just the church intelligentsia and bureaucracy. His prolific writing, multiple meetings, and connection with even the most conservative Mennonite communities in Mississippi and elsewhere suggest that all groups, from the grass roots to the executive level, had to negotiate or respond to the critique raised by Harding.

8. Note in particular Toews's description of Harding's 1967 Mennonite World Conference speech as "riveting." See Toews, *Mennonites in American Society*, 259—61. For evidence of other African-American males with charismatic presence, see Brown, "The Larks"; Vincent Harding et al., "Church and Race in 6 Cities," *The Mennonite*, February 12, 1963, 98—101; "Record of the Meeting of Church Leaders." Mennonite historian Perry Bush also notes the preeminent role that Harding played and writes of him, "Indeed, the leadership had begun to digest the not entirely comfortable knowledge that having inaugurated a prophet in their midst, they could not always contain the direction of his fire." See Bush, *Two Kingdoms, Two Loyalties*, 215. Note that Bush describes Harding in terms of his charismatic capacity, expressed in prophetic pronouncement. While I reposition Harding in this chapter, Bush's work stands in its own right as an excellent summary of the wide-ranging impact Harding had on white Mennonite orientation to the civil rights movement.

9. Writing as a student at Associated Mennonite Biblical Seminaries in 1970, J. Denny Weaver offered a groundbreaking history, "The Mennonite Church and the American Negro" that positioned 1963 in a period during which Mennonites accepted past avoidance of race relations issues and increased their readiness to engage in action. Interestingly, he made no direct mention of Vincent Harding. See Weaver, "The Mennonite Church." As an undergraduate at Goshen College in 1977, Jan Bender Shetler wrote a brilliant and exhaustive paper on Guy Hershberger and Vincent Harding. Although I focus on Harding's earlier years in the church for an explanation of his readiness to leave the Mennonite community well before the advent of the black power movement, Shetler's overarching examination of Harding's failure to act as a conscience to the movement and Hershberger's failure to draw the church into the civil rights movement bears significant attention. See Shetler, "A Prophetic Voice."

10. Payne, *I've Got the Light*, 376.

11. Chapman, *Christianity on Trial*, 73.

12. Haury, *Quiet Demonstration*, 90—91.

13. Vincent Harding and Rosemarie Harding, "Visit to Camp Landon, March 1 to March 6, 1963," memorandum, April 18, 1963, VII.R GC Voluntary Service, Series 11 Gulfport VS Unit, box 1, folder 7, Correspondence—General Conf. 1963, MLA.

14. Alongside Vincent Harding's story, another tale remains largely untold in this chapter. For the first number of years of their Mennonite sojourn, Vincent and Rosemarie's names often appeared together in print. From early 1963 forward, however, Rosemarie's presence in official Mennonite church sources declined. The demands of caring for a newborn combined with the patriarchy and sexism of the Mennonite church turned attention away from Rosemarie and toward Vincent. Although she remained active in both Mennonite and civil rights groups for the period under study here, she received significantly less attention from church leaders than did her husband. Despite evident patriarchy and sexism among groups like the Student Nonviolent Coordinating Committee, the Southern Christian Leadership Conference, and the Congress of Racial Equality, Rosemarie found more ways to exercise leadership among civil rights groups than in the Mennonite community. Thus even though she had been a Mennonite far longer than her husband and rarely critiqued the church in as direct a manner, she became more identified with civil rights groups and less so with the Mennonite church. She thereby became less a border dweller and received little official church attention. In this chapter, Rosemarie appears as an early, but later absent, partner in Vincent's story. In actuality, her voice remained strong and influential in non-Mennonite circles through the period of this study.

15. Harding, "Vincent Harding"; "Harding, Vincent Gordon (1931–)," Martin Luther King, Jr., Research and Education Institute, Stanford University, http://mlk-kpp01.stanford.edu/index.php/encyclopedia/encyclopedia/enc_harding_vincent_gordon_1931/ (accessed January 7, 2010).

16. Harding, "Vincent Harding," 86.

17. Rose Marie Berger, "I've Known Rivers: The Story of Freedom Movement Leaders Rosemarie Freeney Harding and Vincent Harding," *Sojourners*, www.sojo.net/index.cfm?action=news.display_archives&mode=currentopinion&article=CO_040311_berger (accessed February 27, 2008).

18. Harding, "Vincent Harding," 88.

19. Berger, "I've Known Rivers."

20. Paul and Lois King served with James and Rowena Lark at Bethel Mennonite in Chicago beginning in 1955, but (Old) Mennonite Church leaders drew relatively less attention to the integrated team ministry there than General Conference leaders did at the nearby Woodlawn congregation. See Bechler, *Black Mennonite Church*, 93–94.

21. Rich, *Walking Together in Faith*, 101.

22. Bechler, *Black Mennonite Church*, 44.

23. Delton Franz to Orlo Kaufman, September 4, 1958, VII.R GC Voluntary Service, Series 11 Gulfport VS Unit, box 2, folder 30, Correspondence—non-conf 1958, MLA; "Aids for Southern Tour," memorandum, 1958, VII.R GC Voluntary

Service, Series 11 Gulfport VS Unit, box 2, folder 30, Correspondence—non-conf 1958, MLA.

24. Vincent Harding, "To My Fellow Christians: An Open Letter to Mennonites," *The Mennonite*, September 30, 1958, 597–98; Weaver, "The Mennonite Church," 33.

25. Delton Franz, "Island of Hope in a Sea of Despair," *The Mennonite*, February 24, 1959, 119.

26. Guy F. Hershberger, "Nonresistance, the Mennonite Church, and the Race Question," *Gospel Herald*, June 28, 1960, 577–78, 581–82.

27. "Aids for Southern Tour"; Harding, "To My Fellow Christians."

28. I here suggest that, contrary to Paul Toews's position, Harding's challenge to Hershberger emerged alongside rather than subsequent to J. Lawrence Burkholder's articulation of a more socially engaged pacifism. Toews misses that Harding had been advocating for greater social involvement from 1958 through his 1967 Mennonite World Conference speech. See Toews, *Mennonites in American Society*, 261–63.

29. Hershberger, *The Way of the Cross in Human Relations*.

30. Schlabach, "Race, and Another Look," 12, 19, 22–23, 38.

31. Harding, "To My Fellow Christians."

32. Ibid.

33. "Seminar on Race Relations: Representation as of March 18, 1959," memorandum, March 18, 1959, CESR papers I-3-7, box 7, folder 58, AMC.

34. Documents reporting on the event list the names of forty-nine participants, eleven of them African-American. See "Seminar on Race Relations Representation," memorandum, April 17–19, 1959, IX-12-3, PS, folder Race Relations: Christ, the Mennonite Churches & Race, Seminar, AMC. Three other African Americans, Charles Flowers, Gerald Hughes, and Warner Jackson, were quoted in a report by Guy F. Hershberger as also having been present. See Guy F. Hershberger, "Report of the Chicago Race Relations Seminar," memorandum, July 16, 1959, CESR papers I-3-7, box 7, folder 58, AMC.

35. Vincent Harding, "The Task of the Mennonite Church," memorandum, 1959, 29, 31, Hist. Mss. 1-48, box 60, John H. Yoder (1927–1997) Collection Race/Urban issues, file 60/1, AMC.

36. Bush, *Two Kingdoms, Two Loyalties*, 213; Harding, "Biography, Democracy, and Spirit," 689; Harding, "Vincent Harding," 89.

37. Rosemarie Harding and Vincent Harding, "An Experiment in Peace," *The Mennonite*, January 22, 1963, 52–53.

38. Rosemarie Harding and Vincent Harding, "Pilgrimage to Albany," *The Mennonite*, January 22, 1963, 50–52.

39. Vincent Harding, "The Christian and the Race Question," memorandum, August 6, 1962, IX-7-12, file 2, box 6, Race Relations 1955–70, AMC.

40. Harding and Harding, "Pilgrimage to Albany."

41. Ibid.

42. Harding, "The Christian and the Race Question," 3, 4—5.

43. Harding and Harding, "An Experiment in Peace."

44. C. Norman Kraus et al., "Personal Responsibility in Improving Race Relations," *Gospel Herald*, February 5, 1963, 116—17, 32—34.

45. Daniel Hertzler, "Brotherhood at a Distance?" *Christian Living*, February 1963, 2.

46. "Mennonite Faith Called 'Total Love,'" *Gospel Herald*, August 14, 1962, 720—21; Victor Stoltzfus, "A Talk with Vincent Harding," *Christian Living*, October 1962, 10—11, 37—38, 40.

47. Vincent Harding and Rosemarie Harding, "Reflections of a Visit to Virginia," memorandum, 1962, CESR papers I-3-7, box 4, folder 1, AMC.

48. Mahlon L. Blosser to Nelson E. Kauffman, March 4, 1963, CESR papers I-3-7, box 7, folder 7, AMC. Interestingly, as mentioned below, thirteen months later the Virginia Conference proudly promoted a Conference on the Christian and Race. Only white Mennonite men spoke in the conference sessions. See "Conference on the Christian and Race at Chicago Avenue Mennonite Church," memorandum, March 31, 1964, box Broad Street 1936—1979 Richard & Virginia Weaver, VAMC.

49. Haury, *The Quiet Demonstration*, 1.

50. Orlo Kaufman, "The Gulfport Story: Accent on Challenge," memorandum, February 1966, VII.R GC Voluntary Service, Series 11 Gulfport VS Unit, box 6, folder 214, Reports, misc, MLA.

51. Orlo Kaufman to Leo Driedger, January 13, 1960, VII.R GC Voluntary Service, Series 11 Gulfport VS Unit, box 1, folder 4, Correspondence—General Conf. 1960, MLA.

52. Orlo Kaufman, "News in Brief," *Gulfbreeze*, March—April 1960, 2—3.

53. Ibid.

54. Orlo Kaufman to Oswald Klassen and T. B. Schmidt, March 14, 1960, VII.R GC Voluntary Service, Series 11 Gulfport VS Unit, box 2, folder 31, Correspondence—non-conf 1960, MLA; Orlo Kaufman to Orlando Waltner and Leo Driedger, November 12, 1959, VII.R GC Voluntary Service, Series 11 Gulfport VS Unit, box 1, folder 3, Correspondence—General Conf. 1959, MLA.

55. Harold Regier to Mel Flickenger, October 31, 1962, VII.R GC Voluntary Service, Series 11 Gulfport VS Unit, box 4, folder 125, Fresh Air, 1963, MLA.

56. Edna Kaufman, "When You Pray," *Gulfbreeze*, January—February 1963, 1.

57. Orlo Kaufman, "Camp Landon General Report #25 First Quarter, 1963," memorandum, 1963, VII.R GC Voluntary Service, Series 11 Gulfport VS Unit, box 6, folder 215, Reports, quarterly, MLA; Orlo Kaufman to Vincent Harding, February 20, 1963, VII.R GC Voluntary Service, Series 11 Gulfport VS Unit, box 1, folder 7, Correspondence—General Conf. 1963, MLA.

58. Orlo Kaufman to Andrew Shelly, April 11, 1963, VII.R GC Voluntary Service, Series 11 Gulfport VS Unit, box 1, folder 7, Correspondence—General Conf. 1963, MLA.

59. Orlo Kaufman to Verney Unruh, April 30, 1963, VII.R GC Voluntary Service, Series 11 Gulfport VS Unit, box 6, folder 224, Retreats 1963, MLA.

60. Orlo Kaufman, "Issues Faced Squarely," *Gulfbreeze*, March–April 1963, 5.

61. Harding and Harding, "Visit to Camp Landon," 4.

62. Ibid.

63. Orlo Kaufman to Herman Dueck, May 14, 1963, VII.R GC Voluntary Service, Series 11 Gulfport VS Unit, box 2, folder 34, Correspondence—non-conf, Jan.–July 1963, MLA; Orlo Kaufman, "Meeting at Tougaloo," *Gulfbreeze*, January–February 1963, 4.

64. Orlo Kaufman to Daniel Guice, June 27, 1963, VII.R GC Voluntary Service, Series 11 Gulfport VS Unit, box 2, folder 34, Correspondence—non-conf, Jan.–July 1963, MLA.

65. Haury, *The Quiet Demonstration*, 65.

66. Orlo Kaufman, "NAACP Meeting Protested," *Gulfbreeze*, November–December 1963, 2.

67. Harold Regier to Board of Christian Service, March 24, 1964, VII.R GC Voluntary Service, Series 11 Gulfport VS Unit, box 1, folder 8, Correspondence—General Conf. 1964, MLA.

68. Harold R. Regier to Stanley Bohn, May 30, 1968, VII.R GC Voluntary Service, Series 11 Gulfport VS Unit, box 1, folder 25, Correspondence—General Conf., CHM 1968–1971, MLA.

69. Rosemarie Harding and Vincent Harding, "Mississippi Delta Trip March 6–11 (Confidential)," memorandum, April 25, 1963, 10, CESR papers I-3-7, box 7, folder 18, AMC.

70. Harding, "Biography, Democracy, and Spirit."

71. Photo of Vincent and Rosemarie Harding at Broad Street, 1963, uncatalogued box named Broad Street 1936–1979 Richard & Virginia Weaver, VAMC.

72. "Night Services at Broad St. Church," memorandum, 1963, box Broad Street 1936–1979 Richard & Virginia Weaver, VAMC.

73. Promotional flier, "Hear VINCENT HARDING, interracial leader from THE MENNONITE HOUSE, Atlanta, Georgia," 1963, uncatalogued box Broad Street 1936–1979 Richard & Virginia Weaver, VAMC.

74. "Conference on the Christian and Race at Chicago Avenue Mennonite Church."

75. Brunk et al., *Conference on the Christian and Race*.

76. Vincent Harding, "Birmingham, Alabama," memorandum, May 30, 1963, box Clarence E. Lutz, MCC Peace Section, 1963–1969, LMHS.

77. Ibid.

78. Paul Peachey and Ellen Peachey, interview with author, April 1, 2005.

79. Harding, "Birmingham, Alabama," 2.

80. Ibid. The final agreement provided for desegregation of local businesses, hiring of African Americans in sales and clerical positions, releasing prisoners on reduced bail, and maintaining communication between African-American and white leaders. See Bains, "Birmingham, 1963," 182.

81. Patterson, *Grand Expectations*, 481.

82. Findlay, "Religion and Politics," 71.

83. Mae Schrag, "Mennonite Prejudice," *Gulfbreeze*, May–June 1963, 5.

84. Esther Groves, "Gulfport at the Crossroads," *The Mennonite*, November 19, 1963, 697–99; Gary Stenson and Elsie Stenson to Harold Regier, April 3, 1963, VII.R GC Voluntary Service, Series 11 Gulfport VS Unit, box 2, folder 34, Correspondence—non-conf, Jan.–July 1963, MLA.

85. Height, "We Wanted the Voice of a Woman to Be Heard," 84.

86. Edgar Metzler to Peace Section Members, June 28, 1963, CESR papers, I-3-7, box 7, file 7 1963, J–M, AMC.

87. Sandage, "A Marble House," 158.

88. Payne, *I've Got the Light*, 269.

89. Lee, "Anger, Memory, and Personal Power," 151; Nicholas Targ, "Human Rights Hero: Fannie Lou Hamer (1917–1977)," American Bar Association, Section of Individual Rights and Responsibilities, *Human Rights Magazine*, www.abanet.org/irr/hr/spring05/hero.html (accessed February 27, 2008).

90. Berger, "I've Known Rivers."

91. Guy F. Hershberger, "Mennonites and the Current Race Issue: Observations, Reflections, and Recommendations Following a Visitation to Southern Mennonite Churches, July–August, 1963, with a Review of Historical Background," memorandum, September 10, 1963, 11–12, author's personal collection.

92. C. Norman Kraus, "Report on Assignment in the South," memorandum, July 16–August 4, 1963, IX-12-3, Mennonite Central Committee, Data Files, folder Race Relations I, AMC.

93. lhk, "Mennonite Hour to Interview Harding," Mennonite Central Committee and Mennonite Church USA Historical Committee, www.mcusa-archives.org/plowshares/atlanta/8.7.1963.html (accessed February 27, 2008).

94. "Mennonite General Conference Proceedings, August 20–23, 1963, Kalona, Iowa," memorandum, 1963, 87, IX-7-12, file 2, box 6, Race Relations 1955–70, AMC.

95. Nelson E. Kauffman to Guy F. Hershberger, August 26, 1963, CESR papers I-3-7, box 5, folder 165, AMC.

96. Hershberger, "Mennonites and the Current Race Issue."

97. Maynard Shelly, editorial, *The Mennonite*, August 6, 1963, 499; John M. Drescher, "Our Mission and Race," *Gospel Herald*, August 6, 1963, 667; Vincent Harding, "The Christian and the Race Question," *Gospel Herald*, August 6, 1963, 669–71; "Reconciliation," memorandum, August 23, 1963, CESR papers I-3-7, box 6, folder 11, AMC.

98. Guy F. Hershberger, "Letter to the United States Congress on Civil Rights," *Gospel Herald*, August 13, 1963, 705; Edgar Metzler, "The Mennonite Churches and the Current Race Crisis," *Gospel Herald*, August 6, 1963, 683–84; James Reston, "The First Significant Test of the Freedom March," *Gospel Herald*, October 8, 1963, 889; "Schoolmen Aid Race Witness," *The Mennonite*, August 6, 1963, 492–93; John D. Unruh Jr. and Esko Loewen, "Is This Our Revolution?" *The Mennonite*, September 10, 1963, 534–36.

99. Vincent Harding, *Martin Luther King*, vii.

100. Salmond, *My Mind Set on Freedom*, 70.

101. Carson, *In Struggle*, 66.

102. "Meeting of Church Leaders for a Discussion of the Course Which Should Be Followed in This Time of Social Revolution," memorandum, September 14, 1963, 2, CESR papers I-3-7, box 5, folder 165, AMC.

103. Although Rosemarie Harding's name does not appear on the official meeting roster of the day, a later report quotes her observation about the need for reconciliation in the name of love such as that demonstrated by Clarence Jordan at Koinonia Farms. See Dyck, "Dialogue on Race"; "Record of the Meeting of Church Leaders." A third report, in which the speakers' identities were replaced by alphabetized labels, attributes her comment anonymously to "Brother V." In the interest of anonymity, the editors erased Harding's gender. See C. J. Dyck, "Pronouncements—Then What?" *Gospel Herald*, October 22, 1963, 939, 49.

104. "Record of the Meeting of Church Leaders," 3.

105. Shetler, "A Prophetic Voice," 35.

106. Ibid.

107. "Record of the Meeting of Church Leaders," 5.

108. "From Words to Deeds in Race Relations (Tentative Draft)," memorandum, 1963, Hist. Mss. 1-48, box 60, John H. Yoder (1927–1997) Collection Race / Urban issues, file 60/2, Peace Section binder noted '63, AMC; Guy F. Hershberger, "From Words to Deeds in Race Relations," *Gospel Herald*, February 16, 1965, 121, 30.

109. "The Church Facing the Race Crisis," memorandum, December 4, 1963, 18, CESR papers I-3-7, box 5, folder 168, AMC.

110. Ibid.; "Regional Meeting on Race and Cultural Relations," memorandum, September 21, 1963, CESR papers I-3-7, box 5, folder 165, AMC.

111. Items (that is, reports, feature articles, and editorials) referring to or written

by Harding appeared in the *Gospel Herald* on February 5, March 26, and August 6 (three times), in *The Mennonite* on January 22 (two times), February 12 and 26, March 5 and 26, June 25, July 9 (two times), and August 6 (two times), and once in *Christian Living* magazine in February. In general, the *Gospel Herald* focused more on Harding's critique of the church and *The Mennonite* on Harding's civil rights activities. Other than the *Gospel Herald*'s editor's preference for writing about racism as a theological problem and *The Mennonite*'s editor's focus on legislative response, the two publications' coverage of race and civil rights is surprisingly similar given an expectation of greater interest in worldly affairs on the part of Mennonites from the General Conference. In the course of the year both magazines denounced those who used the Genesis passage known as the "curse of Ham" to support racial discrimination, argued for involvement with civil rights as a means to maintain integrity for overseas mission, included a similar number of items on race-related matters (approximately thirty-one for the *Gospel Herald* and thirty-four for *The Mennonite*), and featured articles by white pastors chastising Mennonites for their participation in racial discrimination. See "Birmingham Troubles Mennonite Conscience," *The Mennonite*, October 8, 1963, 604–5; Hubert Schwartzentruber, "Where Do We Stand?" *Gospel Herald*, July 23, 1963, 631. In terms of their printed publications, the white Mennonite response again looked very similar across the community.

112. Edgar Metzler and Vincent Harding, "Race Relations Project," memorandum, 1963, IX-7-12, no. 2, box 6, entitled Race Relations 1955–70, AMC.

113. Edgar Stoesz, "Vince Harding Visit to Akron," memorandum, August 14, 1962, MCC Correspondence, IX-6-3, Inter-Office Peace Section, PS 1962, AMC. Oral history interviews also corroborate the informal criticism that had begun to mount about Harding. See, for example, Paul G. Landis, interview with author, April 28, 2005.

114. Metzler and Harding, "Race Relations Project."

115. Ibid.

116. Elvin L. Martin, "Love in Atlanta," *Volunteer*, September 1963, 4–5.

117. Anna Marie Peterson, "I Came—You May Too," *Volunteer*, October 1963, 1, 10.

118. Metzler and Harding, "Race Relations Project."

119. Vincent Harding to white church members, April 14, 1963, box Clarence E. Lutz, MCC Peace Section, 1963–1969, folder M.C.C. Peace Section Reports, LMHS.

120. Vern Preheim, "Staff Report," memorandum, November 1, 1963, B-23, 1963 Report and Materials for the [General Conference Mennonite Church] Board of Christian Service [meeting] held at Newton, Kansas, December 4–6, 1963, in bound volume shelved with serials, MLA.

121. "From Words to Deeds in Race Relations (Tentative Draft)."

122. Metzler and Harding, "Race Relations Project."

123. Ibid., 6.

124. "Church Facing the Race Crisis," 18.

125. A thorough search of Harding's published addresses and articles from 1958 through 1963 reveals no previous references to his departure from the church.

126. "Church Facing the Race Crisis," 19–21, 21.

127. Ibid., 21.

128. Larry Kehlert, "Southern Churches Probe Race Issue," *Mennonite Weekly Review*, March 12, 1964, 1, 6.

129. "Mennonite Churches in South Hold Conference on Race," *The Mennonite*, March 31, 1964, 203–4.

130. "North America Race Relations," memorandum, 1964, box Clarence E. Lutz, MCC Peace Section, 1963–1969, LMHS.

131. Edgar Metzler to Peace Section Members, April 6, 1965, CESR papers I-3-7, box 7, folder 12, AMC.

132. Vincent Harding, "What Answer to Black Power?" *Gospel Herald*, December 27, 1966, 1114–15.

133. Vincent Harding, "Do We Have an Answer for Black Power?" *The Mennonite*, February 7, 1967, 82–83; Vincent Harding, "The Beggars Are Rising . . . Where Are the Saints?" *Mennonite Life*, October 1967, 152–53; Vincent Harding, "The Peace Witness and Revolutionary Movements," *Mennonite Life*, October 1967, 161–65; Vincent Harding, "Voices of Revolution," *The Mennonite*, October 3, 1967, 590–93; Vincent Harding, "Where Have All the Lovers Gone?" *Mennonite Life*, January 1967, 5–13.

134. Metzler to Peace Section Members, 1965.

135. Ibid.

136. Harding, "The Christian and the Race Question," 2. His commitment to integrity also explains why church leaders invited Harding to speak to the 1967 Mennonite World Conference even though he had cut official ties two years earlier.

137. Paul G. Landis, interview with author, March 8, 2003; Shetler, "A Prophetic Voice," 60.

138. "Black (Studies) Vatican," *Newsweek*, August 11, 1969, 38.

139. Harding, "Biography, Democracy, and Spirit."

140. Guy F. Hershberger to Vincent Harding, December 29, 1971, Guy F. Hershberger Hist. Mss. 1-171, box 14, folder 6, AMC; Albert J. Meyer to Guy Hershberger et al., March 5, 1970, Guy F. Hershberger Hist. Mss. 1-171, box 14, folder 3, AMC; John Powell to Vincent Harding, July 9, 1971, Elkhart, Indiana, IV-21-4, box 1, MBM Minority Ministries Council, Data File 1, A–K, folder General Correspondence 1969–72, AMC.

141. Rachel J. Lapp and Sarah E. Phend, "God's Table: A Precious Piece of Fur-

niture," MPress on the Net, www.goshen.edu/mpress/07-04–2003/story_table
.php (accessed February 27, 2008).

142. Harding, "Biography, Democracy, and Spirit."

Chapter 5. The Wedding March

1. "Hughes-Conrad," *Gospel Herald*, Tuesday, December 21, 1954, 1222.

2. "Christian Race Relations," memorandum, 1955, IX-7-12, file 2, box 6, Race
Relations 1955–70, AMC; Annabelle Hughes and Gerald Hughes, interview
with author, August 29, 2006.

3. Hughes and Hughes, interview.

4. Guy F. Hershberger to John E. Lapp, August 28, 1967, author's presonal collection.

5. D. W. B., "Do You Want Your Daughter to Marry a Negro?" *The Mennonite*,
October 28, 1952, 684; Paul Erb, "Interracial Marriage," *Gospel Herald*, June 24,
1952, 611; Levi C. Hartzler, "Race Problem Unnecessary," *Gospel Herald*, February
8, 1955, 137, 40; Esko Loewen, "What Do You Want to Do, Marry a Negro?" *The
Mennonite*, February 6, 1951, 95; Luke G. Stoltzfus, "Is Christianity a Hindrance to
Good Race Relations?" *Missionary Messenger*, July 1952, 5, 14; Mary Toews, "Forgetting Our Own," *The Mennonite*, December 4, 1951, 763.

6. Between 1889 and 1971, not a single article written by a white Mennonite
and published in any of the national Mennonite church publications took up the
question of the legality or illegality of interracial marriage. For a complete listing of
these publications see Shearer, "A Pure Fellowship," 410–31. Sixteen states had
laws against interracial marriage in 1967: Alabama, Arkansas, Delaware, Florida,
Georgia, Kentucky, Louisiana, Mississippi, Missouri, North Carolina, Oklahoma,
South Carolina, Tennessee, Texas, Virginia, and West Virginia. See Cruz and Berson, "The American Melting Pot?" For a complete listing of Mennonite congregations in those states, see Zook, *Mennonite Yearbook and Directory*, vol. 59, 85–90.

7. William Y. Bell, "The Question of the Races," *Gospel Herald*, January 7, 1926,
835–36. Here and throughout this chapter, I contend that the appearance or absence of published articles on interracial marriage reflected significant changes in
Mennonite thought. Although official church statements and the experiences of
couples like Gerald and Annabelle Hughes corroborate those shifts, the evidence
from printed articles establishes official church positions. Mennonite editors
printed only those articles that fell within accepted church doctrine.

8. The following texts about interracial marriage focus on legislation: Cruz and
Berson, "The American Melting Pot?"; Higginbotham and Kopytoff, "Racial Purity
and Interracial Sex"; Moran, *Interracial Intimacy*; Pascoe, "Miscegenation Law"; Sollors, *Interracialism*.

9. See, for instance, the absence of attention to churches and ministers in Walter Wadlington's study of the primary legal test case in Virginia, the *Loving* case, which eventually made state-based prohibitions against interracial marriage illegal. Wadlington, "The *Loving* Case."

10. Romano, *Race Mixing*, 50.

11. Ibid., 176–77, 214.

12. Haury, *The Quiet Demonstration*, 78; Landes, "But Would You Want Your Daughter to Marry One?"; Weaver, "The Mennonite Church."

13. Simon Gingerich and Lynford Hershey, "Minutes Counsel and Reference Committee for Minority Ministries Education," memorandum, March 5, 1971, 1, IV-21-4, box 1, MBM, Minority Ministries Council, Data File 1, A–K, folder Cross Cultural Relations 1971–1972, Lyn Hershey, AMC; Guy F. Hershberger to Stanley Kreider, May 24, 1968, CESR papers I-3-7, box 7, folder 38, AMC; Lynford Hershey, memorandum, "Report #3 to Counsel and Reference Committee for Minority Ministries Education Program," 1970, fourth cabinet of row on far left wall upon entering room, second drawer, unmarked, folder Minority Ministry Council 1970–71, EMM record room; Harold Regier and Rosella Regier, "Learning by Leaving," *Gulfbreeze*, January–April 1968, 6.

14. Articles from the following publications provided background information for this study: *Christian Living, Gospel Herald, Herald of Truth, The Mennonite, Mennonite Life, Mennonite Weekly Review, Missionary Messenger, Pastoral Messenger,* and *Volunteer.* Also referenced are statements passed by Bethel College, Bluffton College, the Eastern Mennonite Board of Missions, Eastern Mennonite College, the General Conference Mennonite Church, the Indiana-Michigan Conference, the Lancaster Conference, Menno Housing, the Mennonite Board of Missions and Charities, the Mennonite Central Committee, the (Old) Mennonite Church, the Ohio Conference, the South Central Conference, the Southwest Pennsylvania Conference, the Urban Racial Council, and the Virginia Conference.

15. "Christian Race Relations," iii.

16. Moran, *Interracial Intimacy*, 11.

17. Aldine Carpenter Brunk, "Our Duty to People of Other Races," memorandum, 1930, 6, 7, Christian E. Charles Collection, Race Relations, LMHS; S. M. Grubb, editorial, *The Mennonite*, February 6, 1930, 3; "Improving Our Attitude toward the People of Other Races," *The Mennonite and the Christian Evangel*, January 15, 1935, 14–15.

18. Grubb, editorial; "Improving Our Attitude toward the People of Other Races."

19. Abram B. Kolb, "The Race Troubles," *Herald of Truth*, November 15, 1889, 341–43.

20. Sam Steiner, "Kolb, Abram B. (1862–1925)," Global Anabaptist Mennonite Encyclopedia Online, www.gameo.org/encyclopedia/contents/K6442.html (accessed August 23, 2006).

21. Landes, "But Would You Want Your Daughter to Marry One?" 9–10.

22. Israel D. Rohrer, "The Work of the Lord at Andrews Bridge," *Missionary Messenger*, January 1946, 6.

23. Ministers and bishops recalled the differentiation in dress restrictions at Andrews Bridge and other African-American mission stations such as South Seventh Street in Reading. See Paul G. Landis, interview with author, April 28, 2005; William M. Weaver, e-mail message to author, January 30, 2003.

24. Ira J. Buckwalter, minutes of the Colored Workers Committee, 1947–1953, 8, file cabinets far wall, first cabinet, top drawer, drawer marked Home Missions Locations and Other General 1956–1964, four numbered notebooks, EMM record room.

25. Daniel Kauffman, editorial, *Gospel Herald*, January 7, 1943, 865.

26. Reynold Weinbrenner, "From the Editor's Point-of-View," *The Mennonite*, February 5, 1946, 2; Daniel D. Wert, "What About Our Negro Missions?" *Missionary Messenger*, January 1946, 2.

27. J. Harold Breneman, "On Race Prejudice: Behold the Field!" *Missionary Messenger*, October 1949, 11; Paul Erb, "The Race Question," editorial, *Gospel Herald*, January 27, 1948, 75; Irvin B. Horst, "Mennonites and the Race Question," *Gospel Herald*, July 13, 1945, 284–85; Harry L. Kraus, "Will You Dare to Be Christian?" *Gospel Herald*, May 10, 1949, 444–45.

28. Graybill, "The View of the Mennonite Church on Marriage."

29. William L. Stoltzfus, "The Unequal Yoke in the Social and Marriage Relation," *Gospel Herald*, February 23, 1939, 1006, 12.

30. Annabelle Conrad, "What Are You Doing for Christ?" *Gospel Herald*, June 9, 1953, 552.

31. Hughes and Hughes, interview.

32. Loewen, "What Do You Want to Do?"

33. Guy F. Hershberger, memorandum, notes from 1951 Laurelville Conference on Race, July 24–27, 1951, CESR papers I-3-7, box 2, folder 35, AMC.

34. Toews, "Forgetting Our Own."

35. J. N. Smucker, "Mennonites and the Race Question," *The Mennonite*, January 8, 1952, 19.

36. William Keeney, "Woodlawn Mennonite Church," *Mennonite Life*, April 1953, 66–67.

37. William Keeney, "Reborn Color-Blind," *The Mennonite*, January 8, 1952, 22, 25.

38. Erb, "Interracial Marriage."

39. Stoltzfus, "Is Christianity a Hindrance."

40. D. W. B., "Do You Want Your Daughter to Marry a Negro?" 684.

41. Hughes and Hughes, interview.

42. Ibid.

43. Wallenstein, *Tell the Court I Love My Wife*, 204.

44. Gullickson, "Black/White Interracial Marriage Trends," 308–9.

45. Yancey and Yancey, introduction to "Don't Just Marry One," xiv.

46. Root, *Love's Revolution*, 179.

47. Gullickson, "Black/White Interracial Marriage, Trends," 299, 309.

48. I arrive at the figure of fewer than one hundred interracial marriages in General Conference and (Old) Mennonite congregations based on evidence provided in oral history interviews, period reports, and local commentaries. Such weddings were notable enough that they left a clear, though nonsystematized, evidence trail.

49. Golden, "Social Control," 269; Pavela, "An Exploratory Study," 209.

50. "Christian Race Relations."

51. Hughes and Hughes, interview.

52. "A Welcome and a Blessing Awaits Us," *The Mennonite*, June 29, 1954, 407; Harriet Amstutz, "A Look at Woodlawn Children," *The Mennonite*, October 5, 1954, 619; Paul Erb, "The Minority Prevails," *Gospel Herald*, June 8, 1954, 531; Orlo Kaufman, "Reaction to Supreme Court Decision," *The Mennonite*, August 3, 1954, 475; Orlo Kaufman, "The Decision to End Segregation," *Gospel Herald*, September 7, 1954, 860; Carl Kreider, "Negro Segregation," *Christian Living*, August 1954, 36–37; Millard Lind, "Bible Principles Governing Race Relations in the Church," *Gospel Herald*, October 12, 1954, 961–62, 81.

53. "Group Discussion: 'A Race Relations Program for the Mennonite Church'," memorandum, ca. 1954, CESR papers I-3-7, box 6, folder 41, AMC.

54. Hughes and Hughes, interview.

55. Hartzler, "Race Problem Unnecessary." Although the Hugheses entered the church's public gaze as a couple, when opinions about interracial marriage shifted and Gerald accepted nationally prominent church positions with ever greater frequency, Annabelle received less and less attention. Although she established Gerald's credentials through her union with him, she received no offers to sit on national boards and committees.

56. Christian Race Relations," iii.

57. Kraus, "Scriptural Teachings on Race Relations," 33–34, 35–36.

58. "Christian Race Relations," 23.

59. Although Guy Hershberger has received credit for writing the 1955 statement, "The Way of Christian Love in Race Relations," and clearly had a definitive hand in its formation, oral history evidence points to Paul Peachey as the original drafter of the document.

60. "Christian Race Relations," 71.

61. "The Way of Christian Love in Race Relations," memorandum, August 24, 1955, author's personal collection.

62. For example, Episcopalians passed a statement against segregation in

1955 but made no mention of interracial marriage. See Shattuck, *Episcopalians and Race*, 68.

63. "Attitude of Bluffton College on Relationships between Races on the Campus," memorandum, May 1955, III-25-8, box 3, Bethesda Mennonite Church, St. Louis, Missouri, H. Schwartzentruber Files—data files, folder Race Relations Data, AMC.

64. John Fisher to Guy Hershberger, May 14, 1955, CESR papers I-3-7, box 6, folder 16, AMC; Abe Hallman to Guy Hershberger, May 14, 1955, ibid.; Paul Peachey to Guy F. Hershberger, May 14, 1955, ibid.

65. Gerald Hughes, e-mail message to author, January 19, 2007; Miller, "Building Anew in Cleveland," 84.

66. John D. Zehr, "The Sin of Race Prejudice," *Christian Living*, July 1956, 27–29.

67. Elaine Teichroew, "Paul Learns: A Story Based on Observations During Six Weeks of Summer VS in Chicago," *The Mennonite*, March 12, 1957, 171.

68. Paul Erb, "Witnessing in Race Relations," *Gospel Herald*, January 28, 1958, 75.

69. Hughes and Hughes, interview.

70. Guy F. Hershberger, "Report of the Chicago Race Relations Seminar," memorandum, July 16, 1959, CESR papers I-3-7, box 7, folder 58, AMC.

71. Vincent Harding, "The Task of the Mennonite Church in Establishing Racial Unity," memorandum, April 17–19, 1959, Hist. Mss. 1-48, box 60, John H. Yoder (1927–1997) Collection Race/Urban issues, file 60/1, AMC. Harding was most likely paraphrasing his friend and mentor Martin Luther King Jr., who the year before had written, "[The church] can point out that the Negro's primary aim is to be the white man's brother, not his brother-in-law." See King, *Stride toward Freedom*, 206.

72. Barrett, *The Vision and the Reality*, 243.

73. "A Christian Declaration on Race Relations," memorandum, August 17, 1959, IX-7-12, file 2, box 6, Race Relations, 1955–70, AMC; Elmer Ediger to Guy Hershberger, May 13, 1955, CESR papers I-3-7, box 6, folder 16, AMC.

74. The General Conference leaders' seven-year silence on interracial marriage ended in 1962. On April 24 of that year, Leo Driedger, the secretary of the denomination's Peace and Social Concerns Committee, distributed a mass mailing in which he brought up the subject. Members of the Race Relations Committee requested that Driedger attend to the topic, though their study paper released the previous year studiously avoided any mention of interracial marriage. Rather than drafting a new position, Driedger included the section of the Mennonite Church statement dealing with interracial marriage along with the 1959 General Conference statement. Driedger concluded his discussion of marriage between racial groups by

noting, "Such words remind us that Christian brotherhood reaches into the very depths of our lives." See Leo Driedger to Fellow Christians, April 24, 1962, VII.R GC Voluntary Service, Series 11 Gulfport VS Unit, box 6, folder 211, Race Relations, MLA; Vincent Harding et al., "The Christian in Race Relations."

75. Gerald Hughes, "A Negro Mennonite Looks at Integration," *Mennonite Weekly Review*, January 28, 1960; John T. Neufeld, "What About Racial Intermarriage?" *Mennonite Weekly Review*, January 7, 1960.

76. Hughes, "A Negro Mennonite Looks at Integration."

77. Paul G. Landis, "Building Interracial Churches," *Missionary Messenger*, January 1960, 6–7; William Pannell, "The Evangelical and Minority Groups," *Gospel Herald*, March 8, 1960, 205–6; Vern Preheim, "Steps to Integration," *The Mennonite*, April 12, 1960, 232; Harold Regier, "Roots of Prejudice," *The Mennonite*, April 5, 1960, 215–16.

78. Vern Miller to Guy F. Hershberger, October 29, 1961, I-3-7 CESR, 5/140, Correspondence with individuals, II Miller, Vern, 1961–62, AMC.

79. Guy F. Hershberger to Vernon L. Miller, January 25, 1962, I-3-7 CESR, 5/140, Correspondence with individuals, II Miller, Vern, 1961–62, AMC.

80. Miller to Hershberger, 1961.

81. Guy F. Hershberger, "A Mennonite Analysis of the Montgomery Bus Boycott," memorandum, March 1962, 10, author's personal collection.

82. Virgil Vogt, "Emergent Church in Cleveland," *Christian Living*, October 1961, 14–17, 34–35.

83. Bechler, *The Black Mennonite Church*, 174–77.

84. Ibid., 43–44.

85. From 1958 through 1962, eighty-six articles with identifiable racial themes appeared in the *Gospel Herald*, *The Mennonite*, *Christian Living*, and *Mennonite Life*. In 1953 thirty-two such articles appeared in the same four magazines in the course of one year. For a complete listing of these articles, see Shearer, "A Pure Fellowship."

86. "Race and Mennonites," *The Mennonite*, December 31, 1963, 799–800.

87. Martin Louw, "Our Children Are Part Negro," *Christian Living*, November 1963, 12–14.

88. C. J. Dyck, "Dialogue on Race," *The Mennonite*, October 29, 1963, 648–49; C. J. Dyck, "Pronouncements—Then What?" *Gospel Herald*, October 22, 1963, 939, 49.

89. The Baptist community, for example, focused on civil rights involvement to the exclusion of other race relations issues. See Chrisman, "The Price of Moderation," 161–62. Members of the Roman Catholic community did, however, use civil rights agitation to take a stand against antimiscegenation laws in 1963. See Wallenstein, *Tell the Court I Love My Wife*, 203.

90. O. O. Wolfe, Mark Lehman, and Vern Miller, "Integration—What It Will Mean for the Church," *Gospel Herald*, August 6, 1963, 671–72.

91. Dyck, "Dialogue on Race."

92. Cornelius J. Dyck to Ed Riddick et al., September 3, 1963, CESR papers I-3-7, box 5, folder 165, AMC; "Record of the Meeting of Church Leaders for a Discussion on Racial and Civil Rights Problems to Discover Which Course Should Be Followed by the Mennonite Church in This Time of Social Revolution," memorandum, September 14, 1963, MCC Peace Section, Conjoint and Related Minutes, box I, file 1, Reports, 1952−68, AMC.

93. "The Church Facing the Race Crisis," memorandum, December 4, 1963, CESR papers I-3-7, box 5, folder 168, AMC.

94. Minutes of the Mennonite General Conference, August 20−23, 1963, 87, IX-7-12, file 2, box 6, Race Relations, 1955−70, AMC.

95. "MBMC and CPSC Consultation," memorandum, July 29, 1968, Paul G. Landis Coll., Mennonite General Conference Committee on Peace and Social Concerns, 1968−1971, Workbook Committee on Peace and Social Concerns, Washington, D.C., November 7−9, 1968, LMHS.

96. "Interracial Council Approved," *Gospel Herald*, July 23, 1968, 669.

97. John H. Mosemann, "Why an Urban-Racial Council?" *Gospel Herald*, November 25, 1969, 1026−27.

98. The members were John Powell, Gerald Hughes, and Lee Roy Berry. See minutes of the Committee on Peace and Social Concerns, April 27−29, 1969, Paul G. Landis Coll., Mennonite General Conference Committee on Peace and Social Concerns, 1968−1971, LMHS.

99. J. M. B., "Minority Ministries Council Holds First Annual Meeting," memorandum, November 6, 1970, fourth cabinet of row on far left wall upon entering room, second drawer, unmarked, folder Minority Ministries Council 1970−71, EMM record room.

100. During the most active years of the Minority Ministries Council, African-American men married to white Mennonite women continued to dominate staff appointments and committee leadership. In addition to Gerald Hughes, Hubert Brown, Tony Brown, Charles McDowell, Sylvester Outley, Richard Pannell, John Powell, Warner Jackson, and others, all came to serve important roles in the Mennonite Church. See Hubert Brown, "Report on the Church and Urban Development Seminar," memorandum, April 1970, IV-21-4, box 1, MBM, Minority Ministries Council, Data File 1, A−K, folder Church and Urban Development 1970, Seminars, AMC; Warner Jackson to Hubert Schwartzentruber, February 23, 1971, Hist. Mss. 1-784, box 1, Hubert Schwartzentruber Collection, Miscellaneous, folder Minority Ministries Council 1970−71, AMC; "New York City Peacemaker Workshop," memorandum, March 15−16, 1968, author's personal collection; John Powell, "AFRAM to Bring Blacks Together," *Gospel Herald*, July 31, 1973, 592; John Powell, "Urban-Racial Concerns Statement," memorandum, August 19, 1969, I-1-1, Mennonite General Conference, 1898−1971, 1969 Session materials, folder

5/8, AMC; J. N. Smucker, "Pale-Face Religion," *The Mennonite*, October 27, 1953, 659; "We They Coming Together: A Cross-Cultural Experience," memorandum, 1971, fourth cabinet of row on far left wall upon entering room, second drawer, unmarked, folder Minority Ministries Council 1970–71, EMM record room. With the exception of the last four of Vincent Harding's articles in 1967 and 1968, this same group of men wrote most of the few articles penned by African Americans to appear in the church press through 1971. See Curtis E. Burrell Jr., "Causes for Urban Rebellion," *Gospel Herald*, June 18, 1968, 534–36; John Powell, "The Compassion Fund Is," *Gospel Herald*, March 24, 1970, 271; John Powell, "The Minority Ministries Council: A Call to Action," *Gospel Herald*, March 31, 1970, 294; John Powell, "The Urban Racial Council," *Missionary Messenger*, September, 1969, 14–15. In 1969 two articles written by African-American women did appear in the Lancaster Conference's *Missionary Messenger*. See Georgia Lovett, "Others See Christ in Me: At School," *Missionary Messenger*, October 1969, 3; Hazel Sheppard, "Others See Christ in Me: In My Neighborhood," *Gospel Herald*, October 1969, 2.

101. John T. Akar, "An African Views America," *Mennonite Life*, January 1967, 19–23; Melvin L. Lehman, "Mennonites and Pittsburgh," *Christian Living*, March 1970, 2–7; Harold Regier, "Understanding the Southern Viewpoint," *Mennonite Weekly Review*, May 14, 1964; Polly Sedziol, "A Little Knowledge," *The Mennonite*, February 13, 1968, 118–19.

102. Minutes of the Colored Workers Committee, 1964–1969, 222, file cabinets far wall, first cabinet, top drawer, drawer marked, Home Missions Locations and Other General 1956–1964, four numbered notebooks, EMM record room.

103. Gingerich and Hershey, "Minutes Counsel and Reference Committee," 1; Hershberger to Kreider, 1968; Hershey, "Report #3 to Counsel and Reference Committee."

104. Lynford Hershey, "What Is the Mennonite Attitude on Race Relations," *Gospel Herald*, March 23, 1971, 262–64.

105. In response to the somewhat awkwardly worded statement, "There is nothing morally wrong with interracial marriage if both partners are Christian," 49 percent of the respondents to Hershey's survey agreed, 32 percent were uncertain, and the remaining 19 percent disagreed. Ibid.

106. "Statement on Racism," memorandum, July 23, 1971, Lancaster Conference, Statements, LMHS.

107. Barrett, *The Vision and the Reality*, 245.

108. Moriichi, "Woodlawn Mennonite Church," 36–39. For more detail on Curtis Burrell and the Woodlawn congregation, see chapter 6.

109. Haury, *The Quiet Demonstration*, iv.

110. Two other Mennonites offer examples of those who spoke in favor of interracial marriage out of their involvement with (Old) Mennonite Church African-

American congregations. An unnamed member of the Colored Workers Committee spoke out at a meeting in Lancaster, Pennsylvania, on May 23, 1964. See minutes of the Colored Workers Committee, 1964–1969. Three years later housing activist A. Grace Wenger noted in the pages of the *Missionary Messenger* that interracial marriage is not a problem for people who have lived in cross-cultural settings. See A. Grace Wenger, "No Room—in Lancaster?" *Missionary Messenger*, May 1967, 8–10.

111. Hartzler, "Race Problem Unnecessary."

112. Keeney, "Reborn Color-Blind."

113. For example, a Canadian reader, responding to comments made by Vincent Harding in support of interracial marriage, wrote that Harding's position had to have stemmed from "an unwarranted inferiority complex." See "We Mennonites and the Race Problem," memorandum, October 2, 1962, IX-7-12, file 2, box 6, Race Relations 1955–70, AMC.

114. Hughes and Hughes, interview.

115. Mennonites did nothing new here by associating young women's chastity with sexual purity. As Paul Ricoeur notes, purity and virginity have long been linked together, and, conversely, sexuality has from the earliest of times been central to the exercise and description of defilement. See Ricoeur, *The Symbolism of Evil*, 28–29.

116. "Readers Say," *Gospel Herald*, February 17, 1970, 158.

117. Lee Roy Berry and Beth Berry, interview with author, August 29, 2006.

118. Ibid.

Chapter 6. Congregational Campaign

1. Oral histories indicate that Harding visited Community Mennonite on a Sunday soon after the group moved into their new facility in 1959. See Ronald Krehbiel, interview with author, April 25, 2007.

2. Delton Franz, "Why Is Woodlawn Church in the Middle of Chicago's Civil Rights?" *Mennonite / Central District Reporter*, February 15, 1966, A-8–A-9.

3. Delton Franz, "King Comes to Woodlawn," *The Mennonite*, September 28, 1965, 607–8.

4. Franz, "Why Is Woodlawn Church in the Middle of Chicago's Civil Rights?"

5. Franz, "King Comes to Woodlawn."

6. King, *Stride toward Freedom*, 207.

7. Ibid. In comparison to Protestant denominations, the Catholic Church included a greater number of parishes with some degree of racial diversity during this period. See Evans, Forsyth, and Bernard, "One Church or Two?" 235. I have chosen

not to examine Catholic congregations in this chapter because of two factors. First, the parish system in the 1950s and '60s designated specific congregations at which Catholics were expected to worship. Thus Catholic parishioners cannot be said to have chosen to worship in an integrated setting. I instead focus on two congregations at which both African-American and white congregants chose to worship, even though other options were available to them. Second, John T. McGreevy takes up the question of racial integration within Roman Catholicism in the United States at great length. See McGreevy, *Parish Boundaries*. Although McGreevy addresses the first question, about internal developments in integrated congregations, owing to the parish system he is less equipped to explore questions concerning sustainability. This chapter thus expands on McGreevy's work into Protestantism and initiates new exploration of the sustainability of integrated congregations when other options are available.

8. A similar assumption of the inherent value of integration is clearly evident in a booklet published by the American Baptists in 1957 that enthusiastically encourages their congregations to become racially integrated in worship, service, and fellowship. See Cofer, *Racial Integration in the Church*. See also the near euphoria expressed by white Methodist clergy at a 1955 conference in Woodlawn as they related their experiences of welcoming African Americans to their congregations: United Methodist Church, "The Methodist Church and Changing Racial Patterns," 34.

9. "The Church Facing the Race Crisis," memorandum, December 4, 1963, 8, CESR papers I-3-7, box 5, folder 168, AMC.

10. For example, in a 1964 survey of more than five thousand Presbyterian churches, a thousand pastors claimed "some minimal interracial quality." See United Presbyterian Church in the U.S.A., *A Survey of Racial Integration in Local Congregations*, 3. As Michael Emerson suggests in his study of contemporary churches that purport to be integrated, however, those claims are often unsubstantiated. See Dart, "Hues in the Pews." Overall, within American Protestantism during the late 1950s and 1960s, few white churches had more than a handful of African-American congregants, and rarely did the numbers approach 20 percent, the proportion considered by sociologists to represent authentic racial integration. See Christerson, Edwards, and Emerson, *Against All Odds*, 185.

11. Higham and Guarneri, *Hanging Together*, 132.

12. King, *Stride toward Freedom*, 207.

13. One exception, Nancy Ammerman and Arthur Farnsley's *Community and Congregation*, provides helpful insight into one community—Oak Park in Chicago— that successfully integrated and the congregations that continue to worship within it. Her otherwise comprehensive study, however, purposefully avoids examination of Oak Park congregations that dealt with white flight and studies Oak Park in the

latter two decades of the twentieth century rather than the earlier period taken up here. Ammerman asserts that much work has already been done on white churches dealing with white flight in their community. The studies she refers to, however, focused on sociological questions rather than historical ones and were written during the period of the greatest transition, thereby affording little historical distance or perspective.

14. Even otherwise exemplary work, such as Andrew Wiese's *Places of Their Own*, treats African-American suburban homeowners as entirely nonreligious. He offers no explanation as to whether or where African-American suburbanites went to worship once they had relocated to white-dominated suburbs. For an example of a thorough interrogation of the assumptions behind racial integration in the public schools, see Watras, *Politics, Race, and Schools*.

15. Marsh, *Beloved Community*, 2.

16. Barrett, *The Vision and the Reality*; Pannabecker, *Faith in Ferment*; Pannabecker, *Ventures of Faith*; Rich, *Walking Together in Faith*; Smith, *Mennonites in Illinois*; Toews, *Mennonites in American Society*.

17. Community Mennonite receives much less attention in works such as Barrett, *The Vision and the Reality*; Pannabecker, *Faith in Ferment*; Smith, *Mennonites in Illinois*.

18. Moriichi, "Woodlawn Mennonite," 7. Both Community Mennonite and Woodlawn Mennonite were jointly sponsored by the General Conference and (Old) Mennonite denominations. The General Conference had its headquarters in Newton, Kansas, not far from where both Voth and Franz spent their childhoods.

19. Delton Franz, "The Mennonite Church on Trial," *The Mennonite*, May 21, 1957, 324–25.

20. Ibid.

21. Lancaster Conference Board of Bishops, "Cut Hair," *Pastoral Messenger*, October 1964, 8; John W. Eby and Norman Shenk, "Minutes Voluntary Service and I-W Committee," memorandum, January 18, 1967, Paul G. Landis Coll. VS Committee Minutes 1964–1974, LMHS; photo of Camp Landon unit, March 1960, Photo collection, folder Mississippi—Gulfport, MLA.

22. Andrew R. Shelly, "This Is Chicago," *Mennonite Life*, April 1953, 52–55.

23. John T. N. Litwiler, "Iglesia Evangelica Mennonita," *Mennonite Life*, April 1953, 63.

24. A 1940 study of Mennonites in Chicago showed that 92 percent had come from other than Mennonite families. See Barrett, *The Vision and the Reality*, 110. Litwiler's "Iglesia Evangelica Mennonita" shows that this proportion remained roughly constant through the following decade in most congregations in Chicago, except in the case of those students who clustered in the Woodlawn neighborhood to attend Mennonite Biblical Seminary or the University of Chicago.

25. John T. Neufeld, "The Grace Mennonite Church," *Mennonite Life*, April 1953, 65–66; Richard Ratzlaff, "Brighton Mennonite Church," *Mennonite Life*, April 1953, 64–65.

26. William Keeney, "Woodlawn Mennonite Church," *Mennonite Life*, April 1953, 66–67; Shelly, "This Is Chicago."

27. The General Conference provided funding for the East Harlem Protestant Parish in New York City from 1950 through 1956. Efforts there focused on social services rather than evangelism and were not tied to a General Conference congregation. See Barrett, *The Vision and the Reality*, 244. The (Old) Mennonite Church denomination did support African-American missions during this period, as witnessed by the Bethel Mennonite Church that had been planted by James and Rowena Lark to evangelize an African-American neighborhood. That work continued in 1953 under the leadership of Paul King, while Lark raised funds for a new church building. See Levi C. Hartzler, "Bethel Mennonite Church," *Mennonite Life*, April 1953, 60–61. Even at Bethel, however, King and Lark focused on developing an African-American church supported by white workers rather than an integrated congregation that evangelized both white and African-American members.

28. Camacho and Joravsky, *Against the Tide*, 44–45; Keeney, "Woodlawn Mennonite Church."

29. S. F. Pannabecker, "Mennonite Seminary in Chicago," *Mennonite Life*, April 1953, 68–71.

30. Moriichi, "Woodlawn Mennonite," 3–4.

31. See photo of summer bible school, Woodlawn, Chicago, 1954, Photo collection, folder Voluntary Service—North America, MLA.

32. Miller, *Wise as Serpents*, 47–48.

33. Guy F. Hershberger to John Oyer, October 9, 1953, Guy F. Hershberger Hist. Mss. 1-171, box 10, folder 8, AMC.

34. John T. Neufeld, "Problems of Integration," *Mennonite Weekly Review*, December 31, 1959, 11.

35. Moriichi, "Woodlawn Mennonite," 13–14; Pannabecker, *Ventures of Faith*, 55–56.

36. Franz, "The Mennonite Church on Trial."

37. Delton Franz, "Notes on a Southern Journey," *The Mennonite*, January 6, 1959, 4–6; Vincent Harding, "The Task of the Mennonite Church in Establishing Racial Unity," memorandum, April 17–19, 1959, Hist. Mss. 1-48, box 60, John H. Yoder (1927–1997) Collection Race / Urban issues, file 60/1, AMC; "The Mennonite Churches and Race," *Gospel Herald*, May 19, 1959, 460, 77.

38. Rich, *Walking Together in Faith*, 101.

39. Birdie Preheim, "Tok," *The Mennonite*, February 24, 1959, 121; Ed Riddick, "Matterhorn," *The Mennonite*, July 19, 1960, 463; "Woodlawn World," *The Mennonite*, October 15, 1957, 652.

40. Pannabecker, *Ventures of Faith*, 53.

41. Vincent Harding, "Peace Witness to Racial Strife," *The Mennonite*, November 8, 1960, 718, 27.

42. Barrett, *The Vision and the Reality*, 97; Pannabecker, *Faith in Ferment*, 279.

43. "Preliminary Report on Title Guarantee Policy Application Number 45-59-339," memorandum, August 3, 1956, second file cabinet, third drawer, marked Admin, folder Building, CMC, Tax, Deeds, Titles, etc., CMC pastor's office.

44. John T. Neufeld to Paul J. Saengert, July 9, 1956, second file cabinet, third drawer, marked Admin, folder Building, CMC, Tax, Deeds, Titles, etc., CMC pastor's office.

45. John T. Neufeld to Chicago Title & Trust Co., September 24, 1956, second file cabinet, third drawer marked Admin, folder Building, CMC, Tax, Deeds, Titles, etc., CMC pastor's office.

46. Gerald Mares and Dolores Mares, interview with author, September 17, 2006.

47. "Ledger with Handwritten Minutes from Early Church Board Meetings," memorandum, 1956, black unmarked ledger book with red stripe top and bottom and green striping top and bottom, CMC pastor's office.

48. "Dedication," memorandum, August 2, 1959, second file cabinet, third drawer marked Admin, folder Building, CMC, Tax, Deeds, Titles, etc., CMC pastor's office.

49. Donald Burklow, Community Mennonite Church, ca. 1959, framed photo from CMC displayed at church.

50. Don Burklow and Grace Burklow, interview with author, April 15, 2005.

51. Krehbiel, interview.

52. Ibid.

53. Ibid.

54. Tec-Search, "Comprehensive Plan, Markham, Illinois," memorandum, March 1967, large tabloid-size plastic bindery cardboard-covered tan book, 6-2, CMC pastor's office.

55. Ibid.

56. Lawrence Voth, "Markham Introduction," memorandum, May 19, 1964, box Church Bulletins 1970–73, Missions CCM Reports 1974, 1975, 1976, Church Board Records Thru 1974, Binder Board Records 1961–64, CMC second-floor storage area; Lawrence Voth, "The Story of the Markham Day Care Center," memorandum, July 22, 1969, 1, Marlene Suter's personal file.

57. Helen Dick, "King of Fundraising to Retire," *Bethel College Collegian*, February 16, 2001, 1.

58. Marlene Suter, "Church History Notes," memorandum, November 3, 2001, second file cabinet, third drawer, marked Admin, folder Church History, CMC pastor's office; Jane Voth to author, December 2006. Although this chapter focuses

on Larry Voth as a key motivator and agent in maintaining and developing the prospects for racial integration at Community Mennonite, Jane Voth also served a critical role in nurturing relationships with many African-American women at Community. As of this writing, she continues to maintain those relationships through periodic visits to Markham from her home in Newton, Kansas.

59. Suter, "Church History Notes."

60. Ibid.

61. Voth, "Markham Introduction," 2–3.

62. Suter, "Church History Notes"; Lawrence Voth, "Markham and the Race Revolution," *Mennonite Church in the City*, November 15, 1963, 5–6.

63. Peter J. Ediger, "Report on an Informal Meeting at Markham, Illinois," memorandum, September 24, 1963, second file cabinet, third drawer, marked Admin, folder Markham—Race—Village—Issues—General, CMC pastor's office; Wiese, *Places of Their Own*, 121–22; Wiese, "The House I Live In," 118.

64. Karen Daigl, "Markham: Integration Worked Here," memorandum, 1970, second file cabinet, third drawer, marked Admin, folder Markham—Race—Village—Issues—General, CMC pastor's office; Ediger, "Report on an Informal Meeting."

65. "Supplementary Information," memorandum, March, 1965, second file cabinet, third drawer, marked Admin, folder Markham—Race—Village—Issues—General, CMC pastor's office.

66. Louis G. Freeman, "History of the Land and People," memorandum, June 24, 1970, second file cabinet, third drawer, marked Admin, folder Markham—Race—Village—Issues—General, CMC pastor's office.

67. Voth, "Markham and the Race Revolution."

68. Mares and Mares, interview.

69. Voth, "Markham and the Race Revolution"; Mares and Mares, interview; Burklow and Burklow, interview.

70. Voth, "Markham and the Race Revolution."

71. Suter, "Church History Notes."

72. Voth, "Markham and the Race Revolution."

73. Mares and Mares, interview.

74. Freeman, "History of the Land and People," 8.

75. Ediger, "Report on an Informal Meeting," 1.

76. "Community Mennonite Church Church Board Meeting," memorandum, December 15, 1962, box Church Bulletins 1970–73—Missions CCM Reports 1974, 1975, 1976—Church Board Records Thru 1974, Binder Board Records 1961–64, CMC second-floor storage area.

77. Voth, "Markham and the Race Revolution."

78. Burklow and Burklow, interview.

79. Ibid.

80. Mares and Mares, interview. The speaker here quoted the first part of a racially offensive children's rhyme that ends with the phrase, "pick a Nigger by his toe."

81. Mertis Odom, interview with author, July 3, 2005.

82. Note also that Larry and Jane Voth were close friends with Delton and Marian Franz. Jane and Marian roomed together in college, and the couples built on their friendship while both were in the Chicago area. See Voth to author, 2006.

83. Harold Regier, "Where to from Here?" *Gulfbreeze*, September−October 1963, 2.

84. Ediger, "Report on an Informal Meeting." The predominance of white men at General Conference−level leadership meetings during this period is striking. White and African-American women exercised leadership at congregation-level gatherings at Community Mennonite, but rarely did men in leadership positions include women in official church gatherings.

85. Ling, "Gender and Generation," 117.

86. "Community Mennonite Church Church Board Meeting," memorandum, January 17, 1964, 2, box Church Bulletins 1970−73−Missions CCM Reports 1974, 1975, 1976−Church Board Records Thru 1974, Binder Board Records 1961−64, CMC second-floor storage area.

87. Ibid.

88. Although oral history participants recalled this time period as full of a significant number of departures—as many as a third of the congregation by one account—church records indicate that both membership and offerings increased from 1962 through 1963 by 17 percent. See: "Community Mennonite Church Church Board Meeting," 1964; Mares and Mares, interview; Suter, "Church History Notes." The earlier mass departures after Vincent Harding's visit may have become conflated in memory with this latter conflict.

89. Anonymous, interview with author, 2005.

90. Smith's statement that African-American members did not want to marry across racial lines parallels other African-American responses to intermarriage during this period. African Americans recognized the danger of supporting such unions in white settings but accepted interracial couples in their own neighborhoods and communities. See Romano, *Race Mixing*, 83−84, 107−8.

91. "Community Mennonite Church Church Board Meeting."

92. Lawrence Voth, Andrew F. Taylor, and Duane Zehr, "Visit with Alfred Levreau Family," memorandum, March, 1964, 2, box Church Bulletins 1970−73−Missions CCM Reports 1974, 1975, 1976−Church Board Records Thru 1974, Binder Board Records 1961−64, CMC second-floor storage area.

93. Margaret Carr, "Community Mennonite Church Board Meeting," memo-

randum, March 7, 1964, box Church Bulletins 1970–73—Missions CCM Reports 1974, 1975, 1976—Church Board Records Thru 1974, Binder Board Records 1961–64, CMC second-floor storage area.

94. Lawrence Voth to Central District Conference Ministers, April 30, 1964, box Church Bulletins 1970–73—Missions CCM Reports 1974, 1975, 1976—Church Board Records Thru 1974, Binder Board Records 1961–64, CMC second-floor storage area.

95. "Woodlawn World"; Franz, "The Mennonite Church on Trial"; Preheim, "Tok"; Riddick, "Matterhorn"; and, from *The Mennonite*, Harriet Amstutz, "A Look at Woodlawn Children," October 5, 1954, 619; "Church Serves Coffee," January 8, 1963, 25; Esther Groves, "Chicago Volunteers," December 24, 1963, 776–77; Vincent Harding, "To My Fellow Christians: An Open Letter to Mennonites," September 30, 1958, 597–98; Peter Kehler, "The Unwanted," March 3, 1959, 139; Elmer Neufeld, "That the World Might Recognize Christ," November 12, 1957, 709; Elmer Neufeld, "Visitation at Woodlawn," May 21, 1957, 325–24; J. N. Smucker, "Pale-Face Religion," October 27, 1953, 659.

96. "Church Facing Race Crisis," 8.

97. Delton Franz, "What Stance for the Church in the Civil Rights Struggle?" *Mennonite Church in the City*, November 15, 1963, 9–10.

98. Jacoby, *Someone Else's House*, 50.

99. Pannabecker, *Faith in Ferment*, 279; Marlene Suter, e-mail message to author, November 10, 2006. Teachers who relocated to Markham included Vicki Bryant, Lavonne Goessen, Jo Hinz, Winnifred Kauffman, Esther Preheim, Janel Preheim, David Regehr, Cheryl Steiner, Rudi Steiner, and Sandra (Raber) Wingert. See Suter, "Church History Notes."

100. Suter to author, 2006.

101. Suter, "Church History Notes."

102. Burklow and Burklow, interview; Suter to author, 2006; Mary Ann Woods, interview with author, April 29, 2005.

103. "Church Serves Coffee."

104. Moriichi, "Woodlawn Mennonite," 29.

105. Groves, "Chicago Volunteers."

106. "Church Serves Coffee."

107. Moriichi, "Woodlawn Mennonite," 29; Smith, *Mennonites in Illinois*, 394.

108. Groves, "Chicago Volunteers."

109. Smucker, "Pale-Face Religion," 659; photo of summer bible school, Woodlawn, Chicago.

110. Delton Franz to Parents of Chicago Children and to the Host Parents, 1959, VII.R GC Voluntary Service, Series 11 Gulfport VS Unit, box 1, folder 4, Correspondence—General Conf. 1960, MLA.

111. See photo of Margaret Harder and Joyce Goertzen of Mountain Lake with eleven Chicago children from Woodlawn, 1964, Photo collection, folder Churches—Illinois, MLA.

112. "Youth Services Council Memos," memorandum, October 8, 1965, second file cabinet, third drawer marked Admin, folder Markham—Race—Village—Issues—General, CMC pastor's office.

113. Lois Rensberger, "A Weekend in Chicago," *Mennonite / Central District Reporter*, June 17, 1969, A-3–A-5, A-12–A-14.

114. Barrett, *The Vision and the Reality*, 247.

115. Burklow and Burklow, interview; Suter, "Church History Notes."

116. Burklow and Burklow, interview; Mares and Mares, interview; Odom, interview; Woods, interview.

117. Marie J. Regier, "Lots of Education Needed," *The Mennonite*, August 31, 538.

118. Franz, "King Comes to Woodlawn"; Marie J. Regier, "Lots of Education Needed," *The Mennonite*, August 31, 538; Rich, *Walking Together in Faith*, 101–2; Voth to author, 2006.

119. Voth to author, 2006.

120. "Jeremiah Appears in Chicago," *The Mennonite*, July 20, 1965, 467–68.

121. Guy F. Hershberger, "Report of the Chicago Race Relations Seminar," memorandum, July 16, 1959, 7, CESR papers I-3-7, box 7, folder 58, AMC.

122. "Jeremiah Appears in Chicago."

123. "Burrell New Associate at Woodlawn," *The Mennonite / Central District Reporter*, February 15, 1966, A-1; "Jeremiah Appears in Chicago."

124. Curtis E. Burrell Jr. to Hubert Schwartzentruber, January 2, 1958, III-25-8 Bethesda MC 1/10, H. Schwartzentruber Files—Corres., Misc. incoming 1957–59, AMC.

125. Jim Fairfield, "Curtis Burrell: A Bullet Hole in the Window," *Christian Living*, May 1971, 20–24.

126. Rosemarie Harding and Vincent Harding, "They Went to Atlanta," *The Mennonite*, March 5, 1963, 157–59; Linden M. Wenger and Virgil Brenneman, "Program of Witness to and with Negroes," memorandum, April 16, 1959, III-25-8, box 3, Bethesda Mennonite Church, St. Louis, Missouri, H. Schwartzentruber Files—data files, folder Race Relations Data, AMC; "Why Do White Folks Hate Us? Urban-Racial Meetings, Youngstown, Ohio, March 4, 5, St. Louis, Missouri, March 11, 12," *Mission Service Newsletter*, May 9, 1965, 1–4.

127. "Mennonite General Conference Proceedings, Kalona, Iowa," memorandum, August 20–23, 1963, 87, IX-7-12, file 2, box 6, Race Relations 1955–70, AMC.

128. Curtis E. Burrell Jr., "How My Mind Has Changed About Whites," *Christian Living*, September 1966, 28–29.

129. Curtis Burrell, "Response to Black Power," *The Mennonite*, October 11, 1966, 620–21.

130. Curtis Burrell, "The Conscience of a Heavyweight," *The Mennonite*, June 13, 1967, 397–98.

131. Mrs. V. Flaming, "Slander of Country," *The Mennonite*, July 18, 1967, 461; Ronald W. Woelk, "Not Every Black Man," *The Mennonite*, July 18, 1967, 460.

132. Flaming, "Slander of Country"; Mrs. Kathy Mast, "Disgusted with Clay," *The Mennonite*, July 18, 1967, 461; Woelk, "Not Every Black Man."

133. Delton Franz, "Dangers of 'Get Tough'," *The Mennonite*, June 18, 1968, 431; Delton Franz, "Island of Hope in a Sea of Despair," *The Mennonite*, February 24, 1959, 119; Franz, "King Comes to Woodlawn"; Franz, "Notes on a Southern Journey"; Delton Franz, "Senate Committee Hears Chicago Mennonite Pastor," *Mennonite Weekly Review*, September 3, 1970, 2; Franz, "The Mennonite Church on Trial"; Franz, "What Stance for the Church?"; Franz, "Why Is Woodlawn Church in the Middle of Chicago's Civil Rights?"; Vincent Harding et al., "Church and Race in 6 Cities," *The Mennonite*, February 12, 1963, 98–101.

134. Memorandum by Hershberger, "Report of the Chicago Race Relations Seminar," 9.

135. Franz, "Why Is Woodlawn Church in the Middle of Chicago's Civil Rights?"

136. "Interracial Church Tested," *The Mennonite*, December 5, 1967, 739.

137. Rich, *Walking Together in Faith*, 102.

138. Moriichi, "Woodlawn Mennonite," 35–38.

139. Rensberger, "A Weekend in Chicago."

140. Curtis E. Burrell Jr., "A Primer on the Urban Rebellion," *The Mennonite*, June 18, 1968, 418–20.

141. "White Society Saved When Miss America Is Black," *The Mennonite*, August 6, 1968, 495.

142. Warren Moore, "Ethnic Mennonites?" *Mennonite Life*, January 1967, 25.

143. Mrs. Melvin Rensberger, "Woodlawn Pastor Heads $3,500,000 South Chicago Renewal Plan," *Mennonite / Central District Reporter*, February 18, 1969, A-1-2.

144. Ibid.

145. Moriichi, "Woodlawn Mennonite," 32.

146. Fish, *Black Power/White Control*, 118–19.

147. Black, *Bridges of Memory*, 418.

148. Ibid., 564; Fish, *Black Power/White Control*, 118.

149. Black, *Bridges of Memory*, 564; Fish, *Black Power/White Control*, 119.

150. Rich, *Walking Together in Faith*, 102.

151. Burrell, quoted in Moriichi, "Woodlawn Mennonite," 32.

152. Ibid., 34.

153. Fish, *Black Power / White Control*, 251.

154. Rensberger, "Woodlawn Pastor Heads $3,500,000 Plan."

155. Rensberger, "A Weekend in Chicago."

156. Moriichi, "Woodlawn Mennonite," 33; Smith, *Mennonites in Illinois*, 395–96.

157. "Arsonists Set Fire to Woodlawn Church," *The Mennonite*, August 25, 1970, 507–8.

158. Ibid.

159. Note, for example, the tremendous outpouring of support for the Native American Mennonites at Nanih Waiya, Mississippi, after their church building was bombed and burnt in 1964, 1966, and 1969. See John A. Lapp, "Mississippi Report 1969," memorandum, November 22, 1969, Clarence E. Lutz MCC Peace Section 1969–1970, folder Clarence Lutz, Peace Section—November 22, 1969, YMCA Hotel, Chicago, Illinois, LMHS.

160. Rich, *Walking Together in Faith*, 102.

161. "Arsonists Set Fire to Woodlawn Church."

162. "$25,000 Fire in Chicago's Woodlawn Church," *Mennonite Weekly Review*, August 6, 1970, 1; Moriichi, "Woodlawn Mennonite," 37.

163. Franz, "Senate Committee."

164. Jacob T. Friesen, "Pastor in Chicago Ghetto Identifies with Community's 'Hurts and Fears,'" *Mennonite Weekly Review*, August 20, 1970, 5, 10.

165. In chapter 5 I develop the argument that by 1970 the Mennonite community had begun to accept the marriage of African-American men to white women.

166. Fairfield, "Curtis Burrell."

167. Ibid.

168. Smith, *Mennonites in Illinois*, 396.

169. Rich, *Walking Together in Faith*, 102.

170. Madelyn Bonsignore et al., "Veteran's Administration Policy with Regards to Race in Its Repossessed Housing Program in the South Suburbs," memorandum, March 1, 1965, second file cabinet, third drawer, marked Admin, folder Markham—Race—Village—Issues—General, CMC pastor's office; Louis G. Freeman, "Human Relations Summary July 1966," memorandum, July 1966, 3, second file cabinet, third drawer, marked Admin, folder Markham—Race—Village—Issues—General, CMC pastor's office; "Supplementary Information," 1.

171. Freeman, "Human Relations Summary," 3.

172. Ibid., 1, 3.

173. "Community Mennonite Church Directory," memorandum, October 6, 1969, Marlene Suter's personal file; Voth, "Markham Introduction."

174. Woods, interview; Odom, interview; Suter to author, 2006.

175. Smith, *Mennonites in Illinois*, 430.

176. Suter lists the following African-American members who visited or joined the church in the early 1960s and through the 1970s: Jo and Lacie Alien, Orell and Joanne Mitchell, Ivorie Lowe, Mertis Odom, Essie DuBois, Fran Netterville, Richard and Louise Dearman, Andre and Aggie DaCosta, Robert and Mary Ann Woods, Barbara Gibbs, Willie and May Fauther, Judith McCall, Phyllis McKemey, Robert Williams, and Russell and Eva Bell. See Suter, "Church History Notes."

177. Ibid.

178. Mares and Mares, interview.

179. Rensberger, "A Weekend in Chicago"; Voth, "The Story of the Markham Day Care Center."

180. Michael Devine, "Community Mennonite Day Care Center," memorandum, January 22, 1984, Marlene Suter's personal file.

181. Freeman, "History of the Land and People," 8.

182. Daigl, "Integration Worked Here"; Pannabecker, *Faith in Ferment*, 279.

183. Freeman, "History of the Land and People," 10, 12.

184. Odom, interview.

185. Barrett, *The Vision and the Reality*, 246; Rich, *Walking Together in Faith*, 102.

186. Smith, *Mennonites in Illinois*, 396.

187. Miller, *Wise as Serpents*, 47.

188. In addition to Franz, Toews lists the following as having come through the seminary in Woodlawn and gone on to hold influential church postings: Leo Driedger, Cornelius J. Dyck, Marian Franz, Leland and Bertha Fast Harder, J. Howard Kauffman, Robert Kreider, Elmer Neufeld, Betty Jean Pannabecker, Calvin Redekop, and Leola Schulz. See Toews, *Mennonites in American Society*, 259.

189. "Cross-Cultural Theological Consultation," memorandum, April 26–29, 1973, Paul G. Landis Papers, SCCO minutes and report, 1966–71, Cross-Cultural Theological Consultation, 1973, Kitchener 71, LMHS.

190. David Ewert, "The Story of Community Mennonite Church," memorandum, December 1990, second file cabinet, third drawer, marked Admin, folder Church History, CMC pastor's office; David Ewert, "Twenty-Five Years: A Presence with a Difference," memorandum, 1982, Marlene Suter's personal file.

191. Smith, *Mennonites in Illinois*, 430.

192. Jerry DeMuth, "Pastor Sparks Markham: There Goes Neighborhood . . . Upward," 1973, Marlene Suter's personal file; Lynford Hershey, "Report #6 To Counsel and Reference Committee for Cross-Cultural Relations Program," memorandum, August 2, 1971, fourth cabinet of row on far left wall upon entering room, second drawer unmarked, folder Minority Ministry Council 1970–71, EMM record room; Suter, "Church History Notes."

193. Suter to author, 2006.

194. Marsh, *The Beloved Community*, 2.

195. Voth to author, 2006.

196. Franz, "Why Is Woodlawn Church in the Middle of Chicago's Civil Rights?"

197. Marie J. Regier, "Focus on Demonstrations," *The Mennonite*, October 5, 1965, 624.

198. Lawrence Voth, "Woodlawn Church," memorandum, March 10, 1972, box 3, General S–Z, folder Woodlawn Church—MDS, CMC Files. Interestingly, Mennonite Disaster Service had worked successfully with a community organization committed to black self-determination in Pittsburgh. See Clyde Jackson and James Burkholder, "Interacting Where Asked," *Christian Living*, March 1970, 7–9.

199. Payne, *I've Got the Light*, 389.

200. See, for example, Barrett, *The Vision and the Reality*, 245–46.

201. Voth, "Woodlawn Church."

202. Fairfield, "Curtis Burrell."

203. Bechler, *Black Mennonite Church*, 174–75.

204. Burrell's purported joking about having two wives—a white one and an African-American one—could be raised as an example of his misjudgment in a morally conservative community. See Moriichi, "Woodlawn Mennonite," 39. Chuck Neufeld, a member of the pastoral team at Community Mennonite in 2007, reported that Larry Voth once proposed that the church store cadavers in its walk-in freezer on Saturdays, when the facility remained empty. The congregation turned him down.

205. King, *Stride toward Freedom*, 207, 208.

Chapter 7. The Manifesto Movement

1. Newman, *Getting Right with God*, 188.

2. On an official level, those conversations took place between African-American and white men. Oral histories completed for this study suggest that white women in the Mennonite Church were less concerned than white men about the prospect of takeovers.

3. Findlay, *Church People in the Struggle*, 201–2; Murray, *Methodists and the Crucible*, 212–14; Newman, *Getting Right with God*, 188; Shattuck, *Episcopalians and Race*, 195; Williams, "Christianity and Reparations."

4. Bittker, *The Case for Black Reparations*, 5.

5. McGreevy, *Parish Boundaries*, 221; Murray, *Methodists and the Crucible*, 214; Shattuck, *Episcopalians and Race*, 191–92.

6. I am indebted to the work of Kenneth T. Andrews, Robin D. G. Kelley, and George Mariscal for modeling an approach to the civil rights and black power era that evaluates historical actors by what they offered and not by whether they succeeded or failed. See, for example, Andrews, *Freedom Is a Constant Struggle*, 17, 39; Kelley, *Freedom Dreams*; Mariscal, *Brown-Eyed Children of the Sun*.

7. The following authors—historians of religion and historians of the civil rights movement alike—refer to the Black Manifesto from within various permutations of a success or failure paradigm. Clayborne Carson claims that the impact of the Black Manifesto was short lived and not radical enough. See Carson, *In Struggle*, 294–95. He is joined in more recent works by Lawrence Williams and C. Eric Lincoln, who assert that the document was in general a failure and not historically significant. See Lincoln, *Race, Religion*, 115–16; Williams, "Christianity and Reparations," 40. R. Laurence Moore, on the other hand, asserts that the manifesto successfully demonstrated the "phoniness of purported white beneficence." See Moore, *Religious Outsiders*, 195. Robert Weisbrot joins Moore in evaluating a positive component of the manifesto when he notes that it freed up financial resources that had not been previously available. See Weisbrot, *Freedom Bound*, 284. Although Lincoln says that the document was not historically significant, he does note that it exposed to the world what African-American people in the United States had to "endure." See Lincoln, *Race, Religion*, 116. Yet another analyst, Hugo Adam Bedau, offers a convincing argument that the manifesto was based on sound legal principle of unjust enrichment and therefore had successfully established a legal basis for its claims. See Bedau, "Compensatory Justice and the Black Manifesto." Although he disagrees with Williams's and Lincoln's assessments of the historical significance of the Black Manifesto by noting that it was the "first systematic, fully elaborated plan for reparations to emerge from the black freedom movement," Robin Kelley also falls into a success-failure paradigm in his discussion of the Black Manifesto when he notes, "If bringing the issue of reparations to a national audience was one of the goals of the 'Black Manifesto,' it proved to be a stunning success." See Kelley, *Freedom Dreams*, 120–23.

8. The Black Manifesto goes unmentioned in each of these three significant volumes: Bechler, *Black Mennonite Church*; Bush, *Two Kingdoms, Two Loyalties*; Toews, *Mennonites in American Society*.

9. Simon G. Gingerich to H. Howard Witmer, March 23, 1965, fourth cabinet of row on far left wall upon entering room, third drawer unmarked, folder Urban Racial Council, EMM record room; Nelson E. Kauffman to Dear Brother, October 13, 1964, fourth cabinet of row on far left wall upon entering room, third drawer unmarked, folder Urban Racial Council, EMM record room.

10. Paul G. Landis, interview with author, March 8, 2003.

11. Landis traveled with pastors John Kraybill from New York City, William

Yovanovich from Steelton, Pennsylvania, and William Weaver from Reading, Pennsylvania—all of whom served at integrated mission posts—as well as Voluntary Service director John Eby and long-time bishop and missionary to Africa Elam Stauffer. See John Eby, interview with author, February 28, 2003; H. Howard Witmer to Simon Gingerich, February 19, 1965, fourth cabinet of row on far left wall upon entering room, third drawer unmarked, folder Urban Racial Council, EMM record room.

12. "Program for Urban-Racial Conference to Be Held at Berean Mennonite Church, 1321 Lansdowne Blvd., Youngstown 5, Ohio," memorandum, March 4–5, 1965, fourth cabinet of row on far left wall upon entering room, third drawer unmarked, folder Urban Racial Council, EMM record room.

13. The delegates from the Lancaster Conference also heard from few women. The meeting thus began a male-dominated conversation. Although women like Fannie Swartzentruber and Rowena Lark had been holding frank conversations across racial lines for much of the previous three decades, men initiated, led, and controlled interracial public exchanges about the Black Manifesto. In this regard, the Youngstown meeting reflected the sexism present in the black power movement in particular and the civil rights movement more generally. Women did speak and express opinions about the problem of how best to respond to urban racial concerns, but the voices of men around them often squelched their contributions. In this regard, Paul Landis and his white male colleagues from the Lancaster Conference acted as would John Powell and other African-American leaders of the Minority Ministries Council.

14. "Why Do White Folks Hate Us? Urban-Racial Meetings, Youngstown, Ohio, March 4, 5, St. Louis, Mo., March 11, 12," *Mission Service Newsletter*, May 9, 1965, 1–4.

15. Ibid.

16. Simon G. Gingerich, "Report of the Findings Committee Urban Racial Meeting, Youngstown, Ohio," memorandum, March 4–5, 1965, 3, fourth cabinet of row on far left wall upon entering room, third drawer, unmarked, folder Urban Racial Council, EMM record room.

17. Gingerich to Witmer, 1965.

18. D. R. Yoder, "How I Am Making Up My Mind About Negroes," *Christian Living*, September 1966, 30–31.

19. John A. Lapp, "The Coming of Black Power," *Christian Living*, October 18–19, 1966.

20. See, for example, Vincent Harding, "Where Have All the Lovers Gone?" *Mennonite Life*, January 1967, 5–13; George E. Riddick, "Black Power in the White Perspective," *Mennonite Life*, January, 1967, 29–34; Howard Yoder, "Reflections on Riots," *Gospel Herald*, October 3, 1967, 894–95.

21. Mrs. Lloyd Weaver, "With Afro-Americans," *Missionary Messenger*, August 1967, 4–5.

22. Arden Almquist, "Whitey, Your Time Is Running Out," *Missionary Messenger*, November 12–15, 1967.

23. Paul G. Landis, "Tribute Lauds King's Life, Work," *Gospel Herald*, April 23, 1968, 374.

24. "Collective Guilt in Dr. King's Death Called a Mischievous Myth," *Sword and Trumpet*, July 1968, 19; James A. Goering, "Martin Luther King and the Gandhian Method of Nonviolent Resistance," *Sword and Trumpet*, October 1968, 1–5; Vincent Harding, "The History of a Wall," *Gospel Herald*, June 18, 1968, 543–45; Daniel Hertzler, "On the Death of King," *Christian Living*, June 1968, 40; John A. Lapp, "The Greatness of Martin Luther King, Jr.," *Christian Living*, June 1968, 18–19; Frank H. Littell, "Martin Luther King, Jr.," *Mennonite Life*, July 1968, 99; Vern Miller, "We Shall Overcome," *Gospel Herald*, May 14, 1968, 425; John C. Rezmerski, "For Martin L. King, Jr.," *Mennonite Life*, July 1968, 99; Edgar Stoesz, "A Mennonite Reflects on Martin Luther King," *Gospel Herald*, May 14, 1968, 437; "The Death of Martin Luther King, Jr.," *Sword and Trumpet*, June 1968, 1–2; "The Task of Reconciliation," *Sword and Trumpet*, May 1968, 45–50; "Who Was He?" *Gospel Herald*, May 21, 1968, 449; and, from *The Mennonite*, "A Time to Learn Compassion," May 7, 1968, 325–26; Sandra Froese, "The American Dream," May 7, 1968, 329; Vincent Harding, "Wall of Bitterness," June 18, 1968, 424–26; William G. Leber, "Slow on Race Relations," April 23, 1968, 300; Carol Loganbill, "One Night in Alabama," November 19, 1968, 725; William Robert Miller, "The Misunderstanding of Martin Luther King," November 19, 1968, 714–17; Harold Regier, "He Lives On," May 7, 1968, 336; Marie J. Regier, "Bitter Harvest of Hate," November 26, 1968, 732; Marie J. Regier, "To Preach or Demonstrate?" April 30, 1968, 319; Paul Unruh, "Deceived for a Long Time," December 10, 1968, 772; "White Racism Blamed for City Riots," April 2, 1968, 237.

25. Landis, interview, 2003.

26. "Urban Pastors Meet to Air Views," *Gospel Herald*, June 18, 1968, 552.

27. Ibid.

28. See, for example, Leroy Berry, "Of Such Is the Kingdom," *Christian Living*, July 1968, 8–9; Carl L. Good, "Time for Radical Servanthood," *The Mennonite*, June 18, 1968, 432–34; Levi Keidel, "Where Our Race Troubles Began," *The Mennonite*, June 4, 1968, 397–99; Hubert Schwartzentruber, "No One Will Escape," *The Mennonite*, June 18, 1968, 423.

29. John W. Eby, "Witnessing While Working in Washington," *Volunteer*, July 1968, 4–6; Eugene Shelly, "Inner City Growth," *Missionary Messenger*, June 1968, 17; Chester L. Wenger, "Home Missions and Evangelism," *Missionary Messenger*, June 1968, 14–16.

30. Gene Shelly, "Report from the Urban Racial Council," memorandum, 1968, 1, Paul G. Landis Coll., New York—Glad Tidings 1967–68, LMHS.

31. John Powell, "Minutes Minority Ministries Council Executive Committee," memorandum, December 17, 18, 1970, fourth cabinet of row on far left wall upon entering room, second drawer unmarked, folder Minority Ministry Council 1970–71, EMM record room.

32. Shelly, "Report from the Urban Racial Council," 1, 2.

33. Powell, "Minutes Minority Ministries Council Executive Committee." Although I focus on the African-American leadership of the Minority Ministries Council in this chapter, John Ventura and other Latino leaders like Mac Bustos, Ted Chapa, Lupe DeLeón, Criselda Garza, Lupe Gonzales, Tito Guedea, and Sammy Santos served critical leadership roles as the Minority Ministries Council began to develop. Thanks to Felipe Hinojosa for historical insight on this point.

34. Annabelle Hughes and Gerald Hughes, interview with author, August 29, 2006. Note also, as discussed in chapter 5, that John Powell, Gerald Hughes, and Lee Roy Berry were all married to white Mennonite women.

35. Richard Danner, "Bishop Board Meeting," memorandum, August 21, 1969, box Bishop Board Minutes 1964–1969, LMHS; I. Merle Good, "From across the Tracks," *The Mennonite*, February 11, 1969, 93; Ruth, *The Earth Is the Lord's*, 1071–72.

36. Paul G. Landis, "Bishop Board Meeting," memorandum, March 10–12, 1969, box Bishop Board Minutes 1964–1969, LMHS; Leon Stauffer, "Then They Are Brethren," *Volunteer*, March 1969, 3. The 1-W program was administered by the Lancaster Conference but provided a government-sanctioned alternative to military service for young Mennonite men.

37. Carson, *In Struggle*; Williams, "Christianity and Reparations," 41–42.

38. Williams, "Christianity and Reparations," 42.

39. James Forman, "Black Manifesto to the White Christian Church and the Jewish Synagogues in the United States of America and All Other Racist Institutions," memorandum, April 26, 1969, 5, VII.R GC Voluntary Service, Series 11 Gulfport VS Unit, box 3, folder 71, Black Manifesto, MLA.

40. Forman and those who followed him chose to focus on white mainline denominations far more than the Jewish groups originally named in the manifesto document. From the onset, the Jewish community, in the main, reacted more negatively to the Black Manifesto and experienced far fewer interruptions in their services than did the Christian community. Contemporary and historical accounts make no mention of synagogue services' being interrupted by Forman or his associations. See Lecky and Wright, "Reparations Now?" 17.

41. "Black Manifesto," memorandum, 5.

42. "Blacks Defy Church to Read Demands," *Intelligencer Journal*, May 5, 1969; Rose, "Putting It to the Churches," 98.

43. "Blacks Defy Church to Read Demands."

44. See the following articles from the *Intelligencer Journal*: "8 Clergymen Arrested for Occupying Church," July 11, 1969; "$50 Million Asked of Presbyterians," May 19, 1969; "Black Claims Rejected by Baptist Body," June 14, 1969; "Blacks Defy Church to Read Demands"; George W. Cornell, "$500 Million Demand Shocks Church Leaders," May 10, 1969; "Ex-Local Pastor Target of Sit-In," July 12, 1969; "Forman Asks $200 Million from Catholics," May 10, 1969; "Forman Lauds Pastor after Rights Sermon," May 12, 1969; "Judge Lectures Eight Dissenting Ministers," July 17, 1969; "Manifesto Read by Dr. McIntire," July 21, 1969; "Manifesto Rejected by Church," July 24, 1969; "Offices of Church Occupied," June 6, 1969; Joy Owens, "Rights Panel Asks Justice, Opportunity for Black Man," June 16, 1969; "Parley Slated on Negro Fund Demands," July 3, 1969; "Pastor Urges Housing Fund," July 7, 1969; "Presbyterians Reply to Black Manifesto," May 22, 1969; "Protesters Arrested in Churches," June 16, 1969; "Reparations Case Presented," May 16, 1969; Gil Scott, "Black Manifesto Is Direct Attack," May 26, 1969; "Typewriter Given Back to Church," June 12, 1969; "Typewriter Taken as Reparation," June 5, 1969; "UCC Denies Reparation to Forman," June 21, 1969; "UCC Funds for Forman Group Aired," June 27, 1969.

45. "8 Clergymen Arrested for Occupying Church"; "Forman Lauds Pastor after Rights Sermon"; "Protesters Arrested in Churches."

46. "Typewriter Taken as Reparation."

47. Henry Poettcker to Orlo Kaufman and Orlando Waltner, June 27, 1969, VII.R GC Voluntary Service, Series 11 Gulfport VS Unit, box 3, folder 71, Black Manifesto, MLA; "Presbyterians Reply to Black Manifesto"; "Resolutions Adopted by Mennonite Board of Missions July 2–6, 1969," memorandum, I-1-1, Mennonite General Conference, 1898–1971, 1969 Session materials, folder 5/8, AMC; Sousa, "The White Christian Churches' Responses to the Black Manifesto."

48. Frye, "The 'Black Manifesto' and the Tactic of Objectification," 68.

49. Lecky and Wright, "Reparations Now?" 3; Forman, *Control, Conflict and Change.*

50. Juhnke, *Vision, Doctrine, War,* 208–42; Ruth, *The Earth Is the Lord's,* 865–66, 979–83; Toews, *Mennonites in American Society,* 107–53.

51. Peace Problems Committee, *The Christian Nonresistant Way of Life,* 32.

52. Ibid., 41.

53. Edgar Metzler, "The Mennonite Churches and the Current Race Crisis," *Gospel Herald,* August 6, 1963, 683–84; Ruth, *The Earth Is the Lord's,* 1100–1101.

54. "Lancaster Conference Peace Committee Responds to Black Manifesto," *Gospel Herald,* August 12, 1969, 702; Paul G. Landis and Norman Shenk, "Peace and Industrial Relations Committee," memorandum, July 10, 1969, Peace Commit-

tee Minutes, 1962–1974, LMHS; Zook, *Mennonite Yearbook and Directory*, 1969, 65.

55. Landis's letter includes three sentences identifying economic reparations as the Black Manifesto's subject, five referring to race relations, and thirteen discussing nonviolent methods.

56. Noah G. Good and Paul G. Landis to Lancaster Conference Ministers, July 1969, box Conference Statements, LMHS.

57. "Forman Lauds Pastor after Rights Sermon"; "Protesters Arrested in Churches."

58. Good and Landis to Conference Ministers, 1969.

59. Toews, *Mennonites in American Society*, 149, 173.

60. Good and Landis to Conference Ministers, 1969.

61. Smith, *The Story of the Mennonites*, 784.

62. Ruth, *The Earth Is the Lord's*, 993–94, 99.

63. Mahlon M. Hess, editorial, *Missionary Messenger*, August 1969, 24, 23.

64. Ibid.

65. "Lancaster Conference Peace Committee Responds to Black Manifesto."

66. Powell, "Minutes Minority Ministries Council Executive Committee."

67. "A Response to Racial Tensions," *Hi-Lights*, Tuesday, August 19, 1969, 1; John Conventry Smith, "Chronicle of Events At '475,'" May 14-July 5, 1969," memorandum, July 5, 1969, Hist. Mss. 1-48, box 60, John H. Yoder (1927–1997) Collection Race / Urban issues, file 60/4, AMC; Sousa, "The White Christian Churches' Responses to the Black Manifesto."

68. "A Brief Statement on Mennonite Draft Resistance," memorandum, August 15–19, 1969, author's personal collection.

69. John Powell, interview with author, March 16, 2003; Zehr, "The Mennonite Church, 1970," 5.

70. Paul Zehr, interview with author, March 1, 2003.

71. Leonard E. Schmucker to John Powell, September 11, 1969, IV-21-4, box 1, MBM Minority Ministries Council, Data File 1, A–K, folder General Correspondence 1969–72, AMC.

72. Shearer, "A Pure Fellowship."

73. Mattie Cooper Nikiema et al., interview with John Sharp, July 17, 2004, AMC; Powell, interview.

74. John Powell, "Urban-Racial Concerns Statement," memorandum, August 19, 1969, I-1-1, Mennonite General Conference, 1898–1971, 1969 Session materials, folder 5/8, AMC.

75. Findlay, *Church People in the Struggle*, 212.

76. According to the 1970 *Mennonite Yearbook*, congregations were asked to forward about fifty dollars per member to church-wide agencies. The largest percent-

age of that amount, thirty-three dollars per member, went to the Mennonite Board of Missions and Charities that in 1969 received just over $2,200,000. Financial planners in the church thus anticipated receiving budget amounts from the equivalent of 80,000 of the church's 114,000 members in 1969. At that rate, as promoters of the Urban Racial Council fund would soon note, $500,000 a year amounted to an asking of $6 per member if contributions came in at the same rate as they did for the rest of the Mennonite church agencies. See Zook, *Mennonite Yearbook*, vol. 61, 11–12, 44, 50.

77. Powell, "Urban-Racial Concerns Statement," 2.

78. Ibid.

79. "Resolution on Urban-Racial Concerns," memorandum, August 19, 1969, I-1-1, Mennonite General Conference, 1898–1971, 1969 Session materials, folder 5/8, AMC.

80. Ibid.

81. "Urban Racial Concerns," Mennonite Historical Society, www.mcusa-ar chives.org/library/resolutions/BlackManifesto1969.html (accessed November 15, 2006).

82. Ibid.

83. "Reporting Guide for Mennonite General Conference," *Hi-Lights*, Tuesday, August 19, 1969, 3.

84. John Powell, "The Urban Racial Council," *Missionary Messenger*, September 1969, 14–15.

85. Paul G. Landis, "Peace and Industrial Relations Committee," memorandum, October 9, 1969, Peace Committee Minutes, 1962–1974, LMHS.

86. Minutes of the Colored Workers Committee, memorandum, 1964–1969, file cabinets far wall, first cabinet, top drawer, drawer marked Home Missions Locations and Other General 1956–1964, four numbered notebooks, EMM record room.

87. "Evangelist Urges Gospel for Black Community," *Mennonite Weekly Review*, January 15, 1970.

88. Melvin Delp, "Nonconformity Committee Statement to Conference," *Pastoral Messenger*, April 1969, 5–6; Lloy A. Kniss, "Worse or Better?" *Pastoral Messenger*, January 1969, 2; "Report to the Lancaster Mennonite Conference, Mellinger Mennonite Meetinghouse, Lincoln Highway East, Lancaster, Pennsylvania, September 18, 1969," *Pastoral Messenger*, October 1969, 2–4; Aaron M. Shank, "Purpose and Objective of the Mennonite Messianic Mission," *Pastoral Messenger*, April 1969, 7; Norman Shenk, "Pulpit Echoes," *Pastoral Messenger*, October 1969, 8; Aaron O. Stauffer, "Liberalism or Conservatism," *Pastoral Messenger*, January 1969, 1–2; "The Lancaster Mennonite Conference, Weaverland Mennonite Church, East Earl, Pennsylvania, March 18, 1969," *Pastoral Messenger*, April 1969, 1–3; "Worth Noting," *Pastoral Messenger*, January, 1969, 7–8.

89. John Powell, "The Compassion Fund Is," *Gospel Herald*, March 24, 1970, 271.

90. John Powell, "The Minority Ministries Council: A Call to Action," *Gospel Herald*, March 31, 1970, 294.

91. Hubert Brown, "Report on the Church and Urban Development Seminar," memorandum, April 1970, IV-21-4 box 1, MBM Minority Ministries Council, Data File 1, A–K, folder Church and Urban Development 1970, Seminars, AMC.

92. John Powell, "Hesston College Visit," memorandum, April 16, 1970, Hist. Mss. 1-784, box 1, Hubert Schwartzentruber Collection, Miscellaneous, folder Minority Ministries Council, 1970, AMC.

93. Chester L. Wenger to Lancaster Conference Pastors, August 24, 1970, fourth cabinet of row on far left wall upon entering room, second drawer unmarked, folder Minority Ministers' Appointments 1970, EMM record room.

94. A number of the ten men listed in Wenger's August 24, 1970, letter to every pastor in the Lancaster Conference—Richard Pannell, Harold Davenport, George Richards, James Harris, Macon Gwinn, Raymond Jackson, Larry Crumbley, Artemio DeJesus, Jose Gonzalez, Jose Santiago—did go on to fulfill a variety of leadership posts in the Conference and throughout the church, but as of Wenger's letter, none of these Lancaster Conference pastors of color had held formal leadership posts with the Minority Ministries Council.

95. James Thomas and Leon Stauffer, "Peace Committee," memorandum, October 15, 1970, 2, Peace Committee Minutes, 1962–1974, LMHS.

96. Lynford Hershey, interview with author, March 2, 2003.

97. Leon Stauffer, "Special Meeting Lancaster Conference Bishop Board Leaders and Peace Committee with Linford Hershey Director Race Education Program, Minority Ministries Council, Elkhart, Indiana," memorandum, November 13, 1970, Clarence E. Lutz Peace Committee Lanc Conf, MCC, VS—IW, LMHS.

98. "C.P.S.C. At Minneapolis," *Hi-lights of the Mennonite Publishing House*, November 25, 1970, 1.

99. Lynford Hershey, "Report To: Home Missions Council," memorandum, 1970, fourth cabinet of row on far left wall upon entering room, second drawer, unmarked, folder Minority Ministry Council 1970–71, EMM record room.

100. Leon Stauffer to Lynford Hershey, July 14, 1971, IV-21-4, box 1, MBM Minority Ministries Council, Data File 1, A–K, folder Education Program 1970–72, Lynford Hershey, AMC.

101. John Powell to Vincent Harding, July 9, 1971, IV-21-4, box 1, MBM Minority Ministries Council, Data File 1, A–K, folder General Correspondence 1969–72, AMC.

102. Lynford Hershey to Leon Stauffer, July 18, 1971, IV-21-4, box 1, MBM

Minority Ministries Council, Data File 1, A–K, folder Education Program 1970–72, Lynford Hershey, AMC.

103. Chester L. Wenger to Mahlon Hess, July 27, 1971, fourth cabinet of row on far left wall upon entering room, second drawer, unmarked, folder Minority Ministry Council 1970–71, EMM record room.

104. "Minority Ministries Council Annual Assembly," memorandum, October 15–16, 1971, fourth cabinet of row on far left wall upon entering room, second drawer, unmarked, folder Minority Ministry Council 1970–71, EMM record room.

105. John Powell, "Compassion Fund Report," memorandum, 1971, fourth cabinet of row on far left wall upon entering room, second drawer, unmarked, folder Minority Ministry Council, 1970–71, EMM record room.

106. "Minority Ministries Council Black Caucus," memorandum, October 15, 1971, fourth cabinet of row on far left wall upon entering room, second drawer, unmarked, folder Minority Ministry Council 1970–71, EMM record room.

107. Ibid.

108. Ibid.

109. "Minority Statement to Mennonite Church," memorandum, 1971, fourth cabinet of row on far left wall upon entering room, second drawer, unmarked, folder Minority Ministry Council 1970–71, EMM record room.

110. "Minority Ministries Council Latin Concilio," memorandum, October 15, 1971, fourth cabinet of row on far left wall upon entering room, second drawer, unmarked, folder Minority Ministry Council 1970–71, EMM record room.

111. Although minutes of the October 30, 1972, Lancaster Conference Peace Committee make reference to plans to explore holding such an event, no follow-up activity appears in the minutes through 1975. See Ray Geigley, "Peace Committee," memorandum, October 30, 1972, Peace Committee Minutes, 1962–1974, LMHS.

112. Peace Committee, "Of All Nations One People," 1972.

113. Ibid.

114. "Harold Davenport Talks with Kids," photo by Paul Angstadt, 1973, file cabinets middle isle, drawer marked Information Services Picture File, file Archives—Home Ministries, Children's Visitation Program, EMM record room.

115. John Powell, "AFRAM to Bring Blacks Together," *Gospel Herald*, July 31, 1973, 592.

116. Urie A. Bender, "Where Color Doesn't Matter," *Missionary Messenger*, February 1974, 8–9.

117. "Racism Statement by Anabaptists at 'Liberty and Justice' Workshop," memorandum, October 1976, Christian E. Charles Collection, Race Relations, LMHS.

118. "Black Manifesto," memorandum.

119. Russell J. Baer, editorial, *Pastoral Messenger*, January 1970, 4; Good and Landis to Conference Ministers, 1969; Landis, "Bishop Board Meeting"; "Minority Statement to Mennonite Church"; Powell to Harding, 1971.

120. "Statement of Christian Doctrine and Rules and Discipline of the Lancaster Conference of the Mennonite Church," memorandum, July 17, 1968, 22, LMHS.

121. Powell, "Urban-Racial Concerns"; "Minority Statement to Mennonite Church."

122. Bechler, *Black Mennonite Church*, 41; Ira J. Buckwalter, minutes of the Colored Workers Committee, memorandum, 1947—1953, file cabinets far wall, first cabinet, top drawer, marked Home Missions, Locations and Other General 1956—1964, four numbered notebooks, EMM record room; "Seventh Avenue Mennonite Church: Self-Analysis of Congregation in Response to Questionnaire Titled 'Some Questions to Ask When Describing a Church,'" memorandum, September 10, 1965, 10, Paul G. Landis, New York—Seventh Ave, LMHS.

123. "Minority Statement to Mennonite Church."

124. Christian Smith and Michael Emerson note that the history of race relations in evangelical communities has often been hampered by a focus on an individualistic "relationalism" in which interpersonal relationships hold primacy over all else and by an "anti-structuralism" in which members of that community refuse to focus on structural realities. Those tendencies were present at both the grassroots and leadership levels among the Lancaster Conference Mennonites. See Emerson and Smith, *Divided by Faith*, 76.

125. "A Historical Timeline of Minority and Urban Ministry in the United States, 1910—1997," Historical Committee, Mennonite Church USA, www.mcusa-archives.org/Resources/mimorityministriestimeline.html (accessed May 18, 2008).

126. John Powell, "Among Chaos, a Place to Belong," *The Mennonite*, September 25, 1973, 543—44.

127. "A Historical Timeline of Minority and Urban Ministry."

128. Ibid.

129. Historian Felipe Hinojosa correctly notes that the demise of interracial conversation between blacks and whites did not mean that important dialogue within the African-American and Latino communities disappeared. He traces how religious affiliation served an important role in forming multiethnic coalitions and racial and ethnic nationalisms through conversations that continued after Minority Ministries Council members had turned their attention away from talking with white Mennonites. Issues of gender also figure prominently in his exploration of council members' identities. For more information, see Hinojosa, "Making Noise among the 'Quiet in the Land.'"

130. Faith Hershberger, "MCC / Black Caucus Representative Meeting," memorandum, December 4, 1979, I-6-7, African-American Mennonite Association, Records, 1969, 1976—91, box 28 (large), folder Mennonite Central Committee, 28/1, AMC; Faith Hershberger, "MCC / Black Caucus Representatives Meeting," memorandum, October 8, 1979, I-6-7, African-American Mennonite Association, Records, 1969, 1976—91, box 28 (large), folder Mennonite Central Committee, 28/1, AMC; Dwight McFadden to William T. Snyder, June 14, 1979, I-6-7, African-American Mennonite Association, Records, 1969, 1976—91, box 28 (large), folder Mennonite Central Committee 28/1, AMC.

131. "Lancaster Conference Bishop Board Minutes," memorandum, May 17, 1977, LMHS; "Lancaster Conference Bishop Board Minutes," memorandum, July 15, 1982, LMHS.

132. Ruth, *The Earth Is the Lord's*, 1106—16.

133. Thomas and Stauffer, "Peace Committee," 3.

134. "Three Serve Summer Urban Program in Philadelphia," *Gospel Herald*, September 21, 1982, 643.

135. Hershey to Stauffer, 1971.

136. Paul G. Landis, interview with author, April 28, 2005; Landis, interview, 2003; Nikiema et al., interview.

137. "A Historical Timeline of Minority and Urban Ministry in the United States, 1910—1997."

138. Ibid. In 1994 Powell joined the Reference Committee for the Racism Awareness Program of the Mennonite Central Committee.

Chapter 8. A New Civil Rights Story

1. "Mennonite Church Organized Here," *St. Louis Argus*, Friday, November 29, 1957, 1.

2. Bristol, "The Pruitt-Igoe Myth," 354—55.

3. K. Ford to Hubert Schwartzentruber, ca. 1957, III-25-8, Bethesda MC 1/10, H. Schwartzentruber Files—Corres., Misc. incoming 1957—59, AMC.

4. Schwartzentruber and Schwartzentruber, "A Pocket of Hope in St. Louis," 100.

5. Hubert Schwartzentruber, "Will Freedom Ring in the Pew?" *Gospel Herald*, June 18, 1968, 550—51.

6. Emerson and Smith, *Divided by Faith*.

7. Nelson E. Kauffman, "Light Shines out from the Inner City," *Gospel Herald*, June 6, 1961, 516—17.

8. Barnett, "Invisible Southern Black Women"; Collier-Thomas and Franklin, *Sisters in the Struggle*; Fosl, *Subversive Southerner*; Harrison, "Women's and Girls' Ac-

tivism in 1960s Southwest Georgia"; Height, "We Wanted the Voice of a Woman to Be Heard"; Kirk, "Daisy Bates"; Knotts, "Bound by the Spirit"; Ling and Monteith, "Gender and the Civil Rights Movement"; Payne, *I've Got the Light*; Stanton, *Journey toward Justice.*

9. Hubert Schwartzentruber, "No One Will Escape," *The Mennonite*, June 18, 1968, 423; Schwartzentruber, "Will Freedom Ring?"

10. Findlay, "Religion and Politics in the Sixties."

11. Burns, *Disturbing the Peace*; Findlay, "Churches Join"; Gottlieb, *Joining Hands*; Marsh, *Beloved Community.*

12. Schwartzentruber, *Jesus in Back Alleys*, 38.

13. Hubert Schwartzentruber and Mary Schwartzentruber, interview with Leonard Gross, August 2, 1986, 9, I-3-3.3 (see tape in Hist. Mss. 6-234), Historical Committee Mtg. with Hubert Swartzentruber, AMC.

14. Curtis E. Burrell Jr., "How My Mind Has Changed About Whites," *Christian Living*, September 1966, 28–29; Schwartzentruber and Schwartzentruber, interview; Schwartzentruber, *Jesus in Back Alleys.*

15. Joseph, "Dashikis and Democracy"; Kelley, *Freedom Dreams*; Wilmore, *Black Religion and Black Radicalism.*

16. Foner, *The Black Panthers Speak*; Joseph, *Waiting 'Til the Midnight Hour.*

17. Hubert Schwartzentruber to Malcolm Wenger, September 15, 1967, St. Louis, Missouri, VII.R GC Voluntary Service, Series 11 Gulfport VS Unit, box 1, folder 14, Correspondence—General Conf. July–Dec., 1967, MLA.

18. Baxter, "On the American Civil Rights Movement's Origins"; Findlay, *Church People in the Struggle*; Salmond, "*My Mind Set on Freedom.*"

19. Jim Fairfield, "Curtis Burrell: A Bullet Hole in the Window," *Christian Living*, May 1971, 20–24.

20. "South Seventh St. Mennonite Church Annual Report," memorandum, 1968, box South Seventh Street, Reading, Calendars, Clippings, articles, correspondence, historical notes, history, 50th anniv'y tapes, folder South Seventh Street, Reading—Annual Report, 1968, AMC.

21. Paul G. Landis, "Growing Congregations in New York City," *Missionary Messenger*, November 1966, 2–4.

22. Payne, *I've Got the Light*, 102.

23. Hubert Schwartzentruber, "Let Me In!" *Gospel Herald*, May 4, 1971, 396–98.

24. Ibid.

25. Mattie Cooper Nikiema et al., interview with John Sharp, July 17, 2004, AMC.

26. Ann Jennings Brunk to Guy F. Hershberger, June 10, 1952, I-3-7, CESR 7/33, Race Relations Islands of Sanity, AMC.

27. Miller, "Building Anew in Cleveland," 84.

28. Betty Gwinn, interview with author, April 26, 2008.

29. Truman Brunk et al., *Conference on the Christian and Race*; "Mennonite Race Relations: Still at a Low Point," memorandum, August 7, 1970, 4, I.Z.1, folder 77, Race—Articles/reports, box 6, MCA, Peace and Social Concerns Committee of the General Conference Mennonite Church, MLA.

30. Quoted in "Additional Personnel Requested for Atlanta Unit," memorandum, June 7, 1963, IX-12-6 MCC, Reports 1961—1974, box 1, folder Atlanta Mennonite Central Committee, AMC.

31. Hubert Schwartzentruber to Lynford Hershey, September 22, 1970, St. Louis, Missouri, III-25-8, Bethesda MC 1/39, Church Outreach Ministries—MBMC, Misc. Outgoing corr. 1969—71, AMC.

32. Paul G. Landis, interview with author, April 28, 2005.

33. Harold Regier and Rosella Wiens Regier, interview with author, July 12, 2005.

34. Findlay, "Churches Join the Movement"; Harris, *Something Within*; Marsh, *The Beloved Community*; Savage, *Your Spirits Walk Beside Us*.

35. Chapman, *Christianity on Trial*; Chrisman, "The Price of Moderation"; Lewis, *Massive Resistance*; Marsh, *God's Long Summer*; Murray, *Methodists and the Crucible*.

36. Ammerman, *Baptist Battles*; McGreevy, *Parish Boundaries*; Murray, *Methodists and the Crucible*. See also Shattuck, *Episcopalians and Race*; Willis, *All According to God's Plan*.

37. Chappell, *Inside Agitators*.

38. Guy F. Hershberger, "Islands of Sanity," *Gospel Herald*, March 25, 1952, 293—94; Irvin B. Horst, "Mennonites and the Race Question," *Gospel Herald*, July 13, 1945, 284—85; Smith, "Mennonites in America," 92; Smith, *The Story of the Mennonites*, 540; John I. Smucker, "Can Christians Purge Themselves?" *Gospel Herald*, September 12, 1972, 715—16.

39. Bechler, *Black Mennonite Church*, 41.

40. Andrew Schulze to Guy F. Hershberger, July 22, 1955, CESR papers I-3-7, box 6, folder 14, AMC.

41. Marvin Miller, "Churches and Social Agencies Work in Slum Area with Little Success," *New Era*, October 16, 1963.

42. Lind and Scheuer, "Glad Tidings Mennonite Church."

43. Leo Driedger, "Christian Witness in Race Relations," *Mennonite Life*, April 1960, 81—86.

44. Hershberger, "Islands of Sanity."

45. I base this claim on a close reading of more than 850 Mennonite church press articles on race. See Shearer, "A Pure Fellowship," appendix 1.

46. Willis, *All According to God's Plan*.

47. Knotts, "Bound by the Spirit," 191.

48. Frye, "The 'Black Manifesto' and the Tactic of Objectification," 68–69; Wilmore, "Identity and Integration," 227.

49. Harry A. Brunk, "Harry A. Brunk 1944 Diary," memorandum, July 24, 1944, box I-MS-13, Harry A. Brunk Collection Diaries—John Brunk, Joseph Heatwole, Lena Burkholder Brunk, Harry A. Brunk, box 4, VAMC.

50. Goldie Hostetler, interview with author, March 14, 2002.

51. Ibid.

52. Brunk, "1944 Diary."

53. Harry A. Brunk, "Harry A. Brunk 1941 Diary," memorandum, December 24, 1941, box I-MS-13, Harry A. Brunk Collection Diaries—John Brunk, Joseph Heatwole, Lena Burkholder Brunk, Harry A. Brunk, box 4, VAMC.

54. Clarence Fretz, "YPCA Report, City Workers Band I," memorandum, November 3, 1936, box II-G-1e, box 1, YPCA Inclus. Dates 1926–42, folders A–Z, folder City Workers Band 1926–42, EMU.

55. Martin, "City Missions," 57.

56. Ernest L. Swartzentruber and Fannie Swartzentruber to *Gospel Fellowship*, March 13, 1941, box I-MS-13, Harry A. Brunk Collection Materials related to Virginia Menn. Conf., box 1, folder 8, Colored Work Broad Street Mennonite Church, VAMC.

57. Ernest Swartzentruber, "History of the Colored Mission of Harrisonburg, Virginia," *Missionary Light*, April 1943, 4.

58. Lyons, "A Mother's Love," 4.

59. "Testimonies: Mission Children Visitation Program of Lancaster Conference," *Missionary Messenger*, May 1951, 11; Milo Dailey, "Mississippi Negro Boy Is Enjoying Life from Farm Family near Freeman," *Yankton Press and Dakotan*, Friday, August 1, 1969, 10; Delmer Hofer, "Towards Better Understanding between Races," *Northern Light*, September 1969, 2; Chester L. Wenger, "Home Missions and Evangelism," *Missionary Messenger*, June 1968, 14.

60. John H. Kraybill to Paul G. Landis, September 23, 1965, box Paul G. Landis, New York—Seventh Ave, LMHS.

61. Wallace Best makes a similar argument regarding changes brought about in Chicago by the migration of thousands of rural African Americans into the city. See Wallace D. Best, *Passionately Human*, 4, 6, 9, 72, 82–84, 95–97, 117, 184.

62. Findlay, "Religion and Politics," 66.

63. Bush, *Two Kingdoms, Two Loyalties*, 11–12.

64. Harry A. Brunk, "Harry A. Brunk 1964 Diary," memorandum, box I-MS-13, Harry A. Brunk Collection diaries 1953–1967, box 5, VAMC.

65. Best, *Passionately Human*; Savage, *Your Spirits Walk Beside Us*.

66. Moore, *Touchdown Jesus*.

67. Chappell, *A Stone of Hope*, 87.

68. Meier, "Synthesis of Civil Rights History," 211.

69. Kelley, *Race Rebels*, 9–10.

70. "Racism Statement by Anabaptists at 'Liberty and Justice' Workshop," memorandum, October 1976, Christian E. Charles Collection, Race Relations, LMHS.

71. Joseph, *Waiting 'Til the Midnight Hour*, 183–84.

72. "Racism Statement by Anabaptists."

73. Carmichael and Hamilton, *Black Power*, 4; Joseph, *Waiting 'Til the Midnight Hour*, 199.

74. "Racism Statement by Anabaptists."

75. Ibid.

76. Dwight McFadden, "Black Caucus Reviews History, Looks to Future," *Gospel Herald*, November 18, 1975, 834.

77. "Racism Statement by Anabaptists."

78. Ibid.

79. Ibid.

80. *A Historical Timeline of Minority and Urban Ministry in the United States, 1910–1997*, Historical Committee, Mennonite Church USA, September 12, 2006, www.mcusa-archives.org/Resources/mimorityministriestimeline.html (accessed May 18, 2008). The Mennonite Board of Congregational Ministries was one of the first (Old) Mennonite Church organizations to join the Damascus Road Anti-racism Process that emerged within the Mennonite community in the 1990s.

81. Kanagy, *Road Signs for the Journey*, 120; Nikiema et al., interview.

Bibliography

Alvis, Joel L., Jr. "A Presbyterian Dilemma: Ecclesiastical and Social Racial Policy in the Twentieth-Century Presbyterian Communion." In *The Diversity of Discipleship: Presbyterians and Twentieth-Century Christian Witness*, edited by Milton J. Coalter, John M. Mulder, and Louis Weeks, 187–208. Louisville, KY: Westminster John Knox Press, 1991.

Ammerman, Nancy Tatum. *Baptist Battles: Social Change and Religious Conflict in the Southern Baptist Convention*. New Brunswick, NJ: Rutgers University Press, 1990.

Ammerman, Nancy Tatum, and Arthur Emery Farnsley. *Congregation and Community*. New Brunswick, NJ: Rutgers University Press, 1997.

Andrews, Kenneth T. *Freedom Is a Constant Struggle: The Mississippi Civil Rights Movement and Its Legacy*. Chicago: University of Chicago Press, 2004.

Arthur, Linda B. *Religion, Dress, and the Body (Dress, Body, Culture)*. Oxford, UK: Berg Publishers, 1999.

Bains, Lee E., Jr. "Birmingham, 1963: Confrontation over Civil Rights." In *Birmingham, Alabama, 1956–1963: The Black Struggle for Civil Rights*, edited by David J. Garrow, 151–289. Brooklyn, NY: Carlson Publishing, 1989.

Barnett, Bernice McNair. "Invisible Southern Black Women Leaders in the Civil Rights Movement: The Triple Constraints of Gender, Race, and Class." In *Race, Class, and Gender: Common Bonds, Different Voices*, edited by Esther Ngan-ling Chow, Doris Y. Wilkinson, and Maxine Baca Zinn, 265–87. Thousand Oaks, CA: Sage Publications, 1996.

Barrett, Lois. *The Vision and the Reality: The Story of Home Missions in the General Conference Mennonite Church*. Newton, KS: Faith and Life Press, 1983.

Baxter, Anthony G. "On the American Civil Rights Movement's Origins, Nature, and Legacy: Framing the Struggle for the 'Pearl of Great Price.'" Paper presented at the National Association of African American Studies and National Association of Hispanic and Latino Studies conference, History and Civil Rights Section, Houston, TX, February 21–26, 2000.

Bechler, Le Roy. *The Black Mennonite Church in North America, 1886–1986.* Scottdale, PA: Herald Press, 1986.

———. "Facts, Considerations, and Membership of Negroes in the Mennonite Church, 1955." Negro Evangelism Committee, 1955.

Bedau, Hugo Adam. "Compensatory Justice and the Black Manifesto." In *Injustice and Rectification,* edited by Rodney C. Roberts, 131–46. New York: Peter Lang Publishing, 2002.

Best, Wallace D. *Passionately Human, No Less Divine: Religion and Culture in Black Chicago, 1915–1952.* Princeton, NJ: Princeton University Press, 2005.

Biondi, Martha. *To Stand and Fight: The Struggle for Civil Rights in Postwar New York City.* Cambridge, MA: Harvard University Press, 2003.

Bittker, Boris I. *The Case for Black Reparations.* Boston: Beacon Press, 2003.

Black, Timuel D. *Bridges of Memory: Chicago's First Wave of Black Migration.* Evanston, IL: Northwestern University Press, 2005.

Bowman, Carl Desportes. *Brethren Society: The Cultural Transformation of a Peculiar People.* Baltimore: Johns Hopkins University Press, 1995.

Bristol, Katharine G. "The Pruitt-Igoe Myth." In *American Architectural History: A Contemporary Reader,* edited by Keith L. Eggener, 352–64. New York: Routledge, 2004.

Brown, Hubert. *Black and Mennonite: A Search for Identity.* Scottdale, PA: Herald Press, 1976.

———. "The Larks: Mission Workers." In *1991 Mennonite Yearbook and Directory,* edited by James E. Horsch, 8–9. Scottdale, PA: Herald Press, 1991.

Brunk, Harry Anthony. *History of Mennonites in Virginia, 1900–1960.* Vol. 2. Harrisonburg, VA: H. A. Brunk, 1972.

Brunk, Truman, Nelson Burkholder, Paul G. Landis, Grant M. Stoltzfus, Richard Weaver, and J. Otis Yoder. *Conference on the Christian and Race.* Harrisonburg, VA: Virginia Mennonite Conference, March 31, 1964.

Buckridge, Steeve O. *The Language of Dress: Resistance and Accommodation in Jamaica, 1760–1890.* Kingston, Jamaica: University of the West Indies Press, 2004.

Burns, Jeffrey M. *Disturbing the Peace: A History of the Christian Family Movement.* Notre Dame, IN: University of Notre Dame Press, 1999.

Bush, Perry. *Two Kingdoms, Two Loyalties: Mennonite Pacifism in Modern America.* Baltimore: Johns Hopkins University Press, 1998.

Byrd, Ayana, and Lori L. Tharps. *Hair Story: Untangling the Roots of Black Hair in America.* New York: St. Martin's Press, 2001.

Camacho, Eduardo, and Ben Joravsky. *Against the Tide: The Middle Class in Chicago.* Chicago: Community Renewal Society, 1989.

Carmichael, Stokely, and Charles V. Hamilton. *Black Power: The Politics of Liberation in America.* New York: Random House, 1967.

Carson, Clayborne. *In Struggle: SNCC and the Black Awakening of the 1960s.* Cambridge, MA: Harvard University Press, 1981.

Chapman, Mark L. *Christianity on Trial: African-American Religious Thought Before and After Black Power.* Maryknoll, NY: Orbis Books, 1996.

Chappell, David L. *Inside Agitators: White Southerners in the Civil Rights Movement.* Baltimore: Johns Hopkins University Press, 1994.

———. *A Stone of Hope: Prophetic Religion and the Death of Jim Crow.* Chapel Hill: University of North Carolina Press, 2004.

Chidester, David. *Authentic Fakes: Religion and American Popular Culture.* Berkeley: University of California Press, 2005.

Chrisman, David Keith. "The Price of Moderation: Texas Baptists and Racial Integration, 1948–1968." Ph.D. diss., Texas A&M University, 2001.

Christerson, Brad, Korie L. Edwards, and Michael O. Emerson. *Against All Odds: The Struggle for Racial Integration in Religious Organizations.* New York: New York University Press, 2005.

Cofer, Bernice. *Racial Integration in the Church.* New York: American Baptist Home Mission Societies, 1957.

Coles, Robert. *Children of Crisis: A Study of Courage and Fear.* Boston: Little, Brown, 1967.

Collier-Thomas, Bettye, and V. P. Franklin. *Sisters in the Struggle: African American Women in the Civil Rights—Black Power Movement.* New York: New York University Press, 2001.

Cone, James H. *Black Theology and Black Power.* New York: Seabury Press, 1969.

Countryman, Matthew J. *Up South: Civil Rights and Black Power in Philadelphia.* Philadelphia: University of Pennsylvania Press, 2006.

Cruz, Bárbara C., and Michael J. Berson. "The American Melting Pot? Miscegenation Laws in the United States." *Organization of American Historians Magazine of History* 15, no. 4 (2001). www.oah.org/pubs/magazine/family/cruz-berson.html (accessed March 24, 2009).

Cunningham, Michael, and Craig Marberry. *Crowns: Portraits of Black Women in Church Hats.* New York: Doubleday, 2000.

Dart, John. "Hues in the Pews." *Christian Century* 118, no. 7 (2001): 6–8.

D'Emilio, John, and Estelle B. Freedman. *Intimate Matters: A History of Sexuality in America.* New York: Harper and Row, 1988.

Drake, Thomas E. *Quakers and Slavery in America.* New Haven, CT: Yale University Press, 1950.

Dudziak, Mary L. *Cold War Civil Rights: Race and the Image of American Democracy.* Princeton, NJ: Princeton University Press, 2000.

Eby, Omar. *Fifty Years, Fifty Stories: The Mennonite Mission in Somalia, 1953–2003.* Telford, PA: Cascadia Publishing, 2003.

Emerson, Michael O., and Christian Smith. *Divided by Faith: Evangelical Religion and the Problem of Race in America.* New York: Oxford University Press, 2001.

Epp, Marlene. "Carrying the Banner of Nonconformity: Ontario Mennonite Women and the 'Dress Question,' 1989–1960." *Conrad Grebel Review* 8, no. 3 (1990), 237–57.

Erb, Alta Mae. *Studies in Mennonite City Missions.* Scottdale, PA: Mennonite Publishing House, 1937.

Evans, Rhonda D., Craig J. Forsyth, and Stephanie Bernard. "One Church or Two? Contemporary and Historical Views of Race Relations in One Catholic Diocese." *Sociological Spectrum* 22, no. 2 (2002): 225–44.

Fairclough, Adam. *To Redeem the Soul of America: The Southern Christian Leadership Conference and Martin Luther King, Jr.* Athens: University of Georgia Press, 1987.

Findlay, James. "Churches Join the Movement." In *The Civil Rights Movement,* edited by Paul A. Winters, 141–49. San Diego: Greenhaven Press, 2000.

———. *Church People in the Struggle: The National Council of Churches and the Black Freedom Movement, 1950–1970.* New York: Oxford University Press, 1993.

———. "Religion and Politics in the Sixties: The Churches and the Civil Rights Act of 1964." *Journal of American History* 77, no. 1 (1990): 66–92.

Fish, John Hall. *Black Power / White Control: The Struggle of the Woodlawn Organization in Chicago.* Princeton, NJ: Princeton University Press, 1973.

Foner, Philip S., ed. *The Black Panthers Speak.* Cambridge, MA: De Capo Press, 1970.

Forman, James. *Control, Conflict, and Change: The Underlying Concepts of the Black Manifesto.* Detroit, MI: National Association of Black Students, 1970.

Fosl, Catherine. *Subversive Southerner: Anne Braden and the Struggle for Racial Justice in the Cold War South.* New York: Palgrave Macmillan, 2002.

Freed, Sarah Ann. "Mennonites in the Fresh Air Program: An Early Expression of the Mennonite Social Conscience." Term paper, Goshen College, 1967.

Frye, Jerry K. "The 'Black Manifesto' and the Tactic of Objectification." *Journal of Black Studies* 5, no. 1 (1974): 65–76.

Garrow, David J. *Bearing the Cross: Martin Luther King, Jr., and the Southern Christian Leadership Conference.* New York: HarperCollins, 1986.

Gilfoyle, Timothy J. "Street-Rats and Gutter-Snipes: Child Pickpockets and Street Culture in New York City, 1850–1900." *Journal of Social History* 37, no. 4 (2004): 853–62.

Gingerich, Jeffery Phillip. "Sharing the Faith: Racial and Ethnic Identity in an

Urban Mennonite Community." Ph.D. diss., University of Pennsylvania, 2003.

Gingerich, Melvin. *Mennonite Attire through Four Centuries.* Breinigsville, PA: Pennsylvania German Society, 1970.

Gjerde, Jon. *The Minds of the West: Ethnocultural Evolution in the Rural Middle West, 1830–1917.* Chapel Hill: University of North Carolina Press, 1997.

Golden, Joseph. "Social Control of Negro-White Intermarriage." *Social Forces* 36, no. 3 (1958): 267–69.

Good, Robert W. "Forty Years on Diamond Street: A Historical Research of Diamond Street Mennonite Church and Mennonite Mission to Philadelphia." Master's thesis, Eastern Mennonite College, 1982.

Gottlieb, Roger S. *Joining Hands: Politics and Religion Together for Social Change.* Cambridge, MA: Westview Press, 2002.

Graybill, Beth E. "Mennonite Women and Their Bishops in the Founding of the Eastern Pennsylvania Mennonite Church." *Mennonite Quarterly Review* 72, no. 2 (1998): 251–73.

———. "To Remind Us of Who We Are: Multiple Meanings of Conservative Women's Dress." In *Strangers at Home: Amish and Mennonite Women in History,* edited by Kimberly D. Schmidt, Diane Zimmerman Umble, and Steven D. Reschly, 53–77. Baltimore: Johns Hopkins University Press, 2002.

Graybill, J. Lester. "The View of the Mennonite Church on Marriage, Divorce, and Remarriage." Term paper, Goshen College, 1958.

Greene, Christina. *Our Separate Ways: Women and the Black Freedom Movement in Durham, North Carolina.* Chapel Hill: University of North Carolina Press, 2005.

Gullickson, Aaron. "Black/White Interracial Marriage Trends, 1850–2000." *Journal of Family History* 31, no. 3 (2006): 289–312.

Habermas, Jürgen. *The Structural Transformation of the Public Sphere: An Inquiry into a Category of Bourgeois Society.* Translated by Thomas Burger and Frederick Lawrence. Cambridge, MA: MIT Press, 1989.

Hall, Jacquelyn Dowd. "The Long Civil Rights Movement and the Political Uses of the Past." *Journal of American History* 91, no. 4 (March 2005). www.history cooperative.org/journals/jah/91.4/hall.html (accessed March 16, 2009).

Harding, Rachel E. "Biography, Democracy, and Spirit: An Interview with Vincent Harding." *Callaloo* 20, no. 3 (1998): 682–98.

Harding, Vincent. *Martin Luther King: The Inconvenient Hero.* Maryknoll, NY: Orbis Books, 1996.

———. "Vincent Harding: A Black Historian." In *Peace-Makers: Christian Voices from the New Abolitionist Movement,* edited by Jim Wallis, 85–97. San Francisco: Harper and Row, 1983.

Harding, Vincent, Delton Franz, Curtis Janzen, Ed Riddick, Julius Belzer, Paul King, Richard Harmon, and John Miller. "The Christian in Race Relations." Paper presented to the General Mennonite Conference Church and Society Study Conference, Chicago, October 31-November 3, 1961.

Harris, Fredrick C. *Something Within: Religion in African-American Political Activism.* New York: Oxford University Press, 2001.

Harrison, Alisa Y. "Women's and Girls' Activism in 1960s Southwest Georgia: Rethinking History and Historiography." In *Women Shaping the South: Creating and Confronting Change,* edited by Angela Boswell and Judith N. McArthur, 229–58. Columbia: University of Missouri Press, 2006.

Haury, David A. *The Quiet Demonstration: The Mennonite Mission in Gulfport, Mississippi.* Newton, KS: Faith and Life Press, 1979.

Hawes, Joseph M., Constance B. Schulz, and N. Ray Hiner. "The United States." In *Children in Historical and Comparative Perspective: An International Handbook and Research Guide,* edited by Joseph M. Hawes and N. Ray Hiner, 491–522. New York: Greenwood Press, 1991.

Height, Dorothy I. "We Wanted the Voice of a Woman to Be Heard: Black Women and the 1963 March on Washington." In *Sisters in the Struggle: African American Women in the Civil Rights–Black Power Movement,* edited by Bettye Collier-Thomas and V. P. Franklin, 83–91. New York: New York University Press, 2001.

Hershberger, Guy F. *The Way of the Cross in Human Relations.* Scottdale, PA: Herald Press, 1958.

Higginbotham, A. Leon, Jr., and Barbara K. Kopytoff. "Racial Purity and Interracial Sex in the Law of Colonial and Antebellum Virginia." In *Interracialism: Black-White Intermarriage in American History, Literature, and Law,* edited by Werner Sollors, 81–139. New York: Oxford University Press, 2000.

Higham, John, and Carl Guarneri. *Hanging Together: Unity and Diversity in American Culture.* New Haven, CT: Yale University Press, 2001.

Hine, Darlene Clark. *Hine Sight: Black Women and the Re-Construction of American History.* Brooklyn, NY: Carlson Publishing, 1994.

Hinojosa, Felipe. "Making Noise among the 'Quiet in the Land': Mexican American and Puerto Rican Ethno-Religious Identity in the Mennonite Church, 1932–1980." Ph.D. diss., University of Houston, 2009.

Hollenweger, Walter J. *Pentecost between Black and White: Five Case Studies on Pentecost and Politics.* Belfast, Ireland: Christian Journals Ltd., 1974.

Horst, Samuel. *Mennonites in the Confederacy: A Study in Civil War Pacifism.* Scottdale, PA: Herald Press, 1967.

Hostetler, Beulah Stauffer. *American Mennonites and Protestant Movements: A Community Paradigm.* Scottdale, PA: Herald Press, 1987.

Hunter, Tera W. *To 'Joy My Freedom: Southern Black Women's Lives and Labors after the Civil War.* Cambridge, MA: Harvard University Press, 1997.

Jackson, Kenneth T. *Crabgrass Frontier: The Suburbanization of the United States.* New York: Oxford University Press, 1985.

Jacoby, Tamar. *Someone Else's House: America's Unfinished Struggle for Integration.* New York: Free Press, 1998.

Jones, Jacqueline. *Labor of Love, Labor of Sorrow: Black Women, Work, and the Family from Slavery to the Present.* New York: Basic Books, 1985.

Joseph, Peniel E. "Dashikis and Democracy: Black Studies, Student Activism, and the Black Power Movement." *Journal of African American History* 88, no. 2 (2003): 182–203.

———. Introduction to *The Black Power Movement: Rethinking the Civil Rights Black Power Era,* edited by Peniel E. Joseph, 1–25. New York: Routledge, 2006.

———. *Waiting 'Til the Midnight Hour: A Narrative History of Black Power in America.* New York: Holt Paperbacks, 2007.

Juhnke, James C. *Vision, Doctrine, War: Mennonite Identity and Organization in America, 1890–1930.* Scottdale, PA: Herald Press, 1989.

Kanagy, Conrad L. *Road Signs for the Journey: A Profile of Mennonite Church USA.* Scottdale, PA: Herald Press, 2007.

Kelley, Robin D. G. *Freedom Dreams: The Black Radical Imagination.* Boston: Beacon Press, 2002.

———. *Race Rebels.* New York: Free Press, 1994.

Kelly, Brian. *Race, Class, and Power in the Alabama Coalfields, 1908–1921.* Urbana: University of Illinois Press, 2001.

King, Martin Luther. *Stride toward Freedom: The Montgomery Story.* New York: Harper, 1958.

King, Wilma. *African American Childhoods: Historical Perspectives from Slavery to Civil Rights.* New York: Palgrave Macmillan, 2005.

Kirk, John A. "Daisy Bates, the National Association for the Advancement of Colored People, and the 1957 Little Rock School Crisis: A Gendered Perspective." In *Gender in the Civil Rights Movement,* edited by Peter J. Ling and Sharon Monteith, 17–40. New York: Garland Publishing, 1999.

Klarman, Michael J. *From Jim Crow to Civil Rights: The Supreme Court and the Struggle for Racial Equality.* New York: Oxford University Press, 2004.

Klassen, Pamela E. "Practicing Conflict: Weddings as Sites of Contest and Compromise." *Mennonite Quarterly Review* 72, no. 2 (1998): 225–50.

———. "The Robes of Womanhood: Dress and Authenticity among African American Methodist Women in the Nineteenth Century." *Religion and American Culture* 14, no. 1 (2004): 39–82.

K'Meyer, Tracy Elaine. *Interracialism and Christian Community in the Postwar South:*

The Story of Koinonia Farm. Charlottesville: University Press of Virginia, 1997.

Knotts, Alice G. "Bound by the Spirit, Found on the Journey: The Methodist Women's Campaign for Southern Civil Rights, 1940–1968." Ph.D. diss., Illiff School of Theology, University of Denver, 1989.

Kraus, C. Norman. "Scriptural Teachings on Race Relations." In *Conference on Christian Community Relations,* 31–42. Goshen, IN: Mennonite Community Association, Committee on Economic and Social Relations of the Mennonite Church, 1955.

Kraybill, Donald B. "Mennonite Woman's Veiling: The Rise and Fall of a Sacred Symbol." *Mennonite Quarterly Review* 61, no. 3 (1987): 298–320.

Landes, Henry D. "But Would You Want Your Daughter to Marry One? Marriage and Institutional Racism in the Mennonite Church." Term paper, Associated Mennonite Biblical Seminaries, 1974.

Lecky, Robert S., and H. Elliott Wright. "Reparations Now? An Introduction." In *Black Manifesto: Religion, Racism, and Reparations,* edited by Robert S. Lecky and H. Elliott Wright, 1–32. New York: Sheed and Ward, 1969.

Lee, Chana Kai. "Anger, Memory, and Personal Power: Fannie Lou Hamer and Civil Rights Leadership." In *Sisters in the Struggle: African American Women in the Civil Rights–Black Power Movement,* edited by Bettye Collier-Thomas and V. P. Franklin, 139–70. New York: New York University Press, 2001.

Lewis, George. *Massive Resistance: The White Response to the Civil Rights Movement.* New York: Oxford University Press, 2006.

Lincoln, C. Eric. *Race, Religion, and the Continuing American Dilemma.* New York: Hill and Wang, 1999.

Lind, Loren, and James H. Scheuer. "The Glad Tidings Mennonite Church Makes Living a Little Bit Easier for Poor." 90th Cong., 1st sess., *Congressional Record: House,* 113 (January 15, 1967): H1367–H1368.

Ling, Peter J. "Gender and Generation: Manhood at the Southern Christian Leadership Conference." In *Gender in the Civil Rights Movement,* edited by Peter J. Ling and Sharon Monteith, 101–29. New York: Garland Publishing, 1999.

Ling, Peter J., and Sharon Monteith. "Gender and the Civil Rights Movement." In *Gender in the Civil Rights Movement,* edited by Peter J. Ling and Sharon Monteith, 1–16. New York: Garland Publishing, 1999.

Loescher, Frank Samuel. *The Protestant Church and the Negro: A Pattern of Segregation.* New York: Association Press, 1948.

Loewen, Royden K. *Family, Church, and Market: A Mennonite Community in the Old and the New Worlds, 1850–1930.* Chicago: University of Illinois Press, 1993.

Longenecker, Stephen L. "Antislavery and Otherworldliness in the Shenandoah

Valley." Paper presented at the conference After the Backcountry: Rural Life and Society in the Nineteenth-Century Valley of Virginia, Virginia Military Institute, March 23–25, 1995.

Lyons, Linda. "A Mother's Love: Female Influences Passed Down from Generation to Generation." Term paper, Georgia State University, 2001.

MacMaster, Richard K. *Land, Piety, Peoplehood: The Establishment of Mennonite Communities in America, 1683–1790.* Scottdale, PA: Herald Press, 1985.

MacMaster, Richard K., and Donald R. Jacobs. *A Gentle Wind of God: The Influence of the East Africa Revival.* Scottdale, PA: Herald Press, 2006.

Mahmood, Saba. *Politics of Piety: The Islamic Revival and the Feminist Subject.* Princeton, NJ: Princeton University Press, 2005.

Mariscal, George. *Brown-Eyed Children of the Sun: Lessons from the Chicano Movement, 1965–1975.* Albuquerque: University of New Mexico Press, 2005.

Marsh, Charles. *The Beloved Community: How Faith Shapes Justice, from the Civil Rights Movement to Today.* New York: Basic Books, 2005.

———. *God's Long Summer: Stories of Faith and Civil Rights.* Princeton, NJ: Princeton University Press, 1997.

Martin, Betty Marie. "City Missions." In *Shenandoah*, 57. Harrisonburg, VA: Eastern Mennonite College, 1948.

McDannell, Colleen. *Picturing Faith: Photography and the Great Depression.* New Haven, CT: Yale University Press, 2004.

McGreevy, John T. *Parish Boundaries: The Catholic Encounter with Race in the Twentieth-Century Urban North.* Chicago: University of Chicago Press, 1996.

Meier, August. "Toward a Synthesis of Civil Rights History." Epilogue to *New Directions in Civil Rights Studies*, edited by Armstead L. Robinson and Patricia Sullivan, 211–24. Charlottesville: University Press of Virginia, 1991.

Mennonite General Conference. *The Nurture and Evangelism of Children.* Scottdale, PA: Mennonite Publishing House, 1955.

———. "The Way of Christian Love in Race Relations." Paper presented at the Twenty-Ninth Mennonite General Conference, Heston, KS, August 23–26, 1955.

Miller, Keith Graber. "Complex Innocence, Obligatory Nurturance, and Parental Vigilance: 'The Child' in the Work of Menno Simons." In *The Child in Christian Thought*, edited by Marcia J. Bunge, 194–226. Grand Rapids, MI: Eerdmans Publishing, 2000.

———. *Wise as Serpents, Innocent as Doves: American Mennonites Engage Washington.* Knoxville: University of Tennessee Press, 1996.

Miller, Vern. "Building Anew in Cleveland." In *Being God's Missionary Community: Reflections on Mennonite Missions, 1945–1975*, 82–86. Elkhart, IN: Mennonite Board of Missions, 1975.

Moody, Anne. *Coming of Age in Mississippi*. New York: Dell Books, 1976.

Moore, R. Laurence. *Religious Outsiders and the Making of Americans*. New York: Oxford University Press, 1986.

———. *Touchdown Jesus: The Mixing of Sacred and Secular in American History*. Louisville, KY: Westminster John Knox Press, 2003.

Moran, Rachel F. *Interracial Intimacy: The Regulation of Race and Romance*. Chicago: University of Chicago Press, 2001.

Moriichi, Shuji. "Woodlawn Mennonite Church: Mennonites, Civil Rights Movement, and the City." Term paper, Associated Mennonite Biblical Seminary, 1995.

Morris, Aldon D. *The Origins of the Civil Rights Movement: Black Communities Organizing for Change*. New York: Free Press, 1984.

Murray, Peter C. *Methodists and the Crucible of Race, 1930–1975*. Columbia: University of Missouri Press, 2004.

Nasaw, David. *Children of the City: At Work and at Play*. New York: Anchor Press, 1985.

Newman, Mark. *Getting Right with God: Southern Baptists and Desegregation, 1945–1995*. Tuscaloosa: University of Alabama Press, 2001.

O'Neal, Gwendolyn S. "The African American Church, Its Sacred Cosmos and Dress." In *Religion, Dress, and the Body*, edited by Linda B. Arthur, 117–34. Oxford, UK: Berg Publishers, 1999.

Orsi, Robert A. "Everyday Miracles: The Study of Lived Religion." In *Lived Religion in America: Toward a History of Practice*, edited by David D. Hall, 3–21. Princeton, NJ: Princeton University Press, 1997.

Pannabecker, Samuel Floyd. *Faith in Ferment: A History of the Central District Conference*. Newton, KS: Faith and Life Press, 1968.

———. *Ventures of Faith: The Story of Mennonite Biblical Seminary*. Elkhart, IN: Mennonite Biblical Seminary, 1975.

Pascoe, Peggy. "Miscegenation Law, Court Cases, and Ideologies of 'Race' in Twentieth-Century America." In *Interracialism: Black-White Intermarriage in American History, Literature, and Law*, edited by Werner Sollors, 178–204. New York: Oxford University Press, 2000.

Patterson, James T. *Grand Expectations: The United States, 1945–1974*. New York: Oxford University Press, 1996.

Pavela, Todd H. "An Exploratory Study of Negro-White Intermarriage in Indiana." *Journal of Marriage and the Family* 26, no. 2 (1964): 209–11.

Payne, Charles M. *I've Got the Light of Freedom: The Organizing Tradition and the Mississippi Freedom Struggle*. Berkeley: University of California Press, 1995.

Peace Committee. "Of All Nations One People: A Study Guide on Race Relations." Lancaster Conference of the Mennonite Church, 1972.

Peace Problems Committee. *The Christian Nonresistant Way of Life.* Lancaster, PA: Peace Problems Committee and Tract Editors of Lancaster Conference District, 1940.

Raboteau, Albert J. *Slave Religion: The "Invisible Institution" in the Antebellum South.* New York: Oxford University Press, 1978.

Ransby, Barbara. *Ella Baker and the Black Freedom Movement: A Radical Democratic Vision.* Chapel Hill: University of North Carolina Press, 2003.

Reed, Harold. "A History of Steelton Mennonite Gospel Mission." Term paper, Eastern Mennonite College, 1961.

Regier, Ami. "Revising the Plainness of Whiteness." *Mennonite Life* 57, no. 2 (2002), www.bethelks.edu/mennonitelife/2002june/regier.php (accessed February 6, 2010).

Reimers, David M. *White Protestantism and the Negro.* New York: Oxford University Press, 1965.

Reynolds, Margaret C., and Simon J. Bronner. *Plain Women: Gender and Ritual in the Old Order River Brethren.* University Park: Pennsylvania State University Press, 2001.

Rich, Elaine Sommers. *Walking Together in Faith: The Central District Conference, 1957–1999.* Bluffton, OH: Central District Conference, 1993.

Ricoeur, Paul. *The Symbolism of Evil.* Translated by Emerson Buchanan. New York: Harper and Row, 1967.

Rivera, Tomás. *And the Earth Did Not Devour Him.* Translated by Evangelina Vigil-Piñón. Houston, TX: Arte Publico Press, 1992.

Robnett, Belinda. "Women in the Student Non-Violent Coordinating Committee: Ideology, Organizational Structure, and Leadership." In *Gender in the Civil Rights Movement,* edited by Peter J. Ling and Sharon Monteith, 131–68. New York: Garland Publishing, 1999.

Romano, Renee Christine. *Race Mixing: Black-White Marriage in Postwar America.* Cambridge, MA: Harvard University Press, 2003.

Rooks, Noliwe M. *Hair Raising: Beauty, Culture, and African American Women.* New Brunswick, NJ: Rutgers University Press, 1996.

Root, Maria P. P. *Love's Revolution: Interracial Marriage.* Philadelphia, PA: Temple University Press, 2001.

Rose, Gillian. *Visual Methodologies: An Introduction to the Interpretation of Visual Materials.* Thousand Oaks, CA: Sage Publications, 2001.

Rose, Stephen C. "Putting It to the Churches." In *Black Manifesto: Religion, Racism, and Reparations,* edited by Robert S. Lecky and H. Elliott Wright, 96–104. New York: Sheed and Ward, 1969.

Ruth, John Landis. *The Earth Is the Lord's: A Narrative History of the Lancaster Mennonite Conference.* Scottdale, PA: Herald Press, 2001.

Salmond, John A. *My Mind Set on Freedom: A History of the Civil Rights Movement,*
    1954–1968. Chicago: Ivan R. Dee, Publisher, 1997.
Sandage, Scott. "A Marble House Divided: The Lincoln Memorial, the Civil Rights
    Movement, and the Politics of Memory, 1939–1963." *Journal of American*
    History 80, no. 1 (1993): 135–67.
Savage, Barbara Dianne. *Your Spirits Walk Beside Us: The Politics of Black Religion.*
    Cambridge, MA: Harvard University Press, 2008.
Schlabach, Theron F. *Gospel versus Gospel: Mission and the Mennonite Church, 1863–*
    1944; Studies in Anabaptist and Mennonite History. Eugene, OR: Wipf and
    Stock Publishers, 1980. Reprint, Scottdale, PA: Herald Press, 1998.
———. "Race, and Another Look at Nonviolent Resistance." In "A Biography of Guy
    F. Hershberger." Working draft, 2009.
Schmeisser, Iris. "Camera at the Grassroots: The Student Nonviolent Coordinating
    Committee and the Politics of Visual Representation." In *The Civil Rights*
    Movement Revisited: Critical Perspectives on the Struggle for Racial Equality in the
    United States, edited by Patrick B. Miller, Therese Frey Steffen, and Elisa-
    beth Schäfer-Wünsche, 105–25. New Brunswick, NJ: Transaction Pub-
    lishers, 2001.
Schmidt, Kimberly D. " 'Sacred Farming' or 'Working Out': The Negotiated Lives
    of Conservative Mennonite Farm Women." *Frontiers: A Journal of Women*
    Studies 22, no. 1 (2001): 79–102.
Schultz, Debra L. *Going South: Jewish Women in the Civil Rights Movement.* New York:
    New York University Press, 2001.
Schwartzentruber, Hubert. *Jesus in Back Alleys: The Story and Reflections of a Contem-*
    porary Prophet. Telford, PA: Dreamseeker Books, 2002.
Schwartzentruber, Hubert, and June Schwartzentruber. "A Pocket of Hope in St.
    Louis." In *Being God's Missionary Community: Reflections on Mennonite Missions,*
    1945–1975, 97–103. Elkhart, IN: Mennonite Board of Missions, 1975.
Sensbach, Jon F. *A Separate Canaan: The Making of an Afro-Moravian World in North*
    Carolina, 1763–1840. Chapel Hill: University of North Carolina Press,
    1998.
Shattuck, Gardiner H. *Episcopalians and Race: Civil War to Civil Rights; Religion in the*
    South. Lexington: University Press of Kentucky, 2000.
Shearer, Tobin Miller. "A Pure Fellowship: The Danger and Necessity of Purity in
    White and African-American Mennonite Racial Exchange, 1935–1971."
    Ph.D. diss., Northwestern University, 2008.
Shenk, Wilbert R. *By Faith They Went Out: Mennonite Missions, 1850–1999.*
    Elkhart, IN: Institute of Mennonite Studies, 2000.
Shetler, Jan Bender. "A Prophetic Voice in Race Relations? The Mennonite Church-
    Missions to Minority Ministries." Term paper, Goshen College, 1977.

Sitkoff, Harvard. *The Struggle for Black Equality: 1954–1980.* New York: Hill and Wang, 1981.

Smith, C. Henry. "Mennonites in America." In *Mennonites and Their Heritage: A Handbook of Mennonite History and Beliefs,* 79–148. Scottdale, PA: Herald Press, 1964.

——. *The Story of the Mennonites.* Berne, IN: Mennonite Book Concern, 1941.

Smith, Willard H. *Mennonites in Illinois.* Scottdale, PA: Herald Press, 1983.

Sokol, Jason. *There Goes My Everything: White Southerners in the Age of Civil Rights, 1945–1975.* New York: Alfred A. Knopf, 2006.

Sollors, Werner. *Interracialism: Black-White Intermarriage in American History, Literature, and Law.* New York: Oxford University Press, 2000.

Sousa, William Noel. "The White Christian Churches' Responses to the Black Manifesto." Master's thesis, University of the Pacific, 1973.

Stanton, Mary. *Journey toward Justice: Juliette Hampton Morgan and the Montgomery Bus Boycott.* Athens: University of Georgia Press, 2006.

Steinhorn, Leonard, and Barbara Diggs-Brown. *By the Color of Our Skin: The Illusion of Integration and the Reality of Race.* New York: Dutton, 1999.

Stoltzfus, Louise. *Quiet Shouts: Stories of Lancaster Mennonite Women Leaders.* Scottdale, PA: Herald Press, 1999.

Swartz, David R. "Mista Mid-Nights: Mennonites and Race in Mississippi." *Mennonite Quarterly Review* 78, no. 4 (2004): 469–502, 511.

Taves, Ann. "Sexuality in American Religious History." In *Retelling U.S. Religious History,* edited by Thomas A. Tweed, 27–56. Berkeley: University of California Press, 1997.

Thomas, Anita Jones, Karen McCurtis Witherspoon, and Suzette L. Speight. "Toward the Development of the Stereotypic Roles for Black Women Scale." *Journal of Black Psychology* 30, no. 3 (2004): 426–42.

Toews, Paul. *Mennonites in American Society, 1930–1970: Modernity and the Persistence of Religious Community.* Scottdale, PA: Herald Press, 1996.

Tully, Alan. "Patterns of Slaveholding in Colonial Pennsylvania: Chester and Lancaster Counties, 1729–1758." *Journal of Social History* 13, no. 3 (1973): 284–305.

Tweed, Thomas A. *Retelling U.S. Religious History.* Berkeley: University of California Press, 1997.

United Methodist Church. "Report of an Interracial Conference: The Methodist Church and Changing Racial Patterns." Chicago, March 8–9, 1955.

United Presbyterian Church in the U.S.A., Commission on Religion and Race. *A Survey of Racial Integration in Local Congregations of the United Presbyterian Church in the U.S.A.* New York: Commission on Religion and Race, 1964.

Van Slyck, Abigail A. *A Manufactured Wilderness: Summer Camps and the Shaping of*

American Youth, 1890–1960. Minneapolis: University of Minnesota Press, 2006.

Veer, Peter van der. *Imperial Encounters: Religion and Modernity in India and Britain.* Princeton, NJ: Princeton University Press, 2001.

Verney, Kevern. *The Debate on Black Civil Rights in America.* Manchester, UK: Manchester University Press, 2006.

Virginia Mennonite Conference. *Minutes of the Virginia Mennonite Conference Including Some Historical Data, a Brief Biographical Sketch of Its Founders and Organization, and Her Official Statement of Christian Fundamentals, Constitution, and Rules and Discipline: A Publication Authorized by the Conference in a Session Held at Weavers Church, August, 1938.* Vol. 2. Harrisonburg, VA: Virginia Mennonite Conference, 1950.

Wadlington, Walter. "The Loving Case: Virginia's Anti-Miscegenation Statue in Historical Perspective." *Virginia Law Review* 52, no. 7 (1966): 1189–223.

Wallenstein, Peter. *Tell the Court I Love My Wife: Race, Marriage, and Law; An American History.* New York: Palgrave Macmillan, 2002.

Watras, Joseph. *Politics, Race, and Schools: Racial Integration, 1954–1994.* New York: Garland Publishing, 1997.

Weaver, John Denny. "The Mennonite Church and the American Negro." Term paper, Associated Mennonite Biblical Seminaries, 1970.

Weber, John S. "The History of Broad Street Mennonite Church, 1936–1971." Senior thesis, Eastern Mennonite College, 1971.

Weber, Max. *The Sociology of Religion.* Translated by Ephraim Fischoff. Boston: Beacon Press, 1964.

Weisbrot, Robert. *Freedom Bound: A History of America's Civil Rights Movement.* New York: W. W. Norton, 1990.

Wenger, J. C. *The Prayer Veil in Scripture and History.* Scottdale, PA: Herald Press, 1964.

West, Traci C. *Disruptive Christian Ethics: When Racism and Women's Lives Matter.* Louisville, KY: Westminster John Knox Press, 2006.

Wiese, Andrew. "The House I Live In: Race, Class, and African American Suburban Dreams in the Postwar United States." In *The New Suburban History,* edited by Kevin Michael Kruse and Thomas J. Sugrue, 99–119. Chicago: University of Chicago Press, 2006.

———. *Places of Their Own: African American Suburbanization in the Twentieth Century.* Chicago: University of Chicago Press, 2004.

Williams, Carol. *Framing the West: Race, Gender, and the Photographic Frontier in the Pacific Northwest.* New York: Oxford University Press, 2003.

Williams, Lawrence H. "Christianity and Reparations: Revisiting James Forman's 'Black Manifesto,' 1969." *Currents in Theology and Mission* 32, no. 1 (2005): 39–46.

Willis, Alan Scot. *All According to God's Plan: Southern Baptist Missions and Race, 1945–1970*. Lexington: University Press of Kentucky, 2005.

Wills, David W. "An Enduring Distance: Black Americans and the Establishment." In *Between the Times: The Travail of the Protestant Establishment in America, 1900–1960*, edited by William R. Hutchinson, 168–92. Cambridge, UK: Cambridge University Press, 1989.

Wilmore, Gayraud S. *Black Religion and Black Radicalism: An Interpretation of the Religious History of African Americans*. Maryknoll, NY: Orbis Books, 1998.

———. "Identity and Integration: Black Presbyterians and Their Allies in the Twentieth Century." In *The Diversity of Discipleship: Presbyterians and Twentieth-Century Christian Witness*, edited by Milton J. Coalter, John M. Mulder, and Louis Weeks, 209–33. Louisville, KY: Westminster John Knox Press, 1991.

Yancey, George A., and Sherelyn Whittum Yancey. Introduction to *Just Don't Marry One: Interracial Dating, Marriage, and Parenting*, edited by George A. Yancey and Sherelyn Whittum Yancey, xiii–xix. Valley Forge, PA: Judson Press, 2002.

Zehr, Howard J. "The Mennonite Church, 1970." In *Mennonite Yearbook and Directory*, vol. 61, edited by Ellrose D. Zook, 5–22. Scottdale, PA: Mennonite Publishing House, 1970.

Zook, Ellrose D., ed. *Mennonite Yearbook and Directory, 1946*. Vol. 37. Scottdale, PA: Mennonite Publishing House, 1946.

———, ed. *Mennonite Yearbook and Directory, 1956*. Vol. 47. Scottdale, PA: Mennonite Publishing House, 1956.

———, ed. *Mennonite Yearbook and Directory*. Vol. 56. Scottdale, PA: Mennonite Publishing House, 1965.

———, ed. *Mennonite Yearbook and Directory*. Vol. 59. Scottdale, PA: Mennonite Publishing House, 1968.

———, ed. *Mennonite Yearbook and Directory, 1969*. Vol. 60. Scottdale, PA: Mennonite Publishing House, 1969.

———, ed. *Mennonite Yearbook and Directory*. Vol. 61. Scottdale, PA: Mennonite Publishing House, 1970.

———, ed. *Mennonite Yearbook and Directory*. Vol. 62. Scottdale, PA: Mennonite Publishing House, 1971.

Index

cape dress, 16, 29, 37–38, 46–47
Carmichael, Stokely, 100, 177, 187, 227, 247–48
Carr, Margaret, 172
Carter, Cloyd, 5
Carter, Mary Elizabeth, 5
Carter, Robert, 5
catholics. *See* Roman Catholics
Chaney, James, 242
Chappell, David, xii, 234, 273n129
Chicago: African-American population of, 46; Bethel Mennonite in, 9, 40, 44, 163; congregations in, 163; Fresh Air programs in, 66; Martin Luther King campaign, xvii; Larks' move to, 38; marches in, 23, 242; nonconformity conference in, 12; seminary move from, 20; Ada Webb's move to, 44; white Mennonites in, 46; Woodlawn Mennonite and, 14, 19
children, ix, x; African-American, xviii, 2, 10, 13–14, 18, 22, 34, 61, 81, 275n15; agency of, 274n4; civil rights movement and, 64–65, 228, 231, 274n8; disruption by, 63; Fresh Air, xvii, 14, 63, 81, 89; hair and, 63; innocence of, 274n7; Latino/a, 14; prayer coverings and, 73; scripture about, 282n120; urban areas and, 240; white, 14
churches: African-American, 49; Mennonite, x, xx; in Chicago, 303n24; civil rights activity in, viii, x, xi, xx, 57, 128, 273n129; integrated, 102, 302n13; as staging grounds, xii, 128; state relationship to, 245; as testing grounds, 47, 49
Church of the Brethren, 4
Church Peace Mission, 115
city. *See* urban areas
Civilian Public Service, 9, 42, 105, 202
Civil Rights Act of 1964, 120, 225, 239, 241, 243
Clark, Septima, 242
Cleaver, Eldridge, 227

clothing, xiv, xvi, 11–13, 15, 28, 30, 34; African-American, 47, 265n16; double standard of, 48, 295n23; hijab and, 33; Rowena Lark's use of, 37, 59; Mennonites and, xvi, 16, 13, 32, 48, 264n98; missionaries', 43; negative effect of, 37; plain coat and, 27, 32, 37, 240; urban areas and, 240
cold war, 18–19, 50
Colored Workers Committee, 14, 16, 19, 51, 198; Black Manifesto and, 209; Fresh Air program of, 66, 275n15; Gerald Hughes and, 135; interracial marriage and, 152, 301n110; retirement communities and, 259n29
Committee on Economic and Social Relations, 14, 143
communion, 18, 36–37, 40, 42, 58, 225
communists, 8, 19, 50
Community Mennonite (IL), 23, 159, 160, 166–76, 183–86, 303n17; African-American members of, 183–84; Christmas controversy at, 172; civil rights movement and, 175; daycare center at, 173, 187; demonstrations and, 224; departures from, 307n88; Vincent Harding and, 301n1; history of, 162; integration at, 167, 169–71, 175, 183, 185, 226, 232; interracial marriage and, 170, 172, 307n90; photos of, 168, 184; restrictive covenant at, 166; service and, 187, 224; sheltered care workshop at, 185; tensions at, 171; Jane Voth and, 306n58; Larry Voth and, 169; white volunteers at, 174, 184, 187
Compassion Fund, 212–13, 216
conferences: Atlanta, 1964, 125; Board of Christian Service, 1963, 282n125; Goshen College, 1955, 143–44; Laurelville, PA, 1951, 269n62; Mennonite World, 1967, 286n28; Prairie Street, 1963, 151; Virginia, 1964, 113, 287n48; Woodlawn, 1959, 105–6, 147–48, 165

congregations, integrated. *See* integrated
   congregations
Congress of Racial Equality, 20, 25, 143,
   285n14
Connor, Bull, 65
Conrad, Jacob, 134
Conrad, Sadie, 134, 139
conscientious objection, xv, 120, 243. *See
   also* nonresistance
converts, African-American, 12–13, 15,
   49, 51
CORE. *See* Congress of Racial Equality
country. *See* rural areas
coverings. *See* prayer coverings
Crossroads Mennonite (MS), 111
Crumbley, Larry, 321n94
Curry, Billy, 18, 52, 113
Curry, Peggy, 12, 51, 52

DaCosta, Aggie and Andre, 312n176
Davenport, Harold, 213, 321n94
Dearborn Street Mennonite (IL), 38, 46
Dearman, Louise and Richard, 312n176
DeJesus, Artemio, 321n94
Demere, Charles, 125
demonstrations: church's response to, 22;
   civil rights movement, viii, x, 24, 31, 58,
   226; coercion by, xvi; definition of, 63;
   forms of, 31, 218; Fresh Air as, 93; Vincent Harding and, 120; Mennonite participation in, 23, 28, 83, 93; Mennonite
   versions of, vii, ix, xvi, 23, 28, 220, 222,
   224; numbers of, 117; opposition to, 24;
   Hubert Schwartzentruber and, 225; sites
   of, xi, 230; as staging grounds, xii, 225
desegregation, public schools of, 50
Diamond Street Mennonite (PA), 18, 51,
   54
discipleship, 1, 4
Double V campaign, 36
Drescher, John M., 118
dress. *See* clothing
Driedger, Leo, 235, 283n7, 297n74

DuBois, Essie, 312n176
Dyck, Cornelius J., 312n188

Eastern Mennonite Board of Missions
   and Charities, 8, 10–11, 14, 259n29,
   260n44
Eastern Mennonite College, xv, 10–11,
   20; desegregation of, 45, 244, 269n72;
   Vincent Harding at, 109; Goldie
   Hummel at, 238–39; segregation at,
   40, 68, 237; Ada Webb and, 44–45,
   58
Eby, John, 315n11
Eby, Sem, 7
Eden Mennonite Church (KS), 77, 79
Ediger, Peter, 22, 171, 196
Eisenhower, Dwight D., 50
Ekstrom, Florence, 174
Ekstrom, R. A., 174
Elkhart, IN, 20, 98, 119, 163, 197, 225
Emerson, Michael, 323n124
Episcopalians, xvii, 236, 296n62
Eshleman, Merle W., 1
Ethiopia, 49
eugenics, 7, 134–35
evangelism, 6–7, 9, 11–12, 18, 155, 164
Evers, Medgar, 116, 232, 242
evidence: material culture, 257n35; photo-
   graphs as, xx, 22, 44, 50, 257n34
Executive Order 8802, 41
Executive Order 11063, 170

Fairclough, Adam, 283n5
farms, 71, 83, 87, 93
fascism, 36
Fast, Henry A., 62, 96, 241
Fauther, May and Willie, 312n176
Florida, 19
foot washing, 36, 40
Forman, James, xvii, 25; background, 199;
   Black Manifesto delivery, 190; Christian
   focus, 219, 234, 317n40; and Powell,
   reference to, 206; reparations increase

Leadership Conference and, 114; southern tours of, 22; urban areas and, 240; at Woodlawn, 19, 21, 102

Harris, James, 18, 100, 194, 198, 321n94

Harrison, Alisa, xii

Harrisonburg, VA, 6, 20, 29, 34, 37, 45, 50, 237, 239

Hartzler, Levi C., 154

hats, 33

Hawthorne State Hospital, 130–31, 141

Hernley, H. Ralph, 130, 143

Herr, Rebecca, 271n96

Hershberger, Guy F., 10, 13–14, 17, 20–23; activism of, 27; Board of Christian Service and, 282n125; civil rights movement and, 104, 120, 264n4, 284n9; Committee on Economic and Social Relations and, 143; "From Words to Deeds in Race Relations," 123; Vincent Harding and, 101, 117, 121, 128, 286n20; Gerald Hughes and, 131; interracial marriage and, 130, 133, 143–45, 149; Martin Luther King and, 24; Mennonite prejudice and, 235; nonconformity and, 28; nonresistance and, 105, 116, 201; nonviolence and, 104, 120; at Prairie Street, 119; southern tours of, 117–18; *Way of the Cross in Human Relations*, 104, 296n59

Hershey, Lynford, 23, 26, 152, 211–12, 216, 225, 232; civil rights movement and, 263n86; rural areas and, 242; Hubert Schwartzentruber and, 233

Hertzler, Daniel, 109

Hess, Mahlon, 203–4, 207

Hesston College, 44, 177

Hinojosa, Felipe, 3, 264n97, 323n129

history, Mennonite race relations, 257n36

Hochstedler, Eli, 23, 263n88

holy kiss, xiv, 36, 112

homes, as civil rights site, viii, x, xi, xx, 57

homosexuality, xix

Horst, E. G., 68

Horton, Rondo, 1–6, 8–9, 11, 13, 17, 19, 21, 23–25, 27–28; photo of, 149

Hostetler, Beth, 158

Hostetler, Goldie. See Hummel, Goldie

housing: restrictive covenants, 6; segregated, 14

Hughes, Annabelle (née Conrad), 17; attention to, 296n55; demonstrations and, 224; at Gladstone Mennonite, 137–38, 143, 145; interracial conversations and, 192; interracial marriage and, 130, 137, 139, 141, 144, 227, 243; Ohio Conference and, 145; photo of, 142; response to attention, 146; rural areas and, 242

Hughes, Gerald, xiii, 17, 25, 27–28, 220; Anabaptist theology and, 230; at Andrews Bridge, 135; board appointment of, 151–52; bravery of, 232; childhood of, 134; at college, 137; as conscientious objector, 130; demonstrations and, 224; at Gladstone Mennonite, 131, 135, 138, 143, 145; interracial conversations and, 192; interracial marriage and, 130, 137, 139, 141, 144, 243; leadership by, 296n55; Minority Ministries Council and, 152; Ohio Conference and, 145, 230; photos of, 137, 142, 148; at Prairie Street, 98; rural areas and, 242; as song leader, 135, 149; Urban Racial Council and, 152, 198

Hummel, Goldie, 237–38, 245–46

Inman, KS, 74, 77

integrated congregations, xviii, 9, 31, 57, 102, 162

integration. See racial integration

interracial fellowships, 32

interracial relationships, xii, 31, 32, 38; at Camp Landon, 91; Fresh Air and, 75, 79, 85, 93; within Lancaster Conference, 217; tensions in, 64. See also marriages, interracial; sex, interracial

Islam, 33

Neufeld, John T., 166

Newport News, VA, 61, 114

Newton, KS, 10, 62–63, 86, 90, 98, 123, 232

Newtown Chapel Mennonite (FL), 19

New York Herald Tribune, 66

Nickel, Arnold, 79

Nikiema, Mattie Cooper, 51, 265n4

Ninth Street Congregation (MI), 9

nonconformity, xv, xix; baptism and, 16, 37; civil rights movement and, 101; clothing and, 29, 264n98; dancing and, 71; dictates about, 28, 37; doctrine of, 27, 68; earrings and, 71; enforcement of, 43, 261n62; General Conference and, 163; hair and, 27, 54; Vincent Harding and, 106, 118; Lancaster Conference and, 209; life insurance and, 37, 267n43; Mennonite, xv, xvi, xix, 4, 11–12, 15, 20–21, 27–29, 37, 43, 48, 256n22; moustaches and, 16, 261n57; plays and, 27; race and, 229; radios and, 27, 71; Hubert Schwartzentruber and, 248; separation and, 2–4, 7–8, 19–21, 28, 36, 157, 235, 282n119; service and, 116; swimming and, 71; television and, 27; threat to, 64; Virginia Conference survey about, 48

nonresistance: Black Manifesto and, 201, 218, 241; doctrine of, 68, 93; Mennonite, xv, xvi, xvii, 1, 4, 10, 12–13, 48, 156; nonviolence connection to, 103; politics and, 202; World War I and, 201; World War II and, 201–2

nonviolence, 20, 42, 83, 104, 119

North Carolina Mennonite Brethren Conference, 1, 23

North Kenwood, IL, 165, 179

Oak Grove Mennonite (OH), 130, 142, 144, 154, 158

Odom, Mertis, 185–86, 312n176

Ohio Conference, 17; interracial marriage and, 145, 230; racial prejudice and, 131

(Old) Mennonite Church, xiii, 5, 16; African-American congregations in, xiv, 11, 102, 150, 265n6, 304n27; bishops of, xiv; Board of Missions and Charities of, 50; culture of, xiv; editors in, 7; evangelism in, 13–14, 153; Fresh Air program, 64; General Mission Board of, 151; Vincent Harding and, 22, 118; history of, 255n13; interracial marriages in, 27, 138, 144–45, 153, 155; members of, xii, 258n14, 260n42; Minority Ministries Council of, 25; missions by, 69; nonconformity in, 15, 21; nonresistance in, 12; overseas missions by, 18; politics and, 96, 99, 243; polity of, 12; race relations statement by, xvii, 15, 48, 144–45, 155–56; racial prejudice in, 10, 153; segregation in, 6; separated order of, 12; size of, xiii; southern trips by, 19; Turner, OR, and, 25; white members of, 8; Woodlawn conference of 1959, 106, 165

Old Order Mennonite, 5

ordination, 18

Outley, Sylvester, 299n100

pacifism. *See* nonviolence

Pannabecker, Betty Jean, 312n188

Pannell, Richard, 198, 299n100, 321n94

Paradise Mennonite (PA), 209

Peace Section (MCC), 121, 123

Peachey, Paul, 29, 115, 144–45, 296n59

Peachey, Ruth, 45

Philadelphia, MS, 242

Philadelphia, PA, 1, 3, 6–7, 14, 18, 54, 81, 200, 242

Philadelphia Colored Mission, 12, 34

police harassment, 87

Potts, Albert, 65, 74–78, 80; activities of, 76; civil rights movement and, 228; earnings by, 76; photos of, 74–75, 77; police harassment of, 87; privacy of, 77